'ORATOR' HUNT

'ORATOR' HUNT

HENRY HUNT

AND

ENGLISH WORKING-CLASS
RADICALISM

JOHN BELCHEM

CLARENDON PRESS · OXFORD
1985

Oxford University Press, Walton Street, Oxford OX2 6DP
London New York Toronto
Delhi Bombay Calcutta Madras Karachi
Kuala Lumpur Singapore Hong Kong Tokyo
Nairobi Dar es Salaam Cape Town
Melbourne Auckland
and associated companies in
Beirut Berlin Ibadan Nicosia

Oxford is a trade mark of Oxford University Press

Published in the United States
by Oxford University Press, New York

British Library Cataloguing in Publication Data
Belchem, John
'Orator' Hunt: Henry Hunt and English Working-Class Radicalism
1. Hunt, Henry 1773–1835 2. Politician—
Great Britain—Biography
I. Title
322.4′4′0924 DA536-H75
ISBN 0–19–822759–0

Set by Hope Services, Abingdon
Printed in Great Britain
at the University Press, Oxford
by David Stanford
Printer to the University

'A Change is Gonna Come'

Sam Cooke / Otis Redding

To Mary-Rose

Acknowledgements

THIS book is a belated product of the exhilarating experience of studying history at the University of Sussex in the late 1960s and early 1970s. Eileen Yeo, my special subject tutor, inspired my enduring interest in radicalism and social history; Asa Briggs and John Harrison, my postgraduate supervisors, have continued to provide me with much-valued guidance, support and criticism; and Peter Hennock, my inquisitorial internal examiner, and now Liverpool colleague, remains a trenchant critic and heuristic interrogator. Among my student contemporaries, special thanks are due to my good friend and fellow Chartist enthusiast, Jim Epstein, whose recent work on Feargus O'Connor has set a new standard for radical political biography. Sussex apart, I have received advice and encouragement from many other historians and researchers over the years, including John Saville, Dorothy Thompson, Harry Dickinson, John Dinwiddy, Mike Pugh, Ruth Richardson and Mark Harrison. Teaching in Britain and New Zealand has helped clarify my ideas and I owe much to David Sherrington, Jerry Mowat, Philip White and other students. The magisterial studies of Edward Thompson, Gareth Stedman Jones and Iorwerth Prothero have greatly influenced my work: it is impossible to acknowledge such an intellectual debt by footnotes alone.

I would like to express my thanks to the staff of many libraries and record offices, including the departments of printed books, manuscripts, and newspapers of the British Library; Goldsmiths' Library, University of London; Bishopsgate Institute; City of London Guildhall Library; the Bodleian Library, Oxford; Nuffield College, Oxford; John Rylands Library, Manchester; the various American institutions which have sent me material—University of Chicago, University of Illinois at Urbana-Champaign, Widener Library, Harvard, Huntington Library, California, and Adelphi University, Long Island; public reference libraries at Manchester, Preston, Bristol, Bolton, Blackburn, and Carlisle; the Public Record Office and record offices throughout the country, in particular Lancashire, Bristol, Wiltshire, Somerset, and the Corporation of London. A special word of thanks to Ruth and Eddie Frow for their hospitality at the Working Class Movement Library, Manchester, a magnificent collection. I am very grateful to Mr James Stevens-Cox of Guernsey for sending me photocopies of his large private collection of papers relating to Henry Hunt.

Over the years, research on the book has been facilitated by financial assistance from several bodies, to all of whom I wish to express my gratitude: Massey University Humanities Research Fund, University of Liverpool Staff Research Fund, the British Academy, and the Nuffield Foundation who awarded me a Social Science Research Fellowship to cover the cost of replacement teaching for the autumn term 1983, at a time when leave of absence would otherwise have been impossible.

This book has been long in the making, and it is impossible to acknowledge all those who have helped me through this lengthy process. Among the most pleasurable moments was the guided tour of Henry Hunt's Wiltshire provided by Mrs Bunty Horton of Widdington Farm, Henry's birthplace. The least pleasant tasks have been borne by my family without complaint. My parents deserve especial thanks: my mother has typed endless drafts with the greatest proficiency, assisted by my father's proof-reading skills. Mary, my wife and soulmate, has provided me with physical, emotional, and intellectual stimulus and sustenance: it is small recompense, but I dedicate this book to her.

JOHN BELCHEM

Liverpool
June 1984

Contents

Abbreviations

AHH	*Addresses from Henry Hunt, Esq. M.P. to the Radical Reformers of England, Ireland and Scotland, on the measures of the Whig Ministers since they have been in place and power* (1831–2)
BAPCK	British Association for Promoting Co-operative Knowledge
BD	*Black Dwarf*
BL Add. Mss	British Library Additional Manuscripts
BPU	Birmingham Political Union
CPR	*Cobbett's Political Register*
GNU	Great Northern Union
HO	Home Office Papers
MO	*Manchester Observer*
MPU	Metropolitan Political Union
NPU	National Political Union
NUWC	National Union of the Working Classes
PC	Place Collection of Newspaper Cuttings, British Library
PD	*Parliamentary Debates*
PMG	*Poor Man's Guardian*
RRA	Radical Reform Association
SPR	*Sherwin's Political Register*
TFP	*Trades' Free Press*
TN	*Trades' Newspaper and Mechanics' Weekly Journal*
TRR	Henry Hunt, *To the Radical Reformers, male and female, of England, Ireland and Scotland* (2 vols., London, 1820–2)
TS	Treasury-Solicitor's Papers
WFP	*Weekly Free Press*
3730	*Addresses from One of the 3730 Electors of Preston, to the Labouring Classes of Great Britain and Ireland* (The title was varied each week in order to evade the stamp duty, but the number *3730* was always included.)

Introduction

HENRY HUNT has been ill-served by history, damned by the standard sources and conventional historiography of the radical movement. His reputation as a vainglorious, empty demagogue, the marplot of the very cause he professed to espouse, derives from the narrow range of sources upon which historians of English working-class radicalism have been far too dependent, the tendentious papers of Francis Place, and the well-thumbed autobiographies of certain 'respectable' and unrepresentative working-class radicals. To a would be wire-puller and aspiring 'philosophic' radical like Place, Hunt, the popular agitator, appeared 'impudent, active, vulgar': the 'best mob orator of the day', he acted with demagogic irresponsibility as he eschewed the middle-class liberals and intellectuals, and sought to 'inflame the passions of the people against every man who has shown himself at all desirous to do them service'.[1] Looking back on the post-war campaign in his *Passages in the Life of a Radical*, the renegade Samuel Bamford conveniently glossed over his apostasy by anathematizing Hunt, the vain, cowardly and mercenary demagogue, who had misled the people in pursuit of his own self-interest. A similar technique was employed by the quondam Chartist William Lovett in his *Life and Struggles*, with Hunt's successor and emulator, Feargus O'Connor, the villain of the piece.[2] The pioneers of labour history did not question this portrayal of Hunt and O'Connor as braggart demagogues: in their rigid mental and political categories, there was no place for such flamboyant, gentlemanly rabble-rousers. Fabian-inspired historians disapproved of their emphasis on numbers and confrontation; early Marxist historians were disturbed by their social background, populist appeal, and 'pre-industrial' backward-looking message.[3] Whiggish historians, applauding the peaceable, or rather piecemeal, attainment of parliamentary democracy were harsher still in their assessment of the demagogues whose rodomon-tades and braggadocio had discredited and retarded reform.[4] The advent

---

[1] BL Add. MSS 27809 (Place papers), ff. 16 and 22.

[2] S. Bamford, *Passages in the Life of a Radical* (2 vols., Manchester, 1844; rpt. 1 vol. Fitzroy edn., 1967). W. Lovett, *Life and Struggles* (London, 1876; rpt. Fitzroy edn., 1967).

[3] For a critical analysis of early labour history, see Jim Epstein's spirited reassessment of *The Lion of Freedom: Feargus O'Connor and the Chartist Movement, 1832–1842* (London, 1982), 1–3.

[4] See the vehement denunciation of Hunt, drawing heavily on Bamford and Place, in C. B. R. Kent, *The English Radicals* (London, 1899), 276–80. For an updated version, no less critical, see R. J. White, *From Waterloo to Peterloo* (London, Peregrine edn., 1968), 145–6.

of social history produced no significant reassessment: the application of
some elementary Weberian sociology was taken to confirm that popular
but unworthy leaders like Hunt and O'Connor stood outside of and
opposed to formal collective organization, their power resting on 'charisma',
which historians construed as the crude appeal to the prejudices and
emotions of the crowd. The publication of Edward Thompson's monumen-
tal *Making of the English Working Class*, such an important turning-point
in historical studies, still left Hunt unredeemed. 'The demagogue is a bad
or ineffectual leader', Thompson wrote: 'Hunt voiced not principle nor
even well-formulated Radical strategy, but the emotions of the movement.
Striving always to say whatever would provoke the loudest cheer, he was
not the leader but the captive of the least stable portion of the crowd.'[5]
Any rehabilitation of Hunt seems most unlikely in what has been called the
'post-Thompson florescence of social history'.[6] The study of conventional
radical movements has fallen from fashion. Nowadays, historians either
concentrate on de-institutionalized politics, crime, street violence, mental
illness and the like, or ignore the national and instrumental dimension of
radical politics, including such matters as leadership and mass agitation, to
highlight the 'movement culture', the radical counter-culture which
flourished in the localities and offered an alternative and satisfying way of
life within early industrial capitalist society, even for women.[7] Such
'culturalism' has come under structuralist and other attacks, and there is a
new labour history which seeks to return not to the political platform, alas,
but to the workplace and the study of the labour process.[8] A biography of
Hunt, a study in popular leadership and agitation, may be regarded in
some quarters, then, as a backward step in the unhalted forward march of
labour history. But this is an essay in recovery, not in revisionism. The
intention is simply to fill in a gap, to do justice to the popular politics of the
early nineteenth century and its most important leader, who has been
peremptorily dismissed by labour, social and political historians alike. To

---

[5] E. P. Thompson, *The Making of the English Working Class* (London, Penguin edn.,
1968), 690.

[6] G. Eley and K. Nield, 'Why does social history ignore politics', *Social History*, v (1980),
267.

[7] Note the sub-title of the latest symposium on Chartism, J. Epstein and D. Thompson
(eds.), *The Chartist Experience: Studies in Working-Class Radicalism and Culture, 1830–1860*
(London, 1982). See also D. Thompson, *The Chartists* (London, 1984), ch. 7, and David
Jones, 'Women and Chartism', *History*, lxviii (1983), 1–21.

[8] See the debate in *History Workshop Journal*, vii–viii (1978–9), initiated by Richard
Johnson's essay, 'Thompson, Genovese, and Socialist–Humanist History', vi (1978), 79–100.
For the labour process, see the on-going series of articles in *Social History*, including P.
Linebaugh, 'Labour History without the labour process', vii (1982), 319–27; R. Price, 'The
labour process and labour history', viii (1983), 57–75; J. Zeitlin, 'Social theory and the history
of work', viii (1983), 365–74; and P. Joyce, 'Labour, capital and compromise: a response to
Richard Price', ix (1984), 67–76.

transpose Trevelyan's famous remark, this is a study of the politics left out by history.

An athletic, handsome figure of Wiltshire farming stock, 'Orator' Hunt became the most popular and flamboyant figure in radical politics in the early nineteenth century. Under his leadership the popular movement developed the language and programme, ideology and analysis, strategy and class appeal which remained largely unchallenged until the final collapse of Chartism. Not a reformer by upbringing, Hunt did not question his unthinking loyalism until he found himself ostracized by the Wiltshire establishment who resented his social pretensions and conspicuous economic success as a 'gentleman farmer'. After this rebuff, the headstrong Hunt shed his loyalism and progressed rapidly through 'independence' to radicalism. Here he followed a familiar path, similar to that of a better-known disillusioned loyalist, William Cobbett. For Cobbett, Hunt and their like, the war against Napoleonic France provided a thorough political education. Proud of their 'independence', they were offended by the malversation of the 'Pitt System' and the much-flaunted prosperity of the enlarged rentier class of government contractors, sycophants, stock-jobbers and such 'new money'. As 'Old Corruption' reached new levels of extortion and incompetence, widening the gap between the tax-gorgers and the tax-payers, the 'independent' reformers stood forward to champion the interests of the hard-working plundered against the parasitic plunderers. To Cobbett, Hunt and others, it seemed that what separated the economically protected from the economically defenceless, the rich from the poor, was the monopolistic possession of political power. Seen in these terms, economic amelioration, an end to polarization and immiseration, required a political solution through parliamentary reform and the redistribution of power. This simple political analysis, the relevance of which was quickly appreciated by hungry food-rioters and impoverished machine-breakers, continued to dominate radical discourse throughout the first half of the nineteenth century. Discontent was politicized during the war: thereafter, parliamentary reform, the struggle for political power and economic protection, became the very essence of radical protest and the fundamental demand of the Chartist challenge.[9] In his progress from 'independence' to democratic radicalism, Hunt exemplifies the strong political emphasis of English popular protest, an idiom which acquired its vigour and vitality not from the abstract Jacobin language of natural rights in the 1790s but from the harsh economic realities of war-time living.

The popular struggle for parliamentary reform began in earnest amidst the hardship and dislocation of the transition to peace. Hunt's decisive contribution to the remarkable advance of radicalism in the post-war years

[9] See Gareth Stedman Jones's important essay, 'The Language of Chartism' in Epstein and Thompson (eds.), 3–58.

has been overlooked. Other reformers led the way in advocating a new
political departure—the veteran Major Cartwright in his pioneering tours
of the Luddite counties, and Cobbett in his new 'Twopenny Trash'—but it
was Hunt who broke through the restraints of traditional extra-parliamentary
politics and gave the new movement its independent, uncompromising,
democratic tone. His bravura performance at the Spa Fields meetings of
1816–17 opened a new era in popular protest and politics. Fully in control
of the huge crowds, he upstaged the absent moderates and confounded the
insurrectionary plans of the 'Spencean' conspirators, by enrolling the
people in mass agitation for the full democratic programme of constitutional
rights. After Spa Fields, moderate reformers were forced to withdraw:
Hunt and the radicals were adamant that there should be no concessions to
parliamentary allies and no retraction from universal suffrage, annual
parliaments and the ballot. Guardians of the old 'underground' tradition
promptly revised their ways and means following Hunt's great success with
the assembled crowds. The putsch-mentality was cast aside as leaders of
the 'revolutionary party' gave up the conspiracies and plots of the past to
support Hunt's mass platform. Here the people demanded their constitutional rights in a constitutional manner, 'peaceably if we may, forcibly if
we must', employing the strategy of forcible intimidation, an escalating
policy of open agitation which drew upon the rich rhetoric of 'people's
history', celebrating the glorious struggles against absolutism and the
ultimate constitutional right of physical resistance. The format which Hunt
introduced at Spa Fields—constitutional mass pressure from without for
the restoration of the constitutional democratic rights of all—proved
extremely popular and continued to inform radical agitation throughout
the age of the Chartists.[10]

The 'constitutional' nature of this mass platform has been misrepresented
in most studies of the period. Marxist historians have dismissed such
populist historicism as an anachronistic impediment to the development of
a proper revolutionary perspective, while whiggish historians have recast
constitutionalism as a badge of reformist respectability. Such interpretations fail to do justice to the physical strength and confrontationalist
purpose of the popular movement. By drawing upon popular concepts of
the Constitution and the glorious struggles of the past—the myth and

[10] See my earlier papers on 'Henry Hunt and the evolution of the mass platform', *English Historical Review*, xciii (1978), 739–73; 'Republicanism, popular constitutionalism and the radical platform in early nineteenth-century England', *Social History*, vi (1981), 1–32; and '1848: Feargus O'Connor and the collapse of the mass platform' in Epstein and Thompson (eds.), 269–310. See also, T. M. Parssinnen, 'The Revolutionary party in London, 1816–20', *Bulletin of the Institute of Historical Research*, xlv (1972), 266–82; T. M. Kemnitz, 'Approaches to the Chartist Movement: Feargus O'Connor and Chartist strategy', *Albion*, v (1973), 67–73; and the stimulating editorial preface on 'People's history' in R. Samuel (ed.), *People's History and Socialist Theory* (London, 1981), xv–xxxix.

folklore of English libertarian history—Hunt's mass platform reached a wide audience. An excitingly-presented, readily-understood programme, it offered the best means of attracting the normally apathetic, if not those beer-swilling, male chauvinist, xenophobic, flag-waging workers whom historians are no longer allowed to forget. At the very least, it was well pitched at the 'generalized beliefs' or 'birthrights' of the crowd: instinctive anti-absolutist sentiment was soon hardened into radical commitment and solidarity.[11] But popular constitutionalism was not just a useful language with which to attract the crowds and mobilize the masses: it also allowed the radicals to out-manœuvre and discredit the authorities. Through the repertoire of constitutional platform protest, the radicals were able to portray themselves as—and hopefully prove themselves to be—the true upholders of what remained the legitimizing ideology of the ruling class, constitutional freedom and the rule of law. In the great mobilization of 1819, the strategy worked remarkably well. While the radicals indulged in the exciting rhetoric of impending violence, evoking the deeds of the glorious ancestors, the orators carefully proscribed any departure from moral force until all 'constitutional' channels had been explored, so that the discipline and peaceable good order of the monster meetings established a public image of legitimate extra-parliamentary behaviour which the Government had no real right to infringe. In the confrontation of the summer of 1819, each side hoped the other would be the first to overstep the mark, transgress the Constitution, and lose public sanction. The Peterloo massacre was a tremendous moral and propaganda victory for Hunt and the radicals.

The failure of the radicals to advance beyond the vantage ground of Peterloo pinpoints the essential weakness in popular radical strategy. At some point the leaders had to decide whether or not the social contract had been violated, whether the time had come when the oppressed people could and should exercise their sovereign right of physical resistance as allowed by Blackstone and all other authorities. It was this question of timing, this issue of judgement, rather than any absolute commitment to 'moral force' or 'physical force' which divided the radicals at critical moments like the post-Peterloo crisis. At the crucial point Hunt refused to sanction plans for a full-scale confrontation: indeed, he decided to forgo the platform altogether, choosing to rest the radical case on Peterloo itself, looking to public opinion and the courts of law for vindication and victory. The radicals paid dear for this decision to demobilize. In the forum of public opinion it was the established opposition not the radicals who

[11] On 'generalized beliefs' see G. Rudé's essay, 'The "Pre-Industrial" Crowd' in his *Paris and London in the 18th Century: Studies in Popular Protest* (London, 1970), 17–34. For the radical potential of 'vague populism' in contemporary Britain, see H. F. Moorhouse, 'Attitudes to class and class relationships in Britain', *Sociology*, x (1976), 469–96.

benefited from Peterloo, while in the courts the authorities were
exonerated without question, Hunt's unremitting efforts to bring them to
justice notwithstanding. The moral and propaganda triumph of Peterloo
thus proved a pyrrhic victory. The question must remain open as to
whether the radicals would have achieved more by pursuing a course of
physical confrontation, the policy which Hunt proscribed. His behaviour
after Peterloo needs to be scrutinized particularly closely, because it
demonstrates some enduring weaknesses of the English radical movement:
a naïve optimism about the force of public opinion and impartial justice,
and a debilitating obsession with legitimacy. Physical force was not
excluded by Hunt and his successors but they were prepared to use
violence only from a position of strength when there could be no doubt
about its rightfulness or efficiency. With its popular support and 'legal'
posture, the mass platform offered a powerful alternative to other patterns
of collective violence: the unstructured, non-political violence or 'turmoil',
characteristic of pre-industrial protest; and the élitist, spy-ridden 'conspiracies' favoured by the revolutionary underground of the war years.[12]
But the emphasis on legitimacy proved self-defeating. As radicals agonized
over whether they had sufficient constitutional right they lost their physical
might: mass support dwindled, excitement was squandered, and the
initiative passed back to the authorities. In the end, a few ardent stalwarts,
like Thistlewood and the Cato Street 'conspirators', were left to engage in
a hopelessly unequal struggle, driven across the threshold of violence by
despair and anger at the collapse of mass support and the imposition of
repression.

   The failure of the first great mobilization of the mass platform in 1819
was followed by a period of critical self-analysis and internecine argument,
an oft-repeated sequence in the working-class radical movement. The best-
known examples of this process of introspection, dissension, and revision
belong to the Chartist period, but the post-mortem into the collapse of the
post-war campaign was no less important. Amidst the recrimination, some
fundamental questions were raised about the meaning of radicalism and
the nature of protest. Hunt saw no need for any thorough-going revision:
his efforts were directed towards reactivating the platform and strengthening its force through improved organization in the shape of the new Great
Northern Union. This brought him under attack on two fronts: from
Carlile, the incorruptible Paineite ideologue, and Cobbett, the pragmatist
and apologist of gradualism.[13] Carlile, the apostle of rational infidel-

---

[12] For an interesting classification of political violence into turmoil, conspiracy and internal
war, see T. R. Gurr, *Why Men Rebel* (Princeton, 1970), 9–13. See also the discussion of
Chartist attitudes to violence in D. Thompson, 72–4, and D. Goodway, *London Chartism,
1838–1848* (Cambridge, 1982), 123–8.
[13] Little account is taken of these controversies in Joel H. Wiener, *Radicalism and*

republicanism, turned away from the mass platform in disgust, repudiating the volatile crowds, constitutional clap-trap, populist slogans and gentlemanly leaders. His radicalism became purist and individualist: in place of futile agitation, he called upon individual reformers to seek sanctuary in 'temples of reason' where they could strengthen the quality and depth of their ideological commitment through self-discipline and self-education. Hunt's Great Northern Union with its concentration on mere numbers roused him to anger and led to a heated controversy, a neglected precursor of many later debates in the labour movement about how to reconcile ideology with mass appeal, ascetic counter-culture with popular working-class culture. The questions raised remain relevant to this day: should radicals concentrate on ideological rigour, individual mental emancipation and counter-culture, or maximum participation, mass agitation and political challenge? While there is much to commend in Carlile's critique of Hunt and popular constitutionalism, it would be hard to argue that the failure to follow Carlile constitutes a preliminary 'wrong turning' in English working-class history. Carlile, the prophet of a counter-hegemonic ideology of infidel-republicanism, was also the harbinger of the mid-Victorian *rapprochement* between radicalism and liberalism. Too ideological and extreme for popular consumption on the platform, Carlile's ultra-radicalism acquired social respectability in the refined ambience of élite politics and self-help protest: the more committed the lecture-room republican, the more decorous the individual; the more rationalist the debating-hall infidel, the more rational and reasonable he appeared to middle-class liberals. For all its ideological and intellectual weaknesses, the 'constitutional' mass platform offered the best protection against this alluring improvement ethic and middle-class embrace. The bluster and populism notwithstanding, the confrontationalism of the platform preserved the independence of the radical challenge and upheld the integrity of oppositional values. The true radicals in nineteenth-century England were not the ideologues, but the orators, organizers and agitators, among whom Hunt and O'Connor stood supreme.[14]

The dispute with Cobbett also touches upon a recurrent point of tension, although here the controversy was over tactics not ideology, with Hunt the uncompromising fundamentalist at odds with Cobbett the pragmatic

Freethought in Nineteenth-Century Britain: The Life of Richard Carlile (Westport, 1983), and George Spater, *William Cobbett: The Poor Man's Friend* (2 vols., Cambridge, 1982).

[14] On oppositional values and the propensity of their proponents to conform to strict standards of social decorum, see F. Parkin, *Class Inequality and Political Order* (London, 1972), ch. 3, and *Middle Class Radicalism* (Manchester, 1968), 21–32. For the improvement ethic in operation, see Trygve Tholfsen, *Working-Class Radicalism in mid-Victorian England* (London, 1976). For the best discussion of 'purism' and later controversies in the labour movement, see E. P. Thompson, *William Morris: Romantic to Revolutionary* (London, 1976 edn.), Part 3.

opportunist. Throughout his political career, even in the despondent early 1820s, Hunt was a jealous guardian of the radical shibboleth: unlike Cobbett and many others, he refused to regard moderate reform as some kind of instalment; any reform short of universal suffrage, annual parliaments, and the ballot, he dismissed as worthless, if not harmful, to the non-represented people. To Hunt's dismay, Cobbett frequently trimmed his programme and offered his services to discontented groups within the political nation, like the aggrieved agriculturists of the early 1820s, hoping to exploit their influence to gain at least some measure of reform, political or financial. Hunt rejected such opportunism and concentrated on the arduous task of rebuilding the popular movement from below, committed to the full radical programme and nothing less.

These significant controversies were conducted while Hunt was serving his two-and-a-half years prison sentence for his part in the Peterloo meeting. Immured in 'Ilchester Bastile', 'Orator' Hunt turned pamphleteer, journalist and autobiographer in order to retain his leadership of the popular movement. In his voluminous prison writings he displayed insufferable vanity and self-pity verging on paranoia, but the interminable concentration on self, offensive as it sounds to the modern ear, must be read for the most part as political rhetoric. Doubtless he derived some cheap psychological satisfaction from his gasconading exercises in vindication and self-glorification: he was under considerable personal strain at the time, as he battled with the prison authorities for the right to receive private visits from his beloved Mrs Vince, who provided him with the domestic felicity and stability he required to assuage the pressures and tensions of political agitation and public notoriety. But however unbalanced he may have been at this juncture, Hunt accentuated his egotism for a clear political purpose. It was by promoting his own leadership that he sought to defend popular constitutional radicalism against moderate opportunism on the one hand and ideological extremism on the other. His *Memoirs*, published in forty-six instalments, established his credentials with a cumulative—but by no means accurate—record of his early victories over the serried ranks of loyalists, whigs, moderate reformers, renegades and shoy-hoys.[15] Stitched together with his *Memoirs* were his addresses *To the Radical Reformers* in which the martyred Hunt denounced all attempts to revise or undermine the radical challenge.[16] These addresses also served as a diary for his 'gaol politics', recording his heroic battles with the corrupt and sadistic prison authorities. What started as a campaign to secure his 'political status', thereby entitling him to private visits by Mrs Vince, soon widened into an indignant and comprehensive exposure of the manifold

[15] H. Hunt, *Memoirs of Henry Hunt Esq.* (3 vols., London, 1820–2).
[16] H. Hunt, *To the Radical Reformers, male and female, of England, Ireland and Scotland* (2 vols., London, 1820–2).

evils of the prison system which compelled the Government to act—the governor was dismissed and convicted, and the gaol itself condemned for demolition. Hunt, indeed, was unremitting in his labours for prison reform, a task which put him to considerable expense, but characteristically he never concealed or underestimated his contribution to the cause, and expected commensurate public recognition and approval.

Having upheld the cause of democratic constitutionalism against opportunism and revisionism, Hunt left prison hoping to recapture the mass support of the post-war years and to recoup the personal fortune he had lost through agitation and persecution. His business success was quite remarkable, providing him with a sound financial base from which to continue his formidable political struggle. Throughout the 1820s he rarely missed an opportunity to propound the radical programme from any available platform or hustings. By ridiculing the nostrums of the agriculturists, whigs, 'saints', currency cranks, and the newly-named 'liberals', he hoped to reactivate the independent radical platform around the contentious issues of the day. At the same time he extended his campaign to expose the corruption, patronage and concealment that pervaded the political system, and fought a wide-ranging battle for greater accountability in public affairs on the county platform, at the election hustings, in the Guildhall and in his local vestry. Hunt, then, made full use of the various arenas of protest open to freeholders, liverymen, ratepayers and electors in the unreformed political system. His dogged persistence finally paid off. By the end of the decade the problems of 'cash, corn, and catholics' had so transformed high politics that reform came to the top of the parliamentary agenda. Having kept the democratic cause alive throughout the 1820s, Hunt now stood forward to uphold the claims of 'working-class' radicalism against moderate reform and the new liberalism.

The divergence of popular radicalism from liberalism .was the most important 'ideological' development of the 1820s, overshadowing the emergence of Ricardian socialism. In the orthodox pre-history of Chartism, the 1820s feature as the crucial period of intellectual advance towards socialism, into a programme better geared to the grievances and needs of the new industrial workers. The old preoccupation with political corruption was cast aside in favour of a new ideology based on the labour theory of value: the old *petit-bourgeois* emphasis upon the state and taxation was superseded by a more class-based conception of exploitation within the economic process itself.[17] Such a distinction between politics and economics,

[17] It was Marxist labour historians who first drew a rigid distinction between the pre-industrial, middle-class radicalism of the age of Hunt and Cobbett, and the class-conscious socialist radicalism of Chartism, see N. Stewart, *The Fight for the Charter* (London, 1937), 41–62; and A. L. Morton and G. Tate, *The British Labour Movement 1770–1920* (London, 1956), 49–59. See also, P. Hollis, *The Pauper Press* (Oxford, 1970), chs. 6 and 7; and the

petit-bourgeois perspectives and working-class consciousness, the old ideology and the new, obscures the fundamental continuity of radical language, ideology, and endeavour. Hunt's radical programme, so well attuned to popular attitudes and needs, absorbed the rights of labour, the new formulations of the time-honoured labour theory of value, just as readily as it had earlier subsumed the rights of man. Whether directed at the tax-eaters and/or the capitalists, the radical demand remained the same: an end to the system which left labour unprotected and at the mercy of those who monopolized the state and the law. It was liberalism, not proto-Marxism, that Hunt could not accept. Under his leadership, radicalism remained resolutely committed to the struggle for political power as the means to ensure the economic well-being of the common people, or working-classes, as he now called them. Liberalism, by contrast, had no patience with such old notions of political justice and economic equity: it was a progressive creed seemingly at odds with every aspect—death not excluded—[18] of traditional popular experience and culture. It was the increasing number of conflicts with the liberals in the late 1820s which sharpened Hunt's radicalism and highlighted its working-class perspective. Through these political battles with the liberals, he carried traditional radicalism far beyond the confines of petit-bourgeois preoccupation with cheap government into open hostility to the ascendant creed of *laissez-faire* political economy.

Hunt's uncompromising opposition to the Reform Bill and its liberal supporters completed the transition to a fully-fledged class based radicalism. In championing the rights of those excluded by the Bill, he proudly identified himself with the working class. He elicited little support, however: his democratic fundamentalism cost him his health, his business, and the parliamentary seat he had won in potwalloper Preston in 1830. Neither in Parliament nor in the country could he compete with the powerful forces promoting the Bill, but he refused to give up the struggle. Battling against liberal propaganda and the press, reformist sentiment and popular prejudice, he concentrated his efforts on Preston and the north, addressing himself to 'the Working Classes and no other', imploring them to demand equal political rights immediately, and warning them of the dangers of accepting anything less. Although unsuccessful at the time, Hunt's attempt to mobilize the northern workers against the Bill and protect them from the consequences of liberal reform marked the real beginning of Chartism. He died before he could recapture the popular support he had once enjoyed, but shortly thereafter he was accorded pride

critical essay by Gareth Stedman Jones, 'Rethinking Chartism', in his *Languages of Class* (Cambridge, 1983).

[18] See Ruth Richardson's forthcoming study of the Anatomy Act, *Death, Dissection and the Destitute*.

of place in the Chartist pantheon by penitent working-class radicals facing the horrors of the new Poor Law, the defeat of the short-time movement, and the attack on trade unionism. Hunt, the Chartists rued, had been sent to an early grave, broken in heart and spirit by the folly and ingratitude of the people during the Reform Bill agitation.[19]

This book is a political biography of Hunt, not a hagiographic tribute. It is not intended to present him as the definitive radical leader: the aim is simply to ensure that he is accorded proper historical recognition, that his lengthy career in the radical cause is fully noted before any judgements are passed. Any assessment of Hunt must take account of his sheer persistence as a political agitator. What was remarkable about the man was not his notorious vanity or his stentorian lungs, effective though his voice was in silencing crowds, hecklers and opponents,[20] but his perseverance—and integrity—in promoting democratic radicalism. Historians, however, have chosen to ignore or dismiss much of his political life. 'Orator' Hunt is allowed no more than a fleeting appearance, emerging to notoriety at Spa Fields and enjoying a brief moment of glory as the white-hatted star attraction at Peterloo before being summarily dismissed as a self-seeking braggart demagogue.[21] This is hardly fair coverage for the most important and popular figure in early nineteenth-century radical politics, a gentlemanly leader and agitator who contributed so much to the development of English working-class consciousness, a consciousness which derived its strength not from ideological prescription but from collective identification, agitation, organization, and pride.

Hunt was no ideologue or innovative social thinker but he articulated— and personified—an unsophisticated yet uncompromising, libertarian democratic radicalism that drew its oppositional power and popular appeal

[19] Lovett and O'Connor both believed that Hunt was consigned to an early grave by popular ingratitude, see Lovett, 45 and Epstein, 91.

[20] Lovett, 45 quotes a report of Hunt's performance in the Commons, demonstrating the unique power of his voice: 'In vain do all sides of the house unite, cough, and shuffle, and groan . . . he pauses for a moment, until the unanimous clamour of disgust is at its height, and then, re-pitching his notes, apparently without an effort, lifts his halloo as clear and distinct above the storm, as ever ye heard a minster bell tolling over the racket of a village wake.'

[21] Specialist studies such as W. J. Newman, 'Henry Hunt and English Working-Class Radicalism, 1812–1832', unpublished Ph.D. thesis, Princeton University, 1950, and J. W. Osborne, 'Henry Hunt, 1815–1830: the politically formative years of a Radical M.P.', *Red River Valley Historical Journal of World History*, v (1981), 177–94, are restricted in chronological coverage and sources consulted, as is W. J. Baker's entry on Hunt in J. O. Baylen and N. J. Gossman (eds.), *Biographical Dictionary of Modern British Radicals: Volume I, 1770–1830* (Hassocks, 1979), 244–7. The only full-length study, Robert Huish, *History of the Private and Political Life of the late Henry Hunt* (2 vols., London, 1836), was a pot-boiler: appearing soon after Hunt's death, it simply reprinted lengthy extracts from the *Memoirs* and other writings, occasionally punctuated by animadversions on his adultery and excessive zeal in the reform cause, faults which the liberal Huish considered equally unforgivable.

from its very simplicity and immediate relevance to the working class:

His religion was this, that every man, woman and child should be free to exercise
their own religion, without being called to account by any human being. His politics
were, that from the King to the beggar all had equal rights . . . His principle had
always been that a sober, industrious man ought to be able to procure sufficient of
the necessaries, and some of the comforts of life, for his wife and children, and
something, too, to put by for a rainy day. (*Cheers*) When this could not be
obtained, he concluded that there was something rotten in the state of
affairs—(*cheers*)—and he would do his best to bring about a change.[22]

In seeking for change, Hunt was a tireless agitator, unyielding and
irrepressible, driven on no doubt by a restless personality—Bamford noted
that he was 'constantly perhaps through good but misguided intentions,
placing himself in most arduous situations. No repose—no tranquillity for
him.'[23] But whatever personal and emotional satisfaction he derived from
agitation, he never deviated from the path of political principle. His
personal failings, indeed, served to emphasize his commitment to
democratic radicalism. Irascible and temerarious by nature, he could not
suffer opponents of the radical cause, and vehemently rejected any
argument in favour of moderation, gradualism, and compromise. In their
perceptive obituary notice, Hetherington and O'Brien, close friends of
Hunt during the difficult Reform Bill years, drew attention to his
distinguishing quality, his 'utter detestation of cowardice and shuffle':

But this quality, so indicative of a generous spirit—so honourable to the
possessor—is a bitter ingredient of character in times of difficulty and trouble. It
was the bane of Henry Hunt. It made him what the world calls 'impracticable.' It
made it impossible for him to co-operate heartily with knaves, and, as a
consequence, turned all the knaves against him. Hence it is that he was so generally
disliked by the time-serving, fraudulent part of society . . . To sham-reformers he
was particularly obnoxious; while to turncoats and trading politicians he was a
perfect 'raw head and bloody bones.'[24]

Implacable and 'impracticable', 'Orator' Hunt brought the working class
to the forefront of extra-parliamentary politics, much to the horror of
loyalists and reformers alike. His unstinting efforts to mobilize the masses,
his inexhaustible commitment to the democratic cause, place him in a class
apart from earlier gentlemanly leaders of the crowd, not least his most
famous predecessor, John Wilkes. 'Hunt and Liberty' was a very different
cry from 'Wilkes and Liberty'. Wilkes had appreciated the potential of
'personal' politics and succeeded in mobilizing the crowd by associating
himself with the abstract notion of liberty, but the Wilkite agitation
belonged to the era of 'collusion and convergence' in extra-parliamentary

[22] *Preston Chronicle*, 25 Aug. 1832.
[23] Bamford, 20.   [24] *PMG*, 21 Feb. 1835.

politics when the crowd was manipulated to serve the interests of the 'unofficial opposition' within the political nation.[25] Hunt took the process of 'personal' politics a decisive stage further: his name became synonymous with the uncompromising programme of democratic rights and his campaigns transformed the non-represented crowd into an independent, proudly self-sufficient, and organized political force. An independent, gentlemanly leader in the Wilkite tradition, Hunt pointed the way forward to exclusive working-class radicalism and the Chartist challenge.

This study is restricted to England and to men. Scotland and Wales have radical histories of their own but Hunt had many supporters in both countries. Women featured more prominently in radical counter-culture than on the mass platform where orators were invariably male and the programme demanded was always universal *manhood* suffrage, but working-class women attended the mass meetings in their thousands, applauded Hunt's leadership, and regarded the radical political struggle as their own.

---

[25] J. Brewer, *Party Ideology and Popular Politics at the Accession of George III* (Cambridge, 1976), ch. 9; and G. Rudé, 'Collusion and Convergence in Eighteenth-Century English Political Action' in his *Paris and London*, 319–40.

1

The Making of a Radical

I. GENTLEMAN FARMER

HENRY HUNT was born on 6 November 1773 at Widdington Farm, Upavon, 'a lone farm situated upon Salisbury Plain, not within one mile of any other house whatever'. The family was of ancient and respectable standing, but the Wiltshire Hunts were struggling to regain some of their former prosperity. Their ancestry could be traced back to a 'colonel' in William the Conqueror's army (a rather embarrassing credential for a nineteenth-century radical!), for whose part in the imposition of the 'Norman Yoke' the family 'became possessed of very considerable estates in the counties of Wilts and Somerset'. These estates had been passed down from father to son until the civil war when they were confiscated in punishment for the staunch royalism of Henry's great-great-grandfather, Colonel Thomas Hunt, whose dramatic escape to join Charles in exile was the proudest episode in the family's pre-radical history. The restoration of the monarchy brought no restitution of the family property: somewhat aggrieved, the disillusioned colonel retired to a small estate at Enford, Wiltshire, which had been overlooked by Cromwell's agents. By the time Henry's father, Thomas Hunt inherited the Enford estate it was considerably encumbered, but through his other farming ventures he put the family fortunes on the road to recovery, ultimately leaving his son in 'uncontrolled possession of one of the largest farming concerns in the kingdom'.[1]

The return to prosperity began with a good marriage to a wealthy farmer's daughter, after which Thomas Hunt took up the tenancy of Widdington Farm at a rental of £300 p.a., which he decided to retain after he inherited Littlecot Farm and the Enford estate in 1774. A hard-working and efficient farmer, he was well placed to profit from the agricultural boom of the 1790s: he took up the tenancy of Chisenbury Farm in 1795, some 1,000 acres adjoining the family property in Enford and running up to Everleigh. He died in 1797 leaving Henry, the eldest of his six children, in ownership or occupancy of a considerable amount of land: 3,000 acres in the upper Avon valley, Wiltshire, embracing nearly all the tithing of Littlecot, and the tenancies of Chisenbury and Widdington, as well as some property in Bath and Somerset which Henry later claimed was worth 'many

[1] Hunt, *Memoirs*, i, 21–38 and 395.

thousand pounds', including the manor and estate of Glastonbury. On this substantial base Henry Hunt established himself as an extremely successful 'gentleman farmer'.[2]

Henry's decision to follow his father into full-time farming displeased his socially aspiring parents who had higher ambitions for him and duly invested £500 on his education at a number of indifferent boarding and grammar schools to prepare him for Oxford and the Church. His father was already negotiating to purchase him a living when he rebelled: he refused to go up to Oxford and insisted on his right to become a working farmer. His mother never came to terms with this set-back to her social ambitions: she was in poor health and died soon afterwards. His father finally came to respect the decision: he provided his son with a thorough practical apprenticeship in farm labour and management, and entrusted the local clergyman with the completion of his formal education, an arrangement which proved most satisfactory. Henry soon became a 'complete master' of every branch of farming, 'there being no part of it that I had not performed with my own hands'. The Revd. Carrington, an anti-war liberal, tutored him well in the classics and introduced him to the ideas of the 'friends of liberty', although the young Hunt was not particularly interested in politics when there were so many other diversions. An impetuous infatuation with the landlord's daughter at the Bear Inn, Devizes, brought him into conflict with his father again, to spite whom, he resolved to marry the young Miss Halcomb without delay. His father was appalled at the prospect of such a *mésalliance*, a sorry end to his efforts to make his son '*a man of consequence* in the county'. Fortunately there was some reconciliation when Mr Halcomb agreed to raise his daughter's dowry to £1,000, and the newly-weds were installed at Widdington Farm, complete with stock and the rent paid, courtesy of Thomas Hunt. A year later Thomas Hunt died, and Henry decided to leave Widdington and live 'more centrical' on the lands he now controlled. He moved to Chisenbury House, or Chisenbury Priory as it is still known locally, an imposing mansion attached to the remains of the original priory, with five sitting-rooms, twelve bedrooms, fifty-two windows assessed for tax, and a fine eighteenth-century front of brick, noted and admired by Pevsner. Here Hunt lived in great style as a gentleman farmer and 'complete sportsman', enjoying to the full the prosperity of the war years, the 'zenith of the farmer's glory'.[3]

---

[2] Ibid., i, 48, 224, 299, 381–2 and 395–8. *TRR* 12 Jan. 1822.

[3] Hunt, *Memoirs*, i, 41–398, ii, 38 and 63. N. Pevsner, *Buildings of England: Wiltshire* (London, 1963), 240. I am grateful to a previous owner, Mrs Morton-Fisher of Jersey, for information about Chisenbury Priory as it should be called. For a splendid description of this part of the Avon valley, see W. Cobbett, *Rural Rides* (London, 1830; rpt. Penguin edn., 1967), 296–322.

Hunt's success as a capital farmer is worth examining in some detail: his particular position in Wiltshire landed society at the turn of the century helps explain much about his subsequent political career. His income and pretensions antagonized the local gentry and led him to question the established order; his ready rapport with his fellow farmers and the agricultural labourers took him towards reform and popular participation, his financial security allowing him to pursue an 'independent' line in politics. As a minor landowner and substantial tenant farmer, Hunt did not belong to any of the traditional categories of landed society as classified by historians. He was neither established 'gentry' nor prosperous 'yeoman', the latter term causing him great offence when it was applied to him in the Peterloo indictment.[4] Hunt was an early example of the 'gentleman farmer': his combined income from rents and direct farming profits matched that of many squires, but unlike most of the gentry he was a substantial tenant farmer, fully involved in the business of farming. According to his *Memoirs*, the family property in Wiltshire and Somerset was 'of the value of upwards of six hundred pounds a year', but his annual income was around twice this figure.[5] Some details are known about the rents he received in Somerset: he let the farm at Edgerly for £200 p.a.;[6] the manor-house, orchard and fishery at Glastonbury for £36 p.a.;[7] and the annual rights to the Tor Fair for £5;[8] but no figures are available for his farming profits on his own and rented land in Wiltshire. Overall, his income was somewhere between £1,000 and £1,500 a year, a sum which places him comfortably in the ranks of the squires, the middle of the three gentry groups identified by Professor Mingay.[9] In his life-style, however, the young Hunt emulated the very wealthiest members of landed society:

The profits arising from my large well cultivated farms enabled me to vie with men of five or six thousand a year, in my domestic establishment . . . I lived as well, kept as good a house, and had my whole establishment so arranged, as to make quite as good an appearance for a thousand or fifteen hundred a year as many persons make who spend more than thrice that sum.[10]

Hunt's propensity to display his wealth—he delighted in cutting a dashing figure 'at home, at the table, in the field, or on the road'[11]—stemmed from youthful ostentation: it was not some socially motivated exercise in conspicuous consumption. The display was built upon solid economic

---

[4] Huish, ii, 238.   [5] Hunt, *Memoirs*, i, 531.   [6] *TRR*, 25 Sept. 1822.

[7] Hunt, *Memoirs*, iii, 34.

[8] University of Chicago: MS 563, Hunt Correspondence and Papers, item 53, Agreement between Hunt and James Down, 6 Sept. 1822.

[9] G. E. Mingay, *English Landed Society in the eighteenth century* (London, 1963), ch. 2. I would like to thank Professor Mingay for his helpful comments on my findings.

[10] Hunt, *Memoirs*, i, 399.   [11] Ibid., i, 304–5.

foundations: Hunt achieved remarkable success as a working farmer on what was for the most part rather marginal sheep land.

He always took particular pride in his widely acknowledged sheep farming skills, but he also achieved considerable success in arable farming, using progressive methods during the war-time boom. His most successful experiment was at Widdington, where he introduced crops in 1801, growing oats on poor down land which had been 'very highly manured': the oats and straw produced £50 per acre 'while the fee simple of the land would not have sold for £20 per acre'.[12] At Devizes market he always obtained the highest prices for his wheat and barley from his other farms, and regularly chaired the farmers' dinner at the Bear Inn. Some idea of the extent of his farming activities can be ascertained from the inventory of his stock which he drew up in the midst of the invasion scare of 1801: 1,600 sacks of wheat; 1,500 quarters of barley; 400 quarters of oats; 30 cart-horses; 10 draught oxen; 20 cows; 4,200 sheep; 50 pigs; and various wagons and carts. He calculated the total value as £20,000 a little high perhaps for his 3,000 acres, as a good figure for the value of farm stock per acre at this period was around £5 or £6.[13] Hunt certainly made the most of the war-time boom, and really enjoyed his farming to which he was passionately committed, as William Cobbett, who sought his advice on a range of agricultural matters from root crops to mouse poison, clearly realized. 'Those who oppose you', he wrote to Hunt shortly before the Bristol election of 1812, 'little imagine how much more happy you would be upon your farm, if your *duty* did not call you from it.'[14] First and foremost, Hunt was a countryman and farmer, enjoying the pleasures of cultivating the soil, the sports of the field, the wine and 'best old October' of his well-stocked cellars, and the market-day *bonhomie* of the Bear Inn. He was 'doatingly fond of the country, country pursuits, and a country life'.[15]

After his separation from his wife in 1802 he spent much of his time in Bath, away from his beloved farms. His finances took a turn for the worse too, because of the poor performance of the brewery in Bristol in which his father-in-law had persuaded him to invest. He took lodgings in Clifton so that he could supervise the business himself, but his attempt to brew 'genuine beer', using only malt and hops and no drugs or substitute, proved an expensive mistake. The business was finally wound up in 1807, shortly after which he also gave up the tenancy of Chisenbury Farm dividing his time thereafter between his house in Bath and Sans Souci Cottage, a 'sporting cottage' which he had built on his estate at Littlecot.[16] He found

[12] Ibid., i, 533–4.   [13] Ibid., ii, 20–36.
[14] Adelphi University and Nuffield College: Cobbett Papers, Cobbett to Hunt, 10 Feb. 1812. Most of this collection of thirty-five letters from Cobbett to Hunt relate to agricultural matters.
[15] Hunt, *Memoirs*, iii, 43.   [16] Ibid., ii, 83–312.

little satisfaction in an 'inactive life out of business', so he took a large estate at Rowfant, near East Grinstead, 'consisting of a good mansion, a thousand acres of land, and the manorial rights of the whole parish of Worth, extending over upwards of twenty thousand acres'. Here he succeeded in making a quick return, the improvements he effected on the 'poor, hungry, deceitful and barren soil' earning him a clear profit of £2,000 when he disposed of the stock and lease in 1813, a propitious time to quit farming as prices were about to drop dramatically.[17]

For the next few months he devoted all his energies to the sports of the field, for which purpose he acquired the tenancy of Middleton Cottage, Andover, together with the manor of Longparish 'extending over a very fine sporting country, of eight or ten thousand acres'.[18] But he could not keep away from farming, the worsening economic climate notwithstanding. In 1814 he undertook what he later admitted was a 'bad speculation': he bought the three-year lease of Cold Henly Farm, Whitchurch, Hampshire, 300 acres of poor land at £222 a year. Here he intended to 'try the experiment of raising large crops of corn in the manner recommended in Tull's Husbandry'—at this time he was trying to persuade Cobbett to join him in forming a 'Tullian Society'.[19] The system of drilling at wide intervals proved an expensive failure at Cold Henly and later at a farm he took on in Upavon, and the profits of Rowfant were soon lost. He spent vast sums cleaning up and improving the Cold Henly estate, only to have a spurious legal action brought against him for breach of covenant. But this was part of the price he had to pay for his political deviance, his notoriety as 'Orator' Hunt, the radical. The action was hatched up by a coterie of Winchester parsons and attornies who openly boasted to him that they had 'driven Cobbett out of the country, and they would try hard to make me follow him'.[20] After a protracted legal wrangle Hunt petitioned Parliament in 1819 demanding the impeachment of the four judges of the Court of King's Bench and the convening of the committee on courts of justice so that 'all other persons who have suffered in consequence of the maladministration of public justice, may have an opportunity of laying their complaints before such committee, in order that corrupt and partial administrators of public justice may be brought to condign punishment'.[21] The very circumstances which brought an end to his farming career became part of his campaign for reform and accountability in government, administration, and justice.

[17] Ibid., ii, 433–4 and iii, 138–41. University of Chicago: MS 563, Hunt Correspondence and Papers, item 10, Agreement between Hunt and J. Target, 20 Feb. 1811.
[18] Hunt, *Memoirs*, iii, 149.
[19] Adelphi University and Nuffield College: Cobbett Papers, Cobbett to Hunt, 5 July 1814.
[20] Hunt, *Memoirs*, iii, 150–3, 175–8 and 548–50.
[21] 'Impeachment of the Four Judges of the Court of King's Bench', *Medusa*, 5 June 1819.

Cold Henly was Hunt's last venture in full-time farming. After his lengthy imprisonment on the Peterloo charge he was forced to enter business in London to recoup his fortune. Through the sale of one of his products, annatto, a dye used in the colouring of cheese, he retained his links with the west country farming world. Whenever he visited his many agents in the region, he supplied the London press with expert reports on the state of the harvest and other agricultural matters, reflecting his continuing pride in his farming knowledge.[22] Hunt's renown as a successful farmer, indeed, persisted long after he had left the land. In 1830 farmers and labourers looked to him for advice and mediation during the 'Captain Swing' riots.[23] When he broke irrevocably from Cobbett in 1831, after a series of patched-up quarrels in the past, the political origins of the dispute were soon overshadowed by heated polemics about their respective merits as farmers, a matter of the utmost pride to both antagonists.[24]

By this time, Hunt had entered Parliament as MP for Preston and had been away from country living for several years, but he still looked 'half yeoman, half gentleman sportsman'.[25] 'His manner and appearance very good', Charles Greville noted in his diary, 'like a country gentleman of the old school, a sort of rural dignity about him, very civil and good-humoured'.[26] Whenever agricultural matters were under discussion in the House, he was one of the most prominent speakers—he spoke no less than thirty times in one day during the committee stage of the Game Law Amendment Bill.[27] Unequal legislation of this kind, which divided rural society harshly and invidiously, angered him intensely. Some three decades or so earlier he had been led to question his instinctive loyalist politics when the vindictive Wiltshire establishment, resentful of his outstanding success on the land as farmer and sportsman, tried to put him in his place by employing the force of the landowners' law against him.

2. LOYALIST

Brought up as a farmer in the depths of Wiltshire at the time of the French

---

[22] See the copies of Hunt's letters to the *Morning Herald* reprinted in *WFP*, 8 Aug. 1829 (RRA report), *Leeds Patriot*, 1 Aug. and 12 Sept. 1829, and 26 June 1830.

[23] E. J. Hobsbawm and G. Rudé, *Captain Swing* (Harmondsworth, Penguin edn., 1973), 89–90.

[24] Much of the argument was concerned with Cobbett's attempt to introduce maize, see Spater, ii, 431–7.

[25] *New Monthly Magazine*, Mar. 1831, quoted in W. Proctor, 'Orator Hunt, M.P. for Preston 1830–32', *Transactions of the Historic Society of Lancashire and Cheshire*, cxiv (1962), 146–7.

[26] Charles Greville, *The Greville Memoirs* (3 vols., London, 1874), ii, 112.

[27] *PD*, 3rd series, v, 8 Aug. 1831, 940–66.

Revolution, young Hunt was a 'loyal man to the backbone'. In his adolescence he displayed an exaggerated loyalism, a symptom of youthful impetuosity rather than any expression of political commitment. Such hot-headed patriotism, indeed, brought him into conflict with authority at home and in the county. He defied his father and ran away to Portsmouth to attend the royal launching of the *Prince of Wales* when Lord Howe was congratulated by the king for his recent victory over the French fleet. Soon after his return, he clashed with his father again when he decided to enrol in the local yeomanry corps under Captain Astley. The fiery young Hunt joined the Everleigh troop in eager anticipation of the thrill and honour of fighting off the anticipated French invasion, not realizing that the yeomanry saw its purpose in domestic and conservative terms. To his dismay, he found that the troop was preoccupied with 'keeping up the price of corn, keeping down the price of wages, and at the same time keeping in subjugation the labourers, and silencing their dissatisfaction'. As it was, they failed lamentably in this task when confronted with riot and disturbance during the *crise de subsistence* of the mid-1790s. The most inglorious episode was the 'battle of Salisbury' when the troop planned to wreak vengeance upon the market 'mob' who had attacked Dyke, their cornet, after he tried to introduce the 'little bushel' of the Winchester measure, an eight-gallon measure as opposed to the traditional ten-gallon measure which the Hunts, steadfast practitioners of the 'moral economy', still sent to market. In the event, all the officers were suddenly indisposed—Dyke excused himself because of a 'violent pain in the bowels'. Hunt finally resigned in disgust during the invasion scare of 1797, when he publicly criticized Astley, Dyke and the other officers for refusing to serve outside the county. His spirited conduct on the occasion came to the notice of Lord Bruce, colonel of the Wiltshire Yeomanry, who immediately invited him to enrol in the Marlborough troop.[28]

By resigning in such dramatic fashion, Hunt incurred the enduring hostility of Astley, his neighbour and former hunting companion. In league with his fellow 'JUSTASSES', Astley engineered Hunt's removal from the post of principal overseer, a parochial office he had recently taken over after his father's death. The major ratepayer and the largest paymaster in the parish, Hunt had operated a generous relief policy, another instance of his adherence to the old moral economy. After his dismissal from office he protested at the abuse of the allowance system by other employers who eschewed his policy of paying decent non-subsidized wages. Astley's next step in the vendetta was a recourse to the law through an action against

---

[28] Hunt, *Memoirs*, i, 143–258, 333–49. University of Chicago: MS 563, Hunt Correspondence and Papers, item 3, Resolutions of meeting at Enford, 4 May 1798. J. R. Western, 'The Volunteer Movement as an anti-Revolutionary Force', *English Historical Review*, lxxi (1956), 603–14.

Hunt for trespass. By the time it came to court Hunt faced more serious legal charges, the result of a dispute with Bruce, his new commanding officer. The trouble here began with a shooting party to Marlborough Woods during which Hunt's prowess with the gun had disposed of rather too many of Lord Ailesbury's pheasants. He received a letter from Bruce terminating his services in the troop: 'he had no other complaint to make against me', Hunt noted sardonically, 'but that I was too good a shot at his father's pheasants, and consequently a very unfit person to oppose the French in case of an invasion.' Hunt ignored the dismissal and attended the next field-day: when he failed to elicit a public apology from Bruce, he rashly challenged him to a duel. Bruce declined to meet him, preferring to settle the point in the courts. Lengthy legal proceedings followed, during which Hunt's counsel was compelled to protest at the way his client was portrayed as 'some low poacher . . . some low, vulgar, ill-bred or no-bred man, violating the law all over his neighbourhood, and boasting of the triumphs he had over his noble prosecutor'. When Hunt was finally fined £100 and sentenced to six weeks' imprisonment, he decided to publish a full account of the proceedings in order to demonstrate that he had 'in no one instance, disgraced the character of a Gentleman and a Soldier'. Fortunately, he fared considerably better against Astley, who ended up nonsuited: Hunt produced several witnesses who testified to his open agreement with one of Astley's disgruntled tenants to sport on his land at will. Astley's mismanagement of the case angered Ailesbury's legal advisers who were searching for any material to discredit Hunt's apparently exemplary record with the Marlborough troop. What riled them most of all was the way Hunt had been 'passed off as a Gentleman'. Hunt's success on the land notwithstanding, the Wiltshire establishment had clearly decided that he was not one of their kind.[29]

Hunt rather enjoyed his sojourn in the King's Bench Prison, his *'residence in town*, for it is a farce to call it imprisonment'. He negotiated for some comfortable accommodation together with the run of the key, and delighted in the company of some of the leading reformers of the day. Samuel Waddington, the city radical, was his friendly companion at mealtimes, and Waddington's counsel, Henry Clifford, the distinguished liberal lawyer and doyen of Horne Tooke's Wimbledon circle, was a frequent visitor. Clifford took a special interest in Hunt's political enlightenment, and arranged for him to accompany him on visits to other

[29] Hunt, *Memoirs*, i, 402–40, and ii, 312–13; and *The proceedings at large in the Court of King's Bench in the cause the King against Henry Hunt, Esq. for challenging the Rt. Hon. Charles Brudenell Bruce, commonly called Lord Bruce. Addressed to the Officers and Gentlemen of the Wiltshire Yeomanry Cavalry* (London, 1801), v–vii, and 100–1. Wiltshire County Record Office: Savernake MSS, Yeomanry papers, letters from John and Thomas Ward to Ailesbury, 10 Apr., 22 June, 10 July 1799, and 1 Jan. 1801.

clients, including Colonel Despard, then being held in the Tower under the suspension of habeas corpus. Through Clifford, Hunt was invited to Tooke's parties at Wimbledon, but he always declined as he still regarded Tooke and his entourage, most notably Sir Francis Burdett, as dangerous Jacobins. Prison was an important political school for Hunt, but the land remained his absorbing passion: politics was promptly cast aside when he returned to Wiltshire two stone overweight to concentrate his energies on the healthy exercises of farming, the sports of the field, and the general pleasures of life at Chisenbury House.[30]

For the next year or so, Hunt enjoyed a life of 'uninterrupted gaiety and dissipation . . . dinners, balls, plays, hunting, shooting, fishing and driving . . . the very vortex of endless dissipation and folly'. Money was plentiful and business was never neglected, but his marriage was soon under considerable strain. This 'heyday of levity and vanity' was followed by a period of personal and political crisis, which ended with his separation from his wife and his whole-hearted commitment to politics and reform. During the 'giddy round of mirth and folly' he became totally captivated by the charms of Mrs Vince, an unhappily married woman, with whom he soon fell deeply in love. For two years they tried to control and conceal their affection for each other: finally, in the middle of Brighton Race Week, they decided they could no longer live apart and left town together. The elopement marked an important turning-point in Hunt's private life, the rest of which was spent in devoted fidelity with Mrs Vince. The lavish entertaining came to an immediate end, and a formal separation was aranged with his wife, apparently in an amicable spirit—Hunt's private papers, however, suggest that he was less generous than he claims in his *Memoirs*: his wife received an annuity of £250 not £300. With Mrs Vince Hunt found true happiness, but he had flouted social convention, for which heinous solecism he was snubbed by the county establishment: it was this ostracism which carried him into the ranks of the reformers.[31]

On his return from the King's Bench Prison Hunt had tried to establish friendly relations with the county dignitaries. Characteristically, he rather overdid things. During the invasion scare which preceded the peace of Amiens, he embarrassed the neighbouring landowners by offering to place his entire stock and work-force at the disposal of the Government. He repeated the offer in 1803 when the Government introduced a flood of legislation to establish auxiliary forces for home defence. At Enford the landowners had great difficulty raising their quota under the terms of the

[30] Hunt, *Memoirs*, i, 440–529. For details of Waddington and Clifford, Sir Charles Wolseley's brother-in-law, see J. A. Hone, *For the Cause of Truth: Radicalism in London 1796–1821*(Oxford, 1982), 23, 153 and *passim*.

[31] Hunt, *Memoirs*, i, 529–52, and ii, 46–73. University of Chicago: MS 563, Hunt Correspondence and Papers, item 7, Separation agreement, witnessed by Robert Bird, 6 Sept. 1802. Huish, i, 283–98, on this 'deep and damning blot' on Hunt's character.

new Defence Bill until 'Squire' Hunt returned from the Bristol Brewery to assume command. He recruited every able-bodied man available, a tribute to his close and easy relationship with the labourers with whom he had spent so many happy days in 'useful labour and cheerful recreation'. 'We had worked, we had toiled together in the field; we had mingled together in the innocent gay delights of the country wake', he recollected with pride, 'I had been present, and had never failed to patronise their manly sports, at the annual festivals of Easter and Whitsuntide . . . I was so well known amongst the young and old, that they all with one accord exclaimed if Mr. Hunt will be our captain we will follow where he leads, if it be to the farthermost parts of the earth.' The county authorities were scandalized by Hunt's uninvited assumption of command, his latest social enormity. Pembroke, the lord lieutenant, set aside the Government's ruling that all offers were to be accepted, and informed Hunt and the Enford volunteers that their services would not be required. This snub removed what little was left of Hunt's traditional loyalism. Within a few months he became a fervent supporter of Burdett, and an avid reader of Cobbett. The gentleman farmer stood forward as a 'professed politician'.[32]

Hunt's abandonment of loyalism, then, can be explained in local and personal terms within the Wiltshire milieu, where his economic success and pretensions led to social and political ostracism. But this was a time when many loyalists underwent a similar questioning of political allegiance. These were years of considerable flux and confusion as war, patriotism and reform were all undergoing revision and redefinition. Reform was rapidly losing its Jacobin stigma: with the change in the character of the war, reformers of all shades were able to assert their 'patriotic' credentials with some vigour. The anti-war liberals placed themselves to the fore in the volunteering drive of 1803 as Britain was now upholding the cause of liberty against military despotism.[33] The ways and means of radicalism underwent considerable revision once Napoleon's imperial ambitions became apparent. Conspiracy gave way to 'legitimate' activity as the radicals repudiated the French connection on which the success of any physical move depended. Burdett and others now sought to condemn and embarrass the Government by circumventing the repressive legislation imposed in the 1790s. Through his exposure of public scandals, Burdett attracted considerable support and gradually shed the stigma of Jacobinism. When he stood in the famous Middlesex by-election in 1804, his

[32] Hunt, *Memoirs*, ii, 18–28, 114–29, 149 and 178. University of Chicago: MS 563, Hunt Correspondence and Papers, items 4 and 5, Pembroke to Hunt, 20 Aug. 1801, and 14 Aug. 1803; item 6, Hunt to 'My Lord' (Pembroke), 1803; item 8, Pembroke to Sir J. M. Poore, Aug. 1803, and item 90, Hunt to 'My Lord' (Pembroke) n.d. C. Emsley, *British Society and the French Wars 1793–1815* (London, 1979) ch. 6.
[33] J. E. Cookson, *The Friends of Peace: Anti-War Liberalism in England 1793–1815* (Cambridge, 1982), ch. 7.

independent stance was applauded by a number of ex-loyalists, including Hunt and Cobbett. Hunt followed the election closely and admired Burdett's heroic defiance of 'all the magistracy, and all the ministerial aristocracy of the metropolitan county'. Cobbett's volte-face was no less dramatic: Burdett, the Jacobin ogre, was now the patriotic champion battling against the demons of the 'Pitt System'—new money, stock jobbers, contractors, sycophants and the like. The election was a great moral victory for Burdett and reform—he was actually one vote ahead when the poll closed at 5 p.m., but the sheriff declared in favour of the ministerial candidate who had been five votes in front at 3 p.m., the 'customary' closing time. It was Burdett's opponents, the enemies of the reform, who now appeared the real villains with their 'insidious machinations against the constitutional liberties of England'. The patriotic struggle against despotism was beginning to acquire an essentially domestic aspect.[34]

3. 'BRISTOL' HUNT AND THE POLITICS OF INDEPENDENCE AND REFORM

Once he abandoned the last vestiges of traditional loyalism, Hunt progressed rapidly through constitutional 'independence' to democratic radicalism. No longer restrained by the social and political conventions of rural Wiltshire, he was soon to take the lead in the popular politics of one of the most important cities in the land. It was the financial difficulties of the Jacob's Well Brewery which forced him to spend much of his time in Bristol, away from his beloved farms, but he soon acquired an absorbing interest in the politics of this bustling city. In Bristol, Hunt the successful gentleman farmer, discovered his true *métier* as popular political leader.

(i) The Melville affair and the Ministry of All the Talents

Hunt's political education developed rapidly in Wiltshire before he went on to challenge the factions in Bristol. A supporter of Burdett and 'independence' he found himself at odds with the Whig worthies of the county, when a series of war-time scandals relating to malversation, corruption and incompetence in high places prompted a nationwide display of anti-ministerial feeling, expressed through the revival of the platform.[35] At the Wiltshire meeting called to protest at the financial misconduct of Pitt's close friend, Lord Melville, the First Lord of the Admiralty and Treasurer of the Navy, Hunt concluded his maiden speech on the county platform with a string of resolutions expressing 'general condemnation of

---

[34] Hone, ch. 3; Hunt, *Memoirs*, ii, 139–41. See also, Hugh Cunningham, 'The Language of Patriotism', *History Workshop Journal*, xii (1981), 8–33.

[35] H. Jephson, *The Platform: its rise and progress* (2 vols., London, 1892), i, ch. 8.

all peculations and peculators'. His proposals, he later came to understand, were 'too sweeping, as they cut at the Whigs as well as the Ministers': at the time, he allowed himself to be wheedled out of the 'main jet' of his proposals by the more experienced Whigs on the platform.[36] The Whigs gained considerable party advantage from the Melville affair, inhibited though they were by the Grenville alliance: they regained the support of old reformers such as Cartwright and Wyvill; and aroused the hopes of the new critics of the 'Pitt System', including former loyalists like Hunt and Cobbett.[37] The Whigs, Hunt later recalled, became 'popular with the nation at large, and possessed the confidence of the thinking and honourable portion of the people.' By the time the Foxite–Grenville coalition took office in 1806, Hunt was 'one of Mr. Fox's most enthusiastic admirers . . . I own I indulged the most confident hope that he would now realize all his former professions.' These fond expectations were soon blasted. The first act of the new ministry, the bill enabling Grenville to hold the post of First Lord of the Treasury at £6,000 a year and at the same time the office of Auditor of the Exchequer at £4,000 a year 'to audit his *own accounts*' constituted 'a death-blow to the fondly-cherished hopes of every patriotic mind in the kingdom'. In their later actions, Hunt fulminated, the new ministers 'not only trod in Mr. Pitt's steps, by adopting all his measures, but they greatly outdid him in insulting the feelings of the people'. The Ministry of All the Talents revealed the Whigs in their true colours as 'a despicable, a hypocritical, and a tyrannical faction': throughout the rest of his long political life, Hunt constantly reminded the people of this damning record of apostasy, betrayal, profligacy and corruption.[38]

Disillusioned with the Whigs and party politicians in general, Hunt came to take even greater pride in his own 'independence', his freedom from the 'trammels of party': he always cherished the compliment of the old Marquis of Lansdowne that his 'situation in life' rendered him 'one of the most independent men in the kingdom'.[39] Thus, at the general election in November 1806, he tried to arouse the spirit of 'independence' in the county against the corrupt power of the factions. As his 'Address to the independent Freeholders of the County of Wilts.' shows, he regarded 'independence' as the ideal for electors and elected alike. To unseat the time-serving, tax-eating, place-hunters, he appealed to the electors to assert their independence by emancipating themselves from patronage, bribery and deference, to exercise 'those liberties and just rights that were

[36] Hunt, *Memoirs*, ii, 159. University of Chicago: MS 563, Hunt Correspondence and Papers, item 15, Hunt to 'My Lord' (Lansdowne), 30 Apr. 1805.

[37] A. D. Harvey, *Britain in the Early Nineteenth Century* (London, 1978), 155–60. J. R. Dinwiddy, *Christopher Wyvꞏꞏl and Reform 1790–1820* (York, Borthwick Papers, 39, 1971), 14–16.

[38] Hunt, *Memoirs*, ii, 201–12.   [39] Ibid., ii, 9.

so gloriously secured to you by your forefathers'. What was required was a truly independent candidate, 'a man of our own choosing, as free of expense to himself as we would wish him to be honest and true to the confidence reposed in him', a gentleman of sufficient strength and wealth to resist the pull of party and the temptations of place and public money. Hunt's appeal fell on deaf ears: the 'Address', he noted, gave great umbrage 'to the whole of the friends of the Pitt system, which evidently included Whigs as well as Tories; but it produced no beneficial effect upon the senseless and inanimate freeholders of the county of Wilts'.[40] Such was the fate of all appeals to 'independence' in 1806. At Honiton Cobbett displayed his personal independence by pledging his 'firm determination never to receive a farthing of the public money . . . [and] never, in any way whatever, to give one farthing of my own money to any man, in order to induce him to vote, or to cause others to vote for me'; he stood aside at the election when Cochrane took the pledge and was heavily defeated by the local 'Mr Most'.[41] Burdett was rejected by the electors of Middlesex when he adopted the new austere independent manner. Having spent nearly £100,000 on the two previous contests he was particularly keen to dispense with treating and the like, but he rather took matters to extremes, by leaving it entirely up to the 'independent electors' to come forward of their own accord. His vote was halved and he lost the seat. At the next general election a few months later, however, he secured a sensational victory in Foxite Westminster, thanks to the economic efficiency and organizational skills of the new Westminster Committee.[42] Here was a successful model of organized 'independent' endeavour for Hunt to introduce in Bristol, where the general election of 1807 provided him with an object lesson in the duplicity and collusion of the factions.

(ii) The Bristol election of 1807

By the early nineteenth century, Bristol had lost its long-cherished title as the second city of the kingdom, but it remained one of the largest freeman boroughs. Typically for such a constituency, many prominent middle-class families had not been accorded 'freeman' status, whilst the corporation had allowed the dependent poor to take their 'freedoms' according to various local rights and customs. Hunt entered Bristol politics at a time when the middle class were beginning to resent their exclusion from local (and national) political power and the poor freemen were hoping for an end to the long party truce which had so reduced the financial advantages of possessing the franchise. Following the extremely costly contests of 1780,

---

[40] Ibid., ii, 221–5. *CPR*, 15 Nov. 1806, printed the address.

[41] Spater, i, 152–5.

[42] M. W. Patterson, *Sir Francis Burdett and his Times* (2 vols., London, 1931), i, chs. 9 and 10.

1781, and 1784, the local Whigs and Tories had agreed to avoid further conflicts and share the representation. The factions, Hunt regretted, had 'reduced this great City, to a level with the rottenest of rotten *Boroughs*': they 'divided the representation and the loaves and fishes between them, leaving the electors nothing but the empty name of freemen'. In 1807, he was thus surprised and delighted to hear that a third candidate, Sir John Jervis, was prepared to stand. On the hustings he stepped forward to propose Jervis, but the sheriff refused to accept the nomination on the grounds that Hunt was neither a freeman nor a freeholder of Bristol, a ruling which clearly pleased and relieved Jervis. Hunt duly realized that it was all a hoax, that Jervis was 'nothing more nor less than a scape-goat, a mere tool in the hands of the White Lion club, or ministerial faction, a mere scarecrow, whom they had set up to deter any other person from offering himself, or rather to prevent the freemen from seeking another Candidate'. For the third successive occasion, Baillie and Bathurst were returned unopposed, but later in the day there was considerable violence in the city when the frustrated freemen attacked Bathurst's victory procession with 'stones, clubs, oyster-shells and dirt'. Learning of the riots, Hunt returned to the city from Clifton, and managed to draw the crowds away to Brandon Hill where he placated their anger by informing them of his plans to introduce a weekly subscription scheme for poor freemen, his intention to contest the seat personally at the next election, and his readiness to treat them all to three hogsheads of strong beer from his nearby brewery.[43]

A fortnight or so later, Hunt learnt of Burdett's great victory at Westminster. At a cost of less than £800, the artisans, tradesmen and *menu peuple* of the Westminster Committee had successfully challenged the Foxite hold on popular London. A celebratory dinner was held at Bristol at which Hunt presided: congratulatory resolutions were passed in honour of Burdett and the Westminster Committee; a statement of principles was issued, pledging loyalty to the Constitution which, it was hoped, would soon be restored to its 'ancient purity'; and the first steps were taken to encourage the Bristol freemen to recover and assert their just and constitutional rights 'in glorious imitation of those of Westminster'.[44] In the following months, Hunt revitalized popular politics in Bristol, introducing some of the system, method and organization which had

---

[43] H. Hunt, *An Address to all those who wish to preserve their country from the horrors of a sanguinary revolution* (Bristol, 1807). Hunt, *Memoirs*, ii, 234–49. *Bristol Gazette*, 7 May 1807. *Felix Farley's Bristol Journal*, 9 May 1807 and 3 Oct. 1812, for Jervis's later version of events in his address 'To the electors'. J. Latimer, *The Annals of Bristol in the Nineteenth Century* (Bristol, 1887; rpt. 1970) 1 and 29–30. Newman, 173–92. I would like to thank Mark Harrison of Cambridge for his helpful advice on Bristol sources.

[44] Hunt, *An Address to all those*, 8–10, and 15–22; and *Memoirs*, ii, 252–7. *The Proceedings of the late Westminster Election* (London, 1808), 233–46. *Felix Farley's Bristol Journal*, 6 June 1807.

worked so well in Westminster. He began with his promised subscription fund for the poor freemen, whose inability to pay their own fees placed them in the power of those who advanced the money in return for 'a promise of their votes'. In future, by paying a small weekly subscription to his society at the Lamb and Lark, they could take up their freedoms and pay their fees out of their own accumulating funds.[45] His next step was the formation of an electoral society modelled on the Westminster Committee, the Bristol Patriotic and Constitutional Association, which aimed to counteract the 'unwarrantable influence, manœuvre, and deception, which have reduced the electors of this city to mere political cyphers, to passive spectators of the general wreck, freemen with no other appendage of freedom but the empty name'.[46]

By this time, the local loyalists regarded him as an arch-revolutionary, the leader of a desperate gang of adventurers 'who clamour for reform and mean Revolution', the would-be president of the 'committee of public safety for the city of Bristol'. Hunt responded with vigour to such calumny, assuring the good citizens of Bristol that he was 'actuated with the purest and most independent Constitutional motives' and wanted nothing more than the 'permanent establishment of our enviable Constitution as established in 1688'.[47] Some of his own supporters, however, questioned his intentions and turned against him when he followed Burdett into radical reform. Thomas Lee, vice-president of the celebratory dinner in June, accused him of forsaking the values of true independence to establish a Burdettite faction in Bristol, using the freemens' funds and clubs to promote a partisan, radical candidate. A heated controversy ensued during which Hunt derogated Lee's notion of independence and defended the constitutional ways and means of the new popular organizations.[48] His enthusiastic support for Burdett, 'the best friend of the Constitution, the whole Constitution, and nothing but the Constitution of England', continued undiminished, although some of Burdett's reform colleagues were rather embarrassed by their provincial recruit. 'There is one *Hunt*, the Bristol man. Beware of him!', Cobbett warned in a private letter to his publisher in April 1808, 'he rides about the country with a whore, the wife of another man, having deserted his own! A sad fellow! Nothing to do with him!' The letter, the cause of much controversy in later years, was quickly

---

[45] Hunt, *Memoirs*, ii, 260–2.

[46] Hunt, *An Address to all those*, 12–15; and *Memoirs*, ii, 275–9.

[47] Centinel, *The First Six Letters of Centinel . . . containing an exposition of the principles of the Trout-Tavern Dinner Club; of Mr. H. Hunt, the President* (Bristol, 1807). H. Hunt, *An Address to the Public of the City of Bristol, in answer to an anonymous letter, signed Centinel* (Bristol, 1807); and *An Address to all those*, 1–7, and 30–2.

[48] Thomas Lee, *A Letter to Henry Hunt, Esq. Chairman of a Political Club held at the Lamb and Lark* (Bristol, 1808). Letters from Hunt, Lee and others in *Bristol Gazette*, 5–26 May 1808.

forgotten at the time: Hunt and Cobbett, indeed, soon became close friends and allies promoting the reform programme of their hero, Burdett, 'Westminster's Pride and England's Glory'.[49]

(iii) The revival of reform

The campaign for parliamentary reform began to gather momentum as the scandals and blunders accumulated in the years of lengthy war. Cobbett was applauded for his 'democratical and Jacobinical' talk at the Hampshire county meeting called to demand an inquiry into the Convention of Cintra. Then came Gwyllym Wardle's sensational allegations against the Duke of York, Commander-in-Chief of the army, claiming that army commissions had been sold by his mistress, Mrs Clarke. When Parliament acquitted the Duke—he later resigned his office—there was outrage throughout the country: one recent historian has spoken of a middle-class revolt against patrician society.[50] Hunt made a special point of attending the Hampshire meeting where some cautious Whig motions were rejected in favour of Cobbett's anti-establishment resolutions, including the demand for parliamentary reform. He was planning to requisition a meeting of his own in Wiltshire and hoped to become better acquainted with the 'celebrated Mr Cobbett'. In the heavy drinking after the meeting, he managed to have a word with the star of the day, and on his return to Wiltshire he instructed his attorney to prepare a conveyance, giving Cobbett a freehold in the county, thereby allowing him to address the forthcoming meeting. Before the arrangements were finalized, another scandal came to the surface: Madocks's charges of corrupt practice against Perceval and Castlereagh. Parliament refused to investigate the matter, much to the fury of Hunt and Cobbett who addressed the Wiltshire meeting in angry tones. The meeting was a considerable success, although there was a noticeable absence of 'persons of consequence': a series of strongly-worded resolutions was adopted, praising Wardle and Madocks, denouncing all placeholders and pensioners, and demanding 'such a Reform in the Commons' House of Parliament, as shall make that house in reality, as well as in name, the representative of the people, and not an instrument in the hands of a minister'. This 'triumph of the people over faction', as Hunt later described it, marked the beginning of his close friendship with Cobbett, and his unstinting advocacy of 'effectual and Radical Reform'.[51]

The 'revival of reform' at this time did not reflect any ideological conversion or commitment in the nation out of doors: the widespread demand for reform stemmed from anger, impatience and disgust with the

---

[49] Spater, ii, 364–5. Hunt, *An Address to the Public*, 7; and *Memoirs*, ii, 262–4 and 280–1.
[50] Harvey, 245–6.
[51] Hunt, *Memoirs*, ii, 342–69. *CPR*, 29 Apr. and 20 May 1809.

incompetence, corruption and cost of the war effort.[52] Veteran ideologues like Major Cartwright tried to exploit this favourable turn of events, trusting that pressure from without would compel the Whigs to adopt reform as party policy. To precipitate matters, he tried to entice the Foxite or popular Whigs, the so-called 'Mountain', into an alliance with Burdett to head a Wyvill-like association for reform. His well-meaning efforts failed lamentably. The popular Whigs absented themselves from his dinner meeting in May 1809, and few of them voted for Burdett's motion in the Commons shortly afterwards, calling for a tax-paying franchise, equal electoral districts, and parliaments limited to a 'constitutional duration', the standard 'radical' programme of the time.[53] Thereafter, the reform movement lost its momentum. Wardle, it was revealed, had bribed Mrs Clarke to take her stand against the Duke of York, and the reform cause was further discredited by the violence associated with the 'Old Price' riots at the Covent Garden Theatre, in which the Westminster Committee and Hunt's old political instructor, Henry Clifford, were particularly prominent.[54] Then the Government went on the counter-offensive. The recently revived debating clubs were the first target: Gale Jones of the British Forum was committed to Newgate for a breach of privilege. When Burdett protested that Jones's imprisonment was contrary to the spirit of the Constitution, he was ordered to be committed to the Tower until the end of the parliamentary session. Displaying a fine Wilkite sense of popular political theatre, Burdett refused to surrender to the Commons' warrant, and barricaded himself in his house in Piccadilly, where he was finally apprehended reading Magna Carta to his young son.[55] Cobbett was the next victim: the Government brought forward a libel action which had been held in abeyance for nearly a year, and after a rather poor performance at his trial, Cobbett was sentenced to two years' imprisonment and a fine of £1,000.[56] By coincidence, Hunt was serving his second sentence in the King's Bench when Burdett was confined to the Tower and Cobbett was sent to Newgate: he was the victim not of Perceval's stand against reform, but of the malice and political prejudice of his old enemies, the vengeful Wiltshire Tories.

When Hunt returned to Wiltshire from Bristol, after winding up the brewery, he was promptly pursued through the courts by his wealthy landed neighbours who, he claimed, 'made a *common stock purse* in order to defray whatever expenses might be incurred in carrying on actions or prosecutions against me . . . for the declared purpose of putting me down, and, if possible, driving me out of the county'. The first to commence

---

[52] Harvey, 220–50.

[53] N. C. Miller, 'John Cartwright and radical parliamentary reform, 1808–1819', *English Historical Review*, lxxxiii (1968), 712–15.

[54] Hone, 183–5.   [55] Patterson, i, ch. 10.   [56] Spater, i, 233–44.

operations was his old adversary, Astley of Everleigh. This time he took considerable care not to be nonsuited and brought the action for trespass in the name of one of his tenants, but when the writ was executed at Warminster, Hunt cross-examined Simpkins, the hapless tenant, to such considerable effect that the jury returned a special verdict of 'no damages'. This led to a protracted legal battle during which the Court of King's Bench in London twice admonished Wiltshire juries for returning such an unacceptable judgement. Eventually on the third writ, when Hunt was unable to attend the proceedings, a jury finally agreed to award damages against him to the sum of one farthing! Then there were charges brought against him by more powerful neighbours. Hicks Beach, MP for Cirencester, filed an action for trespass which resulted in Hunt having to pay a shilling's damages: the judge was so impressed with Hunt's defence that he refused to award costs against him. This encouraged Hunt to retaliate, and he brought a series of successful actions against some of Hicks Beach's tenants, but he was fleeced by his attorney in the process. Far more serious was the assault charge brought by John Benett of Pyt House, the prospective member for the county. At the Michaelmas Sessions of 1809, a bill of indictment was found against Hunt for an assault on Stone, Benett's gamekeeper, a notorious fighter who had been specially hired to teach Hunt a lesson. In the event, Stone had come off the worse for the encounter, prompting Benett to take the matter to court. Hunt was found guilty of assault and sentenced to three months' imprisonment, thereby precluding his attendance at the Summer Assizes in Salisbury when the third writ in the Astley case was executed.[57]

While in the King's Bench Prison Hunt managed to secure the run of the key again, and was thus able to visit Burdett and Cobbett. His political education developed rapidly in consequence. He came to regard Burdett as the champion of radical or 'real' reform as opposed to the moderate or 'mock' reform proffered by Brand and the popular Whigs. Burdett, however, shared the Whigs' anxiety about uncontrollable activity 'out of doors': on the day of his release, he decided to leave the Tower by the back door and took to the river, thereby avoiding the huge crowds—half a million strong—who waited to fête him on the streets. A few years later, this 'desertion' came to symbolize Burdett's apostasy: Sir Francis *Sly-go* entered radical demonology. At the time, Hunt was disappointed by the day's events, but regarded Francis Place as the real villain of the piece.[58] From Cobbett, Hunt came to understand the urgent economic need for parliamentary reform. Cobbett's imprisonment coincided with the collapse

[57] Hunt, *Memoirs*, ii, 312–405. See also the letter from Hunt in *SPR*, 15 Aug. 1818, protesting at the way Scarlett later misrepresented the facts of the Simpkins's case.

[58] Ibid., ii, 406–25; Hone, 189–94; G. Wallas, *The Life of Francis Place* (London, 4th edn., 1951), 53–6.

of the war-time boom, and he soon set to work on his most famous financial work, *Paper against Gold*, a series of letters exposing the cunning devices of the war-strengthened 'Pitt System'. The war, Cobbett regretted, had consolidated 'the Thing', the system of political corruption and financial plunder which had been tightening its hold since the late seventeenth century at the expense of the unrepresented and heavily taxed poor. Paper money and inflation were but the latest horrors of this funding-system built upon the monstrous national debt, which produced lucrative profits for political peculators and financial speculators, money-men, stockjobbers, Government contractors, pensioners and sycophants, but imposed an intolerable, demand-stifling tax burden on the poor. By 1811, virtually half the Government's annual tax revenue was required simply to meet the interest on this unwanted debt, some £33 million. The only way to return to a healthy metallic currency, Cobbett concluded, was to repudiate the debt, along with the system that produced it and the taxes which serviced it.[59] Through his frequent contact with Cobbett, during this second sojourn in the King's Bench, Hunt returned to active politics with a much sharper economic edge to his radicalism. The rhetoric of constitutional independence was toughened by the language of economic distress as he stood forward to champion the interests of the over-taxed, under-consuming, non-represented poor, and rapidly moved beyond the Burdettite programme and conventions towards unrestrained democratic radicalism.

Hunt made a stormy return to the platform at a county meeting at Wells in March 1811 called to petition the newly installed Regent on the need for reform. The meeting, convened by Hunt at the suggestion of Burdett and the other reformers who attended the regular evening discussion sessions in Cobbett's room at Newgate, provoked the county worthies to unite in full force against the reform threat. Tories and Whigs ordered their tenants to shout Hunt down, a task in which they were ably assisted by the 'black cormorants', the parsons who were so thick on the ground in this cathedral city. Hunt struggled on with his speech, advising the farmers that 'the only remedy to escape *ruin* and distress would be, for the landlords to lower their rents, the parsons to reduce their tithes, and then resolutely join the people in demanding a Reform of the Commons' House of Parliament, which alone would produce a real diminution of taxation'. His radical petition was rejected in favour of 'a mere time-serving piece of fulsome adulation to the Prince Regent', but he refused to regard the occasion as a complete defeat and penned a vindicatory address 'To the Independent

[59] Hunt, *Memoirs*, ii, 480–1. Spater, ii, 314–16. For the strength of 'Old Corruption' and hence the validity of Cobbett's analysis, see Edward Thompson's famous essay 'The Peculiarities of the English', reprinted in *The Poverty of Theory and other essays* (London, 1978), 49–50; and 'Eighteenth-century English society: class struggle without class?', *Social History*, iii (1978) 138–41. See also W. D. Rubinstein, 'The End of "Old Corruption" in Britain 1780–1860', *Past and Present*, ci, (1983), 55–86.

Freeholders and Inhabitants of Somersetshire'. Cobbett, too, believed that the meeting had served a most useful purpose, 'the *exposure of the factions* . . . As if it was a defeat, as if it was not a complete victory, to have compelled the *two factions* to *unite*, to exert all their influence . . . and come barefacedly forward against the people, against reform, against every thing that *menaced corruption!*'[60]

The sharp new edge to Hunt's radicalism was strongly evinced at Cartwright's next dinner meeting, another abortive attempt to bring the radicals and moderate reformers together. While Burdett and the other speakers denounced oligarchy as an evil in itself, a misuse of power that should not be allowed, Hunt drew attention to the dire economic consequence of political corruption. He suggested that the 157 individuals who controlled 307 seats in the Commons, according to the figures in Grey's famous and much-cited petition of 1793, should be publicly named and held responsible for the crippling national debt:

It was they who voted away the public money, and created the debt. It was they who squandered the resources of the country upon their relatives, their friends, their pomp, and their parasites. The people had nothing to do with the anti-jacobin war. That war, and the debt which grew out of it, had been voted by a corrupt House of Commons, chosen by these 157 worthies.

In the discussion of programme and tactics, he was by far the most radical speaker. Here too he shocked the others by ignoring Parliament and the Whigs to concentrate on extra-parliamentary politics and the people. He wanted the meeting to launch a national campaign for radical reform based on petitions to the Regent, dismissing any approach to the corrupt Commons as 'contemptible and ridiculous'. His speech was a splendid example of his mastery of the emotive rhetoric of popular constitutionalism and libertarian history:

If the people were so loyal as to be slow to fly to the sword like their ancestors, let them come forward constitutionally with Petitions to the Throne. The Prince Regent was himself too acute, and was too well advised, not to be well aware that his dearest rights were founded upon those of the people. He had numerous examples in the history of this country to inculcate that sentiment. He had only to look to the case of John, of Charles, and of James II to learn what had been the consequences of infringing the rights of the people, and to be confirmed in his conviction that the best security of the Sovereign is to preserve inviolate the liberties of his people.[61]

Such unrestrained rhetoric and radicalism offended the metropolitan reform establishment and intelligentsia and soon led to Hunt's ostracism. The *Examiner* was the first reform paper to denounce him, doubtless

[60] Hunt, *Memoirs*, ii, 435–62. *CPR*, 16 Mar. 1811.   [61] *The Times*, 11 June 1811.

because the editors—the Hunt brothers—feared they might be confused with their vulgar namesake. They took particular exception to his personal invective directed against Vicary Gibbs, the Attorney-General, who was responsible for the Government's clamp-down on the press. At the annual trial by jury dinner in November 1810, commemorating the anniversary of the acquittal of Tooke and Hardy, Hunt contrasted the enthusiastic reception given to Gibbs in Bristol in 1794 with the riots which had rightly greeted his recent visit, when the walls were chalked 'No Gibbs' and 'Burdett for ever; no Tower'. In 1811, at the next anniversary dinner, he opined that Gibbs would 'admirably grace a lamp-post', a suggestion that the Hunt brothers considered so wilfully irresponsible that they refused to co-operate with Hunt in any way in the future.[62]

But by 1812 the revival of reform had lost momentum and direction: public support had dwindled; the ministers had regained the initiative; and unity had proved unattainable. Cartwright's well-intentioned efforts ended with the formation of two separate reform societies: Northmore's Hampden Club, with its £300 property qualification, was strictly for those who possessed a substantial stake in the country, and it studiously avoided commitment to any specific programme; Cartwright's Union for Parliamentary Reform, by contrast, was more broadly based and identified with the Burdettite programme of direct-taxation suffrage and annual parliaments.[63] Hunt, of course, joined the latter, but there were already indications that his 'popular' interpretation of Burdettite radicalism displeased the delicate and refined sensibilities of the middle-class reformers. The Bristol elections of 1812 completed Hunt's path to democratic radicalism, and placed him in defiant opposition to all moderate reformers.

(iv) The Bristol elections of 1812

Hunt's part in the Bristol elections of 1812, his 'radical' opposition to Sir Samuel Romilly, brought him into open conflict with the middle-class reformers for whom Romilly's candidature was as significant in its way as the campaigns against the Orders-in-Council and the renewal of the Charter of the East India Company.[64] Romilly was adopted by the 'new' middle class of Bristol as an open gesture of protest against the 'high Whigs', the local oligarchs who had chosen one of their kind, Edward Protheroe, to replace Evan Baillie, the retiring Whig member. The 'progressive Whigs' in the Independent and Constitutional Club refused to

[62] *Examiner*, 25 Nov. 1810 and 17 Nov. 1811. Hunt was very active in the campaign to relieve the sufferers of the Government's persecution of the press: he sent a subscription of £17.10s.0d. from Bath to the fund in aid of Peter Finnerty. *The Times*, 21 Feb. 1811

[63] N. C. Miller, 'Major John Cartwright and the Founding of the Hampden Club', *Historical Journal*, xvii (1974), 615–19.

[64] Cookson, *Friends of Peace*, ch. 9. *Felix Farley's Bristol Journal*, 4 Apr. 1812.

endorse Protheroe since he stood for 'No Popery' and 'neutral and
negative whiggism'. By running Romilly against him, the 'modern
reformers' as they were called, were publicly challenging the oligarchic
power exercised by the small group of old-established merchant families
who dominated the Corporation and controlled the electoral politics of the
city. They were strongly supported by popular Whigs and reformers
throughout the country, all of whom held Romilly in high regard: the fund
launched by Lord Folkestone, and managed by 'loan-makers' like Baring
and 'party men' like Whitbread, raised £8,000 with no difficulty at all. A
successful parliamentarian, respected by 'Mountain' and moderates alike,
Romilly was not, however, a very suitable candidate for a large popular
constituency, since he had no aptitude for constituency politics and
disapproved of public dinners, meetings, speeches, and canvassing. Under
sufferance he finally agreed to visit Bristol, 'not for the purpose of
canvassing, but merely to show myself there'. He did not enjoy the
occasion at all. 'Nothing could be more unpleasant to me than all this
parade', he confided to his diary, recording the public procession which
drew him into the city centre. On arrival, he soon gave up the attempt to
address the crowds from the windows of his committee rooms, at which
point the eager Hunt got up on one of the copper pedestals in front of the
Exchange and proceeded to harangue the assembled throng for a good
hour or so. Where Romilly was ill at ease putting himself forward 'out of
the House', Hunt revelled in the politics of the street. Within easy earshot
of Romilly and his supporters, he catalogued the misdeeds of the Ministry
of All the Talents, condemned all Whigs, and boldly proclaimed himself
the 'warm advocate for Radical Reform . . . the staunch friend of Sir
Francis Burdett, and the principles which he professed'. An embarrassed
Romilly was forced to wait until Hunt had finished his pedestal oration
before he could leave for a select dinner at the Assembly Rooms where he
spoke in a very different style. 'I touched upon no topics calculated to court
popular favour,' Romilly recorded with self-denying pride, 'I said nothing
of a reform of Parliament, of pensions, of sinecures, of economy in the
public expenditure, of peace . . . I avowed my attachment to Lord Grey
and Lord Grenville.'[65]

The contrast between Romilly's Whiggery and Hunt's radicalism was
underlined a month later in Bristol when the 'real friends of a radical
reform in Parliament' arranged a Whitsuntide public reception for Hunt.
Huge holiday crowds escorted him to the Exchange, where he delivered his
'second address' from the pedestal and proudly displayed his radical

[65] S. Romilly, *Memoirs* (3 vols., London, 1840), ii, 423–7, and iii, 1–29. *An account of the
entry of Sir Samuel Romilly into Bristol, on Thursday, April 2, 1812* (Bristol, 1812). *Felix
Farley's Bristol Journal*, 11–25 Jan., 8 Feb. and 27 June 1812. *CPR*, 11 Apr. and 4 July 1812.
Hunt, *Memoirs*, ii, 495–509.

independence. 'I am of no party but the people', he proclaimed, 'and I detest all those who plunder that people.' He then entered into a vehement condemnation of all the 'hell-hounds who rob and plunder the people', in particular the 'inhuman advocates of war, devastation and blood . . . all those who do live upon, and who wish to live upon, the sixty millions of additional taxes, annually imposed upon the people during the war'. But it was not just the cost of the war which enraged him: he execrated the very purpose of the conflict. The deployment of the troops against the poor Luddites, the latest and most alarming ramification of the war system, confirmed that the war was directed against the rights and liberties of the people both at home and abroad. 'We are approaching to a military despotism', he warned, protesting at the massive display of military might in the industrial districts: 'we have been at War against Liberty for the last 20 years, which appears likely to end at last in a civil War at home'. He demanded an immediate end to the war, 'the cause of all our sufferings', and in characteristic radical style, put the matter to the vote by a show of hands, thereby securing unanimous and enthusiastic approval for a petition for peace. After the speech, he repaired to the New Assembly Rooms with some hundred supporters, to enjoy a dinner of 'good old English cheer, Roast Beef and Plumb Pudding'. Here to the delight of the guests, including the London shipwrights' leader, John Gast, a Bristol freeman resident in Deptford and former supporter of Romilly, Hunt pledged his 'firm intention never to flinch from the cause he espoused, the Cause of the People . . . to the people he always had appealed, and to the people he always would appeal, not fearing so long as he held the upright principles of Sir Francis Burdett, so long should he receive their support'.[66]

These contrasting public receptions were part of the preparations for the general election which was expected to be called in the spring of 1812. Hunt and his supporters at the Lamb and Lark had started their campaign at the beginning of the year. A committee was appointed in February to secure his return 'free of Expence . . . to follow the glorious example of the Electors of Westminster'; a special subscription was opened to provide funds for those who would lose their jobs by voting for him; and an investigation was begun into the city's charities, from the benefits of which political deviants were always excluded.[67] Hunt took a particular interest in these charities, the lubricant of 'Old Corruption' at city level, and condemned the secret and fraudulent mismanagement of the bequests which served to fund the privileged political position and satiate life-style

[66] *Bristol election: an account of Mr. Hunt's public reception in Bristol, May 18, 1812* (Bristol, 1812). *Bristol Gazette*, 21 May 1812. *Mr. H—t's second Speech without Notes*, undated handbill in Bristol Reference Library.

[67] Hunt's addresses 'To the Freeholders and Freemen of the City of Bristol', in *Felix Farley's Bristol Journal*, 18 Jan. and 15 Feb. 1812, and report of the meeting at the Lamb and Lark in ibid., 8 Feb. 1812.

of the City Corporation. As the first step in a lengthy campaign to force the Corporation to open the books, he issued a *Letter to the Freemen* reminding them that they were the 'real *Owners*', and the Corporation 'merely the *Stewards*', of all the 'large and numerous Estates, and other Property left them at sundry times, under the name of Charities', the details of which he meticulously catalogued in chronological order. Hunt's campaign against malversation and peculation was thus fought on two interlocking fronts in 1812: in the name of independence and the rights of the poor he attacked not only the tax-eating Westminster factions but also the alms-gorging city authorities. His March *Letter to the Freemen* demonstrated how corruption permeated politics at national and local level, as was so well exemplified by the electoral arrangements at Bristol where the factions agreed to share the spoils. 'There is always an *understanding* between the two regular Parties', he explained:

The two PARTIES in this country, like the *foxes* and the *hounds*, though continually at war, have a mutual interest in each other's preservation . . . Their quarrels are, in short, like those of thieves; each wishes to get the largest share of the plunder; but far be it from either to attack his opponent upon *any other score*; far be it from either to make an attack upon the trade of thieving; for, if he were to do that, he would be cutting off the sources of his own existence.

This convenient arrangement, he maintained, still applied despite the disputes among the Whigs: 'The *Whigs* themselves are *divided into two sets,* but neither of the sets attempt to oppose the *Blues*. That would not be fair; that would strike at the root of the trade.'[68] Events soon bore him out.

Before the general election was eventually called, Bragge Bathurst vacated his seat on becoming chancellor of the Duchy of Lancaster. Protheroe and Romilly both refused to contest the vacancy on the grounds that the seat belonged to the 'Blue Interest'. It was assumed that Richard Hart Davis, local banker, 'great monopolizer', and nominee of the White Lion Club would be returned unopposed, but the independent Hunt was determined to force an election. He arrived from Rowfant in a post-chaise to which a long pole was attached, topped by 'a large huge loaf of bread, bearing the motto of "HUNT and Peace"'.[69] On nomination day he tried to swear an oath before the sheriff, pledging himself to keep the poll open till the last moment allowed by law, to demand reform, the exclusion of placemen from the Commons, the abolition of flogging in the army, and never to accept from the crown or its ministers '*Place, Pension, Contract, Title, Gratuity* or *Emolument* of any Kind whatever'.[70] Davis and the loyalist Stedfast Society countered these publicity-seeking radical gimmicks with some hired muscle, in the awesome shape of four hundred or so, burly

[68] H. Hunt, *A Letter from Mr Hunt to the Freemen of Bristol* (London, 1812).
[69] *The Times*, 30 June 1812.   [70] See the handbill in Bristol Reference Library, 10883.

Kingswood colliers, sworn in by the White Lion Club as 'special' constables and equipped with hefty bludgeons painted in Davis's sky-blue colours. These 'mock constables' soon warmed to their task, and Hunt's supporters were given a good drubbing during the first day's polling: they had their revenge in the evening when they rallied *en masse* to attack the White Lion Inn.[71] The next day, Davis's bludgeon-men were dismissed on the magistrates' instructions, after which Hunt decided to take command of the streets himself. When the day's polling was over, he invited the people—'all that is vile and filthy in Bristol', *The Times* reported—to join him in an evening ride through the city as 'a sort of general canvass'. Such behaviour was highly provocative and irresponsible, particularly as he did not deter the crowds from helping themselves to bludgeons and sticks as they passed along the Welsh Back. After he retired to his inn, the inevitable violence began: Davis's house at Clifton was sacked, and in the city itself considerable damage was done to the Council House. The mayor read the Riot Act and then called in the military, much to the concern of Palmerston at the War Office, who was advised by the Solicitor General that the law particularly prohibited the presence of troops 'within any place where an Election is carrying on', a point emphasized by Cobbett who protested in the *Register* that the arrival of the troops was contrary to 'positive law' and 'usage immemorial'. 'This employment of the troops is abominable', he wrote to Hunt: 'It is the last stage of degradation to the system. The nature of that system now stands confessed.'[72] The illegal deployment of the troops at Bristol was a powerful reminder that physical force was the prerogative of the authorities: never again was Hunt to encourage a crowd to riot.

After the arrival of the military, order was restored and the election settled down to a daily routine. As soon as the poll closed each day, Hunt led a procession to the Exchange—on one occasion he was joined at the head of the crowd by a man 'bearing *the Cap of Liberty* before him *à la Francaise*'. Midway through his speech from the pedestal, Davis would appear in his carriage, attended by 'a train of as ill-favoured myrmidons armed with bludgeons, as ever issued from the coal-mines at Kingswood'. At this point, the military duly arrived on the scene to take possession of the key public buildings for the night and prevent any rioting. When the

[71] Bristol Record Office: Election Proceedings 1806–1812 (record book of the Stedfast Society), f. 83; *Bristol Gazette*, 2 July; *Felix Farley's Bristol Journal*, 4 July 1812; and Hunt, *Memoirs*, ii, 509–18.

[72] Ibid., ii, 535–49. *The Times*, 7 July. *CPR*, 11 July. Bristol Record Office: Letters and Miscellaneous Papers, box 1811–1812, Town clerk to Maj. Gen. Oswald, 30 June, and Palmerston to Mayor of Bristol, 3 July 1812, and other correspondence and posting-bills on the riots and the military; Proceedings of the Mayor and Aldermen, 1785–1820, ff. 173–5; and Election Proceedings 1806–12, ff. 93–113. Adelphi University and Nuffield College: Cobbett Papers, Cobbett to Hunt, 27 June and 4 July 1812.

poll finally closed after fifteen days, Davis had secured 1,907 votes and
Hunt 235. The names and occupations of those who voted for Hunt were
published by the White Lion Club, in order, no doubt, to injure them in
business. The vast majority belonged to the gamut of artisan trades,
ranging from peruke-makers, tobacco pipe-makers, toymakers and twine-
spinners to wine-hoopers, brightsmiths, wheelwrights and shipwrights:
students of radicalism will not be at all surprised that the largest individual
groups were twenty-five cordwainers and shoemakers, eighteen carpenters
and joiners, twelve tailors and eleven masons.[73]

The rumbustious by-election in July 1812 widened the breach between
Hunt and the 'respectable' reformers, who were scandalized by his
canvassing, speechifying, and courting of the crowd: the *Examiner*
protested at his 'imitation of Parisian mobs, his caps, his loaves, and his
fish-women'.[74] The local loyalists tried to exploit this dissension in the
reform camp during the election, and issued a list of 'Queries for Mr.
Hunt's Perusal', beginning with the question: 'Has not Sir Francis Burdett
himself declared, that you are too intemperate and too dangerous a man
even for his party to encourage and support?'[75] For the most part,
however, the loyalists preferred to question Hunt's private life rather than
his politics, since this was where scurrility and obloquy were more
effectively employed. 'Ye parents, ye mothers', *Felix Farley's Bristol
Journal* implored, 'is it the fornicator, the seducer of the wife of his most
intimate friend, is it the man who has abandoned an amiable wife and three
young children, that you would support in competition with a native of
your own city, full of charity and good works.' Cobbett tried to retaliate on
Hunt's behalf, and demanded to know whether the 'calumniating crew'
were prepared to 'push their reasoning and their rules up to *peers* and
princes, and to assert that they ought to be put out of power if they cease to
live with their wives'. But the loyalist attacks were unrelenting, since they
regarded Hunt's candidature as a barefaced attempt 'to stir up the minds of
the lower orders of society to riot and rebellion'.[76] No expense was spared
to ensure his defeat, although there was more discretion than usual in the
distribution of bribes and treats to prevent him raising a public cry against
corrupt practices. Even so, the Tories spent £14,362, of which nearly £3,000
was distributed among the constables. Hunt's expenses, by contrast, were
less than twenty-five shillings a day.[77] Against the scurrilous press, the

[73] Hunt, *Memoirs*, ii, 554–68 and iii, 1–19; *The Times*, 9 July; *Bristol Gazette*, 9–30 July;
Felix Farley's Bristol Journal, 11 and 18 July 1812. Bristol Record Office: Election
Proceedings 1806–1812, f. 125.
[74] *Examiner*, 19 July 1812.   [75] *Felix Farley's Bristol Journal*, 4 July 1812.
[76] Ibid., 4–18 July. Cobbett's three letter 'To the Independent Electors of Bristol', *CPR*, 4
July, 1 and 15 Aug. 1812.
[77] Bristol Record Office: Election Proceedings 1806–1812, f. 88. Latimer, 52. Hunt,
Memoirs, ii, 547.

party funds, the hired bludgeon-men, and the pettifogging lawyers, Hunt stood alone, save for the moral support of Cobbett and the physical protection of the crowd. The election, 'a contest between the rich and the poor', added an important social dimension to his radicalism.[78]

The general election in October 1812 was a rather quiet affair by comparison, even though there were four candidates—Davis, Protheroe, Romilly and Hunt. The civic authorities took a number of measures to prevent any repetition of the summer violence, including the positioning of two brass six-pounders in front of the Exchange. Davis and Protheroe, representing the two sections of the West India interest, formed an open (and unassailable) coalition, but no such agreement proved possible on the reform side, despite the willingness of the candidates themselves. Hunt was particularly keen on an alliance and adopted a conciliatory posture which Romilly welcomed and applauded. Radicals were accordingly encouraged to split their votes to promote a united reform front, marshalled by R. A. Davenport, Hunt's agent and friend, whose first task was to call in at the King of Prussia in Deptford, to 'see what is going on at Citizen Gasts'. Romilly's committee, however, refused to reciprocate and vetoed any co-operative endeavour: they openly denounced Hunt as a disreputable and dangerous individual who would 'disunite the ties by which society in a religious, moral, and political point of view, is cemented', and insisted on plumpers for their candidate—Romilly received no less than 767 plumpers, Hunt a mere 11. Even so, Romilly lagged far behind the Davis–Protheroe coalition, and he withdrew from the contest after the eighth day. Two days later, against Hunt's protest, the sheriffs closed the poll, the final figures being Davis 2,910, Protheroe 2,435, Romilly 1,685, and Hunt 455.[79] Hunt decided to petition against the result on a number of grounds, but here too he came into conflict with the middle-class reformers on Romilly's committee who refused to offer any practical assistance and only contributed a miserly £35 to the expenses which topped £600. When the petition was finally heard before a committee of the Commons, it transpired that on one of Hunt's main charges—bribery by the payment for the taking-up of freedoms—it was Romilly and not the elected members who was most at fault![80]

[78] Ibid., ii, 517. During the course of the election Cobbett and Burdett sent R. A. Davenport to Bristol to assist Hunt, ibid., ii, 546.

[79] Bristol Record Office: Proceedings of Mayor and Aldermen, 1785–1820, ff. 179–81. University of Chicago: MS 563, Hunt Correspondence and Papers, item 1, Hunt to Davenport, 1 Oct. 1812. *Bristol Gazette*, 8–22 Oct. *Felix Farley's Bristol Journal*, 3–17 Oct. 1812. C. H. Walker, *An Independent Address to the Electors of Bristol* (Bristol, 1812), viii–ix. Romilly, iii, 54–71. Hunt, *Memoirs*, iii, 67–8 and 90–117. Latimer, 51–3.

[80] Hunt, *Memoirs*, iii, 118–36. *An Authentic Report of the Evidence and Proceedings before the Committee of the Hon. House of Commons, appointed to try the merits of the Bristol Election of October 1812* (Bristol, 1813). Bristol Record Office: Burgesses 1812 to 1818, shows that between 30 Sept. and 16 Oct. 1812, 1,686 new freedoms were taken up.

In the course of collecting evidence for the petition, Hunt obtained a Speaker's Warrant which allowed him access to the accounts of the City Corporation, where he discovered 'a mass of fraud and chicanery', the details of which he revealed at a public dinner in January, when he provided the radicals with 'a peep into the *sanctum sanctorum of the Council House*'. The dinner was Hunt's reward for his independence and radicalism in 1812: the 'Champion of the Rights of Bristol's Sons', he was presented with a crown of oak leaves in accordance with the custom of the ancient Romans 'to reward the meritorious Citizen with an honorary Crown'.[81] He returned to the city in March soon after the Commons committee had declared in favour of the sitting members, whose election had cost £15,000 apiece. He arrived in flamboyant style, in an open carriage drawn by six horses, with the postillions bedecked in purple jackets, his election colour. From the pedestal he pledged to return to contest the seat at the next and every opportunity, adding melodramatically that he would 'bring his Son, a little sturdy boy, and place him at his side to fight for their rights when he should no longer be able'. He then turned to the politics of the day and condemned the examination of the Princess of Wales: he received unanimous support for the address which he intended to present personally to the much-injured Princess. Dinner was then taken at the Talbot and the evening passed off quite peaceably. The next night, however, the statue of the King in Portland Square was demolished by a crowd to shouts of 'Hunt for ever'.[82] This was the last episode in the stormy proceedings of the Bristol elections of 1812, during which Hunt had served a remarkable political apprenticeship.[83] The champion of the crowd, he had defied the authorities, the factions, and the progressive reformers. 'Bristol' Hunt was soon to enter London politics as a figure of some notoriety, a staunch supporter of the Princess of Wales, and the veritable scourge of all Whigs and moderate reformers.

[81] H. Hunt, *An account of the public dinner of the friends to purity of election . . . January 28, 1813, Henry Hunt, esq. in the chair* (Bristol, n.d.). For Hunt's exposures, see also J. Cranidge, *A Mirror for the Burgesses and Commonalty of the City of Bristol* (Bristol, 1818).

[82] *Bristol Gazette*, 25 Mar.; *Felix Farley's Bristol Journal*, 27 Mar. 1813. For details of the presentation of the address, see University of Chicago: MS 563; Hunt Correspondence and Papers, item 92, Lady Charlotte Lindsay to Hunt, n.d.; and *TRR*, 25 July 1820.

[83] Legal disputes over the expenses continued for several months, see *CPR*, 11 Sept. 1813.

2

The Establishment of the
Mass Platform

THE war years were of considerable importance in the shaping of popular politics and protest. Hunt's path to democratic radicalism must be studied in the context of the general hardening of opposition attitudes following the collapse of the patriotic consensus of the invasion scare years of 1803–5. Foxite Whigs, fearing that it would prove impossible to restrain the Crown if the war continued, offered the principle of party, the programme of economical reform, and the practice of aristocratic exclusiveness as the best defence against absolutism.[1] The anti-war liberals, the flag-bearers of middle-class consciousness, protested against oligarchy and the war system, which was producing dangerous concentrations of wealth and power in 'Fortress Britannica' at the expense of the provincial middle class, the particular victims of the financial demands, economic uncertainties and social consequences of an unnecessary conflict.[2] The patrician Burdett stood forward for reform as an independent gentleman seeking to purge corruption and oligarchy by restoring 'purity' to the Commons, much in line with the programme and ideology of the old country party.[3] While speaking the same language as Burdett, 'Bristol' Hunt was moving towards a more democratic view of reform in which the economic well-being of the common people—the real victims of wartime taxation, inflation and dislocation—was the first consideration. By extending traditional extra-parliamentary politics to embrace the economic needs and political rights of the common people, Hunt accomplished the breakthrough to mass radicalism that the Jacobinism of the 1790s had been unable to secure.

Hunt was able to attract a mass audience because of the fundamental changes in popular protest which occurred during the war, the crucial transition period in the secular process known as the modernization of protest. Eighteenth-century or 'pre-industrial' protest was characterized by spontaneity, direct action, violence and a backward-looking *mentalité*: the riotous crowd was rebellious in defence of custom and the old 'moral

---

[1] F. O'Gorman, *The Emergence of the British Two-Party System 1760–1832* (London, 1982), ch. 1.

[2] Cookson, *Friends of Peace*, 41 and *passim*.

[3] J. R. Dinwiddy, 'Sir Francis Burdett and Burdettite Radicalism', *History*, lxv (1980), 17–31.

economy', seeking the redress of grievances through the restoration of a happier, doubtless mythical, golden past. All this gave way to on-going organization and forward-looking ideology in modern or 'industrial' protest, as the workers began to campaign for reform to improve their condition.[4] During the war, food-rioting, the most characteristic form of 'pre-industrial' protest, became increasingly intertwined with political radicalism and trade unionism: in the post-war years it disappeared as a separate entity.[5] At the same time, the urban crowd began to assert its independence and radicalism: 'No Corruption' replaced 'No Popery' as the most popular cry on the streets.[6] In the industrial districts too, discontent became politicized during the war: here, the Luddite crisis completed the process as the aggrieved workers found themselves denied the protection of old paternalist legislation and confronted by the full physical power of the state when they resorted to collective bargaining by riot. Henceforward working men came to regard democratic control of the state as an essential means to protect and improve their lot.[7]

The post-war radical movement gave mass expression to this politicization of discontent. Cartwright's pioneering tours of the Luddite counties and Cobbett's new popular journalism emphasized the importance of parliamentary reform to the labouring man, but it was Hunt's platform campaigning which led to the mass mobilization of the people in the radical cause. The transition to peace completed his disillusionment with the traditional channels of extra-parliamentary politics: he recoiled in disgust from the hypocrisy, self-interest and opportunism displayed in the exclusive platform campaigns for the abolition of the Property Tax and the introduction of the Corn Bill. In working alliance with the 'revolutionary party',[8] he broke through the conventional constraints and welcomed the involvement of all in the demand for the rights of all. At Spa Fields, Hunt brought the open, constitutional mass platform into being, a structure of radical endeavour which was to remain largely unchallenged until the collapse of Chartism.

---

[4] G. Rudé, *Protest and Punishment* (Oxford, 1978), 13–26 and 52–8; and *Ideology and Popular Protest* (London, 1980), 146–57. See also J. Foster, *Class Struggle and the Industrial Revolution* (London, 1974), 41–3. For recent criticism of this modernization thesis, see R. J. Holton, 'The crowd in history: some problems of theory and method', *Social History*, iii (1978), 219–33; and J. Bohstedt, *Riots and Community Politics in England and Wales 1790–1810* (London, 1983), 209–23.

[5] A. Booth, 'Food riots in the north-west of England 1790–1801', *Past and Present*, lxxvii (1977), 84–107. J. Stevenson, 'Food riots in England 1792–1818' in J. Stevenson and R. Quinault (eds.), *Popular Protest and Public Order* (London, 1974).

[6] Thompson, *Making*, ch. 13.

[7] J. R. Dinwiddy, 'Luddism and politics in the northern counties', *Social History*, iv (1979), 33–63.

[8] Parssinnen, 'Revolutionary party', 266–82.

I. HUNT AND THE MODERATE REFORMERS

The moment he entered London politics, 'Bristol' Hunt became embroiled in conflict with the reform establishment. He disapproved of the obeisance to the 'Mountain' and the Whigs, and the neglect of the rights and interests of the common man. A democratic radical, he was dissatisfied with the pecuniary protests of the *petite bourgeoisie* in the Common Hall, and the moderate reform proclivities of the Westminster Committee. As the war entered its third decade, he demanded a more vigorous and independent radical challenge to the rapacious and repressive 'Pitt System'. Government expenditure from 1812 to 1815 totalled £550 million, an amount surpassing that spent from 1793 to 1796 by over three and a half times. Repression and reaction stood clearly revealed as the nation's war aims: troops were sent against the poor Luddites, the free Americans were engaged in conflict, and no effort was spared to restore the Bourbons in France. The final throes of war served to harden Hunt's democratic radicalism.

It was at Burdett's suggestion that Hunt entered the Common Hall, that great arena of ratepayers' democracy, to advocate 'general not partial liberty', and expose the factionalism of Robert Waithman, the 'City Cock'. Waithman, the patriotic linen-draper, had fought long and hard to transform the city from a bastion of Pittite loyalism into a stronghold of peace, retrenchment and reform, but his close connections with the Whigs disturbed Burdett, Cobbett and many other reformers. Hunt agreed to become a liveryman of the Loriners' Company in order to register his protest at Waithman's co-operation with Whitbread and Brougham in support of the Princess of Wales in 1813, and consequent refusal to join Cobbett in a great popular campaign on her behalf. As it happened, the affair ended in anti-climax when the Princess accepted the Government's bribe and departed for Europe.[9]

The self-appointed scourge of the Whigs, Hunt also involved himself in Westminster politics where the Committee were trying to retain the support of the increasingly prosperous electorate through a *rapprochement* with the Mountain. The 'Rump', as the Committee were known, following the removal of the old London Corresponding Society members, wanted to enhance their reputation and influence by providing a seat for Brougham, master tactician of the successful 'petition and debate' campaign against the Orders-in-Council.[10] They seized their opportunity with unseemly

[9] J. R. Dinwiddy, '"The Patriotic Linen-Draper": Robert Waithman and the Revival of Radicalism in the City of London, 1795–1818', *Bulletin of the Institute of Historical Research*, xlvi (1973), 72–94. Hunt, *Memoirs*, iii, 159–64; and his speech at Farringdon, tracing his career in city politics, in *WFP*, 10 Jan. 1829.

[10] W. Thomas, 'Whigs and Radicals in Westminster: the election of 1819', *Guildhall Miscellany*, iii (1970), 174. Cookson, *Friends of the People*, ch. 9. P. Fraser, 'Public Petitioning and Parliament before 1832', *History*, xlvi (1961), 207–9.

haste when Thomas Cochrane, Burdett's lack-lustre and inefficient fellow member, was charged in connection with the Stock Exchange hoax of 1814. Place managed to persuade Brougham to commit himself in writing to Burdett's famous radical programme of 1809, and his election in Cochrane's place seemed assured. Hunt, however, was quite unconvinced by Brougham's sudden conversion to the cause, and promptly informed the Rump that he would stand himself and force them to the expense of a full fifteen-day poll if they dropped Cochrane or replaced him with a candidate other than Major Cartwright, the most venerable of radicals. Looking back on the affair, Cobbett considered that Hunt's intervention was decisive in thwarting the Rump's plans, but in truth, Cochrane's success in the Westminster election in July was very much his own doing. After his conviction for what was at most an unwitting involvement in the scandal, he became the great hero and martyr of the day. The Rump decided to swim with the popular tide: Brougham was dropped and Cochrane was swept to victory unopposed. The Government had no wish to provoke another 'Wilkes and Liberty' furore, and duly allowed the election of the convicted Cochrane to stand.[11]

These preliminary skirmishes with the Waithmanites and the Rump prepared Hunt for his outright opposition to the moderate reformers when the war finally gave way to peace, and a series of platform campaigns developed over the Property Tax, the Corn Bill, and distress. Hunt soon came to realize there was no place for his independent, uncompromising radicalism in the traditional arenas of extra-parliamentary politics, the city, popular Westminster, and the county platform.

The campaign against the Property Tax began as soon as peace was concluded with France in 1814, and demonstrated the power of middle-class 'pressure from without' in the unreformed system when the various mechanisms of the platform—meetings, petitions, press coverage—were closely co-ordinated and linked to the efforts of the opposition in the Commons. Hunt found himself at cross purposes with Waithman when he supported his petition to discontinue the Tax at the Common Hall in December. Where Waithman looked to the Whigs for support and leverage, Hunt used the occasion to remind the livery of the taxation record of the Ministry of All the Talents, thereby demonstrating that there was 'an equality of demerit between Whigs and Tories, between those who had introduced, and those who had continued this inquisitional institution, between those who left it at 6½, and those who raised it to 10 per cent'. Waithman opposed the principle and incidence of the Tax which caused such resentment amongst the middle classes, but Hunt fulminated against the very purpose of the Tax, the revenue from which was 'lavished in the

[11] Patterson, i, ch. 14. A. Aspinall, 'The Westminster Election of 1814', *English Historical Review*, xl (1925), 562–9. *CPR*, 22 Feb. 1817 and 3 Jan. 1818. Hunt, *Memoirs*, iii, 283–303.

support of corruption, and in a division of spoil between both parties'. To prove the point, he resorted to personalities, a favourite device, listing some twenty prominent figures, including such eminent Whigs as Erskine and Ponsonby, who were 'fattening upon the public purse', enjoying pensions to the tune of some £200,000 per annum, a sum that would support '5,000 families at 15s. a week, or in other words would maintain 20,000 persons through the year'. His embarrassing speech ended amidst uproar and disapprobation.[12]

On the Whig-sponsored county platform, his intervention was most unwelcome as he tried to broaden and radicalize the issue. His speech on the Somerset platform in January 1815 caused great offence when he welcomed the conclusion of peace with the Americans whom he pointedly eulogized as 'the only remaining free Government in the universe'.[13] At the Hampshire meeting later that month, he seconded Cobbett's radical petition, calling for the repeal of all war taxes and 'all the laws passed during the war which diminished the liberties of the people'. He pulled no punches in his speech, accusing the supporters of the anti-Property Tax campaign of narrow self-interest, hypocrisy, and opportunism, since they had been ardent advocates of the evil war until the very end, pledging their '*last shilling* and their *last drop of blood*'. The speech was ignored, and all references to Cobbett's rejected petition were carefully excluded from Whig press reports of the meeting.[14] A month later, the Government bowed to the pressure from without and announced that the Tax would be discontinued, but Napoleon's return from Elba denied the repealers their victory, and the campaign against the Tax had to be fought again a year later.

The renewal of hostilities against Napoleon roused Hunt to fury. At the Common Hall he joined Waithman, a veteran anti-war campaigner, in condemning this 'war of the most unjust oppression'. Once again, a suitably dramatic rendering of domestic history reinforced his argument:

Our ancestors had claimed the right of choosing and dethroning Kings, and in one instance of *dispensing* with their heads. He thought that by the principles of our revolution, it was decided that the power of choosing Sovereigns remained with the people. Why should we, then, endeavour to force upon France a government which all the French nation detested and abhorred? (a mixed tumult of hisses and applause interrupted Mr. H. for a considerable time).[15]

He came into conflict with the Rump again as they delayed holding a meeting to protest at the resumption. Cobbett offered an explanation for

[12] *The Times*, 14 Dec. 1814. See also Fraser, 207–11; and A. Briggs, 'Middle-Class Consciousness in English Politics', *Past and Present*, ix (1956), 67–9.
[13] *CPR*, 21 Jan. 1815. Adelphi University and Nuffield College: Cobbett Papers, Cobbett to Hunt, 19 Jan. 1815. Hunt, *Memoirs*, iii, 245–50.
[14] *CPR*, 4 Feb. 1815.   [15] *The Times*, 28 Apr. 1815.

their tardiness. 'The petty aristocrats of the Strand will feel uncommon alarm at the revolutionary movement you are making', he wrote privately to Hunt, 'I should not at all wonder if they were to give up the idea of Meeting to avoid so dangerous a man as you, whose very name seems to signify pistols and lamp-posts.'[16] When the meeting was finally held, Hunt found himself having to defend the great Napoleon against a string of opprobious charges. After Waterloo, he clashed with Brougham and the popular Whigs when they defended the detention of Napoleon on St Helena, a policy which Hunt condemned as a 'disgraceful, damnable, imperishable blot on the escutcheon of England's character'.[17]

The second campaign against the Property Tax gathered force in 1816 when it became known that the Government intended to continue with a modified version of the Tax as part of its peacetime fiscal policy. Unable to raid the sinking fund, the sacred cow of ministerial finance, Vansittart, probably had no alternative to the unpopular course of continuing the war taxes to meet the interest payments on the debt, but town and country taxpayers protested vehemently as deflation developed apace. The customary social divisions, so strongly evinced in the Corn Bill controversy, were swept aside as agriculturists, merchants, and manufacturers joined together to demand a reduction in taxes along with a cut-back in government salaries and public expenditure generally.[18] The second campaign against the Property Tax was thus much wider than the first, but it was still not sufficiently radical for the likes of Hunt and Cobbett. On the Hampshire platform, they lost an amendment calling for parliamentary reform as the essential first step to enforce the necessary general retrenchment.[19] Two days later, however, Hunt scored a sensational victory for the radical cause at a Westminster meeting on the Property Tax issue. The Rump were hoping to use the occasion to implement the plan they had been forced to abandon in 1814: the whole point of the exercise was to provide a favourable image of Brougham to the Westminster electors. All went well at the meeting in Palace Yard until Hunt interposed with what Place described as his 'usual impudence and malice'. He itemized the misdeeds, broken promises, corrupt and profligate practices of Fox and his ministers in such lurid detail that the embarrassed Whigs, Brougham, Brand and Bennet, soon quit the hustings. Hunt, Place recorded with dismay, was left 'in possession of the field'. Place tried to repair the damage and continued to seek Brougham's favour, since the

[16] Adelphi University and Nuffield College: Cobbett Papers, Cobbett to Hunt, 5 May 1815.
[17] *CPR*, 24 June 1815 and 3 Jan. 1818. Hunt, *Memoirs*, iii, 259–60 and 308–10.
[18] J. E. Cookson, *Lord Liverpool's Administration: The Crucial Years 1815–1822* (Edinburgh, 1975), 35, 45 and 58–69. B. Hilton, *Corn, Cash, Commerce: the economic policies of the Tory governments, 1815–1830* (Oxford, 1970), 31.
[19] *CPR*, 24 Feb. 1816.

second campaign against the Property Tax resulted in another victory for his 'petition and debate' tactics, demonstrating his effectiveness in the Commons, where Burdett and Cochrane had nothing to show for their half-hearted labours. The unrepentant Hunt had no illusions about Brougham's latest parliamentary success: the Tax was repealed because so many MPs were personally interested in its abolition and therefore 'kindly condescended to listen, or at least they pretended to listen, to the prayers of the people'.[20]

The campaign against the new corn Bill was far less successful: here was an issue on which the Parliament of landowners was quite unyielding to pressure from without. Hunt was a vehement critic of the Bill, objecting to 'the injustice of making the mechanic and the labourer pay a war price for his bread in time of peace'. To his surprise, he found that Burdett prevaricated over the issue, and that Cobbett was slow to appreciate that reform and retrenchment would render protection unnecessary.[21] Hunt campaigned against the proposed Bill from the outset, and was soon locked in controversy with his old Wiltshire adversary, John Benett of Pyt House, a landowner of over £10,000 p.a., who had impressed the committees of both houses of parliament with his protectionist arguments. Benett tried to mobilize support for the Bill in the county and arranged a meeting at Warminster to petition for protection. Hunt confounded his plans by forcing his way into the meeting, 'a "Conclave of Cardinals with closed doors"'. Benett's petition, Hunt protested, was intended 'especially to benefit the landholder, even the farmer was of secondary consideration, and it was decidedly hostile to the interest of every other class of society, and if acted upon would prove ruinous to the litle tradesman, the mechanic, and the labourer'. The landlords, he continued, were the last group in need of protection, their rents having increased 'in proportion as the rest of the community had suffered privations; the nearer the mechanic and the labourer had approached to starvation and beggary, the higher were the profits and the more efficient the means of the landholder'. Some graphic figures based on Enford where he had a small estate and where Benett was the largest landowner, clinched the argument, showing that 'at the present price of land, corn, bread, and labour, the landlord is benefited three times as much as the farmer, and six times as much as the labourer . . . within the last 30 years, labour has risen from 6*s*. to 8*s*. per week, 33 per cent, the quartern loaf from 5*d*. to 10½*d*., 105 per cent, the rent of land from £400 to £1,260, 212 per cent'. He cautioned the farmers against supporting a bill, the sole object of which was 'the benefit and

[20] *CPR*, 2 Mar. 1816 and 3 Jan. 1818. *Examiner*, 25 Feb. 1816. BL Add. MSS 27809 (Place papers), f. 14, and 37949 (Place papers), f. 37, Place to Brougham, 23 Mar. 1816. Hunt, *Memoirs*, iii, 308.
[21] Hunt, *Memoirs*, iii, 217–19.

aggrandizement of a few rapacious landholders, whilst it was calculated to shift the odium of a dear loaf off their own shoulders, and fix it upon the back of the farmer'. After this powerful speech, Benett's petition was promptly defeated, but that was by no means the end of the matter as the Enford figures were hotly disputed in the correspondence columns of the local press. Hunt collected the letters together and published them in a cheap pamphlet available to 'all classes of society'. In his commentary, he contested every aspect of Benett's case for protection in a highly technical and detailed manner, a reminder that Hunt the radical was still Hunt the successful gentleman farmer. 'My whole dependence is on land, and the cultivation of it,' he concluded, 'but I will never consent to petition for a Corn Bill, purposely to raise the price of bread, thus conferring a temporary and unnatural benefit upon the landholders, at the cruel expense of the hitherto too greatly oppressed community.'[22]

As a farmer opposed to protection, Hunt found himself in a difficult position when the Common Hall met to denounce the Corn Bill, the 'Bill to destroy Trade and Manufactures'. Such was Waithman's vehemence against the protectionist landed interest that Hunt felt compelled to protest, pointing out that there were many farmers and landowners like himself who opposed the Bill. He failed to convince the livery and was forced to withdraw an amendment substituting Waithman's censure of the agriculturists with the demand for radical reform.[23] Back in Wiltshire, his position was better understood. Huge crowds attended the county meeting which he requisitioned to petition the Lords against the Bill, and the proceedings had to be transferred to the open air. In a vigorous speech, he denounced protection as an evil consequence of the Pitt System: the war-time growth of government expenditure was to be maintained in peace-time by persisting with war taxes upon the farmer. The meeting was a great success, an impressive and peaceable display of anti-protectionist feeling. Cobbett was particularly struck by Hunt's handling of the large crowds at a time when there was considerable rioting against the Bill in London and elsewhere. The collection of signatures then proceeded apace: in less than four days some 21,000 names were appended to the petition. But the Wiltshire petition, along with many others, was ignored by Parliament. The Corn Bill, Hunt protested angrily, was passed 'under the protection of a military force, in defiance of the prayers, the petitions, and the remonstrances of a great majority of the people of England'.[24]

The Bill proved of little benefit to the over-capitalized and over-

---

[22] H. Hunt, *Corn Laws. The Evidence of John Benett . . . An Impartial Report of the Meeting of Landowners at Warminster. Mr. Benett's Letter . . . Mr. Bleeck's Letter . . . Together with an inedited letter from Mr. Hunt* (Salisbury, 1815); and *Memoirs*, iii, 225–35.
[23] *The Times*, 24 Feb. 1815.
[24] *CPR*, 11 Mar. 1815. Hunt, *Memoirs*, iii, 236–45.

producing agriculturists. Protectionism, as far as the Government was concerned, was simply a pragmatic means to assist the transition from war to peace, and from a depreciated paper currency to a metallic standard, but no thought was given to the dangers of over-production.[25] After a handsome harvest in 1815, corn prices fell drastically in 1816. When Hunt attended the annual meeting of the Bath and West of England Agricultural Society in December 1815, he found the protected agriculturists already in disgruntled and discontented mood. Accordingly, he tried to draw their attention to the close connection between corn and cash, and the consequent need for wholesale retrenchment and reform of the funding-system as the Government began the return to bullionism. Distress, he informed the farmers, had a political cause: the financial policy of the corrupt and unrepresentative government.[26]

As war gave way to peace and economic conditions deteriorated, Hunt appeared on a variety of platforms to propound his essential radical message: distress was political in origin and thus required a political solution. The problem here of course was that those who suffered most from the ravages of distress had no right of access to the traditional extra-parliamentary platform to hear and endorse the radical programme. It was the common people who felt the full force of military demobilization, the cessation of Government orders, and deflation, not to mention the introduction of the Corn Law and the repeal of the Property Tax which meant dearer bread and increased indirect taxation, both of which hit the poor disproportionately hard. On top of all this, the weather was atrocious, removing any hope of 'peace and plenty'. The spring and summer of 1816 were the worst in recorded history, the result of unprecedented volcanic eruption in the Pacific which obscured the sky throughout the northern hemisphere for months on end. In April and May there were 'bread or blood' riots in several counties, accompanied by a revival of arson and machine-breaking.[27] Such traditional protest was soon overshadowed, however, by the emergence of a modern mass radical movement based on the extension of the constitutional platform to 'members unlimited', the product of Hunt's final breach with the moderate reformers and new working alliance with the 'revolutionary party'.

The Government denied all responsibility for the distress, the unavoidable and temporary consequence of the transition from war to peace, and refused to sanction any intervention beyond a traditional exercise in philanthropy, that much-used instrument of social control.[28] Hunt took

---

[25] Hilton, ch. 1.   [26] *CPR*, 6 Jan. 1816 and 7 Oct. 1819.

[27] J. D. Post, *The Last Great Subsistence Crisis in the Western World* (Baltimore, 1977), xii–iii, 14, 16, 27 and 84–5. A. J. Peacock, *Bread or Blood: a study of the agrarian riots in East Anglia in 1816* (London, 1965).

[28] J. Stevenson, 'Social Control and the Prevention of Riots in England 1789–1829' in A. P. Donajgrodski (ed.), *Social Control in Nineteenth-Century Britain* (London, 1977).

strong exception to the much-vaunted 'sinecure-soup project', the fund opened at the City of London Tavern under the patronage of the Duke of York. At the Common Hall in August, he subjected the first subscription list to some telling scrutiny, once again demonstrating his mastery of personalities in political argument. He was at his most cutting when he noted that his 'old friend' Lord Camden, the teller of the exchequer, was on the list of 'munificent subscribers':

The noble lord's receipts for the last year amounted to £38,400; and he found, upon a little examination, that his donation of £100 was just three farthings in the pound out of this enormous sum extracted from a distressed and impoverished people. (*Applause.*) . . . This was the comparative rate at which the great paupers thought it their duty to contribute to the support of the little paupers . . . He had looked at the subscription list of the gentry of the London Tavern, and found it amounted that day to the sum of £33,000; so that it appeared Lord Camden received, in the course of a year, from the public, much more than was subscribed in a month by all the rich paupers to its distresses. (*Applause.*)

He continued in fine oratorical form as he traced the origins of distress back through 'a long and unjust war, waged against the liberties of all mankind' to its true political source in 'a profligate system of borough-dealing . . . a system that took the wages of industry to give them to idleness . . . a system which was first generated in the corrupt bosom of one of the greatest villains that ever existed—he meant Sir Robert Walpole; and had been brought to maturity by another Minister, Mr. Pitt'. The meeting proved to be Hunt's greatest triumph in the Common Hall. Waithman was ill and unable to attend, and Hunt had little difficulty in persuading the livery to adopt the radical proposals he had been forced to withdraw in 1815 when the Corn Bill was under discussion. A petition was adopted, berating the distress and calling for the 'Constitutional Right of a full, free and frequent representation', which was to be presented to the Regent 'seated on the throne'.[29] In October the sheriffs reported back that they had been unable to comply with these instructions, as Sidmouth had ruled that only the Corporation of London and not the livery had the privilege of personal access to the sovereign. This produced an angry response in the Common Hall: the livery resented what they regarded as a violation of their traditional rights, and the battle lines were drawn for an eighteenth-century-style conflict between the city and the court. Waithman returned to head the city challenge, trusting that this would assist the Whigs in their attack on the Government's handling of distress. There was no place here, of course, for Hunt's independent radicalism, and his militant proposals were voted down by the livery in October under Waithman's instructions. Hunt, *The Times* reported, 'got a severe reprehension'.[30] At the next Common Hall, held after the first Spa Fields

[29] *The Times*, 22 Aug. 1816.   [30] *The Times*, 9 Oct. 1816.

meeting, Waithman pressed home his advantage: Hunt's radical programme and methods were decisively rejected.

In the city the distress of 1816 produced what Halevy described as the 'final manifestation of the traditional warfare between the City and the Court'.[31] In popular Westminster, distress led to an important change of tactics: reformers turned their attention away from the Mountain and planned a major exercise in extra-parliamentary politics. For some while old Major Cartwright had been working along these lines in the Hampden Club, but it was not until the summer of 1816 that reform intellectuals and the Rump gave serious consideration to a national campaign for the Burdett reform programme, by which time their hopes for Brougham had suffered a final set-back when the 'celebrated gownsman' absented himself from the annual purity of election dinner on learning of Hunt's presence.[32] A 'committee of public safety' was formed, bringing Benthamites, radicals and members of the Rump together to institute and co-ordinate a campaign for reform throughout the country, beginning with a public meeting in Westminster itself. Peevish as ever, Place criticized the arrangements for the meeting, particularly the invitation which had been extended to Hunt by some of the 'inexperienced' members of the Committee. To prevent any further damage, he arranged a private interview with Hunt in order to impress on him the need for moderation. He reported the conversation to his mentor, James Mill, who had already resigned from the Committee and was firmly of the opinion that 'such men as Hunt do infinite harm to the good cause':

Hunt says his mode of acting is to dash at good points, and to care for no one that he will mix with no committee, or any party, he will act by himself, that he does not intend to affront any body, but cares not who is offended, and he is weak enough to suppose the parliament may be induced to pass an act to destroy sinecures, he seems detirmined [sic] to do all he can to inflame people against individuals . . . he is a very pretty sample of an ignorant, turbulent, mischiefmaking, fellow, a highly dangerous one in turbulent times.

Place had no understanding of Hunt's independent, uncompromising radicalism and character: he feared he would be manipulated by Burdett, Cochrane and Cartwright, all of whom were ill-disposed towards Place at this stage.[33] Hunt's conduct at the Westminster meeting was exemplary: he was by far the most effective speaker in favour of reform, repeating much that he had said so successfully at the Common Hall three weeks previously: copies of the speech were reprinted in several parts of the

[31] E. Halevy, *The Liberal Awakening 1815–1830*, trans. E. I. Watkin (London, 2nd edn., 1949), 19.

[32] *CPR*, 1 June 1816 and 22 Feb. 1817.

[33] BL Add. MSS 35152 (Place papers), f. 206, Mill to Place, 26 Aug., ff. 207–16, Place to Mill, 30 Aug., 2 Sept. and 15 Sept. 1816.

country and enjoyed a wide circulation. While Hunt provided the best analysis of distress, it was Cochrane, the prison-hardened radical, who pointed the way forward in terms of a national campaign for reform. He insisted that something more than conventional petitioning was required: he therefore suggested that on the opening day of Parliament, two deputies from 'all the counties, and all unrepresented, and all misrepresented cities and towns' should assemble in London to present remonstrances.[34] With some modifications, this proposal was taken on board by the Hampden Club at its next committee meeting.

Under Cartwright's leadership, the Hampden Club had changed dramatically in recent years, as the old major concentrated his energies on the creation of a national reform movement, beginning with his famous petitioning tours of the Luddite counties.[35] In March 1815 he instituted a mass petitioning campaign under the auspices of the Hampden Club, using the name of the society to promote an image—far removed from reality—of strong central leadership by wealthy, independent gentlemen. Burdett, chairman of the committee supervising the campaign, sent out a circular letter explaining that the special printed petitions were in support of a direct-taxation suffrage, but the signatures of those excluded by such a reform would be most welcome. Over the next few months an impressive number of petitions was collected, but attendance at Club meetings in London remained abysmally low. Cartwright took heart from the success achieved by the small central committee which had led the campaign against the Slave Trade, and persuaded Burdett to approve a further extension of activity in the provinces. At the general meeting in June 1816 it was agreed that the next round of petitioning should be accompanied by public meetings and the establishment of Hampden clubs or societies in every county, town, and parish. Cochrane's deputy scheme was incorporated into these ambitious plans for a great display of reform opinion in the provinces when the committee met in November. They decided to prepare a draft bill for reform which they would present to the next full meeting of the Club in March and also to 'any Meeting of Persons who may be deputed from petitioning Cities, Towns, or other Communities, to confer together in the Metropolis, on the best means of effectuating a constitutional Reform'. Here was the origin of the famous Hampden Club convention of January 1817.[36]

---

[34] *National Distress. Speech of Mr. Hunt, made at the meeting of the electors of Westminster . . . September 11th, 1816* (Holt, n.d.), broadsheet distributed in Bristol. *Examiner*, 15 Sept. 1816 reported 'a specimen of more ability than usual given by our vociferous namesake of Bristol'. *CPR*, 21 Sept. and 20 Nov. 1816. Adelphi University and Nuffield College: Cobbett Papers, W. Cobbett junior to Hunt, 13 Sept. 1816.   [35] Miller, 'John Cartwright', 718–23.
[36] This account is based on the papers of Thomas Cleary, a collection of pamphlets, handbills, reports and letters, bound in the British Library as *Proceedings of the Hampden Club 1812–1822.*

Two points must be noted straight away. First, as far as Cartwright and Burdett were concerned, the scheme was rigidly identified with the declared programme of the Hampden Club, direct-taxation suffrage, equal electoral districts, and annual parliaments, a programme endorsed by Cobbett in his influential *Register*:[37] the technical details of the draft bill were open to discussion, but not the principle. Second, the convention was not intended as an exercise in independent popular politics from below. In his circular letters, Burdett always called upon the 'Gentlemen of landed property' to stand forward at the head of the reform movement, and when he endorsed the convention scheme he pointedly referred to the precedent of Wyvill's association movement of 1780-1. To the veteran Cartwright, the old notion of the 'association' remained the desideratum. By bringing the masses into the Hampden Club, he hoped to force the landed classes to assume their rightful role as leaders: with such gentlemanly leadership and a huge popular membership, the Hampden 'association' would be more representative than Parliament and its demands could not be ignored. To this end, he tried to arrange an assembly of dignitaries at the Mansion House who would be ready to take the lead once the humble delegates arrived in London with their petitions.[38] Before the provincial delegates were elected, however, the convention scheme was totally transformed by Hunt's initiation of the mass platform at Spa Fields. Through Hunt's working alliance with the 'revolutionary party', the radical movement of 1816 committed itself to universal suffrage and mass pressure from below.

2. HUNT AND THE 'REVOLUTIONARY PARTY'

In September 1816, Hunt received a letter from Arthur Thistlewood requesting a personal interview. After making some inquiries about Thistlewood he decided to ignore the letter altogether. Thistlewood's past was certainly somewhat chequered: he had been involved with the revolutionary underground for some time, but was also a heavy gambler and something of a scoundrel. What particularly disturbed Hunt, was his membership of the Society of Spencean Philanthropists, a group which had come into being after the death of Thomas Spence in 1814. Radical as he now was, Hunt wanted no contact with those who looked to insurrection to implement a revolutionary 'plan' based on the abolition of private property in land. In equating Spenceanism with revolution Hunt made what was a common mistake at the time and amongst historians later. Recent work has shown that Spence was more traditional than revolutionary in his parish-based programme and millennial 'plan': Spenceanism acquired its identifi-

[37] *CPR*, 12 and 19 Oct. 1816.   [38] Miller, 'John Cartwright', 723-4.

cation with revolutionary conspiracy because of its medium rather than its message. Spence's novel methods of propaganda were well-suited to the tavern world of the ultra-radicals and 'revolutionary party' in central and east London, where he was a popular and respected figure. After his death, his more doctrinaire followers took little part in political agitation, insurrectionary or otherwise. They believed that without a major redistribution of landed wealth and power within each parish, parliamentary reform, even on Paineite republican lines, would leave the masses as poor and powerless as before. Such thorough-going Spenceanism was very much a minority creed, the preserve of Thomas Evans and his son, who concentrated on education and propaganda until the Peterloo massacre prompted them to rethink their position. Other tavern radicals turned to more instrumental politics. By the autumn of 1816, most so-called 'Spenceans' were more interested in the immediate prospects for insurrection than in the long-term merits of Spence's plan for a fundamentally reordered economic and social system. Disciples of Spence or not, they were veterans of and heirs to the great underground tradition of the war years. As the post-war distress deepened, they hoped to obtain mass involvement in their insurrectionary designs by exploiting the popular appeal of a crowd-puller like Hunt, who had made quite a name for himself by his controversial behaviour in the traditional arenas of popular politics.[39]

The so-called 'revolutionary party' now believed that a well-attended public meeting would serve as the best springboard for insurrection. Once the multitude had assembled, attracted by the presence of some celebrities on the platform, the conspirators would be able to set to work. Dr Watson, the impecunious surgeon, and his profligate son James would so inflame the crowd that vast numbers would follow the appointed leaders or 'generals' in attacking several key buildings—for example, Thistlewood, the 'Head General' was to capture the Bank of England, and young Watson was to lead a contingent to sack the gunsmiths' shops and take the Tower.[40] Like many conspirators before and since, the revolutionary party in post-war London assumed that their central 'coup' would precipitate the rising of the whole people, unprepared though they were. As events turned out, it was not until the second Spa Fields meeting on 2 December that Thistlewood and young Watson tried to put this plan in effect, by which time most of their fellow 'revolutionaries' had decided to cast aside

[39] Hunt, *Memoirs*, iii, 327–28. Parssinnen, 'Revolutionary party'. H. T. Dickinson's introduction to his edition of *The Political Works of Thomas Spence* (Newcastle, 1982). T. R. Knox, 'Thomas Spence: The Trumphet of Jubilee', *Past and Present*, lxxvi (1977), 75–98. I. Prothero, *Artisans and Politics in early nineteenth-century London: John Gast and his Times* (London, 1981 edn.), 88–91.

[40] A. Calder-Marshall, 'The Spa Fields Riots, 1816', *History Today,* xxi (1971), 407–15.

Spencean ideology and insurrectionary politics to support Hunt and the constitutional mass platform. In agreeing to attend the first Spa Fields meeting, Hunt had spelt out terms which forced the leaders of the revolutionary party to revise their plans quite drastically.

Hunt was invited to Spa Fields by Thomas Preston, the 'Bishop' as he was known to his fellow Spencean Philanthropists. Preston was also involved with a group of Spitalfields silk-weavers and poor workmen who met at the Carlisle in Shoreditch, and campaigned for the abolition and regulation of machinery. It was through this group that the plans were announced for a public meeting of the 'Distressed Manufacturers, Mariners, Artisans, and others, of the Cities of London and Westminster, the Borough of Southwark, and the parts adjacent, at Spa Fields'.[41] As secretary, Preston wrote to all the leading reformers of the day, including Hunt, Cobbett, Burdett and Waithman, requesting their attendance. Hunt alone accepted once Preston had confirmed that the object was 'to agree to a memorial to the Prince Regent, setting forth their grievances, and praying for relief'. After consulting Cobbett, Hunt drew up some resolutions of his own together with a 'proper address to be presented to his Royal Highness upon the occasion'. It was while trying to make contact with Preston that he met two other members of the organizing committee, Thistlewood and Dr Watson, who reluctantly agreed to show him a copy of the memorial they intended to present to the Regent. To his horror, Hunt found that the whole affair was 'made up of Spencean principles, relating to the holding of all the land in the Kingdom as one great farm belonging to the people'. It was arbitrary and unjust, and he admonished Thistlewood and Watson, for suggesting that one set of people could dictate to any other what the law should be. The radicals should concentrate on obtaining a full representation of the people: only when this had been achieved could such principles as those in the memorial be discussed. Furthermore, he refused to countenance their proposed mass march to Carlton House to enforce an audience with the Regent. The presentation of the memorial, just like its contents, should be scrupulously 'constitutional'. A small deputation should be sent to the Regent with an address outlining the distressed state of the people and calling for reform upon the principles of universal suffrage, annual parliaments, and the ballot, to 'save the wreck of the constitution'. Dr Watson was happy to defer to Hunt on all these points. Unlike Evans he was not a doctrinaire Spencean: he was prepared to shelve the 'plan' in order to support a campaign for universal suffrage. Unlike Thistlewood and his own son, he was not obsessed with the traditional putsch-type strategy: he was prepared to postpone the 'coup' in order to concentrate on a campaign which would facilitate mass mobiliz-

---

[41] T. Preston, *The Life and Opinions of Thomas Preston, patriot and shoemaker* (London, 1847), 24–8. W. Hone, *The Riots in London* (London, 1816).

ation.[42] After Hunt's impressive performance on 15 November, most members of the revolutionary party followed Dr Watson's lead and endorsed the working alliance with Hunt. Some revolutionaries, however, were furious that Hunt had been able to dictate the terms at Spa Fields. Thistlewood and the young Watson made sure that a second meeting was called so that they could go ahead with their original insurrectionary plan, every last detail of which was well-known to the Government through Castle and other informers.[43] It was not until the disastrous failure of precipitate insurrectionism on 2 December that the more recalcitrant members of the revolutionary party came to accept the utility of Hunt's constitutional mass platform.

The working alliance between Hunt and the revolutionary party proved a very satisfactory arrangement right up until Peterloo. The young Watson and his group were forced to abandon their immediate plans for insurrection, but otherwise there was little sacrifice of principle or strategy. Admittedly, Hunt's radicalism was constitutionally phrased: it lacked the rational conviction of Paineite republicanism, and was quite devoid of the socio-economic analysis of Spenceanism, narrowly focused though that was on landed wealth. But Hunt's commitment to universal suffrage, as Spa Fields made clear, was forthright, unequivocal, and very popular with the people at large. Thereafter, ultra-radicals willingly supported his constitutional programme because it represented such an uncompromising challenge for political power: it mattered little that they viewed political reform as but a necessary first stage, whilst he regarded universal suffrage as in itself the desideratum. Furthermore, it was quickly appreciated that Hunt's constitutional campaign of mass pressure from without offered the best security against the tricks and traps of the informers and *agents-provocateurs* who plied their trade all too easily in the tavern world of revolutionary conspiracy. By promoting Hunt's campaign of mass mobilization, the ultra-radicals turned away from conspiracy and coups in order to engineer an open, propitious and decisive confrontation with the authorities.[44] For Hunt, too, the alliance worked well, allowing him to break through the confines of traditional extra-parliamentary politics and challenge the moderate reformers. Having clashed with the ratepayers in the Common Hall, the relatively well-to-do electors in popular Westminster, and the landowners and freeholders at county meetings, he went to Spa Fields, the first wholly 'unlimited' demonstration of a radical character in

[42] Hunt, *Memoirs*, iii, 328–34. *CPR*, 18 Oct. 1817. See also Watson's speech at the Crown and Anchor, 31 July 1817 in PC, set 39, i, f. 125.

[43] HO, 44/4, ff. 360–421, narrative by John Castle in four parts.

[44] For an excellent analysis of ultra-radical confrontationalist strategy, see I. Prothero, 'William Benbow and the concept of the "General Strike"', *Past and Present*, lxiii (1974), 149–55.

London since 1795, to institute a campaign which was open to all and demanded the rights of all. Backed by the organizational skill of Dr Watson, he was able to reach a mass audience and seize the initiative from the reform establishment.

3. SPA FIELDS

Popular radicalism was transformed by the three Spa Fields meetings of 1816–17. Pittite repression had followed quickly in the wake of the pioneering monster protest meetings of the 1790s, and it was not until the post-war years that the mass meeting became established as the principal arena in popular politics. At Spa Fields Hunt brought the mass platform into being: constitutional protest open to all for a constitutional programme acknowledging the political rights of all. After Spa Fields there could be no retraction from the complete radical programme of universal suffrage, annual parliaments and the ballot: the direct-taxation programme endorsed by Burdett, Cobbett, Cartwright and the other luminaries of the Hampden Club was denied popular support. From Spa Fields onwards, the radicals sought to achieve their uncompromising demands by mounting such a display of overwhelming mass support in the country as would coerce an otherwise inexorable Government. Forcible intimidation, mass agitation situated on the borderline of legality, became the fundamental strategy of the popular radicals, who deliberately exploited ambiguities in the law and Constitution to develop mass pressure from without and thereby embarrass and menace the authorities. These 'politics of disorder', to use the terminology of the social scientist, supplanted both the 'politics of order', as exercised by Francis Place and the Westminster reformers in dutiful orchestration with Brougham and other favourably disposed Whigs in the Commons, and the 'politics of violence', the precipitate insurrectionism of Thistlewood and the revolutionary party, which served only to facilitate governmental repression.[45] The efficacy of these new tactics, barely glimpsed before the repression of 1817, was to be demonstrated dramatically in the great radical mobilization of 1819.

The importance of the Spa Fields meetings is seldom acknowledged by historians: instead of hailing the transformation of popular politics, they condemn the advent of 'Orator' Hunt, the demagogue, the bane of reform. Such criticism is both unjust and unhistorical since it fails to acknowledge the deliberate transmogrification of 'Bristol' Hunt into 'Orator' Hunt by the ministerialists and moderate reformers of the time, an all too effective means of discrediting his achievements at Spa Fields where he forced open

[45] On the politics of disorder, see J. Wilson, *Introduction to Social Movements* (New York, 1973), 229–31.

the arena of extra-parliamentary politics to the crowd, established the programme of universal suffrage, and formulated a strategy which no longer required the patronage and controlling influence of those within the political nation. Cobbett was appalled by the torrent of abuse directed against Hunt after the success of the first Spa Fields meeting. '*I am defending you this week*', he wrote to him privately, 'the atrocious villains shall not calumniate you at this rate without my speaking.' But the press attacks continued, portraying 'Orator' Hunt as an immoral adventurer, a mercenary, self-seeking, deluder of the good people. Speaking at the third Spa Fields meeting in February 1817, Hunt drew attention to this fundamental change in anti-radical propaganda, the full force of which was now borne by himself. Previously, he noted, terms like the 'rabble' and the 'swinish multitude' had been much employed: now, 'they find out some other epithets, they call you a well-disposed, a good sort of people; but say that you are deluded'. To stigmatize the reform cause, the anti-radicals of the post-war years vilified the leaders and orators, the demagogues who 'retired to their homes in comfort, leaving the deluded audience to their suffering'.[46] Perspectives have changed dramatically, but sympathetic historians of the popular movement still condemn the radical leadership. The actions of the 'mob' have been decoded to reveal the political crowd, but the demagogue has yet to be de-stigmatized. A study of Hunt's great speeches at Spa Fields reveals that there was far more purpose and principle and much less vanity and demagoguery in his oratory and leadership than historians have assumed.

Hunt's first task at Spa Fields on 15 November was to inform the huge crowds of the futility and irrelevance of the various responses so far displayed to the unprecedented economic distress.[47] Philanthropy was summarily dismissed after a brief reference to the paltry sum subscribed by those who 'gorged themselves with the public spoils . . . and called their

[46] The first reference to 'Orator' Hunt that I have come across is in Southey's article 'Parliamentary Reform', *Quarterly Review*, xvi (1816), 248, which was reprinted in pamphlet form in Manchester in 1817. The sobriquet was widely and quickly adopted, see for example *A Few Little Truths; Or, the Orator HUNT-ed from Spa Fields to his old Earth at the Cottage* (Bath, n.d.), a loyalist poem distributed in Bristol soon after the 2 December Spa Fields meeting ('WHAT riots, what tumults, what *shocking* confusion / Has London just witness'd from Hunt's *vile* intrusion'), which included 'A Few Little Truths Forgot by Mr. Orator Hunt': one line reads 'O! orator, orator, orator Hunt'. For the vilification of Hunt by the moderate reformers at this time, see the editorial in *Examiner*, 24 Nov. 1816. In Hunt's defence, see Adelphi University and Nuffield College: Cobbett Papers, Cobbett to Hunt, 20 Nov. 1816; *CPR*, 23 Nov. 1816; H. Hunt, *Plain Facts. Is he a Traitor? Being a defence of Mr. Hunt from the calumnies of the London Newspapers* (London, n.d.); and W. Hone, *Full Report of the Third Spa-Fields Meeting* (London, 1817), 7 and 15.

[47] This account of the 15 November meeting is based on: *Fairburn's Account of the Meeting in Spa-Fields* (London, 1816); *The Times*, 16 Nov. 1816; *Examiner*, 18 Nov. 1816; and Hunt, *Memoirs*, iii, 334–42. Estimates of the attendance vary between 5,000 and 15,000. William Clark, a journeyman-coachmaker was the chairman of all three meetings.

conduct benevolent'. Food-rioting was shown to be pointless and mis-
directed since bakers and butchers were not responsible for the current
high prices and were suffering almost as much from the weight of taxes as
the people themselves. Moderate reform was the next target. He ridiculed
the 'milk and water reformers' who were so vocal in their cosy conclaves
but refused to join the people at Spa Fields. Such reformers, he warned,
were 'false friends . . . wolves in sheep's clothing . . . the greatest enemies
the people ever had'. To prove the point, he employed the device later
labelled 'consistency by contrast' by his successor and imitator, Feargus
O'Connor.[48] Time after time he contrasted his own readiness and sacrifices
to attend the meeting with the unexplained absence of supposed reformers
who were doubtless to be found 'slinking behind their counters':

On the present occasion where were all these pretended friends? What had become
of all the great city patriots, that the distressed population of the metropolis had
been obliged to send 100 miles for him to preside at their deliberations?

This was a crude but effective means of legitimizing his leadership as he
called for a campaign of escalating platform activity and cautioned the
crowd against any hasty, physical struggle with the authorities:

He well knew what ought to be done in such a crisis. He knew the superiority of
mental over physical force; nor would he counsel any resort to the latter till the
former had been found ineffectual. Before physical force was applied to, it was
their duty to petition, to remonstrate, to call aloud for timely reformation . . .
Those who resisted the just demands of the people were the real friends of
confusion and bloodshed; but if the fatal day should be destined to arrive, he
assured them that, if he knew anything of himself, he would not be found concealed
behind a counter, or sheltering himself in the rear.

Hunt, then, regarded the first Spa Fields meeting as a marshalling exercise
for a legal but confrontationalist platform campaign of mass pressure from
without. Believing that the way to achieve radical reform was through mass
meetings like the present gathering, he criticized the new delegate scheme
of the Hampden Club which, he feared, would be infiltrated by
Government agents, although he welcomed the drafting of a reform bill by
Burdett and Cartwright with whom he was proud to ally as an enemy of the
Whigs—'Sir Francis Burdett had exposed them in the House of Commons,
Major Cartwright in his publications, but he took to himself the proud task
of exposing them in public.' His main recommendation was for a national
campaign of open mass meetings for reform as soon as Parliament
assembled. The present meeting on distress, he advised, should adjourn
until the first day of the new Parliament, when a petition for radical reform
should be adopted as part of a nationwide display of strength:

[48] *Northern Star*, 31 Mar. 1849.

. . . our fellow-countrymen of Bristol, Liverpool, Manchester, Birmingham, Nottingham, Leicester, Glasgow, Paisley, and of every City, Town, and populous place in the United Kingdom, are hereby invited, and requested by this Meeting to assemble and meet on the *same* day, at the same hour, and for the SAME PURPOSE.

Much to his annoyance, young Watson successfully moved an amendment reconvening the meeting on 2 December to receive the Regent's answer to their present petition on distress.

This amendment apart, Hunt was in full control of the 15 November meeting. The petition to the Regent bore no trace of the original Spencean memorial: it was the familiar demand for the recall of Parliament, retrenchment and reform. Spa Fields, indeed, provided Hunt with a mass audience for his well-rehearsed analysis of the dire economic consequences of the war, the debt, and the boroughmonger-system. Specially for the occasion he read out extracts from what was to become his famous *livre rouge*, a certain report of the House of Commons which he had bound and placed in his library under the title 'Splendid Paupers':

. . . the cause of our misery was not to be traced in a transition from war to peace; but in supporting the establishments and the expenditure of war during a peace, and in filling this little book (Loud applause). Taxes here appeared to be expended, not only in paying the judges etc; but in pensioning the fathers, the brothers, the mothers, the sisters, the cousins, and bastards of the borough-mongers (*loud applause and laughter*), and all sorts of paupers.

Excessive taxation, he continued, exhausted the capital of the small employer and thus led to unemployment and suffering for the poor. He therefore called upon the employer, 'the man who wore a good coat' to join the worker, 'the artisan, with a dirty apron upon his waist' in the campaign for radical reform and retrenchment. But the mass platform proved to be the preserve of the artisan and the labourer: Spa Fields was the parting of the ways for radicals and moderates, a political division which split the ranks of the industrious along socio-economic or 'class' lines.

After the success of the first meeting, Cobbett enjoined on Hunt the need to be 'very *cautious*' as the unplanned 2 December meeting approached. The press and the Government, Cobbett was convinced, would stop at nothing to goad the peaceable radicals into folly and violence, and he feared that Hunt might be provoked into some unwise action by the 'common howl of foul abuse and viperous calumny' directed against him. Hunt was well aware of the dangers. He resolved to have nothing more to do with Dr Watson and Thistlewood if they continued to keep company with the likes of John Castle, who had behaved most suspiciously at the dinner after the 15 November meeting. Hunt kept himself apart from Watson and his group until 2 December itself when, *en route* to Spa Fields, he encountered Castle who pleaded with him to forget the meeting and hurry instead to the assistance of young Watson who had 'got possession of the Tower'. Hunt was not to be caught in this well-laid plot. He denounced Castle as a '— scoundrel', and dashed on to Spa Fields where he dwelt at length on the supremacy of moral over physical force.[49] Aware that Hunt would object to their plans, Thistlewood and young Watson had arrived at Spa Fields early in the morning in order to proceed with their insurrection unimpeded. Crowds returning from the execution of four criminals at the Old Bailey provided a ready audience when they stationed their cart, specially hired for the occasion by the now absent Castle, on the site of the old Pie House, well away from Merlin's Cave where Hunt was scheduled to speak at 1 p.m. Young Watson soon worked the crowd up into a suitable frenzy. 'If they will not give us what we want,' he catechized in a dramatic climax, 'shall we not take it: ("Yes!") are you willing to take it? ("Yes!") If I jump down among you, will you follow me? (Universal cries of "Yes!" and loud shouts).' Several hundred followed him and the cordwainer John Hooper through the streets to Smithfield, where a customer was accidentally shot in the groin during a raid on a gunshop, the only serious casualty in the riots. Numbers fell away, and 'Head General' Thistlewood was forced to beat a sorrowful retreat at the Tower when he found that the troops, whom he had treated so lavishly in the pubs, had no intention of joining the people. Minor disturbances continued throughout the afternoon and early evening in some parts of the city, the most prominent participants being the distressed demobilized seamen who had made their way to London to claim their arrears in pay and prize money.[50]

By the time Hunt arrived in his tandem at 12.55 p.m. huge crowds were assembled on Spa Fields which had all the appearance of a fair with 'stalls for the sale of fruit, gingerbread, etc.'[51] The day was a great triumph for Hunt's brand of popular platform radicalism, the antics of the '*Pie-House* conspirators' notwithstanding. In his speech he skilfully steered the people towards open, mass agitation for the radical programme. He began by detailing his single-handed efforts to present the 15 November petition to

[49] Adelphi University and Nuffield College: Cobbett Papers, Cobbett to Hunt, 20 Nov. 1816. *CPR*, 20 Nov. 1816. Hunt, *Memoirs*, iii, 343–6 and 365–6.

[50] W. Hone, *Riots in London*; and *Hone's Riots in London, Part Two* (London, 1816). Dr Watson also arrived at Spa Fields early, but he refused to join the insurrectionists much to Thistlewood's fury; he was very critical of his son, whom he considered imprudent and insane, and had apparently tried to stop him moving the 2 December amendment at the first meeting. See his speech at the Crown and Anchor, 31 July 1817 in PC, set 39, i, f. 125; and Prothero, *Artisans and Politics*, 91.

[51] This account of the 2 December meeting is based on: W. Hone, *The Meeting in Spa Fields* (London, 1816); *Examiner*, 8 Dec. 1816; BL Add. MSS 27809 (Place papers), ff. 22–5; and Hunt, *Memoirs*, iii, 365–74. All reports agree that the attendance was much larger than on 15 November: the radicals later claimed that the meeting attracted 100,000, see *People*, 28 June 1817.

the Regent, reading every last sentence of his correspondence with Sidmouth so that the people could judge for themselves 'whether I disgraced myself or you'. Reports such as these became a characteristic feature of his speeches: at a time when no formal channels of accountability existed, he felt the need to legitimize his leadership on every public occasion, by recounting in full detail his actions on the people's behalf. Other techniques to legitimize his position pervaded the speech: 'consistency by contrast', and the proud emphasis on his independence and gentlemanly status. 'I am a private country-gentleman, with a small fortune,' he informed the crowds, 'but I take care to live within my means and spend whatever I do for my poor countrymen, that they may share in it.' The independent country gentleman held a revered position in popular libertarian history: Hunt's status was thus the best guarantee of his defiant opposition to corruption, oppression, factionalism, and plunder, and his best retort to anti-radical calumny. It was to satisfy his principles not his vanity that Hunt spent so much time at Spa Fields defending himself against the slanderous press and establishing his personal credentials for leadership. In the name of radical reform and no apostasy, he was preparing to challenge the renegade Burdett, his former hero and the acknowledged champion of the people. After the first meeting he had written to Burdett in Brighton to fix a convenient time for them to present the petition to the Regent as deputed by the meeting. Burdett, miffed by inaccurate press reports which suggested that the name of Lady Oxford, his former mistress, had featured in Hunt's list of 'splendid paupers', tersely replied that he had not received any 'authentic account of the petition', and was 'determined not to be made a cat's paw of and not *to insult the Prince Regent*'. Hunt was furious and wanted to make it public knowledge that Burdett was 'backing out', but Cartwright and Cobbett prevailed upon him not to mention the incident and to pocket Burdett's insult.[52] Nevertheless, he was determined to prepare the way for a full-scale radical campaign without Burdett's patronage and leadership.

The centre-piece of his speech was his lively ridicule of the official response, as it were, to the 15 November petition, the Regent's donation of £4,000 to the Spitalfields Soup Committee, 'a base attempt to impose a cheat on you'. 'Which would you prefer, a penny-worth of soup, or a penny-worth of your earnings?', he demanded: 'Shall the thing be given up altogether? (Loud cries of "no, no!") I knew you would say no, and therefore I put the question; for had you said yes, I would have been quite confounded.' Their next step, he suggested, was a petition to the Commons, now scheduled to assemble on 28 January, demanding universal suffrage, annual parliaments, and the ballot. The whole point of the

---

[52] H. Hunt, *The Green Bag Plot* (London, 1819), 4–5; and *Memoirs*, iii, 354–5. *CPR*, 20 Dec. 1817.

exercise was to force Parliament to understand that 'the sentiments of the Petitioners are the sentiments of the People at large'. Corrupt as they were, the Commons would give way, he maintained, once they realized 'the whole people of England were petitioning for their rights . . . As that House are in the habit of saying, "Oh, this or that Petition is only signed by 4 or 5,000", I propose the whole of us shall sign it (*"Yes, we shall"*).' He proposed that Cochrane alone should be accorded the honour of presenting their monster petition, but other speakers, unaware of recent events, insisted that Burdett, the 'tried friend of the people', should be asked as well. The meeting was adjourned until 10 February, the second Monday after the meeting of Parliament, when Burdett and Cochrane were to report back.

The Spa Fields meeting of 2 December inaugurated the mass platform. While the revolutionary party fell into the Government's secret spy trap, Hunt established a new structure of open, popular, constitutional, radical endeavour. From this point on, radicalism was synonymous with mass meetings, mass petitions, and the programme of universal suffrage, annual parliaments and the ballot, a programme for which all could strive and none should hinder by foolish excursions into violence. The impact of Hunt's 2 December speech was immediate: it radicalized the Hampden Club petitioning/delegate scheme and electrified the new provincial clubs and societies. Joseph Mitchell of Liverpool, John Kay of Royton, and other delegates to the forthcoming convention were sent to London to attend the Spa Fields meeting: they returned north, ardent advocates of universal suffrage, convinced that Hunt was the spearhead of the movement.[53] Throughout the provinces there was a discernible change of mood: gone were the days of unquestioning deference to the London Hampden Club, that 'brilliant constellation of Rank, Talent and Respectability'; now Burdett and Cartwright were ordered to prepare their bill forthwith and to incorporate the Spa Fields' programme of universal suffrage.[54] At Middleton on 16 December, Mitchell chaired a meeting of deputies from fourteen petitioning bodies representing the cotton towns in and around Manchester, where weavers' wages were down to four or five shillings a week: they implored Burdett and Cartwright to draft their radical bill without delay; dispatched missionaries to towns yet to hold mass petitioning meetings; and issued a declaration in which the old radical

---

[53] H. W. C. Davis, 'Lancashire Reformers', *Bulletin of the John Rylands Library*, x (1926), 51–4.

[54] *The Addresser Addressed, or a reply to the Townsman of Bolton* (n.p., 1816). *Resolutions, and Petition of the Inhabitants of Manchester* (Manchester, n.d.), a report of the 30 December meeting. For reports of other meetings, and radical pamphlets and handbills, see TS, 24/3; HO, 40/9; and the very useful volume of such material bound in Manchester Central Library as *Parliamentary Reform*.

analysis of underconsumption merged with the labour theory of value to justify the now uncompromising demand for universal suffrage:

They must seek a Power in the Constitution . . . a Power that will curtail luxury—by diminishing Taxation, and will enable the people to buy shoes, stockings, shirts, coats, hats, etc. and then there will be a demand for labour . . . suffrage commensurate with *direct* Taxation, seems to grant, that property only ought to be represented; whereas, labour makes property, and therefore in the name of common sense ought to be represented.[55]

In London, the Hampden Club agreed to a rearranged timetable: Burdett and Cartwright were to present their bill to an extraordinary general meeting on 18 January, prior to submitting it to the convention of petitioning delegates four days later.[56] This re-scheduling prompted a further round of mass meetings in the north-west, which the new radical paper, the *Manchester Political Register*, had insufficient space to report in full. The campaign also gathered momentum across the Pennines where Mitchell and John Johnston, the Manchester delegate, addressed a number of meetings. On 1 January, deputies from twenty-one petitioning bodies met at Middleton again, with John Knight in the chair and Samuel Bamford as secretary: having affirmed their commitment to universal suffrage, they called upon all petitioning bodies to meet again on 10 February to receive reports on the reception of their petitions in line with Hunt's policy at Spa Fields. In a speech at Barnsley, Mitchell took this tactic a stage further and advocated simultaneous meetings on every Monday until a satisfactory answer to their petitions was forthcoming.[57]

As the Hampden Club petitions took on a radical hue, Hunt ensured that the west country played its due part in this first exercise in mass pressure from without. Bristol had not escaped the terrible distress of 1816, and large crowds were expected at the petitioning meeting which 'Spa Fields' Hunt was to address on 26 December. He arrived to find the city 'more like a besieged fortress than anything else': the cavalry corps from Trowbridge and Dorchester were on duty along with the North Somerset Yeomanry and 800 special constables. The mayor refused the use of the Guildhall and forbade the construction of any hustings in the open air. Hunt, however, was neither intimidated nor thwarted. In a lengthy speech from his rain-drenched gig on Brandon Hill, he advised the crowds to resist provocation and thereby confound the irresponsible, alarmist authorities:

We want no tumults, no riots, we want only our rights . . . The partizans of

---

[55] *To the People of England . . . meeting of Deputies . . . Middleton, the 16th Day of December, 1816* (Manchester, n.d.). Bamford, 15.

[56] See the report of the committee meeting, 30 Dec. 1816, in *Proceedings of the Hampden Club*.

[57] *Manchester Political Register*, 4 Jan.–1 Feb. 1817. Bamford, 15–16.

corruption wanted a Plot—they would give any thing for a Plot—but we shall disappoint them . . . Let them surround us with their cavalry and artillery—we will oppose to them the artillery of truth, reason, and justice—(*Great applause*) . . . We are assembled for a legal and constitutional purpose and have nothing to fear. We have been robbed of our rights, and we are assembled to-day to tell the Robbers, '*Give us back our Constitution—we want no Soup Kettles!*'

An uncompromising radical petition for universal suffrage was then adopted which Hunt was deputed to take to the London convention: within a few days, it attracted thousands of signatures.[58]

A week or so later he held a meeting at Bath and was forced once again to depart from the standard procedure. Since the mayor refused to comply with his requisition, he called the meeting in his own name and used his large yard in Walcot Street as the venue. Troops and special constables were much in evidence, and placards were issued requesting masters to keep their servants, apprentices and workmen within doors, but the attendance was so great that the proceedings had to be adjourned to the Grove, where a radical petition on the Bristol lines was adopted unanimously, and Hunt and John Allen were appointed as delegates to the Hampden Club convention.[59]

Hunt introduced himself at the London convention as the delegate from '14,000 petitioners of Bristol, 8,000 of Bath and 100,000 at least at Spa Fields'. Together with Samuel Brooks, the veteran Westminster reformer, he collected the testimonials of the other 'country' delegates who assembled at the Crown and Anchor on 22 January, representing some 151 places in all, and bearing petitions signed by half a million people.[60] Burdett, chairman of the original organizing committee, declined to attend this humble but not unimpressive gathering, having previously informed Cartwright and Cobbett that he would 'never consent to extend the Suffrage beyond householders and those who paid direct Taxes'. Cartwright took the chair in his absence, and advised the delegates to adopt the household suffrage programme advocated by the Hampden Club and endorsed by Burdett who would present the bill in Parliament. Cobbett agreed—he had been hastily elected as a delegate from the Union Society especially to

[58] Bristol Record Office: Letters and Miscellaneous Papers, boxes 1816 and 1817, contain much correspondence on Hunt's visit and the increased charitable efforts in December 1816 to alleviate distress. *Bristol Gazette*, 9 Jan. 1817; *CPR*, 11 Jan. 1817; and Hunt's *Memoirs*, iii, 397–401. Estimates of attendance on this rainy day vary between 900 and 10,000. Hunt had visited Bristol earlier in the year when he spoke briefly from the pedestal, *Bristol Gazette*, 18 July 1816.

[59] *Bristol Gazette*, 9 Jan. 1817. Hunt, *Memoirs*, iii, 401–9. The former put the attendance at 5,000, the latter at 12,000–15,000.

[60] This account of the convention is based on: *Manchester Political Register*, 1 Feb.; *Bristol Gazette*, 30 Jan.; *CPR*, 22 Feb. 1817; Hunt, *Memoirs*, iii, 411–22; Bamford, 19–21; BL Add. MSS 27809 (Place papers), ff. 33–4; and the report in *Proceedings of the Hampden Club*.

advocate the Burdettite programme, his recent conversion to universal suffrage notwithstanding.[61] Hunt, however, stood adamantine on the principle of universal suffrage and refused to subscribe to the '*doctrine of exclusion*':

The instructions he had from the great bodies that deputed him, as well as his own personal feelings, forbade him from giving this limit of elective right his sanction . . . What, he would ask, has called forth the animation that now, like an electric shock, pervaded the empire on the great question of Reform? What but the feelings of Universal Suffrage? By the adoption of a limit such as proposed, one fourth of the worthy persons who have signed these petitions would be excluded.

He was immediately supported by the northern delegates and Cobbett prudently abandoned his rearguard action. Once the convention had voted in favour of a radical bill, embracing universal suffrage, annual parliaments and the ballot, Hunt called for its immediate dissolution lest the Government impute sinister designs to the petitioning radicals. Not all the delegates shared these fears, but in the end his motion was carried dissolving the 'far-famed delegate meeting'.

The next task was to find an MP prepared to present the delegates' petitions. Burdett, of course, refused to have anything to do with them, and Cochrane was reluctant to act on his own. Hunt decided to force the issue in his inimitable way: on the day Parliament assembled, he led a procession of delegates through huge crowds to Cochrane's house, informing the masses *en route* that Cochrane would assuredly present the petitions. The besieged Cochrane was left no choice: to obtain egress he agreed to present Hunt's Bristol petition, whereupon he was carried across Palace Yard aloft in an armchair, bearing the petition and a bundle of sticks, one for each county, symbolizing the strength of the united people.[62] Later that day, however, the window of the Regent's coach was shattered by a missile as he returned from the opening of Parliament: the Government now had the pretext to implement 'alarm', the technique of repression first employed by Pitt.[63]

The press had been preparing the ground for repression ever since the 2 December meeting by refusing to distinguish between the riots in the city and the peaceable events at Spa Fields. Hunt was disgusted by these spurious and flagitious reports, and tried to stop William Hone publishing his broadsheet accounts, wrongly assuming that here too the riots and the meeting would be ominously conflated and he would be portrayed again as the chief incendiary.[64] Hone, in fact, provided an accurate account of events together with a full-scale vindication of Hunt's conduct on the day:

[61] *CPR*, 23 Nov. 1816. [62] Hunt, *Memoirs*, iii, 424–9. Bamford, 22.
[63] White, 113–14 and 156.
[64] Stevens-Cox Collection: Hunt to Hone, 6 and 8 Dec., and Hone to Hunt, 7 Dec. 1816.

This is Mr. Hunt's sin—he preached reform, and recommended patience and perseverance: he saved London from being deluged with blood, by restraining the passions of men pinched with hunger and goaded by distress . . . for this the Corruptionists cannot forgive him while he lives. As long as he conducts himself with the temper and moderation he shewed at the last Meeting, he will have the approbation of all thinking men.[65]

Cobbett, too, appreciated Hunt's great achievement on 2 December in preserving the peace and outwitting the authorities, a point he stressed in his new cheap journalism, his own contribution to the rise of the mass platform and the demise of traditional violent protest. The Government, he delighted, were quite bewildered by the peaceable petitioning platform. 'They sigh for a PLOT', he wrote to Hunt in a famous letter: 'Oh, how they sigh! They are working and slaving and fretting and stewing; they are sweating all over, they are absolutely pining and dying for a plot!'[66] Their embarrassment was relieved by the 'attack' on the Regent, the 'Pop-Gun Plot': sensational ex-parte information was hurriedly passed on to secret committees of both Houses for examination and report, prior to the introduction of repressive legislation to curb the platform.

The third Spa Fields meeting on 10 February took place whilst the committees were still investigating the contents of the famous 'green bags', the 'precious documents got up to prove that sedition, conspiracy and rebellion were close at hand'.[67] Fearing that the platform would soon be suppressed, Hunt used the occasion to justify the conduct of the radicals, impugn the 'alarm' policy of the Government, and expose the apostasy of the moderate reformers. The Government, he remonstrated, had resorted to desperate, fraudulent measures to proscribe and besmear the peaceful petitioning radicals: they had 'trumped up' the story 'about the attack on the Regent, detained the Evanses and other 'deluded followers of the *Spencean Plan*', and given vent to 'dreadful accusations of treason'. The radicals, he insisted, had behaved openly, peaceably, and constitutionally:

No one here will say that we have propagated the doctrines of the Spencean Plan . . . We came here solely to agree to a Petition for Parliamentary Reform. We have already told Parliament, that if our first Petition did not answer the purpose, we should petition twice; and we shall do so again and again, until our prayers have effect. (*Applause*) We shall petition as long as we have a right to do so. It is a privilege due to us by the constitution.

'If it were wished to make him the victim,' Hunt continued, pledging his

---

[65] W. Hone, *Riots in London*.

[66] *CPR*, 2 Nov. 1816 (from which date a cheap broadsheet edition was available)—11 Jan. 1817.

[67] This account of the 10 February 1817 meeting is based on: W. Hone, *Full Report of the Third Spa-Fields Meeting* (London, 1817); and Hunt, *Memoirs*, iii, 443–8.

personal commitment to continue the constitutional struggle, 'he was willing to lay down his life. (*"Never, never, we will protect you!"*).' After this successful deployment of the death motif, one of his favourite rhetorical devices, he called upon the crowds to adopt a petition defending the right of petitioning and demanding the constitutional programme of universal suffrage, annual parliaments and the ballot, first requested by the Duke of Richmond some thirty years previously. The third Spa Fields meeting, then, confirmed the popularity of Hunt's leadership, programme and tactics. The response was deafening when he called for three times three cheers at 2.30 p.m., to coincide with similar demonstrations at meetings throughout the country.[68]

The acknowledged leader of the radicals, Hunt refused to contemplate any reconciliation with the moderate reformers in the face of Government repression. From the platform at Spa Fields, he excoriated the behaviour of Burdett, Waithman and the reform establishment. Burdett was shown to have betrayed the people's trust and instructions: he had not even bothered to reply to the chairman's letter requesting him to present the 2 December petition with its 24,479 signatures; he had simply made it known that he 'could not support a Petition embracing the principle of universal suffrage, or election by ballot', and that it was not convenient for him to attend on 10 February. Waithman stood condemned for his hostility to the Spa Fields meetings and manipulation of the Common Hall, in detailing which Hunt incurred the wrath of some liverymen in the crowd. Throughout the period of the Spa Fields meetings, Hunt was engaged in a running battle with the Waithmanites for the allegiance of the livery. Back in November, Waithman had expressed his strong disapproval of mass meetings which 'professed to call exclusively upon the lowest order of the people, and which, by being held in the open air, would naturally contain loose and suspicious individuals'.[69] In the Common Hall that month, he led the attack on a string of motions based on the Spa Fields resolutions, to which Hunt replied by ridiculing all the talk of 'moderate reform'. What, he wondered, would the livery think of a moderately honest man or a moderately virtuous wife?—'Would they not look upon it as a direct insult, and require that the man should be perfectly honest, and the woman unexceptionally chaste? So it was with the cause of reform: it ought to be pure and above suspicion.' In the name of true reform, he refused to be silenced by any appeal to moderation or unity:

He had heard it said, that it was injudicious to create any division among the reformers. This was about as wise as it would be to desire the farmer not to divide

---

[68] For the Hampshire meeting on 10 February, see *CPR*, 15 Feb., and for the meetings in the north, see *Manchester Political Register*, 15 Feb. 1817.

[69] Dinwiddy, 'Patriotic Linen-Draper', 88.

his corn from the chaff. It was absolutely necessary to draw a line of separation between the real and the sham friends of reform.

But he failed to carry the day, and the livery adopted Waithman's moderate resolutions.[70] Shortly before the third Spa Fields meeting, the Common Hall met again to petition for reform. The proceedings, Hunt reported to the Spa Fields crowds, were 'rigged' by Waithman: radical amendments were dismissed out of hand, and the petition was as anodyne as could be. Hunt, in fact, had left the Guildhall in disgust to address the crowds outside, 'letting them know that the people inside were of no consequence—they [the people in the street] were the only proper advocates of liberty'.[71]

The Spa Fields meetings thus brought Hunt into irreconcilable conflict with Burdett, Waithman and the moderate reformers as he proceeded to mobilize the people out of doors. Reformers who sought to work within the system, found their task much more difficult now that Hunt had raised the spectre of mass pressure from without. The Whigs refused to regard moderate reform as the means to curb this radical threat. Thus when Waithman and his associates formed themselves into a dining-group known as the Friends of Economy, Public Order and Reform, to promote co-operation with the parliamentary opposition, they failed to attract any Whig support—Burdett and Brand were the only MPs to attend the February dinner.[72] Brougham, once the great hope of the Westminster reformers, was delighted to regain party favour by leading the attack on the radical extremists when the reform petitions were presented in the Commons.[73] The potential strength of Hunt's mass platform frightened the Whigs just as it compelled the Government towards repression.

[70] *The Times*, 30 Nov. 1816.
[71] *The Times*, 1 Feb. 1817. *Independent Whig*, 2 Feb. 1817.
[72] Dinwiddy, 'Patriotic Linen-Draper', 89–90.
[73] J. Cannon, *Parliamentary Reform 1640–1832* (Cambridge, 1973), 170.

3

Repression, Risings, and Reform, 1817–1818

THE mass platform was rapidly crushed by the 'dungeon Parliament' of 1817, but repression intensified radical feelings and strengthened the post-war radical challenge: moderate leaders were repudiated; the alliance between Hunt and the revolutionary party was reinforced; and links with the trades were forged. When the radicals started to mobilize again, a process which began before the Seditious Meetings Prevention Act had run its full course, there was a distinct class identity associated with the platform. The language of 'the people' still predominated and the programme remained that of popular constitutionalism, but the working people now took a particular pride in their independent opposition to the corrupt and repressive political system. Without acquiring any new ideology or revolutionary strategy, radical reform, under Hunt's unquestioned leadership, took on a working-class tone.

I. REPRESSION

The reports of the committees of secrecy painted an alarming picture of a 'general plan of rebellion and revolution', gaining in strength since the failure of the first attempt at insurrection on 2 December. Through the Hampden Club convention and other delegate bodies, the radicals were secretly co-ordinating their efforts for a revolutionary rising to destroy the present frame of society by the 'division of the landed, and extinction of the funded property of the country'. Spence's 'plan', as Cobbett had feared, was paraded as the radical, revolutionary 'plot'.[1] Hunt was outraged by this flagrant misrepresentation of the radical campaign: he petitioned Parliament and wrote to Sidmouth to register his personal protest and vindicate his own conduct on the platform:

In standing forward, or, rather in coming forward at the call of my countrymen in distress, I have violated no law. I have used no incentives to riot or to violence of any sort; I have not proposed or given the smallest countenance to, any projects or propositions for 'dividing the land', or for subverting any establishment or institution . . . I have assisted in the promoting of Petitions for a Reform in the

[1] *PD*, 1st series, xxxv, 411–19, and 438–47. *CPR*, 13 Dec. 1816.

Commons' House of Parliament. This I have done with special care to promote, at the same time, peace, good order and a respect for the laws. I belong to, and am connected with, no Clubs, no Conciliabules, no secret Associations, of all which I disapprove.

As well as justifying his own position, Hunt challenged every detail of the lurid accounts of the Spa Fields meetings and the Hampden Club convention, but his itemized confutation of the 'green bag' reports was ignored by Parliament, which gave its approval to a series of repressive measures.[2] The most hated of these was the suspension of habeas corpus, or 'Absolute Power of Imprisonment Act', as Cobbett called it, but the most effective of the new laws was the Seditious Meetings Prevention Act which strictly forbade the practice introduced at Spa Fields of holding and adjourning simultaneous mass meetings, and decreed that any meeting of over fifty people required the prior permission of the local magistrates. Radical clubs and societies were also to be 'utterly suppressed and prohibited as unlawful combinations and confederacies'; and to keep the radical press under control, Sidmouth issued a circular, encouraging magistrates to arrest persons suspected of disseminating seditious libel.[3]

The imposition of repression widened the gulf between the radicals and the moderate reformers. In the radical ranks, feelings ran high against Burdett who was held culpable for the facility with which the ministers had been able to introduce the dreaded new laws. It was Burdett who had called and then deserted the Hampden Club convention, the spectre which haunted the green bag reports: the convention, Place noted, was by far the most useful incident enabling the ministers to 'alarm the timid'.[4] To compound matters, Burdett had then remained in Leicestershire, enjoying his hunting, instead of defending the people in the Commons. This dereliction of duty was roundly condemned by Hunt at a meeting in Westminster to protest at the new laws. The fox-hunting baronet, now back in town, responded angrily and ridiculed Hunt's 'outrageous' notions about the role and function of a popular member of Parliament. 'He had rather be the tool of a Court, than be moved as a puppet, and commanded when to speak, and when to hold his tongue', Burdett proclaimed, eschewing any suggestion that he was the people's delegate in Parliament. Hunt came off the worse for the exchange and suffered further discomfiture

[2] See Hunt's petitions against the mistreatment of Thomas Dugood, a young lad confined to prison for pulling down a scurrilous anti-Hunt posting-bill, and against the committees' reports, *PD*, 1st series, xxxv, 169–73, 210–11, 546–51, 589–90; and his letter to Sidmouth in *CPR*, 8 Feb, 1817.

[3] Jephson, i, 403–12. *CPR*, 19 July 1817.

[4] BL Add. MSS 27809 (Place papers), f. 34. It was the way in which the Government portrayed the convention that led Cobbett to issue his famous advice to the radicals to 'have nothing to do with any *Political Clubs*, any secret *Cabals*, any *Correspondencies*', *CPR*, 15 Feb. 1817; see also *CPR*, 20 Dec. 1817 and 11 Apr. 1818.

when his amendment for universal suffrage failed to attract a seconder.[5]

In the city too Hunt found little support for radicalism despite the widespread disapproval of the new legislation. He was hissed and hooted when he arrived at the Common Hall on 28 February convened to protest at the suspension of habeas corpus, and it was some while before he could secure himself a hearing. Defiant as ever, he then assured the livery that he did not regret and would never retract his radical principles—'They might torture his flesh, they might impair his constitution, yet—and he gloried in the idea—they could not destroy *a noble mind*.'[6] The Common Hall met again in May to oppose any extension of the period of suspension, and to censure the city MPs who had ignored the February resolutions. Hunt seized the opportunity to introduce some long-prepared motions calling upon Alderman Combe, the Whig member, to resign, since his poor health prevented him from attending to his parliamentary duties. Caught unawares, Waithman was furious and 'tried as many tricks as a Monkey, *to Coax, to wheedle, to bully & to threaten the Livery*', but in the end, Hunt's resolutions were carried. Combe duly took the Chiltern Hundreds to be succeeded by Matthew Wood, the popular, reforming lord mayor and Waithman's arch rival. Hunt was delighted with the outcome, but it was the smallest of victories: the livery still refused to sanction radical reform, and the Government continued with its repressive policies.[7]

On the county platform, Hunt faced a problem of a different order: here there were no allies, friendly or otherwise in the campaign against repression, but serried ranks of loyalists, sworn enemies of the radicals, impassioned supporters of the Government's stand against the revolutionary threat. Against the odds, Hunt, initially assisted by Cobbett, tried to unfurl the radical banner in this most hostile but still legal arena of extra-parliamentary politics. They were given a rough ride at the Hampshire meeting in March when they tried to move an amendment to the loyalist address, proposing to add after the word constitution 'as established by Magna Charta, the Bill of Rights, and the Act of Habeas Corpus, for which our forefathers fought and bled'.[8] At the next county meeting in Wiltshire, Hunt had to face the wrath of the loyalists single-handed. He arrived at Devizes to learn that Cobbett had fled the country and taken passage to America. Bewildered and dispirited, he was then subjected to an unmerciful castigation on the platform where Benett, his old adversary, led the calumnious attack. As soon as he tried to defend himself, Benett's

[5] *The Times*, 26 Feb. 1817. *Hone's Reformist Register*, 1 Mar. 1817.
[6] *The Times*, 1 Mar. 1817.
[7] Lancashire Record Office: Hunt Correspondence DDX/113, Hunt to Bryant, 7 June 1817. Hunt, *Memoirs*, iii, 484–91. *The Times*, 31 May 1817. Dinwiddy, 'Patriotic Linen-Draper', 88.
[8] *CPR*, 15 Mar. 1817. Hunt, *Memoirs*, iii, 457–9.

hirelings in the audience 'commenced a bellowing and braying like so many of their four-legged bretheren'. According to plan, the sheriff then dissolved the meeting, ordered the Riot Act to be read, and instructed the magistrates to take Hunt into custody. At this point the crowd came to Hunt's rescue, and the authorities reluctantly gave up the attempt to arrest him, whereupon he was carried in triumph to his inn.[9]

The Government was soon confirmed in its new repressive powers: 'alarm' proved self-fulfilling and the committees of secrecy were set to work again to investigate the provincial risings of 1817. The provincial radicals were generally more hesitant than their 'revolutionary' London comrades to engage in the politics of violence: they wanted to be sure of mass support and popular legitimacy before taking any physical action. One of the most militant radicals in the north-west, John Bagguley, an eighteen-year-old servant, was highly critical of young Watson and his 'precipitate measure' on 2 December: the riots, he regretted, had damaged the petitioning campaign, the legal means of mobilizing support and preparing the masses for the inevitable physical struggle.[10] Bagguley was the main promoter of the March of the Blanketeers, which Bamford believed originated in the evening drinking and discussion sessions at the Cock, Grafton Street, when William Benbow, Mitchell and other northern delegates to the Hampden Club convention were befriended by members of the revolutionary party and plans were mooted for a general rising in the provinces.[11]

Whatever its origins, the Blanketeer scheme was adopted in Manchester in early March at a public meeting protesting at the suspension of habeas corpus and the rejection of the Hampden Club petitions, several hundred of which had now been sent to Westminster, signed by one and a-half million people in all. The Manchester radicals were disgusted by the spurious grounds on which Parliament rejected the clearly-expressed wishes of the people, the most blatant instance being the Speaker's ruling that only 13 of the 600 petitions which Burdett intended to present as his belated contribution to the campaign, conformed to accepted standards.[12] Striking a pose of righteous legality, the Manchester radicals decided to petition in groups of twenty, in strict conformity with Stuart legislation against tumultous petitioning. They agreed to meet again a week later when ten out of every group of twenty were to set off for London to present the petitions, equipping themselves with blankets for the long journey south. The scheme, R. J. White noted, combined all the advantages of legality with all the opportunities of development into

---

[9] Hunt, *Memoirs*, iii, 461–70.
[10] Informant's report of conversation with Bagguley, enclosed in Ethelston, 16 Jan. 1817, quoted in S. Maccoby, *English Radicalism 1786–1832* (London, 1955), 330.
[11] Bamford, 29–30.   [12] *CPR*, 8 March 1817. Cannon, 170.

something else. The authorities took swift and decisive action. On 10 March, a number of leaders were arrested and detained for the next eight or nine months, including John Bagguley, Samuel Drummond, John Johnston, the Manchester tailor, Elijah Dixon, spinner, and William Ogden, the veteran seventy-three-year-old printer; the hunger march itself was quickly broken up, although some poor weavers got as far as Stockport and a few reached Ashbourne. Anger at the detention of the Blanketeer leaders led some radicals to talk of making 'a Moscow of Manchester'. This time the authorities acted rather hastily: a secret committee meeting at Ardwick Bridge was raided on 28 March and other arrests, including Bamford and Healey, followed soon afterwards, but most were discharged within a month or so because of insufficient evidence.[13] Meanwhile, plans for the general rising first discussed at the Cock were taking shape as repression intensified: secret committees were appointed for the various regions and districts; central co-ordination was entrusted to delegate meetings at Wakefield; the date was fixed for 26 May, the first Monday after Burdett's motion for reform; and it was agreed that there should be simultaneous uprisings in the towns of the midlands and the north, a concentration of forces round Nottingham, and then a march on London. To ascertain the support which was likely to be forthcoming, Joseph Mitchell was deputed to tour the country and report back to the central delegates at Wakefield. As is well known, he soon acquired a travelling companion, the infamous Oliver the spy.[14]

The rising, postponed to 9 June, was a limited affair. Provincial radicals did not eschew physical force, but they were determined to cross the threshold of violence only when there was some chance of success. Several district delegate meetings had already been raided, and Oliver was now regarded with the utmost suspicion, but even so, some radicals braved the hopelessly uneven odds on the night. Several hundred clothing workers advanced upon Huddersfield in the Folley Hall rising, but they wisely dispersed before military reinforcements arrived. In Pentrich, home base of Thomas Bacon, the veteran Jacobin who had represented the east midlands radicals at the Hampden Club convention, the discussions at the Cock, and the central delegate meetings at Wakefield, Jeremiah Brandreth heroically led a contingent of men through the pouring rain on the fourteen-mile march to Nottingham, stopping at houses and farms *en route* to demand arms and support: on one occasion, a farm servant was accidentally killed. When they finally reached Nottingham, wet and

---

[13] Davis, 58–62; White, 163–6; and Bamford, 31–112. 'Return of all persons arrested, committed, or detained in England on treasonable charges in the year 1817', *Journals of the House of Commons*, lxxiii (1818), Appendix, 778.

[14] Hunt, *Green Bag Plot*, 8–15. Reports of the committees of secrecy, *PD*, 1st series, xxxvi, 949–56, and 1088–98.

demoralized, they were immediately overpowered by a force of hussars ready in waiting.[15]

Hunt believed that the radicals had a duty to all they could to assist Brandreth and the Pentrich prisoners. He wrote to Thomas Cleary, who served as 'a sort of general secretary to the Westminster Committee', asking him to arrange a public meeting to promote a subscription to defray the expenses of feeing the best counsel for their defence. Cleary refused in the most unequivocal terms—'We, Reformers, are far from wishing to countenance or identify ourselves with any man guilty of murder, robbery or riot . . . I COULD ALMOST HANG THEM MYSELF for playing the game of the tyrants so well.' Hunt was appalled by the inhumanity of this reply. As it was too late to convene a meeting himself, he set off for Derby to offer what personal assistance he could. Defence counsel refused to grant him an interview, but he stayed on to attend the whole of the trial proceedings which confirmed his initial belief that the Pentrich rising was 'a horrible plot, to entrap a few distressed, poor creatures to commit some acts of violence and riot, in order that the Government might hang a few of them for high treason!' He never forgave the Westminster reformers for their desertion of the condemned Derby prisoners. Using material provided by Mitchell and others, he published a pamphlet which traced the rising or 'green bag plot' back to the ill-advised Hampden Club convention, called in Burdett's name, and the treachery of Burdett's mercenary agent, Thomas Cleary, who had sold information to the Government about the evening meetings at the Cock.[16]

Hunt was more successful in his efforts on behalf of the London 'conspirators', Dr Watson, Thistlewood, Preston and Hooper, who faced charges of high treason arising out of the events of 2 December. Watson was the first to be tried, just at the time of the sensational revelations in the *Leeds Mercury* about Oliver and the Government's spy-system. The prosecution case relied heavily on the evidence of John Castle, whose unsavoury past was revealed under cross-examination to have included brothel-keeping, bigamy, forgery and blood money. But it was Hunt's evidence, as the first defence witness, which condemned Castle to perdition and ensured the acquittal of Watson and the others: in graphic detail, he described the deliberate and diabolical trap which Castle had set

[15] For recent and contrasting interpretations of the Pentrich rising and Oliver the spy, see M. I. Thomis and P. Holt, *Threats of Revolution in Britain 1789–1848* (London, 1977), 44–61; J. Stevens, *England's Last Revolution: Pentrich 1817* (Buxton, 1977); and Thompson, *Making*, 711–33.

[16] Hunt, *Memoirs*, iii, 493–507, and *Green Bag Plot*. Cleary's letter was reprinted in *SPR*, 4 July 1818, along with two letters from Dr Watson to Hunt on efforts to assist the Derby prisoners. See also, T. Cleary, *A Reply to the Falsehoods of Mr. Hunt* (London, 1819).

for him after the 15 November meeting.[17] Following the acquittal, Hunt chaired the celebratory dinner at the Crown and Anchor, where the Spa Fields working alliance was publicly acknowledged and warmly reaffirmed. Hunt reminded the radicals that their aim was 'to regenerate, not to destroy the Constitution', and Watson censured his son, who had fled to America, for his foolish conduct on 2 December.[18] From this point on, Hunt could always rely on Dr Watson to quash any plans for insurrection by members of the revolutionary party.

By his conduct in 1817, Hunt assured for himself the deserved leadership of the next radical campaign: he had not only opposed repression, but had also defended its victims. Repression completed what Spa Fields had begun: Hunt and the radical reformers were henceforth irrevocably divided from Burdett and the moderate reformers. It was a division not just of programme and tactics, but also of class. Like the great crowds at Spa Fields, the victims of 1817, the participants in the various risings and conspiracies, were overwhelmingly working class. Thistlewood was the solitary 'gentleman' listed in the return of persons arrested, committed or detained on treasonable charges in 1817. Dr Watson and Bamford's friend, Joseph Healey, were entered as surgeons. All the rest, some ninety odd names, were artisans, labourers and factory workers: there were large numbers of framework-knitters and weavers, trades where Luddism had formerly been strong; half a dozen labourers; spinners, cloth dressers, colliers, masons, cutlers, coopers, hatters, cordwainers, shoemakers, tailors, printers, engravers and various other trades.[19] These were 'the people' with whom Hunt readily identified: it was workers like these that he was determined to mobilize as soon as the repressive restrictions came to an end.

Throughout 1817 Hunt kept to his radical colours and upheld the cause whenever the law allowed: on one such occasion he nearly carried the day when he moved a string of radical amendments at Robert Owen's meeting at the City of London Tavern called to consider his plan to 'relieve distress, re-moralize the lower orders, reduce the poor rate, and gradually abolish pauperism'.[20] Viewing events from America, whence he had fled to escape creditors and repression, Cobbett was much impressed by Hunt's dogged radicalism, his 'perseverance that no discouragement can check'. He continually praised Hunt at the expense of Burdett, the fallen champion, who had turned his back on the real reformers. When Cobbett learnt that Burdett had not even bothered to bring forward a bill for reform at the end

[17] 'The whole proceedings in the case of James Watson' in T. B. Howell (ed.), *State Trials: vol xxxii, 1817* (London, 1824), 1–674.
[18] PC, set 39, i, f. 125.
[19] *Journals of the House of Commons*, lxxiii (1818), Appendix, 778.
[20] *Hone's Reformist Register*, 23 Aug. 1817.

of the great petitioning campaign but had simply moved for a select committee to examine the issue, he decided that the time had come for Burdett to be 'politically put to death'. Hunt, he believed, was just the man to accomplish this task. He sent him a rough draft of an address to the electors of Westminster, and encouraged him to start campaigning in the constituency against the neglectful, indecisive Burdett who had 'abandoned the Reformers and abetted the damnable Corn Bill'.[21] As repression still forbade his taking to the mass platform, Hunt needed little prompting. In 1818 he turned to the election hustings at Westminster, where he was soon in conflict with '*petty shop-keepers*, and little *tradesmen*, who under the denomination of *tax-paying housekeepers*, enlisted themselves under the banner of Sir Francis Burdett, in order to set themselves up as a sort of privileged class, above the *operative* manufacturer, the artizan, the mechanic and the labourer'.[22]

2. WESTMINSTER ELECTIONS, 1818 AND 1819

In 1818 Burdett made a determined effort to restore his reputation as the radical champion. After habeas corpus was resumed, he came forward to chair a much-publicized meeting at the Crown and Anchor to promote a subscription for those who had been imprisoned during its suspension.[23] A few days later, he signed his famous radical pact with Jeremy Bentham, whose conversion to the cause had finally been made public with the publication of his prolix *Plan of Parliamentary Reform* in 1817. Bentham and Burdett came together to promote universal suffrage in the professed belief that 'the most profound philosophy cannot unite in vain with the greatest popularity of the time', although Burdett's intention was simply to regain some of his lost popular appeal and reform credentials as the general election of 1818 approached.[24] Hunt was quite unconvinced by Burdett's new radicalism and challenged him to pledge himself to universal suffrage at a legally convened meeting in Palace Yard in late March. Once again, Burdett refused to be ordered to advocate any particular programme, but he did not object when the meeting adopted a petition for universal suffrage and annual parliaments, drawn up by Major Cartwright.[25] In the Commons in early June, he spoke in favour of universal suffrage, attributing his new stance to Bentham's influence, but then justified the

---

[21] *CPR*, 13 Sept. 1817–11 Apr. 1818. Adelphi University and Nuffield College: Cobbett Papers, Cobbett to Hunt, 17 Oct. 1817 and 8 Jan. 1818. University of Illinois: Cobbett to Hunt, 7 Feb. 1818.

[22] Hunt, *Memoirs*, ii, 75.   [23] PC, set 39, i, ff. 247–77.

[24] W. Thomas, *The Philosophic Radicals* (Oxford, 1979), 41–2.

[25] *The Times*, 24 Mar. 1818. BD, 25 Mar. 1818.

radical programme in terms of history and popular constitutionalism, not utilitarianism.[26] By this time, Cochrane had finally announced that he was leaving the country to take command of the Chilean Navy, and the Westminster electors were faced with a bewildering choice of 'radical' candidates at the forthcoming general election. Hunt was the first to declare himself, eagerly anticipating a face-to-face confrontation on the hustings with 'any supporter of a *Cruel Corn Bill* or any opposer of *Universal Freedom*'.[27] As in the past, the Rump overlooked Cartwright's claims and nominated the Hon. Douglas Kinnaird as Burdett's running-mate. Kinnaird, a young banker and manager of the Drury Lane Theatre, was a member of the Rota, an exclusive dining-group of Burdett's close friends, one or two of whom were now fashionable disciples of Bentham. The aggrieved Cartwright—'Antient Pistol' as he was unkindly labelled by Byron, another member of the Rota[28]—was later nominated by his loyal admirers, with some encouragement, it would seem, from certain members of the Rump who calculated that this was the best way to undermine the Huntites, those 'implacable and wrong-headed friends to our cause'. Encouraged by these divisions in the reform camp, the Whigs decided to run Romilly in the propitious hope of recapturing the former Foxite stronghold of popular Westminster. The ministerialists fielded Sir Murray Maxwell, a naval captain and 'Flogger of Britons by tyranny stung'.[29]

Hunt approached the election in the now standard radical manner. Recognizing his 'duty to come forth from his rural retirement and labour in behalf of the people', he swore an affidavit before the mayor, pledging himself against place and pension, committing himself to universal suffrage and the repeal of the Corn Laws, and promising to keep the poll open for the longest possible period. 'My course is plain and direct', he informed the public-spirited and independent electors in one of his campaign handbills, 'and disdains all subterfuge or studied ornaments of speech—Universal Suffrage and Annual Parliaments, and an opposition to all laws that have a tendency to curtail the Liberties of the People, and oppress and starve the Poor.' He made the fullest possible use of the hustings, and went on speechifying tours of the constituency, delighting the crowds with his

[26] Thomas, *Philosophic Radicals*, 42–3.
[27] 'Mr. Hunt's Address to the Electors of Westminster', *CPR*, 23 May 1818. See also, Lancashire Record Office: Hunt Correspondence, DDX/113, Hunt to Bryant, 26 May 1818.
[28] Byron to Hobhouse, 26 June 1819 in J. Murray (ed.), *Lord Byron's Correspondence* (2 vols., London, 1922) ii, 115–16.
[29] BL Add. MSS 27841 (Place papers), f. 113, A. Galloway to Place, 5 June 1818, and f. 554, 'A New Song', one of innumerable handbills in this volume, a major source for the election. See also the volume in the British Library bound as *A collection of addresses, pamphlets, posters, squibs, etc., relating to the Westminster election, 1818*. For a useful secondary study, see J. M. Main, 'Radical Westminster, 1807–1820', *Historical Studies (Australia and New Zealand)*, xii (1965–7), 186–204.

lampoons of Burdett and his 'understrapper, his *bouche-trou*, his stop gap, his cat's paw, his toad-eater, Kinnaird'.[30] All this was very disturbing to the Rump who preferred to keep radicalism and the non-represented crowds out of the election proceedings to avoid offending the respectable householders who dominated the constituency—the franchise in Westminster was far from democratic despite the city's radical reputation: it was vested in resident householders and excluded all lodgers; many of the parishes were prosperous, even opulent residential areas; and the more humble householders were small tradesmen who serviced the rich and the 'ton', Westminster being the very centre of the nation's wealth and fashion.[31] During the full fifteen days election, the Rump tried various strategems to silence Hunt on the hustings and discredit him with the unwelcome crowds. From the beginning they joined the ministerialists and 'Bully Baldwin's' gang in heckling him with a list of 'delicate questions' about his relationship with Mrs Vince, but their most effective weapon was the spy-charge specially manufactured by Place in the *Gorgon* and amplified by Cleary on the hustings.[32] Cleary, Cartwright's election agent, transferred his services to the Rump because Burdett's return appeared to be in doubt. At the end of the third day's poll, the baronet lagged far behind Romilly and Maxwell, and drastic action was taken: Kinnaird was jettisoned, Cartwright agreed to withdraw, and Cleary took to the hustings to give vent to the spy charge against Hunt. After much taunting, Hunt retaliated by producing Cleary's despicable letter condemning the Pentrich prisoners. Thanks to Place again, Cleary was able to trump this by displaying Cobbett's letter to his publisher John Wright in 1808, advising the reformers to have nothing to do with such a bad character as 'Bristol' Hunt. The Rump trusted that this would not only embarrass Hunt on the hustings but also cause Cobbett to terminate his lengthy campaign against Burdett and themselves. When the news reached America, Cobbett immediately proclaimed the letter a forgery, redoubled his attacks on the Rump, and supported Hunt more fervently than before.[33]

In popular Westminster as in freeman Bristol, Hunt was the undisputed choice of the crowd but not of the electorate. He won the show of hands on nomination day, but finished well at the bottom of the poll with a derisory

[30] BL Add. MSS 27841 (Place papers), f. 63 and f. 201. Hunt, *A correct report of the proceedings of the meeting . . . to take into consideration and adopt the best means to secure the election of Henry Hunt, esq.* (London, 1818), 18–21. 'Revival of the Ancient Mode of Canvassing', *SPR*, 20 June 1818.

[31] Thomas, *Philosophic Radicals*, 85–7.

[32] BL Add. MSS 27841 (Place papers), f. 262, 'Mr. Hunt. Delicate Questions'; f. 151, Place to Cleary, 10 June 1818; and ff. 382–4, Editor of the *Gorgon* to the Gentlemen of Sir Francis Burdett's committee.

[33] *SPR*, 4 July 1818. Hunt, *Memoirs*, iii, 530–7. *CPR*, 28 Nov. 1818. G. D. H. Cole, *The Life of William Cobbett* (London, 1924), 222–4.

eighty-four votes. Despite this poor personal poll, the election demonstrated his ability to disconcert the reform establishment and discomfort
those radicals who preferred politics to principle. Burdett, 'Westminster's
Pride and England's Glory', finished a sorry second to Romilly, thereby
denying the Westminster reformers the position of strength which the
Gorgon considered so important for negotiating an agreement with the
popular Whigs.[34] Hunt's uncompromising radical campaign, so harmful to
the moderate reformers, attracted considerable support from hard-liners
who refused to accept the realities, compromises, machinations and
chicanery of popular politics within the unreformed system. Veteran
Jacobins like Gale Jones allied themselves with Hunt out of their disgust at
the sharp practice displayed by the Rump at the annual purity of election
dinner, the nomination meeting, and the election itself.[35] Hunt's cause was
also upheld by a younger generation of militant radicals, most notably the
publicists who came to the fore in Cobbett's absence. William Sherwin was
most impressed by Hunt's 'unwearied and *consistent* endeavours in
promoting the principles of Universal Suffrage', and ridiculed the new
radical pretensions of the Burdettites—'After *eighteen months* consideration,
the trimming, hesitating, half-measure gentlemen are come up to the
principles laid down at the Spa Fields meetings!! . . . Are ye so dull as not
to see through the shallow contrivance!' Hunt, Sherwin advised in his
Political Register, the favourite paper of Dr Watson and his group,
deserved the support of every true radical since he came forward 'on the
simple ground of public principle destitute of any object except that of
obtaining the rights of the People, determined to sacrifice his time, his
exertions and his fortunes in the cause of liberty'.[36] Sherwin's associate,
Richard Carlile, published Hunt's campaign material and furnished the
famous red flag with 'UNIVERSAL SUFFRAGE as a motto, surmounted by a
Cap of Liberty, surrounded with the inscription of Hunt and Liberty'.[37]
Thomas Dolby, the leading radical bookseller and distributor, brought out
a pamphlet extolling Hunt's virtues and campaigned industriously on his
behalf.[38] The revolutionary party offered considerable assistance: Preston
provided some placards; Dr Watson saw to the bodyguard arrangements;
and W. P. Washington, a leading Lancashire Luddite who had recently
arrived in London to join Watson's group, acted as Hunt's poll-clerk.[39]
Others involved in the campaign included William West, the wire-worker,

[34] *Gorgon*, 18 and 25 July 1818.
[35] See Jones's lengthy speech in *A correct report of the proceedings . . . to secure the election of Henry Hunt, Esq.*, 8–18, and his address 'To the Independent and Public-spirited inhabitants of the city of Westminster' in BL Add. MSS 27841 (Place papers), f. 402.
[36] *SPR*, 30 May–18 July 1818.   [37] Hunt, *Memoirs*, iii, 528.
[38] Thomas Dolby, *Memoirs* (London, 1827), 109–110; and *An appeal to the electors of Westminster* (London, 1818).
[39] Prothero, *Artisans and Politics*, 96.

to whom Hunt had turned to arrange a subscription in London for the Pentrich prisoners after Cleary's rebuttal, and William Giles, the Wych Street baker who had stood Preston's bail in 1817.[40] Up in Lancashire, Samuel Bamford arranged a subscription to help with the expenses, and wrote to the Westminster electors enjoining them to vote for Hunt, the 'People's Man'.[41]

The only notable opposition in the radical ranks came from close associates of Major Cartwright. Thomas Wooler, Cartwright's loyal lieutenant and amanuensis, had co-operated with Hunt earlier in the year when they tried to radicalize Waithman's resolutions in the Common Hall, protesting at the Indemnity Bill to cover the period of the suspension of habeas corpus.[42] During the election, however, Wooler's *Black Dwarf* came out strongly against Hunt whose candidature was deemed to threaten Cartwright's rightful return as Burdett's colleague. Unlike Hunt and his supporters, Wooler and Cartwright never questioned the integrity of Burdett's radicalism or his prescriptive right to the first Westminster seat. This deference to the baronet continued after the election, undiminished by Burdett's specific disavowal of universal suffrage and adoption of the term 'general suffrage' at the 'raree show' and other dinners celebrating his return. As Wooler's animus against Hunt intensified, Cobbett decided to intervene to set the record straight. In a series of open letters to Cartwright, he explained that Hunt was not a rival or an opponent but the redoubtable enemy of the despicable Rump who had always refused to acknowledge the major's indisputable right to a Westminster seat.[43] But Wooler and Cartwright were still far from convinced when a by-election was called in November following Romilly's suicide.

Hunt shed no tears for Romilly. 'You know I always thought, and therefore said, that Romilly was a great *Political imposter*', he wrote to Bryant, his friend and legal adviser:

He *talked* loud & well against corruption yet he took good care never to *do* any thing that would tend effectually to destroy it . . . he *knew* that his *Hypocrisy* must soon be exposed, he *knew* that more was expected from him than he ever meant to perform. It was a different thing to be the *popular Member* for Wes[tr] than to be smuggled into the House for Arundel. He *knew* that the Eyes of the Reformers would be upon him, he *knew* that he should not go to the Palace Yard Meetings & he *also knew* that whether he went there or not, that I should go there, and *he knew* that he would receive *such instructions* from his Constituents there assembled, that

---

[40] Hone, 283.

[41] *A correct report of the proceedings . . . to secure the election of Henry Hunt, esq.*, 6–7.

[42] *The Times*, 25 Feb. 1818.

[43] *BD*, 3 June–26 Aug. 1818. *SPR*, 18 July 1818. Letters to Cartwright in *CPR*, 28 Nov. 1818–15 May 1819. Wooler was also angered by Hunt's efforts to nominate Cobbett for Coventry, a seat he wanted to contest himself.

he would not perform, he *knew* all this, & he *guessed a great deal more*—his Wife died, & *Butcher like*, he CUT HIS THROAT.[44]

After Romilly's departure from the scene, Hunt trusted that a genuine radical would fill the vacancy. He intimated that he was prepared to stand himself, but he hoped that Wooler and his friends would nominate Cartwright as he was in considerable financial difficulties as a result of the last campaign: he faced a court case over his share of the expenses, and there was new legislation pending, purposely designed to 'keep Hunt away', which confirmed the financial liability of candidates for their use of the hustings.[45] Wooler and Cartwright still refused to think ill of Burdett and the Rump and no steps were taken to nominate the major. At the nomination meeting on 17 November, the 'Rump Farce' as it was called, Wooler kept silent when Burdett ruled from the chair that Cartwright's nomination was out of the question. Hunt then tried to propose Cobbett, but was reprimanded by Burdett who was prepared to authenticate the 1808 letter produced by Cleary. The meeting ended by adopting Burdett's own nominee, John Cam Hobhouse, a member of Brooks's Club and also of the Rota, the most suitable compromise candidate acceptable to Whigs and reformers alike.[46]

The election did not take place until February, by which time Hunt had prevailed on Cartwright to stand. There was some reconciliation between the two, now that Cartwright acknowledged that there had been some 'double-dealing' by Burdett and the Rump, but the major still criticized Hunt for his past conduct on the hustings and his generally injurious mode of advocating radical reform.[47] At the last minute, a Whig candidate also came forward, prompted by the publication of a report by Hobhouse's committee in which Place had inserted a long and vituperative history of parliamentary reform and its betrayal by the Whigs. Hobhouse tried to retrieve his position as the compromise candidate by reading out a deliberately ambiguous statement on reform at the start of the election, but he could no longer hold the balance. He failed to appease the Whigs, who

[44] Lancashire Record Office: Hunt Correspondence, DDX/113, Hunt to Bryant, 7 Nov. 1818.

[45] *SPR*, 14 Nov. 1818. Lancashire Record Office: Hunt Correspondence, DDX/113, Hunt to Bryant, 10 and 25 Nov. 1818. For the action brought by the high bailiff, see *MO*, 12 and 19 June 1819. For the Westminster Hustings Bill, see BL Add. MSS 27842 (Place papers), f. 272, Place to H. G. Bennet, 3 Feb. 1819; and Hunt's petition in *PD*, 1st series, xxxix, 1451–6 and 206–8.

[46] *SPR*, 21 Nov. 1819. 'Report of the Proceedings held at the Crown and Anchor . . . 17th of November', in HO, 42/182. *CPR*, 6 Mar. 1819. Hunt, *Memoirs*, iii, 556–8. See also the correspondence between Cleary, Hunt, and Cobbett's publisher in *CPR*, 19 Dec. 1818 and 9 Jan. 1819.

[47] Cartwright's 'Address to the Electors of Westminster', reprinted in *CPR*, 15 May 1819. University of Chicago: MS 563, Hunt Correspondence and Papers, item 17, Cartwright to Hunt, 11 Feb. 1819. Hunt, *Memoirs*, iii, 567–74.

duly continued with Lamb's candidacy, and his obfuscatory 'written declaration' was mercilessly lampooned by the radicals, who concentrated their anger on the one clear assertion, the secondary importance of the extension of the vote compared with the desirability of a standard franchise and equal electoral districts. Hobhouse and his kind, a radical posting-bill explained, would leave the opulent shop-keeper, the master manufacturer and the rich householder in possession of their votes, while they would deprive the honest mechanic, the ingenious artisan, and the humble labourer of their present rights in popular Westminster.[48] Burdett, who had studiously avoided appearing on the hustings during the general election, was soon forced to come forward to present the reform argument in a more favourable light, but he was powerless against the 'contemptible alliance' between Hunt and the Whigs. Cheered by Whig crowds, and applauded by the Whig press, Hunt concentrated his energies not on promoting Cartwright, but on discrediting Hobhouse, the Rump, and 'the giant, the political apostate, Sir Francis Burdett'. In a final bid for the popular vote Hobhouse swung over to the radicals, but Lamb's lead was irreversible. Radical candidates, William Thomas has observed, usually fared badly in by-elections at Westminister since the politically influential classes were not distracted by their own contests in the country but remained in town. Hunt's presence on the hustings served to accentuate the pattern. The triumphal car which the Rump had built before voting started was never seen on the streets of London. Lamb topped the poll with 4,463 votes, followed by Hobhouse with 3,861, and Cartwright a mere 38, a figure which Hunt, with his easily-satisfied vanity, could not resist comparing with the 84 votes he had secured the year before.[49]

3. THE BEGINNING OF MOBILIZATION

At the Westminster elections, Hunt finally succeeded in ousting Burdett from the favour of the non-represented masses, an achievement every bit as important in the history of independent working-class radicalism as Feargus O'Connor's later debunking of Daniel O'Connell.[50] While Hunt's energies were concentrated on popular Westminster, his allies in the revolutionary party were preparing for the next mobilization of the people. In May 1818, Watson arranged another meeting at Spa Fields, within the

[48] The manuscript of Hobhouse's declaration is in BL Add. MSS 27842 (Place papers), f. 326; for radical posting-bills ridiculing it, see ff. 372–82. The other main source for the election is the biased but comprehensive *Authentic narrative of the events of the Westminster Election . . . Compiled by order of the Committee appointed to manage the election of Mr. Hobhouse* (London, 1819). The best secondary study is Thomas, 'Whigs and Radicals'.

[49] Thomas, *Philosophic Radicals*, 86. *Memoirs*, iii, 579–88.

[50] Epstein, 39–42.

terms of the Seditious Meeting Prevention Act, to outline plans for a national mass platform campaign to commence as soon as the Act expired in July. Hunt was invited to chair the meeting, but he was detained on business in Ireland: he sent his apologies and encouraged Watson to take the chair himself. By comparison with the earlier assemblies, the Spa Fields meeting of 4 May 1818 was a rather low key affair, attended by no more than 2,000 people, but for Watson, the reluctant chairman, it was an extremely important occasion.[51] The leading advocate of the working alliance with Hunt, he marshalled the London radicals for a renewed constitutional campaign of mass pressure from without. His influence within the revolutionary party had recently been strengthened since Thistlewood, who still believed in bloodthirsty ways and means, and had a plan ready to murder the ministers, was removed from the scene and sentenced to a year's imprisonment after challenging Sidmouth to a duel.[52] At Spa Fields, Watson used his new authority to promote the mass platform and popular organization. Back in February, in the wake of a number of meetings to celebrate the liberation of the last of the prisoners held under the suspension of habeas corpus, he had outlined his plans for a British Patriotic Association to organize subscriptions throughout the land; such a subscription scheme, he now suggested, would provide the finance and the organizational framework for simultaneous mass meetings as soon as the law allowed. These meetings should restrict their demands to the constitutional rights of universal suffrage, annual parliaments and the ballot, which Cartwright had verified and codified in his recently-published *Constitutional Bill of Rights and Liberties.*[53] Watson was adamant on this point, and spoke at some length of the origins and terms of his agreement with Hunt which, he admitted, had caused displeasure to some of the Spenceans. Popular constitutionalism, Watson still believed, was the surest way of attracting the masses to the radical cause, but his advocacy of the mass platform was now couched in the inchoate language of class. 'They were called together as labourers and mechanics', Watson observed with pride, 'a class of people from whom all the good that men enjoyed was derived.' The labouring classes, he continued, were 'the sole support of the superstructure', the foundation from whence 'all the other classes rise pyramidically to the Throne'. One of the main resolutions adopted by the meeting, deplored the absence of laws and regulations 'to raise industrious labourers to the importance due to their usefulness in society'. Watson's

[51] This account of the 4 May meeting is based on: *British Press*, 5 May; *Independent Whig*, 10 May; and *Shamrock, Thistle, and Rose*, 29 Aug. 1818. For Hunt in Ireland, see *CPR*, 16 May 1818; he returned via Bristol where he spoke from the pedestal again, *Bristol Gazette*, 14 May 1818.

[52] *The Times*, 9 Feb. and 15 May 1818. Prothero, *Artisans and Politics*, 92.

[53] J. Cartwright, *A Bill of Rights and Liberties or An Act for a Constitutional Reform of Parliament* (London, 1817).

hopes for a mass platform campaign did not materialize until 1819, by which time the identification of radicalism with the interests of the working class—'the social and civilized rights of labourers throughout the three Kingdoms'—had been underlined by the prominent role of radicals in the trade union struggles of the latter half of 1818.

During the disputes of 1818, many trades cast aside their traditional sectional and regional jealousies to promote general unionism, and shunned their former hostility or indifference to political agitation.[54] Working-class protest in the post-war years was a cumulative process, the trade union developments of 1818 strengthening the radical mobilization of 1819 in a manner that defies reductionist or compartmentalist interpretation. The spinners' strike was by far the most formidable of a series of well-organized strikes in the north-west in the relative prosperity of the summer of 1818. Radicals of Blanketeer fame like Bagguley, Drummond and Johnston, were in close touch with the strikers, offering practical assistance and political advice. It was this strike too which provided John Doherty, the great trade union leader of the late 1820s and early 1830s with his first experience of wider working-class organization in projects for a general union of spinners, a general union of all trades, and an alliance with the radicals for fair wages, better conditions, and parliamentary reform.[55] In London, Watson and his group played host to the spinners' delegates sent south to collect funds and advocate the formation of a general union of trades in line with the 'Philanthropic Society' established in Manchester. Through their efforts on behalf of the northern trades unionists, the Watsonites reinforced their links with the London trades. When Watson arranged the next mass radical meeting, John Gast, the most important of the London trades leaders, was delighted to appear on the platform alongside an old friend from the Bristol elections of 1812, Henry Hunt.[56]

Poorly attended as it was, the meeting near Palace Yard on 7 September 1818 marks the real beginning of the great radical mobilization of 1819.[57] Hunt took no part in the organization, which was the work of a committee convened by E. J. Blandford, an impecunious hairdresser, but he had already agreed with Watson on the need for a more militant use of the mass platform. On his return from Ireland he had accompanied Watson to Sidmouth's office to present the Spa Fields petition of 4 May. Once again, Sidmouth ruled that the Regent would answer petitions only from certain

---

[54] A. Aspinall, *The Early English Trade Unions* (London, 1949), 248–99. G. D. H. Cole, *Attempts at General Union* (London, 1953), 4–13.

[55] R. G. Kirby and A. E. Musson, *The Voice of the People: John Doherty, 1798–1854* (Manchester, 1975), 181–28.

[56] Prothero, *Artisans and Politics*, 99–103.

[57] This account is based on the reports in HO, 42/180; TS, 11/1055/4673 (3); *The Times*, 8 Sept. 1818; and *SPR*, 12 Sept. 1818.

corporate bodies.[58] Thereupon Hunt and Watson decided that the radicals must present their case more forcibly: demeaning and pointless petitions were to be shunned and the campaign escalated by the adoption of 'final and Public' declarations to the Regent, explaining the people's grievances and sufferings, together with remonstrances to the Regent, listing the 'cruel, illegal and unconstitutional acts of the corrupt and wicked Administration', and demanding the impeachment of this 'favourite junta'.

The Declaration, which Watson read to the Palace Yard meeting, was a potent mixture of natural, contractual and constitutional rights so characteristic of the eclecticism and vigour of popular radical argument. The Crown, the Regent was reminded, was 'a sacred trust and inheritance held only by the free consent and for the sole welfare and benefit of the people'. Resistance to earthly tyranny was proclaimed 'not only a right inherent in the People, and an acknowledged principle of the English Constitution, but a sacred duty enjoined by the laws of God and Man'. The Remonstrance, which Hunt presented to the meeting, was no less emotive but relied for its force on popular libertarian history, celebrating those occasions when the people had risen in rebellion against 'oppression on the part of the Sovereign, or his favourite and confidential Ministers'. Charles I and James II, the Regent was advised, would have enjoyed a very different fate had they 'shown a becoming deference for public opinion'. It was therefore up to the Regent to decide between his private inclinations and his public duty. The old popular myth that the monarch would harken to the people's needs if only they could reach his ear, was thus revitalized by the new language of menace. Alongside the myth and the grandiloquent constitutional rhetoric, was a clear commitment to the interests and well-being of the working classes. Radical reform was essential, the Remonstrance concluded, because 'every industrious labourer, manufacturer and mechanic, has a right to reap the ample and substantial fruits of his virtuous and USEFUL TOIL'. The Remonstrance, indeed, set the tone for the radical campaign of 1819: it was in popular concepts such as the Constitution and the historical struggle for its implementation, that the working-class radicals sought legitimation for their programme and their methods. Gast struck the keynote in his speech when he called upon the 'mechanical classes' to join the radicals and 'go forth as the Barons of old with a Sword in one hand and the Bill of Rights in the other and demand your Birthrights'.

After the Declaration and Remonstrance had been adopted, Watson expatiated on the merits of his penny-a-week subscription scheme which now went under the grandiose title of the Universal Union Fund of the Non-Represented People of the United Kingdom of Great Britain and

---

[58] *Shamrock, Thistle, and Rose*, 29 Aug. 1818.

Ireland. The scheme, based on small groups of ten (later changed to twenty-five) and elected hundredth and thousandth collectors, was designed to provide funds, organization, and a rapid means of communication, thereby mobilizing the collective power of the labouring poor. At Palace Yard, Watson was appointed general secretary and Hunt treasurer of the fund.

The subscription scheme, however, failed to fulfill its promise: the radicals had too many competing claims on their hard-earned pence. Watson himself was dependent on whip-rounds at his weekly meetings at the George to meet the Palace Yard expenses and cover the cost of his various publications, including the new journal, *The Shamrock, Thistle and Rose*, launched to record the transactions of the non-represented people and 'to call the attention of all ranks of industrious people, especially the labouring classes, to their own interests, to shew to them the advantages of unity amongst themselves, against the evident combination of persons who fatten on their labour'. By December, Watson was in severe financial difficulties and was arrested for debt, but he managed to bring out another pamphlet in support of the spinners' committee whose forthcoming trial presented yet another call on radical funds.[59] In the north, Watson's subscription scheme enjoyed some success in the Manchester area, but the main call on scarce resources here was financial assistance for Bagguley, Drummond and Johnston. They were arrested for speeches at Stockport on 1 September when they protested at the arrest of the spinners' committee and recommended the people to arm in readiness for a national convention which should assume the role of an anti-parliament. Bail was set at an impossibly high figure, which the hard-pressed radicals struggled to raise. A national subscription was set up at a public meeting in Stockport, and the Revd Joseph Harrison, secretary of the new Stockport Union Society, devoted all his energies to relieving the plight of Bagguley and his colleagues. Despite these efforts and appeals to wealthy reformers like Sir Charles Wolseley, the three radicals remained in gaol, much to the relief of James Norris, the Manchester stipendiary magistrate. Reporting to the Home Office in mid-November, by which time the defeated strikers had long since returned to work, Norris noted that 'Bagguley & Co' were 'such adepts in the work of sedition and withall have such access to men of their own stamp amongst the *working* classes that if they were at large I think it possible at least that we might be thrown into commotion again'.[60]

[59] Prothero, *Artisans and Politics*, 99–105. T. M. Parssinnen, 'Association, convention and anti-parliament in British radical politics, 1771–1848', *English Historical Review*, lxxxviii (1973), 515–16. Informers' reports in HO, 42/180–182. J. Watson, *The Rights of the People, Unity or Slavery* (London, 1818); and *A Letter to Viscount Lord Sidmouth* (London, 1818).

[60] Norris, 7 Sept., and 'Minutes of the difft. speeches of Messrs. Bagguley & Co', HO, 42/180; Norris, 18 Nov., and Lloyd, 14 Nov., 3, 7 and 29 Dec. 1818, HO, 42/182. *Report of the Proceedings . . . at Stockport, on Monday the 28th Day of September, 1818* (Manchester, n.d.).

The Palace Yard meeting provided the framework for the next radical campaign, but it was not followed by an immediate popular mobilization. Competing financial claims prevented the radicals from adopting Watson's ambitious plans for national organization, and in London concerted action was further hindered by the persistence of old ideological tactical and personal divisions. The Spenceans still met separately from the Watsonites, and there was much ill-will over the Evanses' disproportionate share of the funds collected for the relief of those who had been detained under the suspension of habeas corpus.[61] There was still some support for the old insurrectionary ways and means. At the George on 21 September, a paper was read out containing 'an undisguised plan for effecting a revolution'. Watson saw to it that the paper was destroyed and the plan discarded, reminding the group that 'it was an instruction from Hunt, to claim Radical Reform only: (lest the Law should lay hold of them) and that every thing desired would follow'.[62] While Watson regarded Hunt as the unquestioned leader, some of his group started to look around for other big names to pull in the crowds whenever they could afford to mount the next mass meeting. Sir Charles Wolseley was the main hope, and would have been a good draw, with his title and ready command of popular constitutional rhetoric, as exhibited in his recent address to his fellow Staffordshire landowners: 'The barons of Runnymede—the Hampdens and Sydneys of the Commonwealth—the heroes of 1688 point out where an English gentleman should be found, when the rights of his countrymen, and the freedom of his country are invaded.' But while Wolseley stood defiant against excessive taxation and extended protectionism as agricultural distress intensified, he refused to mount the mass platform. Hunt, therefore, remained the touchstone by which other public figures were judged and found wanting.[63]

After the Palace Yard meeting, Hunt remained in the political limelight. He caused quite a stir in the law courts when he refused to employ counsel in his libel action against the *New Times*, the most scurrilous loyalist rag, or at his trial for an assault on 'Spectacle' Dowling, the vituperative reporter who had given evidence against Watson and the Spa Fields conspirators, and had struck Hunt with a whip on the Westminster hustings before receiving payment in kind. When Sidmouth refused to present the Palace Yard Declaration and Remonstrance to the Regent, he registered his protest in the strongest terms, and demanded the return of the documents which he intended to lay before the Regent by some other means. He then

[61] Prothero, *Artisans and Politics*, 108.
[62] Hanley, 21 Sept. 1818, HO, 42/180.
[63] Stafford, 5 Nov., and C's reports, 2 and 23 Nov., 3 and 21 Dec. 1818, HO, 42/182. Wolseley's address in *SPR*, 10 Oct. 1818.

announced his intention to visit Manchester, taking the Declaration and Remonstrance with him. As the news spread, the radical campaign acquired tremendous momentum.[64]

[64] PC, set 39, i, ff. 304–6. *SPR*, 31 Oct. 1818. Lancashire Record Office: Hunt Correspondence, DDX/113, Hunt to Bryant, 9 Dec. 1818. Hunt, *Memoirs*, iii, 544–8.

4

The Radical Mobilization of 1819

THE radical campaign of 1819 was the most impressive mobilization in pre-
Chartist history. It was Hunt's first trip to the north which initiated the
campaign: his return visit in August brought the mobilization to a climax at
Peterloo. The strength of the challenge derived from its accessibility and
relevance to the working people: the popular constitutional idiom served
the movement well until the events at Peterloo forced the radicals to decide
whether they should exercise the constitutional right of resistance,
transforming the implicit threat of numbers into an outright physical
challenge to the state. Hunt's caution at this juncture cost the movement
dear: 'excitement' was squandered, mass support dwindled, internal
arguments developed and repression was imposed, prompting an embittered
few to cross the threshold of violence out of desperation rather than in
hope.

I. THE PEOPLE'S CHAMPION

For the radicals in the north-west, the new year began in the most
encouraging fashion with a mass meeting of the 'old sort' at Oldham on 4
January. The meeting, 'the first symptom of a revival of the smothered
fire', attracted a crowd of some 6,000 or so. There were many 'old stagers'
on the platform along with some new faces, most notably John Thaxter
Saxton, journalist and sub-editor of the *Manchester Observer*, the lively
radical paper and precursor of the *Northern Star*, which provided extensive
coverage of the movement in 1819 within a popular newspaper format.
Pride of place at the meeting was accorded to one of Hunt's Spa Fields
banners, suitably adorned with a cap of liberty. The crowd, 'XY' reported
to Byng, the military commander, was thrown into a 'transport of joy'
when James Scholefield, the chairman, announced that Hunt was to attend
the next meeting at Manchester on 18 January to petition for reform and
repeal of the Corn Laws.[1]

Hunt was welcomed to the north as the great hero of Spa Fields where,
Bamford apostrophized:

[1] Byng, 9 Jan., HO, 42/183. *MO*, 9 Jan.

> Thou raised thy voice, and the people awaking
> Beheld the foul source of corruption display'd
> And loyal stupidity, quickly forsaking . . .
> The shouts of thousands, for freedom arose.[2]

The meeting on St Peter's Field, attended by crowds of 8,000–10,000, was a regional display of support for Hunt and the radical cause.[3] All the major leaders, organizers, journalists and martyrs of north-west radicalism were on the platform: unfortunately, their combined weight caused the hustings to collapse midway through the proceedings! John Knight, the 'Lancashire Major Cartwright', was the master of ceremonies; Joseph Harrison of the Stockport Union Society introduced himself as their 'Chaplain on the Field of Battle' and reminded the meeting of the plight of Bagguley, Drummond and Johnston; Joseph Mitchell, the first self-appointed political missionary, stressed the need for organization; William Fitton, a Jacobin veteran from Royton, welcomed the demise of Church and King mobs which he attributed to the 'great *moral revolution*' effected by the 'public spirit of such gentlemen as Mr. Hunt'; and poor old ruptured Ogden, the septuagenarian letter-press printer and habeas corpus detainee, addressed his fellow Mancunians on the merits of radicalism. Several towns sent delegates to the meeting, and the magistrates were struck by the number of 'country people' who attended. In Manchester itself many workers were locked in their factories and were thus unable to participate, but the prominence of radicals from the more closely-knit, single industry out-townships was to remain a distinctive feature of the northern movement.

Hunt went to Manchester to bring the northern radicals up to the mark on the new policy of remonstrances and declarations. At Oldham the 'old stagers' had decided to petition once again, although the crowd agreed with Mitchell that it would be pointless asking Burdett to present it—'Sir Francis Burdett he much feared had forsaken the people—(here a great shout of "We have done with him")'. In accepting the Manchester invitation, Hunt informed Whitworth, chairman of the organizing committee, that he had resolved never to petition again after the experience of 1817; the general election of 1818, he added, had not altered matters, since it had strengthened the position of the Whigs, the 'greatest enemies of real reform and the liberties of the people'.[4] At the Manchester meeting, Hunt gave the crowd a clear lead when he asked them how they intended to proceed:

The question for me to submit to you will be whether you will ever again submit to

[2] 'The Welcome', *MO*, 23 Jan.
[3] This account of the meeting and dinner is based on the reports in *MO*, 23 Jan., *BD*, 27 Jan., and HO, 42/183.
[4] Hunt to Whitworth, *SPR*, 16 Jan.

such infamous conduct, whether again you will petition those who ought to be your servants, or whether you will boldly remonstrate to the throne on your manifold grievances (loud applause; cries of 'no petition'—'remonstrate, remonstrate').

The Declaration and Remonstrance which Hunt had brought with him from London were then adopted *nem con*.

The Manchester meeting provided Hunt with the opportunity to confirm and legitimize his leadership on the northern platform. All the rhetorical devices of Spa Fields were given another airing as he sought the direct approval of the Manchester audience:

I am, as you see me, a plain man; I have a little landed property by inheritance. Of the income which I derive from it, I live upon one half, and the other I devote to your service, in endeavouring to recover your rights. If ever I desert the principles which I have hitherto professed, may that colour (*pointing to one of the flags*) be my winding sheet (*Loud applause*).

At the meeting and at the dinner at the Spread Eagle afterwards, he spent some considerable time detailing the history of his political career from his days in the yeomanry corps to his efforts on behalf of the Pentrich prisoners. Throughout, he laid great stress on his gentlemanly status, the best refutation of loyalist calumny:

They have represented me as a most infamous and rascally fellow; yet I have only done what every country Gentleman ought to have done . . . I am an humble country Gentleman, and when I have been before the public I have dared to advocate the cause of truth.

All in all, the day's events were a great triumph for Hunt and the radical cause. He was hailed by the Manchester radicals as 'the intrepid Champion of the people's rights'. In return, he assured them that the memory of the day 'would descend with him to the shades of Hampden, Sydney and the brave heroes that had fought and bled with our forefathers'. 'The good old character of an independent country Gentleman was surely there in him', a correspondent wrote to the *Manchester Observer*:

I had almost compared him to an English Baron in the time of John and Magna Charta, but that Mr. Hunt's motives were so much more praiseworthy; he was not there as they met that worthless King at Runnimede, to advocate the rights of a few, but of all.[5]

At Manchester, Hunt both legitimized his leadership and carried the radical campaign forward by relying upon popular myths about English history, the Constitution, and the heroic role of the independent country gentleman. Proud of his status as an independent wealthy gentleman, he did not seek the deferential support of the crowd: by displaying his

[5] 'A Radical Reformer', *MO*, 6 Feb.

gentlemanly credentials he was identifying himself with, not distancing himself from, the oppressed and suffering people.[6] Like the glorious ancestors, his commitment to the cause was absolute: the opponent of oppression and injustice, he repudiated the factionalism and apostasy of the Whig aristocracy, the people's putative 'natural leaders'. Gentlemanly leadership in the form exercised by Hunt and O'Connor thus served to guarantee the independence and integrity of the radical challenge, thereby preparing the way for exclusive working-class mobilization.

During his visit to Manchester, Hunt 'the people's champion' attracted thousands of northern workers to the radical cause. 'Meaney who was Lukewarm jacks before', one of Col. Fletcher's informers reported, 'now Comes forward and Idlese hunt.' Norris, the Manchester stipendiary magistrate, reported that whilst Hunt was in town the weavers in the over-stocked, low-waged cotton industry 'seemed to hold a different tone and feeling and appeared in *many townships* in the neighbourhood ripe for any tumult or stir etc'.[7] The support Hunt could marshall amongst the low-paid weavers and workers of the out-townships was forcefully demonstrated before he returned south. Having been physically ejected from the Theatre Royal by a group of loyalists and soldiers led by the Earl of Uxbridge, Hunt decided to retaliate at the earliest opportunity. On the following Monday vast numbers assembled outside the theatre. 'Hunt and his party', Norris reported, 'must have sent his emissaries into the country for assistance as *many hundreds* came in during the day'. Bamford headed a specially picked contingent of ten stout fellows from Middleton to 'attend the play—to protect Mr. Hunt if requisite, and to retaliate with punishment, any insult that might be offered to him, or any of his friends'. At Oldham, 150 men were chosen to act as a 'special bodyguard', and around 1,500 radicals in all set off down the Oldham Road towards the theatre in what Chippendale described as a 'Strange Infatuation!!!' When Hunt discovered that the magistrates had ordered the theatre to remain closed, he addressed the huge crowds in impassioned language before advising them to disperse peaceably to avoid the wrath of the 'BLOODY BUTCHERS OF WATERLOO'. Later that evening a dozen loyalist roughs forced their way into his private room and challenged him to a fight.[8] Before returning to London, he tried and failed to gain legal restitution for these various loyalist assaults: the Duke of York, the Commander-in-Chief, took no notice of his formal complaint; his action against one of the special

[6] For an unconvincing analysis of the deferential nature of northern radicalism, see R. N. Soffer, 'Attitudes and allegiances in the unskilled north, 1830–1850', *International Review of Social History*, x (1965), 429–54.

[7] 'B's' report, enclosed in Fletcher, 11 Feb., and Norris, 3 Feb., HO, 42/184.

[8] This account is based on the innumerable letters, press cuttings and handbills in HO, 42/183, and PC, set 40, i; Bamford, ch. 29; and A. Prentice, *Historical Sketches and Personal Recollections of Manchester* (Manchester, 1851: rpt. London, 1970), 147–50.

constables was dismissed and he found himself subjected to a severe cross-examination by John Cross, the lawyer whom he had accused of mishandling Brandreth's defence; finally, the grand jury at Liverpool threw out a bill against the Earl of Uxbridge and his colleagues. Bruised and sore, Hunt left Manchester in a rather disconsolate mood, much to the delight of the local authorities who predicted and rejoiced that he was 'for ever done'.[9] But the country radicals who had come with their clogs and their cudgels to defend their champion and teach the local dandies a lesson, were eagerly awaiting Hunt's return. 'But come, my lads, some other day', Bamford concluded his poem on the theatre affair, 'We'll pin them, e'er they sneak away/And they shall either play or pay/When *Hunt* returns again.'[10]

Stimulated by Hunt's visit to Manchester, radicalism developed apace in the north in early 1819. There was still some hesitation, however, about the London policy of strident remonstrances. At the next mass meeting at Royton on 8 February, Saxton was overruled, and it was decided to petition once more, although all agreed: '*This is the last time that we will Petition*!!!'[11] A week later the radicals met again at Sandy Brow, Stockport, a much larger and altogether more militant affair.[12] The meeting was requisitioned by the local leaders, Harrison and Dr Cheetham, together with a group of four weavers and a tailor. Fitton, the Royton surgeon took the chair and introduced a declaration of rights since they were 'weary of the joke of petitioning the Commons'. Harrison addressed the crowd in emotive style:

You have petitioned long to no effect, now you are *remonstrating*, and perhaps it will be with as little effect. Words are but wind . . . the *cause of freedom* is the *cause of God* . . . Shall I advise you to take up arms and fight for it?—('Yes, yes!' said the people)—No, no, that I will not do. I will not advise you in this case at present.

While Harrison took the crowd to the very verge of violence, the blundering authorities overstepped the mark. The reckless local magistrates ordered Birch and his fellow constables into the midst of the meeting to seize the proudly displayed cap of liberty whilst Saxton was addressing the crowd. With its various historical associations, the cap of liberty was well

[9] Hunt to the Duke of York, Norris, 26 Jan., Lloyd, 26 and 28 Jan., HO, 42/183; and Norris, 3 Feb., HO, 42/184. Hunt returned to London via Birmingham where George Edmonds advised him against calling a mass meeting, Bedford, 8 Feb., HO, 42/184.

[10] The poem is reprinted in R. Walmsley, *Peterloo: The Case Reopened* (Manchester, 1969), 47–9.

[11] *MO*, 13 and 20 Feb. Fletcher, 11 Feb., *HO*, 42/184, which claims the attendance was only 400–500. The meeting was requisitioned by 3 weavers, 2 spinners, a manufacturer and a shopkeeper.

[12] This account is based on *MO*, 20 Feb. and the reports by Lloyd, Prescot, Norris and Byng in HO, 42/184.

chosen as the legitimizing symbol of the post-war radical movement: the Roman badge of freedom, it was an ancient and venerable emblem which had appeared on the coinage of the realm until the 1790s when it became associated with the French revolutionaries.[13] After an heroic struggle the radicals succeeded in defending the cap and the constables retired. The meeting then returned to the business of the day, and a remonstrance was adopted, but it was respectful in tone by comparison with that carried at Manchester, and it was subsequently referred to as the Stockport Petition.

There were no more mass meetings until the rejection of the Manchester Remonstrance and the Stockport Petition at the end of May. In the interim, the radicals in the north concentrated on extending and improving their organization. The first stage here was often the adoption of one of the various subscription schemes. *The Rights of the People*, a pamphlet which enjoyed a wide circulation in the north, provided full details of Watson's Universal Union Fund and Wooler's alternative, locally-based scheme.[14] In an article addressed 'To the Working Class of England', the *Manchester Observer* put forward a scheme of its own which proved very popular: penny subscriptions were to be forwarded to the 'Fund for enabling Messrs *Cobbett*, *Hunt*, *Cartwright* and *Wooler*, to obtain seats in the House of Commons'. Corrupt boroughs were to be purchased to place these men of 'great talent' where they could 'strike at the head of this Leviathan'.[15] The scheme was promptly taken up by the Oldham Union Society when its new rooms were opened at the end of February, and it spread rapidly throughout Lancashire, where the radicals entertained high hopes of what could be achieved in the Commons by one or two true champions of the people.[16] The more alarmist magistrates believed that these funds were simply a cover for far more sinister designs, and they reported that a rising was planned for 10 March, the anniversary of the Blanket meeting. When that day passed peaceably, they spoke of the postponement of plans until Bagguley's trial in mid-April. Although there was undeniably some arming by the rank and file, the reports of alarmists like Ethelston and Lloyd were greatly exaggerated: open organization, not armed conspiracy, remained the radicals' main concern, even after Bagguley's conviction.[17] The Stockport Union Society, which Hunt made a special point of visiting during his January trip to the north,[18] issued a declaration of objects and

---

[13] *BD*, 24 Feb. and 30 June. *CPR*, 23 Oct., 'The Origins and Properties of the Cap of Liberty', *Radical Reformer or People's Advocate*, 13 Oct.

[14] See the Manchester edition of Watson's *Rights of the People*, enclosed in Fletcher, 27 Feb., HO, 42/184. *BD*, 30 Dec. 1818. [15] *MO*, 6 Feb. *BD*, 3 and 17 Mar.

[16] Fletcher, 27 Feb., HO, 42/184, and 30 Apr. HO, 42/186.

[17] See the reports of Ethelston and Lloyd in HO, 42/183–186. For the trial, see *BD*, 21 and 28 Apr.

[18] *MO*, 23 Jan. and 6 Feb., which includes Hunt's letter 'To the Inhabitants of Stockport', praising the Union Society.

principles specially for the guidance of new radical groups like the Manchester Patriotic Union Society, which developed out of the Union Sunday School in Ancoats, and the Blackburn Association for the Diffusion of Political Knowledge, 'established conformably to the principles of the union, that is now so generally adopted throughout the United Kingdom, for the purpose of spreading *Political Information* amongst the useful class of society, the Lower Orders, as the State Paupers term those whose LABOUR supports them in IDLENESS and LUXURY'.[19]

By the time Hunt tried to present the Manchester Remonstrance and the Stockport Petition, radicalism in the north had acquired considerable strength: the new open societies, whether modelled on the Stockport Union Society or the Hull Political Protestants, were able to attract community involvement in the radical cause by offering the kind of cultural and educational provision that was to become such an important part of the Chartist experience.[20] In London, radicalism lacked such a community base. Radical groups like Watson's committee were shunted from one pub to the next as landlords, worried about their licences, denied them the use of their rooms. Furthermore, ideological disputes and personal rivalries ran much deeper in the metropolis. Watson asked the leading publicists, Carlile, Sherwin and Wooler to join his committee to promote a united front, but they all declined. The rigorous Evanses still berated the lax Watsonites, but a disaffected Spencean group, led by the mulatto Robert Wedderburn, joined Watson's camp. Finance remained the major problem and led to the postponement of plans for a general meeting—the proceeds of the subscription fund, the treasureship of which Hunt entrusted to his friend West, fell far short of what was required to mount a public meeting. The Westminster by-election caused a further delay in the plans, just as it occupied all Hunt's time.

As the prospect of holding a general meeting receded, the London radicals turned their attention to Cobbett's plan for a great 'Puff-Out', a massive forgery of notes to undermine the paper money system. The Watsonites still looked to Hunt for leadership here, believing that he alone could be trusted with the forged notes and had 'friends enough to put them about the streets'.[21] Hunt, however, chose a more orthodox path to challenge the 'paper men of the city': in May, he took over the proceedings

[19] *Declaration of the Object and Principles of the Union Society formed at Stockport*, enclosed in Lloyd, 17 Feb., HO, 42/184, and the amended version, approved by Major Cartwright, in *BD*, 28 Apr. For the Union Sunday School and the Patriotic Union Society, see *MO*, 6 Mar., and D. Read, *Peterloo: The 'Massacre' and its Background* (Manchester, 1958), 51–2. 'Blackburn Association for the Diffusion of Political Knowledge', posting-bill enclosed in Bouchier, 23 Apr., HO, 42/186.

[20] Read, 47–54.

[21] See the informers' reports in the bundle marked 'Papers Relating to the Thistlewood Conspiracy', HO, 42/190. 'The Puff Out', *MO*, 3 Apr.; Spater, ii, 368.

at a public meeting at the City of London Tavern, called to petition against the government's new proposals for the resumption of cash payments.[22] To ensure that he would have the necessary support on the floor, he called in at Dr Watson's on the day before, when he spoke too of his hopes to gain a personal audience with the Regent before the end of the month to present the Manchester Remonstrance and Stockport Petition.[23] This was the news for which the northern radicals had been waiting with some impatience.[24] By way of gratitude and encouragement, Joseph Johnson, secretary of the Manchester Patriotic Union Society, dispatched the most flattering address, assuring Hunt of 'our highest approbation and support, so long as you continue the distinguished champion of our cause—that is, the cause of Universal Suffrage and Annual Parliaments'. After penning a fulsome reply to the brave reformers of Lancashire whose support and confidence he cherished as 'one of the most distinguished honours that can be conferred on an Englishman', Hunt, the people's champion, tried yet again to gain access to the Regent on the throne.[25] Once more Sidmouth stood 'sentinel before the ears of the Regent'. Hunt demanded the return of the documents so that he might endeavour to find 'some other means of making the prayers and complaints of the suffering people of Lancashire and Cheshire known to his royal highness the Prince Regent.'[26] According to the Manchester magistrates in their report of the circumstances leading up to the events of 16 August, it was this 'threat' by Hunt that led to the great upsurge in the north in the summer.[27] Certainly, it soon became very clear that Hunt alone could hold together a movement so heightened in feeling by the rejection of the Remonstrance.

2. NATIONAL UNION

There was a remarkable intensification of the radical campaign after the rejection of the Remonstrance, which coincided with a severe economic downturn—the unwelcome return of 'General Distress' who was 'beating up for Recruits in all the Manufacturing Districts of the Kingdom'[28]—and the imposition of new taxes on malt, tea, coffee and spirits. These new taxes, the Government's first stand against the 'parsimony and prejudice' which had dominated public opinion since Waterloo to the detriment of

[22] *BD*, 19 May. *CPR*, 2 Oct.
[23] 'C's' report, 18 May, HO, 42/190.
[24] See Hunt's letter in *MO*, 8 May, explaining the delay.
[25] *MO*, 29 May, for the address and reply.
[26] *BD*, 2 June.
[27] 'Supplementary Statement', 23 Apr. 1820, HO, 42/12 ff. 636–70.
[28] Nottingham posting-bill, enclosed in Enfield, 2 May, HO, 42/187.

financial policy, were deeply resented by the radicals.[29] 'The great mass of the industrious being already on the border of famine,' Cartwright wrote in reply to Johnson and the Manchester radicals, 'the main question to be decided is, whether they shall submit to an additional burthen of taxes, or the boroughmonger usurpers shall submit to a radical reform.' Cartwright's hope was that the people would 'every where hold their meetings, speak their minds, and assert their rights'.[30] A couple of days later, delegates from twenty-eight northern towns met at Oldham and agreed to transform the burgeoning local radical associations into the co-ordinating machinery for a campaign of mass pressure from without. Angered by the rejection of the Remonstrance, they issued a declaration, recommending 'the formation of Union Societies, in every town and village in the Kingdom, for the purpose of acquiring and diffusing political information, and also the frequent holding of public and district meetings, in order to connect, complete and harmonize our political understanding and feeling'.[31] In the following weeks and months there was a tremendous increase in the number of mass meetings as the radicals extended their organization throughout the country, and widened their appeal to secure the partici- pation of all groups within the working community. Union Societies and Political Protestants spread from their respective bases to other industrial centres such as Birmingham and the west midlands, and Newcastle and the north-east. Trades which had earlier eschewed political involvement, now turned enthusiastically to the radical cause, led by the most distressed of all, the handloom weavers of Carlisle, whose only hope previously had been government-assisted emigration to Canada. Particular efforts were made to enlist the support of the growing number of Irish immigrant workers. To overcome the problem of size and communication in London and the large cities, a system of parochial unions was introduced. Special female reform societies were established to emphasize the extent of community involvement in the movement, and the great mass meetings became outings for whole families, trades and communities. The platform, once the preserve of exclusive groups of property-owners and electors, now became the people's own.[32]

The Oldham delegates called for mass meetings to issue addresses or appeals to the people, explaining the true cause of their deplorable plight, and demanding the immediate implementation of the radical programme

---

[29] Cookson, *Lord Liverpool's Administration*, 170. N. Gash, 'After Waterloo: British Society and the Legacy of the Napoleonic Wars', *Transactions of the Royal Historical Society*, 5th series, xxviii (1978), 145–57.

[30] *MO*, 12 June.   [31] Chippendale, 7 June, HO, 42/188. *MO*, 12 June.

[32] For a detailed analysis of the platform campaign of the summer 1819, see J. C. Belchem, 'Radicalism as a "Platform" Agitation in the periods 1816–1821 and 1848–1851: with special reference to the leadership of Henry Hunt and Feargus O'Connor', unpublished D. Phil. thesis, University of Sussex, 1974, 67–143, and Appendices A and B.

embodied in Cartwright's *Bill of Rights and Liberties*. A week later the new campaign began with mass meetings at Ashton (3,000–15,000) and at Hunslet Moor (5,000–10,000), at which the first steps were taken towards the formation of a 'national union'.[33] The incarcerated Bagguley had previously recommended such a course to Harrison, and the promotion of an open national organization of hundreds of thousands was now endorsed by the Stockport Union Society and the Hull Political Protestants, the two 'model' societies, who set aside their petty bickering and concentration on education, to co-ordinate the campaign of mass pressure from without.[34] The 'national union' was an open exercise in forcible intimidation: the Government was to be overawed by the progressive display of radical strength. The appeal of the nation adopted at the Barnsley meeting on 12 July called upon every man, who by useful employment contributed to the necessities of the state to 'join in a National Union, to demand their rights, in a voice which must accomplish their end, and restore freedom and happiness to the country'.[35] 'Form your ranks close and deep', a radical posting-bill at Wigan advised, 'prove to the world that you are the countrymen of Boadicea, Alfred, Hampden, Sidney and Russell.—It is in contemplation to form a general Union throughout the kingdom; *now* is the proper time: genuine Reformers, show yourselves, and let the hordes of corruption tremble at your numbers.'[36] In a particularly militant speech at Hunslet Moor on 14 June, George Petre, the tailor and Spencean poet, recommended 'frequently assembling yourselves in bodies, that you shew the atoms of corruption the immense body of freemen which stand before them: not by arms or petitions. No! that will not do. Nothing but assembling yourselves in bodies . . . will ever release you from the bonds of Borough-mongering Faction.' Petre's speech so horrified the middle-class reformers that Edward Baines, proprietor of the *Leeds Mercury* attended the adjourned meeting on Hunslet Moor on 21 June (10,000) to plead with the radicals to return to petitioning and moderate reform, and give up their unions and mass meetings, 'periodical approximations towards mischief'. Baines's arguments were rejected out of hand, but James Mann, leader of the Leeds radicals, decided to check on Petre's credentials and wrote to Hunt about him. Hunt replied that Petre was unknown in London as well, and cautioned Mann against any 'premature

---

[33] *MO*, 19 June. *Wakefield and Halifax Journal*, 18 June. The figures in parentheses show the range of the estimates of attendance, based on magistrates' reports and anti-radical press cuttings in the Home Office papers, and the reports in the radical press.
[34] Bagguley to Harrison, 6 June, enclosed in Lloyd, 26 June, HO, 42/188. For the squabbles between the two societies, see James Pollitt's letter, *MO*, 15 May. The Stockport Society sent a delegate to the Ashton meeting to recommend a national union; the Hull Political Protestants sent a letter to the same effect to the Hunslet Moor meeting.
[35] *Leeds Mercury*, 17 July. *SPR*, 31 July.
[36] 'BRITONS BE FREE', enclosed in Fletcher, 15 July, HO, 42/189.

movement on the part of the Yorkshire Reformers particularly if they should be instigated to resistance by any Person employ'd by a vigilant and blood thirsty Tyranny'.[37] As the great exponent of mass pressure from without, Hunt was determined to prevent any repetition of the events of 1817: the very openness of the 'national union' was the radicals' best guarantee against the dreaded spy-system.

The mass meetings that promoted the national union belong to the 'politics of disorder': they were situated on the borderline of legality, and were a form of direct action as they by-passed—or rather ignored—the conventional political channels and pointed towards unmediated confrontation with the Government.[38] To prepare for this event, there were plans for a national convention or 'national meeting'. A resolution adopted at Ashton on 14 June called for delegate meetings to arrange 'a general Election of Representatives, to meet in London, or elsewhere, to enter upon such a plan of obtaining a Radical Reform of the people's House of Commons, as they shall deem necessary'.[39] The great meeting at Blackburn on 5 July (30,000–40,000) and the next meeting on Hunslet Moor on 19 July (4,000–15,000) recommended the appointment of representatives 'to join a National Meeting, that the whole may be brought to one general focus, in order that they may devise the best plan to effect a radical reform'.[40] Following the meeting at Stockport on 28 June (8,000–20,000) plans were already proceeding for a 'general meeting of persons from all parts of the nation' to be held at Oldham to arrange for the election of deputies to London.[41] On 11 July a preliminary meeting of delegates was held at Royton, and it was decided to delay the Oldham meeting until after the great mass meeting in Manchester so that 'the orators of high degree who attend the latter may have an opportunity of being present upon the Occasion'.[42] It was to this Manchester meeting that Hunt was invited, where he was expected to preside at the election of a 'legislatorial attorney' for the unrepresented inhabitants.

The legislatorial attorney scheme is the best-known tactic of the radical campaign of 1819; one historian has described it as a brilliant means of dramatizing the reform issue.[43] It was Wooler who first suggested that a board of representatives, elected by the people using the procedure laid down in Cartwright's *Bill*, should be sent to the Commons as legislatorial attornies for the large unrepresented towns. Unlike petition rolls, he explained, the attornies could not be 'got rid of by being *laid* or *put under* their table': the Commons would be forced to discuss reform and the press

---

[37] *Leeds Mercury*, 26 June. *Leeds Independent*, 24 June. Hunt to Mann, 26 June, HO, 42/188.

[38] Wilson, 229–33.   [39] *MO*, 19 June.   [40] *MO*, 10 July. *BD*, 28 July.

[41] *MO*, 3 July.

[42] 'XY's' report, enclosed in Fletcher, 15 July, HO, 42/189.   [43] Cannon, 181.

would report the debate throughout the land.[44] When added to the platform activity of the summer, Wooler's plan acquired a militant, confrontationalist edge, and appealed to many ultra-radicals, including the Spencean Thomas Evans who eagerly anticipated being 'elected' himself.[45] Soon after the scheme was put into effect at the great meeting at Newhall Hill on 12 July (15,000–60,000), the disadvantages of the plan became clear.[46] The election (*in absentia*) of Sir Charles Wolseley to represent Birmingham overstepped the mark of the 'politics of disorder'. The undoubted illegality of holding an election without the monarch's writ provided the Government with an opportunity to intervene at a time when the radical advance appeared unstoppable, and without the bother and embarrassment of introducing special legislation. Edmonds, Maddocks, Lewis, Wooler and Cartwright were indicted for their part in the election; speakers at the Macclesfield meeting on 31 July (1,500–10,000) were later convicted for recommending the scheme even though they had been unable to find a suitable candidate (a common problem); and most disturbing of all, the Manchester magistrates seized upon a reference to a possible election to ban the meeting planned for 9 August.[47] This prompted Watson and others to question their initial enthusiasm for the legislatorial attorney scheme. Within their scenario, the Manchester meeting was of crucial importance: it was to be the provincial climax of the platform activity of the summer, the final preparation for a general meeting of the non-represented millions. The Birmingham radicals, Watson regretted, had displayed 'very bad Generalship': even Thistlewood thought they had been 'very premature'.[48] For Hunt too, the Manchester meeting was of far greater importance than the legislatorial attorney plan, which he later described as 'a foolish and absurd scheme'. Vain as he was, Hunt had no interest in being 'elected' for Manchester, or London for that matter: he agreed to return to the north to offer his services to what should be 'the *largest assemblage* . . . that ever was seen in this country'.[49]

In the summer of 1819, Hunt brought the radicals back into line for a great display of numerical force. Shortly after the Birmingham meeting, he took the chair at Smithfield on 21 July (10,000–80,000), a meeting arranged by the Watsonites. Their original plan was to meet on the hallowed 14 July and then send delegates to the country to organize simultaneous meetings, a

[44] *BD*, 30 June.   [45] W—r's report, 14 July, HO, 42/190.

[46] *A correct report of the proceedings . . . at Newhall Hill, Birmingham, on Monday, July 12, 1819* (Birmingham, 1819).

[47] *MO*, 7 and 14 Aug. *BD*, 18 Aug.

[48] 'BC's' reports, 29 July and 5 Aug., HO, 42/190–91; anon. report, 14 Aug., HO, 42/192.

[49] *Full particulars of the final examination of Mr. Hunt and the other prisoners at Manchester, on a charge of high treason* (London, 1819), 14. Hunt, *Memoirs*, iii, 593–4. Hunt to Johnson, 6 July, HO, 42/191.

'general meeting' of the nation, a fortnight later; but with only £8 or so in the kitty, it was decided to delay the meeting for a week in the hope of raising some cash. All the arrangements were left to a secret committee of thirteen chaired by Blandford, although the placards and posters were issued in the grandiose name of the 'Committee of 200 formed out of the great body of the NON-REPRESENTED PEOPLE of the British Metropolis'. When Hunt accepted the invitation of the 'humble mechanics' to chair the meeting, he called upon Londoners to follow the example of the brave and honest reformers of the north whose great peaceable meetings had both perplexed the loyalists and denied the Government any resort to '*Special Commissions*, *Dungeons* and *Hangings*'. 'By great public meetings being peaceably but firmly conducted', Hunt proclaimed, 'the Public Feeling of the whole country may be so concentrated as to cause the consummation of all our wishes.'[50]

The Smithfield meeting added another chapter to Hunt's 'consistency by contrast'. All the big names were invited to attend, much to Hunt's satisfaction. 'It will give those Gentleman an opportunity of coming amongst them, and by so doing stamp their Professions with sincerity', he noted in his reply to Blandford, 'and it will also give the People an opportunity of knowing in whom they may place reliance on the day of trial which in all human probability cannot be far distant'. Hunt alone accepted and chaired the meeting with masterly control, the provocative behaviour of the authorities notwithstanding.[51] The infamous William Franklin posted up inflammatory bills which began: 'May that day of Trial which our intrepid Leader in his answer to our requisition said could not be far distant *be this day*'. John Atkins, the alarmist lord mayor, was convinced that the meeting was part of a plot which involved '*firing this great city and murdering all its peaceable inhabitants*'.[52] Backed up by a considerable display of military power, he sent the city marshals into the midst of the meeting to arrest Joseph Harrison on a Stockport warrant—Harrison had come to London to second the Smithfield resolutions, stopping *en route* to address the Nottingham meeting on 19 July (3,000–20,000).[53] But for Hunt's command of the crowd, Harrison's arrest would certainly have provoked a major riot. When he later saw several people in the crowd trying to 'kick up a Row', he cut the meeting short since any violence 'would damn the cause altogether'.[54] Hunt emerged from the proceedings with much credit. At the Common Hall a few days later, he scored a victory over the Waithmanites when his stridently worded condemnation

[50] Informers' reports, HO, 42/189–90, which includes Blandford to Hunt, 5 July; Hunt's reply, 8 July, HO, 42/194.
[51] This account is based on: *A report of the meeting held in Smithfield* (London, 1819); and the reports of Atkins and others in HO, 42/190.
[52] 'To our Lord and Saviour', *Theological Comet*, 14 Aug.
[53] *SPR*, 31 July.   [54] 'C's' report, 29 July, HO, 42/190.

of Atkins was carried in preference to their '*milk and water*' motion of censure. The Watsonites even hoped that Hunt might be nominated for sheriff.[55]

As a result of the Smithfield meeting, London came to the forefront of radical agitation. The Palace Yard Declaration was readopted and the resolutions were the most advanced yet carried. They included important provisions for improving radical organization in the capital: a system of parish poll-books was introduced to register the names of the non-represented;[56] and various steps were taken to incorporate the growing number of Irish immigrants, a policy strongly endorsed by Hunt. With typical showman's flair, he picked just the right moment to unfurl a specially prepared tricolour, the 'Union Flag of England, Scotland, Ireland'; he silenced hecklers who objected to the inclusion of resolutions for Catholic emancipation; and he gave his name to a widely-circulated 'Address of the People of Great Britain to the People of Ireland', an appeal for 'Political Union in the cause of Universal Civil and Religious Liberty'.[57] The most important and controversial of the Smithfield resolutions was the call for the non-payment of taxes from 1 January 1820, after which time the radicals would not consider themselves 'bound in equity by any future enactments which may be made by any persons styling themselves our representatives, other than those who shall be fully, freely, and fairly chosen by the voices or votes of the largest proportion of the members of the state'. Hunt strongly supported this course since he 'wished to follow the advice of John Hampden, never to pay taxes which were not imposed on the people by a Parliament of their own choosing'. The Smithfield meeting, then, added yet another confrontationalist tactic to the radical platform whilst preserving the peaceable and 'legal' stance of the movement: the tax-refusal resolution did not immediately infringe the law, but it later became an important part of the prosecution case at the Peterloo trial.[58] Watson was delighted with the day's proceedings and publicly expressed his gratitude to Hunt, their worthy chairman, who had cured Cartwright and Cobbett of apostasy and 'never yet flinched from his public duty'.[59] Relations between Hunt and Watson were particularly

---

[55] *The Times*, 27 July. 'BC's' report, 29 July, HO, 42/190.

[56] See T. Davison's pamphlet, *Smithfield Meeting* (London, 1819), explaining the scheme, and his handbill 'Brave and United Britons' in HO, 42/202. Prothero, *Artisans and Politics*, 114–15.

[57] Thistlewood sent 4,000 copies of Hunt's 'Address' to Dublin and Cork; free copies were available from all political booksellers in London, see 'BC', 2 Aug. and Holmes, 3 Aug., HO, 42/191.

[58] 'Attorney and Solicitor General's Opinion on the Proceedings at the Smithfield Meeting', 17 Aug., HO, 42/192.

[59] After the meeting, Hunt wrote a personal letter of thanks to Blandford and the committee, see HO, 42/193.

cordial at this stage and there had been much friendly co-operation between them in recent weeks. Hunt took the chair at the anniversary dinner to celebrate the acquittal of the Spa Fields 'conspirators', and in the lingering dispute over the relief fund for the sufferers under the Suspension Act he was strongly supported by Watson against Cleary and Evans.[60] Watson also arranged a meeting at the Crown and Anchor to open a subscription fund for Hunt who was in some financial difficulty after costly legal actions over the Westminster hustings expenses and his breach of covenant at Cold Henly Farm. Details of the fund to 'defray the Expenses incurred by that valuable Friend of the People, H. Hunt Esq. . . . and to indemnify that Gentleman for the Pecuniary Sacrifices he has made in advocating the great Cause of Freedom' were sent to Harrison in Stockport with instructions from Watson to do all he could to promote the subscription in the north.[61]

After Smithfield, Watson and the London radicals turned their attention to the Manchester meeting which Thistlewood and Preston expected would provide the long-awaited 'signal to begin'. Watson may have lent a more favourable ear to such revolutionary talk, but his main concern was to ensure that the Manchester meeting would build upon the success achieved at Smithfield. After Hunt set off for the north, he kept him informed of events by post and warned him of the traps being laid by the loyalists and the authorities. Most of his time was spent on plans for a 'final meeting' in London on Hunt's return to be held on Kennington Common on 23 August, when it was hoped the vast numbers would be swollen by some 15,000–20,000 immigrant Irish workers.[62]

Hunt, like Watson, wanted the Manchester meeting to be the greatest display of radical strength in the provinces. From the start he had recommended that it should be 'very publick . . . rather a meeting of the County of *Lancashire* etc. than of Manchester alone'. In his intercepted correspondence with Joseph Johnson, brushmaker and secretary of the Patriotic Union Society, he gave detailed instructions of the kind of 'management' required to ensure that the meeting would be the largest ever, attracting people 'from almost all parts within 20 miles round'. Hunt was particularly anxious to retain the initiative in the provinces where Sir Charles Wolseley was making quite a name for himself after his 'election' at Birmingham and platform debut at Stockport. 'We must cherish him', Hunt wrote begrudgingly to Johnson: 'As for his Title, I think nothing of it,

---

[60] *Medusa*, 26 June and 3 July. 'BC's' report, 24 July, HO, 42/190. I have not been able to locate a copy of J. Watson, *Address to the People of England on the falsehoods of the enemies of Mr. Hunt*.

[61] Watson to Harrison, 30 June, HO, 42/190.

[62] See the reports of 'A', 'BC', 'C', and W—r (George Edwards) in HO, 42/190–1, and the examination of 'B' in HO, 44/5 ff. 7–16. Watson to Hunt, 13 Aug., HO, 42/192. Prothero, *Artisans and Politics*, 115–16.

yet it must go a great way with the Multitude, and it must be a cursed Eye-sore for our Aristocratical Opponents.' Johnson duly assured Hunt that his long identification with the cause far outweighed Wolseley's title, adding that the Smithfield meeting 'has gained you great Applause. The Lancashire Reformers likewise begin to think the Londoners are in earnest.' 'We have nothing to do but concentrate public opinion', Hunt replied as he prepared to leave for the north, 'and if our Enemies will not listen to the voice of a whole People, they will listen to nothing, and may the effects of their Folly and Wickedness be upon their own Heads.'[63]

Hunt went to Manchester in the hopes of mounting a great display of irresistible numerical force, much in line with what he had been advocating ever since he first spoke on the mass platform at Spa Fields. He was not deterred by the attacks on unpopular police officers, the pike-manufactur-ing, and the famous drilling on the moors which came into prominence in Lancashire radicalism at this time, much to the concern of some of the small tradesmen in the Manchester Patriotic Union Society: the anxious Joseph Johnson, it seems, contemplated withdrawing altogether when the magistrates banned the 9 August meeting.[64] Well-versed in the law, Hunt challenged every move of the authorities and redoubled his efforts to bring the radicals into line for a great 'constitutional' display of strength. To counter the Royal Proclamation condemning seditious meetings and unauthorized drilling, he issued his own 'Proclamation' in which he defiantly asserted the legal and constitutional right of public meeting, and lampooned the Manchester magistrates who had ordered the people to 'abstain at their peril' from the banned meeting! In a series of strident addresses he called the Lancashire radicals to order for a rearranged meeting on 16 August. He insisted that they cease 'playing at soldiers', and issued instructions that they must come to the meeting '*armed* with *no other weapon* but that of a self-approving conscience; determined not to suffer yourselves to be irritated or excited, by any means whatsoever, to commit any breach of the public peace'. Having heard a rumour that the magistrates had issued a warrant against him, he offered himself up to the authorities on the Saturday before the meeting, in order to leave them no pretext for breaking up the proceedings.[65] Hunt's efforts to ensure that the radicals would gather peaceably on St Peter's Field on 16 August (30,000–200,000) were truly remarkable and extremely successful.

[63] Between 3 July and 3 Aug. 4 letters from Hunt to Johnson and 6 letters from Johnson to Hunt were intercepted, see HO, 42/189–91.

[64] Depositions of J. Johnson, 19 and 20 Aug., and his letter to Sidmouth, enclosed in Norris, 21 Aug., HO, 42/192. For details of the drilling etc. see TS, 11/1056, Bamford, 130–50, and Read, 113–26.

[65] For a comprehensive collection of Hunt's addresses and radical, loyalist, and official publications, see *Impartial Narrative of the Late Melancholy Occurrences in Manchester* (Liverpool, 1819), 8–31. Hunt, *Memoirs*, iii, 608–9.

The bloody details of the Peterloo massacre have been endlessly rehearsed.[66] At least eleven people were killed and many hundreds injured when the inept magistrates sent in the Manchester and Salford Yeomanry, flailing their recently sharpened sabres, to arrest Hunt and the other leaders on the platform, and then ordered in the 15th Hussars to disperse the peaceable crowd. The concentration on local detail and context, such a feature of work on Peterloo, has tended to obscure the strength of the radical challenge which faced the authorities throughout the industrial districts. In the summer of 1819 the authorities were outmanœuvred by the radicals: they were confronted by a massive mobilization of the working class. As Edward Thompson has argued, a physical encounter was inevitable in these circumstances.[67] That it occurred at Manchester, where class polarization (and hatred) was particularly pronounced, and the inebriated publicans, butchers and shopkeepers of the local yeomanry were apparently such bad horsemen, explains only why it was so bloody.

The vigour of the radical challenge in 1819 stemmed from its rapport with popular political attitudes. In terms of intellectual history, the popular constitutionalism of nineteenth-century working-class radicalism poses something of a problem. Historians are agreed that radicalism could not and did not attract a popular audience until the traditional constitutional language of eighteenth-century political debate had been cast aside. This was the achievement of Tom Paine and the 1790s. Reform was opened up to 'members unlimited' as the appeal to history and constitutional liberties was overborne by the vocabulary of reason and natural rights, and the prospect of a republican constituent convention.[68] Nineteenth-century radicalism, however, was permeated by popular constitutionalism, not by Paine's counter-hegemonic republican ideology. This was not the retraction that it seems, and the most ardent Paineites soon recognized the advantages and utility of a constitutional guise.[69] The mobilization of 1819 was self-righteously constitutional. At the mass meetings the radicals declared that they were 'perfectly satisfied that our Constitution, in its original purity, as it was bequeathed to us by our brave ancestors, is fully adequate to all the purposes of good government; we are therefore determined not to be satisfied with anything short of that Constitution, the whole of our Constitution, and nothing but our Constitution.'[70] Orators like William Greathead Lewis, the Coventry journalist, justified the radical programme as 'the re-establishment of that glorious constitution be-

---

[66] Read remains the best study, despite the number of monographs published to mark the 150th anniversary, including Walmsley's unconvincing exercise in revisionism.

[67] Thompson, *Making*, 751.

[68] Ibid., chs. 1 and 5. H. T. Dickinson, *Liberty and Property: political ideology in eighteenth-century Britain* (London, 1977), chs. 6 and 7.

[69] Belchem, 'Republicanism', 1–3.   [70] Leeds resolution, 19 July, *BD*, 28 July.

queathed to us by the immortal Alfred', and Major Cartwright trusted to settle the issue by actually producing the Constitution in its pristine Saxon form.[71] For the most part, however, radical argument was less concerned with Saxon precedent than with the corpus of laws secured during the struggles against absolutism: not just the sacred Whig canon of Magna Carta, Habeas Corpus, the Bill of Rights and the Act of Settlement, but also innumerable obscure statutes which suggested that annual parliaments, free elections, and no taxation without representation, were once the law of the land. Many radicals delighted in a pedantic display of their encyclopaedic knowledge of the 'law-writers' constitution'; others simply assumed that 'Annual Parliaments and Universal Suffrage constitute essential parts of our Constitution, and are our rightful inheritance'.[72]

As a means of establishing the intellectual rectitude of the radical programme, popular constitutionalism appears somewhat jejune. But it was their tactics rather than their programme that the radicals sought to justify. By legitimizing their protest activity in terms of popular constitutionalism, the radicals were able to galvanize populist anti-absolutism into radical commitment; demystify and discredit the political establishment; and desanctify the apostate Whigs, the people's putative 'natural leaders'. As the great mobilization of 1819 demonstrated, popular constitutionalism placed the initiative with the radicals to the embarrassment of the Government and the annoyance of the Whigs. The radicals appeared in heroic guise as the true loyalists, upholding the Constitution which had been 'won by the valour and cemented with the blood of our ancestors'.[75] Radical poetasters struck the popular chord:

> Shall Englishmen o'ercome each foe,
> and now at home those rights forgo,
> Enjoy'd by none beside?
> Degenerate race! ah! then in vain,
> Your birthrights sacred to maintain
> HAMPDEN and SYDNEY died![74]

The corruption and arbitrary power of the Government, and the apostasy and factionalism of those 'mischievous perfidious and pretended Reformists, the milk-and-water gentlemen, the Whigs', stood exposed and

---

[71] Lewis's speech, Stockport, 28 June, *MO,* 3 July. Cartwright, *Bill of Rights and Liberties,* and 'English Constitution produced and illustrated', serialized in *BD,* from 7 May 1823. See also, C. Hill, 'The Norman Yoke' in J. Saville (ed.), *Democracy and the Labour Movement* (London, 1954).

[72] 'The British Constitution, 1819', print enclosed in Fletcher, 27 Feb., HO, 42/184. *SPR,* 10 May 1817. Leeds, 19 July, *BD,* 28 July.

[73] *Declaration, Rules, and Resolutions of the Birmingham Union Society established for the Restoration of Human Happiness* (Birmingham, 1819).

[74] 'Ode', *MO,* 9 Jan.

condemned by the radicals' guardianship of 'the cause for which HAMPDEN fell in the field and SYDNEY died on the scaffold'.[75] The intimation of impending violence, reinforced by the evocation of the deeds of the glorious ancestors, was an essential—and exciting—part of the popular appeal of the mass platform as the radicals worked through the repertoire of forcible intimidation. At the same time, the radicals were able to present a peaceable public image by proscribing any violent act until all constitutional channels had been explored. By constitutionalism, open associations, and orderly mass meetings, the radicals managed to appease 'public opinion', thereby blunting the Government's legal and repressive powers: the radicals skilfully developed a form of extra-parliamentary behaviour which the authorities had no real rights to infringe. Through popular constitutionalism, indeed, the radicals were able to outmanœuvre the Government, by portraying themselves as, and proving themselves to be, the true upholders of what remained the chosen legitimizing ideology of the ruling class: constitutional freedom and the rule of law. The ruling class were the prisoners of their own rhetoric. History, birthrights, the rule of law, and constitutionalism in general, provided the radicals with a court of appeal that was held in popular reverence and which the political establishment, Tory and Whig alike, could not ignore save by shedding too much of its legitimizing ideology and unmasking its class rule.[76] When the northern workers and their families assembled in their tens of thousands in the greatest good order on St Peter's Field for a legally convened meeting for reform, Hunt and the radicals had succeeded in imposing their interpretation of the dominant value-system.

The authorities were quite confounded by the nature of the radical challenge. After the meeting at Halifax on 2 August (6,000–15,000), Horton, the local magistrate, wrote to Whitehall that he did not consider the 'peaceable Conduct observed by these Meetings is so very favourable a circumstance'. The Home Office agreed, noting that it was 'not the mode in which the English character usually exhibits Discontent'.[77] Despite repeated pleas from magistrates in the north, Sidmouth refused to introduce special legislation to counter what he described as the 'unprecedented Artifice with which the Demagogues of the present day contrive without transgressing the Law, to produce on the Public Mind the same effect which used only to be created by means unquestionably unlawful'.[78] Convinced that Whitehall was being unduly circumspect in dealing with the

---

[75] Nottingham resolutions, 19 July, *BD*, 28 July. *Medusa*, 24 July.

[76] Belchem, 'Republicanism', 6–12. E. P. Thompson, *Whigs and Hunters* (London, Peregrine edn., 1977), 258–69.

[77] Horton, 3 Aug., HO, 42/191. Hobhouse to Horton, 13 Aug., HO, 41/4 f. 468.

[78] See the letters to Norris, 11 June, Chippendale, 2 July, Lloyd, 5 July, and Hay, 14 July, in HO, 79/3; and Hobhouse to Norris, 2 Sept., HO, 41/5.

radical challenge, the Manchester magistrates decided to take matters into their own hands and 'bring the matter to issue'. 'If the agitators of the country determine to persevere in their meeting', Norris announced, 'it will necessarily prove a trial of strength and there must be a conflict.'[79] On 16 August, the magistrates gained their bloody victory. The Government in no way encouraged the Manchester magistrates to act as they did, but they could have taken steps to restrain them.[80] After the massacre, they defended the magistrates to the hilt, although they made sure that there would be no repetition or emulation of their actions. The 16 August, the Home Office explained to magistrates throughout the land was a special case: the extensive drilling made it especially intimidating; there were depositions from respectable inhabitants attesting to the state of terror that gripped the town; and the presence of Hunt, fresh from Smithfield, pointed to a conspiracy of national ramification. The very evidence which was to ensure Hunt's conviction, also served to prevent any repetition of the events of 16 August.[81]

The Peterloo massacre must be set in the context of the radicals' success in outmanœuvring the authorities, and the consequent tension which developed between circumspect central government and harassed magistrates in the north. To understand why the publicans and shopkeepers of the Manchester and Salford Yeomanry displayed such ill-concealed hatred on the day, it is necessary to appreciate another aspect of the radical campaign of 1819: its working-class character. Radical demands were still phrased in the language of 'the people', but the movement was concerned above all with the interests of the manual workers. The radicals still depicted society in terms of a fundamental division between the industrious and the idle, the tax-payers and the tax-gorgers, but amongst the industrious, primacy was accorded to the contribution of the artisan, the mechanic and the labourer, from whom all riches sprang. 'Our Merchants, Tradesmen, and Master Manufacturers are serviceable in circulating the riches which your labours produce', Joseph Brayshaw explained to the labouring classes from the platform at his native Yeadon on 28 June (2,000): 'were it not for the product of your labour, they must be reduced to poverty'. Brayshaw, a Freethinking Christian and radical missionary in the north-east, was an articulate exponent of underconsumptionism, the radical analysis of the economic distress caused by 'Old Corruption' and suffered most severely by the poor labourers, who lost ten shillings in every eighteen through excessive taxation:

All riches spring from labour . . . Now the taxes are laid upon your food, and your

[79] Norris's letters, 14–31 July, HO, 42/188–9.
[80] Hobhouse to Byng, 3–5 Aug., HO, 79/3; and to Norris, 3 and 4 Aug., HO, 42/191.
[81] See the letters to magistrates in HO, 41/5.

clothing, and upon every product of your labour . . . Whenever the taxes press upon any species of manufacture, so as to diminish its consumption, they destroy the market for your labour, and you are deprived of work and of bread. Such is the case at the present time; the load of taxes upon goods of British manufacture has nearly destroyed our Foreign commerce; distress has reduced our Home consumption to almost nothing; by this means you are thrown out of employment, which means nothing less than that you are deprived of bread.[82]

John Knight gave a sharp working-class edge to the traditional denunciation of 'Old Corruption':

Governments are not the *producers* of property, that is done by the labourers, and by the labourers alone: government is only the *manager* and *distributor* thereof— and when it gives more to any individual, than a *manual labourer* CAN *produce*, does it not, by every such act, commit a robbery upon Society?[83]

But it was not just the profligacy and excessive tax-burden of 'Old Corruption' that hit the manual labourers disproportionately hard: they had to endure a number of oppressive laws designed for the economic advantage of those who possessed political power. Property, Joseph Johnson explained to the Ashton meeting on 14 June, 'has usurped the power of legislation; and until the class of labourers have gained a decided preponderance in the House of Commons . . . they have no security whatever for any thing'.[84] At the mass meetings, resolutions were passed condemning the Combination Laws which 'send the industrious labourer to prison for years, for endeavouring to enjoy as much of the fruits of his labour as was necessary for his existence'.[85] The appeal to the nation adopted at Leeds on 19 July spoke strongly against the 'late factory-law, which, under the semblance of kindness towards those who are too young and too tender to be employed therein, legalize a system of oppression destructive to health, and, as we believe, of morals also'.[86] Much was said at the great Blackburn meeting on 5 July about how machinery had become a curse instead of a blessing 'through the perversion of the powers of Government'.[87]

Without undergoing any major revision, the traditional radical analysis was becoming more relevant to the interests and needs of the working class. This is not to suggest that radicalism became class exclusive. When a loyalist armed association was formed in Manchester, the local radicals

[82] J. Brayshaw, *Proceedings of the meeting held at Yeadon . . . To which is added, Advice to the Labouring Classes* (Dewsbury, 1819). For Brayshaw, see Belchem, 'Republicanism', 17–19.
[83] J. Knight, 'Read, Mark, Learn! An Analysis of the Red Book', broadsheet in HO, 42/191.
[84] *BD*, 23 June.
[85] See, for example, the Ashton resolutions in *BD*, 23 June.
[86] *SPR*, 31 July and *BD*, 28 July.   [87] *MO*, 10 July.

implored the middle class not to enrol in its ranks but to join the campaign for reform:

Oh! ye sinking Manufacturers and Shopkeepers, is it the starving Labourers who have ruined you; or is it DEAR Pensions and HIGH rents and Taxes? To enrich the Hive would you destroy the working Bees, or the Drones? Take part then with the People, in their constitutional endeavours to remove the extravagant and avaricious *Placemen, Pensioners, Sinecurists* and *Aristocratic Borough-mongers*— and then, and not till then, will *plenty* and *prosperity* return to you.[88]

It was precisely because the middle class were not automatically excluded from their proceedings that the working-class radicals soon began to acquire a sense of class pride as they realized they were perforce on their own. The mass meetings, indeed, became great working-class carnivals. The meeting at Blackburn on 5 July is a good example of this. Weavers' meetings at Glasgow, Manchester, Paisley and Carlisle had all been won over from emigration to radicalism,[89] but the Blackburn mass meeting was the first radical gathering in a weaving community and it attracted vast crowds. It was the first meeting too at which the new female reform societies took a prominent part: the women arrived in a great procession to present Knight, the chairman, with a 'most beautiful Cap of Liberty, made of scarlet silk or satin, lined with green, with a serpentine gold lace, terminating with a rich gold tassel'. The bands, processions, iconography and community involvement came to typify the appeal of radicalism to the working class.[90] By 16 August 1819, constitutional radicalism under the leadership of a 'people's champion' had acquired a definite working-class tone and perspective. This is the essential context in which the Peterloo massacre must be placed.

3. PETERLOO, THE COURTS, AND PUBLIC OPINION

The Peterloo massacre inflamed radical spirits, aroused middle-class public opinion, and unnerved the Government. The radicals, however, failed to advance beyond this vantage ground. After Peterloo it was the weaknesses

[88] John Rylands Library, English MS 1197: Peterloo material collected by the Revd Hay, f. 14, posting-bill 'To the Inhabitants of Manchester'.
[89] Norris, 21 June, HO, 42/188. *MO*, 26 June. *BD*, 14 July. J. C. F. Barnes, 'The trade union and radical activities of the Carlisle handloom weavers', *Transactions of the Cumberland and Westmorland Antiquarian and Archaeological Society*, new series, lxxviii (1978), 156–7.
[90] *MO*, 10 July. Norris, 4, 6 and 10 July, and Fletcher, 15 July, HO, 42/189. The rules of the Blackburn Female Union served as a model for other female reform societies, as did 'Declaration and Rules of the Female Union Society of Stockport', see *True Briton*, 21 July. See Bamford, 146–50, on community preparation for the 16 Aug. meeting.

and not the strengths of popular constitutionalism that were revealed. The unconstitutional outrage of Peterloo, it was believed, would stir the nation where petitions and remonstrances had failed. Thus, there was tremendous support for Hunt's policy of resting the case for radicalism on Peterloo itself, using the courts of law as a national platform to broadcast the radical programme as the Manchester murderers were brought to condign justice. But popular and hard-fought as it was, this campaign for legal redress served the radical movement ill. By concentrating on the courts and vacating the mass platform, the radicals unwisely transferred confrontation to the authorities' own ground. Furthermore, by relying on the force of public opinion, the radicals found it difficult to preserve their independence and integrity: the impact of the massacre was exploited by the Whigs, the moderate reformers, and various other opposition groups at the expense of any consideration of the radical programme.

In line with the spleenful criticisms of radical renegades like Bamford and Johnson, Hunt has been stigmatized as a self-centred, cowardly demagogue who turned timid and ingratiating after Peterloo in the face of legal proceedings.[91] The truth of the matter is rather different. Before his own trial took place, Hunt explored every legal arena to bring the Manchester authorities to justice, clashing head on in the process with the judiciary and legal establishment. His hard-fought campaign for legal redress began during his eleven-day solitary confinement in the New Bailey where he was taken after his arrest on St Peter's Field when he had displayed dignity, rectitude and restraint, despite being badly manhandled by the authorities, his famous white hat proving insufficient protection against the flailing sabres and staves. While Hunt prepared for all-out battle in the courts, the treacherous Johnson repudiated any links with 'the lower classes of Reformers' and tried to make a deal with the Manchester magistrates by offering them his private correspondence with Hunt![92]

From the New Bailey, Hunt wrote to Sidmouth demanding his immediate release and protesting at the 'illegal conduct of the military towards an unarmed and peaceable people, met for the purpose of exeı ising what they thought they had a perfect right to do'.[93] He sought the professional advice of lawyers in Manchester and London regarding errors in the magistrates' warrant: he wrote to a friend that he was 'panting

[91] Bamford, 179–272. J. Johnson, *Letter to Henry Hunt, Esq.* (Manchester, 1822). Thompson, *Making*, 764.

[92] Norris, 21 Aug., and Byng, 21–23 Aug., HO, 42/192. 'King Harry the Ninth's White Hat' became the symbol of radicalism, apostrophized in ballad and verse, see for example, *The White Hat* (Newcastle-upon-Tyne, 1819). A month after Peterloo, a special meeting of the Anglican Sunday School Committee in Manchester passed regulations 'to prevent any of the Children from coming with White Hats or other Badges which are now used by the disloyal and disaffected as expression of their political sentiments', see Read, 201.

[93] *MO*, 28 Aug.

to be at them in a *Court of Justice* before an *honest Jury*'.[94] He addressed a number of public letters to radicals in London, which set the record straight about the peaceable background to the meeting, and he tried to secure his release to give evidence at the first inquests on the Peterloo victims.[95] At his final examination on 27 August, when he was informed that the charge had been reduced from high treason to seditious conspiracy, he harried the magistrates at every turn, their various infractions of correct legal procedure being recorded by his solicitor, Charles Pearson, the city radical.[96] Fearing the effects of Hunt's release—Norris believed that Manchester would be in 'open rebellion in 24 hours'—the magistrates hurried him off to Lancaster Castle under heavy military guard before bail could be provided.[97] Vast crowds, the largest that Nadin, the infamous deputy constable, had ever seen, lined the route all the way to Lancaster—'It appeared as though the entire population had come forth to greet and cheer Hunt and his party . . . The whole way is a continued scene of populous Townships and villages and they were all equally enthusiastic in their Shouts.'[98] Bail was arranged soon after Hunt arrived—Thomas Chapman and Sir Charles Wolseley provided the sureties—and preparations were made for a triumphal return to Manchester. After an overnight stop at Bolton, Hunt was led into Manchester by a great procession headed by over a thousand Bolton colliers, crofters and weavers. Hunt, Norris reported, was 'in possession of this part of the country'.[99]

There was another display of overwhelming popular support a couple of days later when Hunt set off along the now hallowed route to Lancaster to attend the opening of the assizes, where the legal battle began in earnest. On arrival, he objected to the composition of the grand jury and remonstrated with its foreman, Lord Stanley, about the prejudicial order in which the bills were presented: the bill for seditious conspiracy was to be taken before the bills against the yeomanry for cutting and maiming which had been sent in first. After these unavailing protests, he concentrated his efforts on three bills which indicted the magistrates' leading witnesses for perjury, but these were dismissed by the grand jury along with the bills

---

[94] Manchester Central Library, Archives Dept., Hunt to F. R. Atkinson, 17 Aug., and Atkinson to Hunt, 19 Aug. Letter to Pearson, 20 Aug., *MO*, 28 Aug.; and 'To a friend in London', 26 Aug., *MO*, 4 Sept.

[95] *MO*, 28 Aug.–11 Sept. University of Chicago: MS 563, Hunt Correspondence and Papers, item 18, Hunt to Manchester Magistrates, 18 Aug; see also, item 19, Hunt's letter, 26 Aug., demanding that the magistrates allow his friend West to visit him.

[96] Several pamphlet versions were published, and the proceedings were reported in full in the new journal, *Peter-Loo Massacre*.

[97] Norris, 24 and 25 Aug., HO, 42/193. *Letter from Mr. Hunt to Mr. West* (London, 1819).

[98] Norris, 29 Aug., HO, 42/193.

[99] *MO*, 4 Sept. Hunt's letters in *MO*, 11 Sept., and Norris, 28–30 Aug., HO, 42/193.

against the yeomanry, although a true bill was found against the '*Notorious* Mr. Owen', whose name headed the list of those who had deposed as to their alarm on 16 August.[100] Despite these set-backs, Hunt was fêted by huge crowds when he left Lancaster, having traversed in his own case. He was drawn into Preston, where the occasion was somewhat marred by the death of his favourite horse Bob, and thence right through Blackburn to Bolton, where he again rested overnight. On the morrow some 40,000 to 80,000 people, many wearing green ribbons and white hats with printed labels 'Hunt and Liberty', lined the streets of Manchester to welcome back their champion, who for once was too exhausted to make a lengthy speech. The next day he left for London, after having issued a farewell address 'To the Brave Reformers of Lancashire', pledging himself 'not to taste *one drop* of taxed BEER, SPIRITS, WINE or TEA, till we have brought some of these m—s to justice.'[101]

Back in London, all Hunt's time was given over to preparing a motion to obtain a criminal information against the Manchester magistrates, and he had to decline invitations to address meetings at Bristol, Birmingham, Leeds and elsewhere.[102] At the beginning of the legal term, he tendered several affidavits to the Court of King's Bench but they were rejected on the grounds that only law officers of the crown or gentlemen of the bar could act as the prosecution in such matters. 'No man in future shall obtain criminal justice against an offender', Hunt protested to the judges, 'unless he is able and consents to *buy* it of some hireling belonging to the Courts of Law.'[103] He insisted that at the very least he had the right to address a jury, but he was defeated on this very point again a few days later when he tried to bring in an action against 'Dr. Slop' of the *New Times*.[104] His next move was to request the Attorney-General to bring in the action against the Manchester magistrates; when this was refused, Hunt returned to the Court of King's Bench, seeking an order to compel the Attorney-General, only to be informed that the court possessed no such authority. The next day he was rebuffed yet again when he was refused permission to present the perjury and maiming bills, dismissed at Lancaster, to the assembled Middlesex grand jury, which he claimed had 'co-extensive jurisdiction' with the Court of King's Bench.[105] Finally, he addressed a lengthy,

---

[100] Reports and Hunt's letters in *MO*, 11 Sept. *Letter from Mr. Hunt to Mr. Giles* (London, 1819). Lancashire Record Office: Hunt Correspondence DDX/113, Hunt to Bryant, 7 Sept. Hunt, *Memoirs*, iii, 636–7. Pearson's letter, *BD*, 8 Sept.

[101] *MO*, 11 Sept. *Peter-Loo Massacre*, no. 5. Norris, 9 and 11 Sept., and Nadin, 11 Sept., HO, 42/194.

[102] Hunt to T. Williams, Bristol, 14 Sept., *New Times*, 17 Sept.

[103] *MO*, 13 Nov. Hunt's letter to Sir John Bayley, *Medusa*, 20 Nov.

[104] *MO*, 23 Oct. University of Chicago: MS 563, Hunt Correspondence and Papers, item 20, Hunt to Stoddart, 16 Oct.

[105] *MO*, 20 Nov.

powerfully-worded petition to the Commons, accusing the legal establishment of having acted 'in direct violation of Magna Charta and the Bill of Rights', and asking to be heard at the bar of the House as the only means of securing justice and redress.[106]

Hunt's bravado in the courts delighted the radicals who worshipped him as the 'Undaunted advocate of Freedom's laws!':

> The daring Champion of unrivall'd fame
> The Patriot Hunt (immortal be his name!)
> Has sworn to advocate the suff'rers cause
> And to bring to light the spurners of the laws.[107]

His skirmishes with the judiciary were a cheap and effective means of attracting publicity at a time when more formal legal proceedings like the Lees inquest were proving very expensive and drained money away from the funds collected for the bereaved and injured—when the inquest finally seemed certain to return a verdict of wilful murder, the proceedings were adjourned and subsequently declared null and void![108] After the failure of the various attempts to bring the Manchester authorities to justice, Hunt hoped to make his own trial the decisive inquest, as it were, into the bloody events of 16 August. To ensure a fair trial, he persuaded the Court of King's Bench to transfer the proceedings from Lancashire to the spring assizes at York.[109] His next task was to raise sufficient funds to cover the costs. He had been on bad terms with the Metropolitan and Central Committee for managing the subscription to bring the perpetrators of the Manchester atrocities to justice, ever since the management of the fund had passed from Wooler and Cartwright to the metropolitan reform establishment, the 'worthies who composed the Westminster, the Borough, and the City of London Rump Committees'. In November, when he was voted 100 guineas to assist with his costs, he refused to accept 'the proferred boon . . . from the hands of a self-elected junto, the majority of which are the offscourings of the Old Westminster Rump'. As the reformers prepared for the general election which would follow the King's final demise, Hunt protested at the way the fund was 'polluted by the festering hand of faction, and perverted from its proper cause by the most pitiful intrigues to promote election patronage and bribery'.[110] So, as his

---

[106] *PD*, 1st series, xli, 370–7.

[107] J. F. 'To Henry Hunt, Esq.', *MO*, 25 Sept.

[108] Read, 147–9. Hunt was very critical of Harmer, the solicitor sent by the Metropolitan and Central Committee appointed for the relief of the Manchester sufferers, *Memoirs*, iii, 635–9.

[109] *MO*, 12 and 19 Feb. 1820.

[110] Hunt to Sir Richard Phillips, 16 Nov. in *Political Tracts 1819–20*, a volume of pamphlets and newspaper cuttings in the British Library. Hunt's letter to the subscribers in *Examiner*, 10 Jan. 1820. Hunt, *Memoirs*, iii, 633–5.

trial approached, he promoted a fund of his own, a special subscription to allow the defence to produce an unending stream of witnesses: he spoke in terms of one out of every hundred who had attended Peterloo!

The fruits of the taxes of the poor are being lavished in boundless profusion to obtain our conviction—we want but little for our defence. We want only the means of taking our witnesses to the trial. I want no counsel—I know the cobwebs of the law, and conscious of our innocence, fear not to be taken in their trammels . . . The day is arriving when we shall see whether Corruption has left any virtue in our Courts of Justice, or whether our Constitutional rights were buried in the Tomb of Peterloo.[111]

He proposed that any surplus in the fund should be used to defray his campaign costs at Preston where he stood in the general election of 1820, thereby allowing the electors in this popular constituency the opportunity of 'elevating the intended victim of a foul conspiracy, into that situation where he will never cease his endeavours to obtain justice for an injured and greatly insulted people'. Hunt stood at Preston pledged to secure an immediate parliamentary inquiry into Peterloo together with the implementation of the full radical programme, the only policy which would 'stem the torrent of cruel, partial taxation, which has, in the ramification of its overwhelming power, reduced the farmer and the tradesman to the verge of *pauperism*, and the mechanic, the manufacturer and the labourer, to a state bordering on *starvation*'. His plans to contest the seat in the true radical fashion were cut short, however, when he was called to his trial at York soon after the election began: even so, he polled tolerably well against the old alliance and gained well over a thousand votes.[112]

On arrival at York, Hunt took complete charge of the defence proceedings, much to the subsequent dissatisfaction of Bamford and Johnson. But he was denied the opportunity of bringing the butchers of Peterloo to justice. The court refused to entertain any discussion of the behaviour of the magistrates, yeomanry, constables, or military. The charge was tried 'in the same manner as if no magistrate, no constable, no yeoman, had appeared on the field during the day': the point at issue was 'the original formation of the meeting and the object of those who assembled it'. Hunt was bitterly disappointed: even so, his performance was most impressive, as George Maule, the treasury-solicitor, was the first to admit in his reports to the Home Office, noting that the judge 'seems to have formed a decisive opinion in favour of the Orator'. The judge's charge to the jury pointed towards an acquittal, although Bayley clearly

---

[111] 'To the Brave and Much-Injured Reformers', *MO*, 19 Feb. 1820; and 'To the Persons, Male and Female, who attended the Meeting at Manchester', posting-bill in HO, 40/11 f. 173.

[112] For Hunt's addresses and a full report, see *Collection of Addresses, Squibs, Songs, etc. published during the late Contested Election* (Preston, 1820). The figures were: Horrocks 1,902, Hornby 1,649, Williams 1,525, and Hunt 1,127.

considered that the Smithfield tax-refusal resolutions told heavily against Hunt. In the end, Hunt, Johnson, Knight, Healey and Bamford were convicted on the fourth count of unlawful and seditious assembling for the purpose of exciting discontent.[113] Hunt moved unsuccessfully for a new trial, and in May was sentenced to two and a half year's imprisonment at Ilchester gaol.[114]

Hunt's unremitting efforts to bring the Manchester authorities to justice were completely ineffective. The campaign for legal redress stood no chance of success since the Government had decided to make unquestioning support for the Manchester magistrates the very test of political loyalty and responsibility: hence the unseemly haste with which the magistrates were publicly congratulated in the name of the Regent, and the blunt refusal of any inquiry into the affair.[115] Furthermore, the Government took the opportunity to strengthen its legal powers, by reversing its attitude towards special legislation. 'Parliament and the Country', Sidmouth now opined, 'must make the option between Laws suited to the Danger, a Military Government, or Anarchy'.[116] At the end of November, Parliament was specially convened to pass the infamous Six Acts, an attempt to return to the narrow political participation of the eighteenth century. Attention has generally focused on the laws and taxes curbing the freedom of the press, but the cornerstone of the Six Acts was the new Seditious Meetings Prevention Bill, a far more restrictive measure than the Acts of 1795 and 1817. There were new clauses prohibiting the carrying of banners and flags, and a powerful new provision restricting attendance to those actually resident in the parish where the meeting was held. 'It gets rid of the great evil of itinerant orators, and of all artificial means of excitement', Liverpool explained to Grenville, 'parochial meetings would generally be flat, and in most cases the gentlemen who live in the parish would have influence enough to check those with whom they are so intimately connected.'[117] The Six Acts brought an end to the great radical mobilization of the post-war years. Reinforced by its new repressive powers the Government was able to launch upon the most sustained campaign of prosecution in the courts in British history. By the summer of 1820 all the leading radical orators, organizers, journalists, publishers, and

[113] Several accounts of the trial were published, of which the most popular was Dolby's edition, *The Trial of Henry Hunt, Esq . . . for an alleged conspiracy to overturn the government* (London, 1820). Bamford, 240–68. Johnson, *Letter*. Maule, 21–4 Mar. 1820, HO, 40/11.

[114] *BD*, 10 and 17 May 1820. *MO*, 20 May 1820. *Reports of State Trials*, new series, i (1820–23) (London, 1888), 489–94.

[115] Thompson, *Making*, 750–1.

[116] Sidmouth to Hulton, 2 Sept., HO, 41/5.

[117] Liverpool to Grenville, 14 Nov., quoted in C. D. Yonge, *The Life and Administration of Robert Banks, Second Earl of Liverpool* (3 vols., London, 1868), ii, 430–4.

distributors were confined in prison.[118] After Peterloo, the 'legal' victory was gained by the Government, not by the aggrieved radicals.

The radicals were unable to compensate for their legal defeat in the courts by securing an 'ideological' victory in the country. In terms of public opinion, Peterloo benefited the established opposition, not the radicals. Out-groups, moderate reformers, and popular Whigs were quick to capitalize on the impact of the massacre. 'Who would have speculated on the Manchester affair or on its approval', George Ensor, the Benthamite intellectual, wrote to Place, 'the profit of these two capital blunders is incalculable . . . they were victories gained to us by the enemy over themselves.'[119] But while the Government and the authorities were roundly condemned, Hunt and the working-class radicals received little praise. The old opposition groups in the corporate towns and cities of the unreformed system trusted to benefit from the outrage by restricting discussion at their protest meetings to the need for an inquiry without any mention of radicalism or reform.[120] In popular London it proved more difficult to treat Peterloo in such convenient isolation. The Westminster reformers agonized over the problem of how to exploit the massacre without giving some credit to Hunt, 'a man who had vilified and abused them so outrageously'.[121] Burdett avoided an reference to Hunt in his famous letter condemning the massacre and the 'bloody Neroes', for which he was later prosecuted.[122] Byron wrote to his friend Hobhouse to advise the Westminster reformers against any reconciliation with the likes of Hunt:

If the Manchester yeomanry had cut down *Hunt only*, they would have done their duty . . . our classical education alone should teach us to trample on such unredeemed dirt . . . if to praise such fellows be the price of popularity, I spit upon it as I would in their faces.[123]

After his return from the north, Hunt proved a considerable embarrassment to the metropolitan reformers who were keen to exploit the Peterloo issue. In Southwark, he was not allowed to address a meeting of the electors until Sir Robert Wilson and the other dignitaries had left the platform and the high bailiff had officially dissolved the gathering. The crowd remained to cheer Hunt who caused a sensation when he removed his famous white hat and 'like Mark Antony, exhibiting the mantle of Caesar, pointed out the impressions left by the sabre strokes which he had

[118] Jephson, i, 503–28. Thompson, *Making*, 768.
[119] BL Add. MSS 35153 (Place papers), f. 113, G. Ensor to Place, 19 Nov.
[120] See, for example, the reports of the meetings in Norwich, York, Liverpool, and Lewes in *MO*, 25 Sept.–9 Oct., and HO, 42/195.
[121] BL Add. MSS 27837 (Place papers), f. 186, Hobhouse to Place, 27 Aug.
[122] *BD*, 25 Aug. Patterson, ii, 490–504.
[123] Byron to Hobhouse, 22 Apr. 1820, quoted in Murray, ii, 143–4.

received at Manchester'.[124] In the city there was pandemonium when he arrived at the Common Hall to support the Waithmanites in their demand for an inquiry into Peterloo, while Atkins tried to restrict the business of the day to the election of his successor. Atkins's cronies tried to shout Hunt down whilst the reformers cheered him on. The master of just such occasions, Hunt pulled a nightcap from his pocket with a great flourish, dramatic evidence of his determination to wait all night if necessary to gain a hearing. Atkins and the Court of Aldermen subsequently commenced legal proceedings against Hunt, Waithman, Parkins, Thompson, Bunstead and others for tumultuous rioting at the Common Hall, accusing them of conspiring to obstruct the election of the city's chief magistrate.[125] Any suggestion of unity between Hunt and the Waithmanites was soon dispelled when the Common Hall met again to censure Atkins and defend their right to discuss public issues. Hunt spoke in angry terms, provoked by some person telling him to 'hold his tongue, as he would certainly otherwise spoil all'. He refused to be silent as Waithman had 'taken certain objections to what he chose to call great tumultuous meetings in the open air, just as if it were right for the Livery to assemble when they thought proper, and that it were not right for any persons else to follow their example. (*Question, question from many parts of the Hall*.)' In the ensuing uproar it proved impossible for anyone to gain a hearing: the meeting ended in total disorder.[126]

Despite strong lobbying by the popular Whigs, the Whig party leaders were reluctant to stand forward over Peterloo, dreading some intervention by Hunt and the radicals. 'If matters are left to themselves', Brougham tried to convince Grey, 'we shall have a green bag, which is worse than Hunt. And really the tendency of things at present—to end in a total separation of the upper and middling from the lower classes, the property from the population—is sufficiently apparent and rather alarming.'[127] It was not until Fitzwilliam forced the issue by agreeing to a Yorkshire meeting on the strict issue of an inquiry, that the party decided to take to the county platform.[128] The county meetings produced some grandiloquent rhetoric about the rights of the freeborn Englishman, encouraging many radicals to hope that the Whigs were about to seize the 'glorious opportunity' to head a campaign for 'that timely reform of existing abuses, which alone can save the country from a calamity too dreadful to think

---

[124] *London Alfred*, 29 Sept. and 6 Oct.

[125] *The Times*, 30 Sept. *Gentleman's Magazine*, Nov.

[126] *The Times*, 20 Nov. The case against Hunt, Waithman and others was later discharged, see *MO*, 17 June 1820.

[127] Brougham to Grey, 19 Sept., quoted in A. Aspinall, *Lord Brougham and the Whig Party* (Manchester, 1927), 346–7.

[128] A. Mitchell, *The Whigs in Opposition 1815–1830* (Oxford, 1967), 125–31, gives details of 9 meetings.

of'.[129] But not a word was said about reform: Joseph Mitchell, Hunt's lieutenant in the north was manhandled off the platform at York when he tried to raise the issue.[130] Back in Parliament the party took the first tentative steps on the path to 1832. United in anger by Fitzwilliam's dismissal from his lord-lieutenancy, the Whigs stood opposed to the Government's repressive policy: the 1819 session produced the nearest approach to an effective two-party system in the unreformed Parliament. The Tories won the party battle at Westminster, but the Whigs gained considerable approval in the country, particularly in the large unrepresented towns where Peterloo marked an important turning-point in middle-class political awareness.[131] Henceforward, the Whigs carefully cultivated such support. When Russell introduced a bill for transferring seats from boroughs disfranchised for corruption to large unrepresented towns, he received enthusiastic backing from the leadership. But after the ministers agreed to transfer the Grampound seats, radical Whigs like Lambton tried to push ahead too fast for party approval. He drew up a draft bill embracing household suffrage and the disfranchisement of the rotten boroughs. The party leadership refused to endorse such a thorough programme: the Queen's Affair provided Lambton with a convenient excuse to withdraw. It was with considerable hesitation, then, that the Whigs embraced the cause of middle-class reform in the aftermath of Peterloo.[132]

4. PETERLOO AND FORCIBLE INTIMIDATION

After Peterloo most radicals looked to the courts and public opinion, believing that reform was certain to follow in the wake of a proper inquiry into the events at Manchester. But the ultra-radicals drew a different lesson: Peterloo pointed the way to outright physical confrontation, now that the authorities had spilt the first blood. Evans returned to political activism, and plastered his shutters with posters proclaiming 'To Arms— and avenge the Blood of the Manchester murdered', adding that now 'there must be either a Revolution or a military Despotism.'[133] Sherwin's *Register* was renamed the *Republican*, and in its columns Carlile worked to

[129] 'Address to the Gentlemen and Freeholders of the County of Ayr', posting-bill enclosed in A. F. Smith, 6 Dec., HO, 42/200.
[130] *London Alfred*, 27 Oct. and 3 Nov. Deputy Postmaster, York, 14 Oct., HO, 42/196.
[131] Mitchell, 131-6. Cookson, *Lord Liverpool's Administration*, 198. Prentice, 178-227. J. E. Taylor, *Notes and Observations, critical and explanatory of the Papers Relative to the Internal State of the Country* (London, 1820). Read, 164-72.
[132] A. Mitchell, 'The Whigs and Parliamentary Reform before 1830', *Historical Studies (Australia and New Zealand)*, xii (1965-67), 26-9.
[133] W—r's report, 19 Aug., HO, 42/192.

transform the 'crisis' into a republican revolution, a hope shared by Wedderburn's coterie at the Hopkins Street Chapel.[134] Most of the revolutionary party, however, held fast to the popular constitutional idiom, as they called for a dramatic intensification of mass pressure from without, now that oppression had assuredly passed the undefined point after which—as Blackstone and all authorities allowed—the constitutional right of resistance should be exercised. Peterloo, the people were warned, proved that 'the Social Compact is broken up—that a Conspiracy exists against the Rights and Liberties of the Non-Represented People, that the rich are leagued against the poor; and that a legal tyranny, supported by a military despotism, is prepared to deprive them of every vestige of the freedom guaranteed to them by their forefathers'.[135] To defend their rights and restore their liberties the people should place themselves 'in the most imposing attitude which circumstances will admit of', James Griffin advised in the new ultra-radical paper, the *Cap of Liberty*.[136] The *Democratic Recorder*, another new ultra-radical paper, carried the masthead: 'Are the Masters of Kings! The Creators of Kings!! The Transporters of Kings!!! The Executors of Kings!!!! to submit to a vile faction.'[137]

The bellicose pronouncements of the revolutionary party disturbed those radical leaders who wished to rest their case on Peterloo, and revert to the 'politics of order'. Wooler and Cartwright hailed the events at Manchester as 'our most glorious victory':

We rejoice at the event . . . for it was the triumph of calumniated reform. It was the conquest of the slandered reformers—the victory of temper and principle, over infuriate loyalty and authorised treason. This victory must be ever kept in memory, and its effect stimulate and guide your future conduct.[138]

To preserve this moral victory, they immediately cautioned against any further exercise in forcible intimidation, and criticized the Watsonites for continuing with their mass meeting of the 'two counties', now switched from Kennington Common to Smithfield. They called an indoor meeting of their own at the Crown and Anchor where they instituted the fund to fight Peterloo in the courts, the management of which soon passed into the hands of the Westminster reformers who held their own meeting on 2 September in Palace Yard. Disappointed by the poor attendance at the much-criticized Smithfield meeting on 25 August (8,000–20,000), and encouraged by the promising start to the campaign for legal redress, Watson continued to exercise a moderating influence over the revolution-

---

[134] *SPR*, 21 Aug. *Republican*, 27 Aug.–3 Dec. Reports by 'BC' and others in HO, 42/194–197.

[135] Resolution at Finsbury meeting, 1 Nov., *London Alfred*, 10 Nov.

[136] *Cap of Liberty*, 13 Oct.

[137] *Democratic Recorder*, 2–23 Oct.   [138] *BD*, 17 Nov.

ary party and tried to promote a united reform front. A deputation from the Committee of 200 was sent to the Palace Yard meeting, although it seems that Thistlewood and some others who marched behind the red banner of universal suffrage were hoping for a clash with the authorities.[139] To the disapproval of hardliners in both camps, the Watsonites and the Rump came together to arrange a joint procession and dinner to welcome Hunt back to London. The Rump, recognizing that Hunt would have to be honoured in some way, trusted that a cheap public dinner would suffice. Watson wanted the occasion to be a great display of radical strength in the capital.[140] As events turned out, Hunt's triumphal entry into London on 13 September marked the end of his working alliance with the Watsonites who were convinced that he had forsaken their cause and joined the Burdettites.

The procession was a tremendous success—even the ministerialists spoke of crowds in excess of 200,000.[141] 'There was a good deal of respect at times paid to the man', Place reported to Hobhouse:

How in a mass of 300,000 could it be otherwise? Aye, and he deserved it too . . . If the people—I mean the working people—are to have but one man, they will, as they ought, support that man at least with their shouts . . . Whose fault is it that no better man goes among the people? Not theirs, they will cling to the best man that makes common cause with them . . . If none shows himself but Hunt, Hunt must be their man.[142]

As the undisputed hero of the hour, Hunt's vanity undeniably got the better of him. He insisted on altering the route of the procession which was rather too long and tiring for him. At the dinner, he decided to take the chair himself just as Burdett had done after his liberation from the Tower in 1810. Watson was furious as he had arranged for Gale Jones to chair the proceedings, and had never dreamt that 'the hero of the piece would ever wish to become the master of ceremonies'.[143] To make matters worse, Hunt left Watson holding the bill: three months later he was gaoled for its non-payment. But it was Hunt's carefully-considered after-dinner speech that brought an end to the alliance with the revolutionary party. A sound judge of popular political attitudes, Hunt realized the need to dissociate

[139] *BD*, 25 Aug., which includes Cartwright's letter denouncing the Smithfield meeting. Wolseley declined to chair it, see his letter to Blandford, HO, 42/192. *London Alfred*, 1 and 8 Sept. *Full Report of the Speeches and Proceedings of the Westminster General Meeting* (London, 1819). Prothero, *Artisans and Politics*, 118.

[140] Informers' reports, HO, 42/193–4. *BD*, 15 Sept.

[141] Hunt, *Triumphal Entry of H. Hunt into London . . . September 13, 1819* (London, 1819). Lord Mayor's reports, 13 Sept., HO, 42/194.

[142] BL Add. MSS 27837 (Place papers), f. 192, Place to Hobhouse, 19 Sept. *The Times*, 14 Sept. also put the figure at 300,000.

[143] Watson, 'To the unrepresented inhabitants of the metropolis' in *Political Tracts 1819*, a volume of newspaper cuttings and pamphlets in the British Library.

the radicals from any suggestion of republicanism, Spenceanism, levelling, infidelism or revolution now that Peterloo had stirred the nation and all eyes were upon them in the campaign for legal redress. At the Crown and Anchor, as later in the courts and at the Preston election, Hunt spelt out his basic economic and social philosophy, a creed which touched the right chord with workers throughout the land but displeased the militants and ideologues of metropolitan ultra-radicalism:

He had never said that there should be an equal division of property, and that there should be no poor people. No, the whole front of his offending, was an earnest wish that the man, poor and industrious, who laboured from one end of the week to the other, should have something more than the necessaries of life. If something was not rotten in the Constitution, he contended that such a man should have some little thing to minister to his luxuries, and have by him a something against a wet day.[144]

Previously, Watson and his colleagues had been quite prepared to tolerate Hunt's brand of popular radicalism. After the dinner they cast aside such self-restraint and condemned Hunt for his ingratitude and retraction. They were angered by the way he disclaimed responsibility for organizing any of the mass meetings and called for unity with other reform groups:

He deserved to be considered a mere fool, or dolt and an idiot, if he did not consider that he was now placed on the very pinnacle of popularity; and it would be unworthy of him, while placed on such a distinguished pinnacle, were he not to use his utmost endeavours to conciliate all parties among the Reformers.

Thistlewood regarded Hunt's speech as a 'premeditated insult', and the 'Committee of 500' resolved to have nothing more to do with him. Thomas Preston reminded Hunt that it was Watson and the Committee who had worked hard to raise him to his 'present eminence in society'. Hunt, he regretted, had turned his back on the 'trusty fellows' who protected him 'in the day of danger', and had given himself up to 'a set of Puppies that were your greatest enemies'. 'All seem to agree that Hunt had forsaken the people and gone over to the Burdett party', an informer reported. The deists, republicans and Spenceans who met at the Hopkins Street Chapel promptly announced that Hunt's principles of reform 'would not suit their purposes, which were nothing short of a Revolution'.[145]

[144] 'Principal Part of Hunt's speech at the Crown and Anchor', HO, 42/202. See also his nomination day speech at Preston: 'He had never set the poor against the rich: he knew that both classes must exist, for if all were made equal to-day, they would not remain so to-morrow. In his public life he had become acquainted with the feelings of a great portion of the people, with few exceptions he found them disposed to be satisfied, if they could obtain the means of supporting themselves and their families by their labour from Monday to Saturday', see *A Collection of Addresses, Squibs, Songs etc.* (Preston, 1820), 9. For his repudiation of Carlile's deism, see Bamford, 259–60; and *Republican*, 12 Apr., 1822.

[145] See the letters from Watson, Thistlewood, and the Committee, and from Hunt to W.

After the breach with Hunt, the Watsonites turned their attention to mobilizing the masses while popular anger at Peterloo was still intense. In place of a third meeting in Smithfield in October, Watson and Thistlewood issued a call for simultaneous meetings on 1 November. 'They must decide their own fate!!!', the poster advertising the London meeting advised the friends of freedom in all parts of the kingdom: 'A noble spirit of Independence at Runnymede obtained the Magna Charta!!! . . . let them give *one imposing evidence throughout Great Britain* of their desire and determination to obtain, if possible, by Peace and good order, a redress of their grievances.'[146] Plans for this decisive exercise in forcible intimidation were ruined by Hunt who resorted to the crudest smear campaign to thwart his former allies. Learning of Thistlewood's tour of the north to promote the 1 November scheme, he wrote to the *Manchester Observer* claiming that simultaneous meetings were being advocated by those who 'had their journeys paid by Whitehall'. To the delight of the loyalist press, bitter polemics followed as Thistlewood and Watson countered this spy-charge by accusing Hunt of peculating the Palace Yard subscription fund. Hunt's objections to the 1 November plan were soon lost in the welter of obloquy, but his main concern was to preserve the moral victory of Peterloo against any repetition of what he called the childish events of 2 December 1816—'By cool and temperate conduct the people of Manchester have gained the great victory over their enemies: do not you, therefore, suffer any act of violence to destroy the progress of that victory.' Hunt, the Watsonites fulminated, had 'grown Whiggish and anxious to get rid of the "Ragged Radicals"'. 'He will be laid upon the shelf', Watson predicted, 'and the people must go on as well they can without their *leader* and *champion*.'[147] But the provincial radicals refused to go ahead without Hunt's sanction: meetings planned for 1 November at Newcastle, Carlisle, Leeds, Halifax, Huddersfield, Barnsley, Manchester, Bolton, Wigan, Blackburn, Newcastle-under-Lyme, Nottingham, Leicester and Coventry were all called off.[148] In London, the rain-sodden Finsbury meeting was very poorly attended, and thereafter the Watsonites steadily lost support.[149]

Evans, in *New Times*, 16 and 17 Sept. 'BC's' report, 15 Sept., HO, 42/194. Preston to Hunt, 17 Sept., and 'C's' report, 22 Sept., HO, 42/195.

[146] Informers' reports, 13–31 Oct., and Thistlewood's posting-bill, 'Third Meeting of the People of the Metropolis', HO, 42/196–7.

[147] Hunt's letters in *MO*, 23 Oct. and *BD*, 27 Oct.; replies by Watson and Thistlewood in *Radical Reformer*, 27 Oct.; and a further round of correspondence, 28–31 Oct., printed in the loyalist press and pamphlets, see *Radical Recriminations: The correspondence of Hunt, Thistlewood, Blandford and Watson* (London, n.d.), and *Radical State Papers* (London, 1820). Throughout the controversy, Hunt was strongly supported by two new papers, Teulon's *White Hat* and Mitchell's *Blanketteer*.

[148] Byng, 18 Nov., HO, 42/199.

[149] *London Alfred*, 10 Nov., and the reports in HO, 42/198.

The proposed adjourned meeting on 15 November was given up when Watson reported that 'the communication between himself and the Country Places had dropped, for that they had sided with Hunt'.[150] A crowd of only a few hundred attended the meeting in Smithfield on 24 November, the day after the opening of Parliament, and the group suffered a further blow shortly afterwards when Watson was imprisoned for the dinner debt.[151] By the time the Six Acts were under discussion, the London ultra-radicals were a much depleted force. They had to abandon plans for a protest meeting of their own on Clerkenwell Green, but refused to have anything to do with Hunt's Smithfield meeting on 8 December against the new proposals. Thistlewood, who had taken over the leadership, decided they should attend the joint Whig–Rump meeting at Covent Garden, where their presence was none too welcome. Some of the revolutionary party worked their way from one meeting to another, bearing arms and inflammatory banners in a last attempt to provoke a clash with the authorities, only to have their black flag torn to shreds by the crowds. The time had passed for mass confrontation.[152]

From his prison cell, Watson issued an address castigating Hunt for squandering the excitement generated by Peterloo. Hunt, he maintained, should have taken advantage of the 'popular feelings at the time of his liberation from prison to bring the cause of Reform to a close', particularly as he had 'repeatedly, publicly, and unequivocally declared *"the time was not far distant"* that they would have to *"fight for them* (the people's rights); *that he would not be found in the rear ranks,"* and *"that he would fight for them and die for them"'*.[153] While Watson ruminated on the hollow rhetoric of forcible intimidation, Thistlewood turned his thoughts back to conspiracy and fell easy prey to George Edwards, the *agent provocateur*. Edwards's success in weaving the Cato Street 'conspiracy' stemmed from the intense hatred which Thistlewood's circle felt towards Hunt whom they were sworn to destroy 'as soon as the Ministers were killed'. It was Thistlewood's anger with Hunt, his indignation at being labelled a spy, that spurred him on towards a hopeless attempt at insurrection which even Carlile condemned, serving as it did to strengthen the Government and confirm it in its new repressive powers.[154]

[150] 'C's' report, 10 Nov., HO, 42/198.

[151] Reports of Lord Mayor and others in HO, 42/199, which includes several posters for the meeting attacking 'moderator Hunt'.

[152] W—r's report, 6 Dec., HO, 42/199. 'BC's' reports, 30 Nov. and 1, 5 and 7 Dec., Birnie, 8 Dec. and Lord Mayor, 8 Dec., HO, 42/200. HO, 44/6 ff. 165–9.

[153] 'Address to the Reformers', *Patriot*, 24 Dec.

[154] Reports from George Edwards (W—r) in HO, 44/4, and his lengthy account, 11 Mar. 1820, HO, 44/5 ff. 203–39. Robert Adams's deposition, HO, 44/4 ff. 203–4. See also T. Preston, *Letter to Lord Viscount Castlereagh* (London, 1820); and J. Stanhope, *The Cato Street Conspiracy* (London, 1962). Carlile's attitude surprised several correspondents, *Republican*, 3 Mar.–12 May 1820.

In the provinces Hunt retained the loyal support of the radicals, including those who finally turned to physical force in the spring of 1820. There was a marked contrast, indeed, between the reaction to Peterloo in London and in the provinces. In London, the hardcore of ultra-radicals saw no third possibility between military despotism and revolution. To secure maximum popular participation in the decisive confrontation with the authorities, they retained the language of constitutionalism, employing its full emotive force. In the provinces, constitutionalism ran much deeper: it was the very essence of popular radicalism, not simply an instrumental form of rhetoric. After Peterloo, provincial radicals stepped back from the militant mass platform to emphasize their constitutionalism because they wished to avoid the horrors of 'absolute Despotism on the one hand, or a dreadful Revolution on the other'.[155] On 25 August, delegates met at Oldham and decided against any escalation of radical agitation: they issued instructions that 'all Drilling and mustering in large Bodies with or without Arms should be suspended, and that every Appearance of Resistance to the Laws should be avoided and the Spirit of Violence repressed as much as possible'.[156] Across the Pennines, the details and implications of Peterloo were discussed at unannounced night meetings,[157] but these were followed by a series of mass meetings starting at Wakefield on 30 August, very much in the old style, with the Yorkshire radicals displaying the utmost concern for peace, order and legality.[158] In place of the festive spirit of the summer, however, the meetings were characterized by solemnity and dignity. At Hunslet Moor on 20 September (20,000–40,000), the crowd was dressed in mourning and the banners were draped with black crepe.[159] Sixteen bands, similarly attired, led the people to the Halifax meeting on 4 October (50,000) through pouring rain, 'with the same solemnity as at a funeral'.[160] At these meetings the radicals extolled Hunt, awaited the successful outcome of his campaign for legal redress, and pledged themselves to his policy of abstinence from excisable goods.

There was the same concern for discipline, order and constitutionalism in areas where radicalism acquired new strength after Peterloo. The new union societies of the West Midlands issued a number of constitutional declarations and pamphlets to confute the propaganda of the Birmingham Loyal Association for the Suppression and Refutation of Blasphemy and Sedition. The meeting at Newhall Hill on September 23 was a sombre,

---

[155] 'Declaration of the Political Protestants of North and South Shields', 2 Oct., handbill in HO, 42/196.

[156] 'XY's' report, HO, 42/194.

[157] Leeds Deputy Postmaster, 19 Aug., and Horton, 22 Aug., HO, 42/192. *Medusa*, 28 Aug.

[158] *Leeds Mercury*, 4 Sept.; *MO*, 11 Sept.

[159] *Leeds Reform Meeting Held on Hunslet Moor, September 20th, 1819* (Leeds, 1819).

[160] *MO*, 9 Oct. Horton, 5 and 6 Oct., HO, 42/196.

highly-disciplined occasion: the hustings were covered in black cloth; Sir Charles Wolseley arrived in a mourning coach; and the crowds raised their respectful hands in support of the resolutions, 'some were blacked, some smeared with soot, and others covered in mourning gloves'.[161] In the north-east, the printers and schoolmasters who had first stood forward in the radical cause were joined after Peterloo by a rapidly growing number of ironworkers and pitmen as Political Protestant groups and reformers' reading societies spread throughout the region. The United Committee of Political Protestants ensured that the meeting at the Town Moor, Newcastle on 11 October (40,000) was a great display of discipline and strength. Sixteen thousand marched in procession, headed by the ironworkers of Winlanton, followed by reform societies from Benwell, Fawdon, Gateshead, North and South Shields, led by their class leaders who wore special white hats with black bands. 'The Order and organization of such a Body', the local authorities reported, 'was more frightful as to the future, than violence.'[162]

On the platform after Peterloo the provincial radicals displayed their discipline and constitutionalism as they demanded an inquiry into the events at Manchester, supported Hunt's campaign in the courts, and reaffirmed their commitment to Cartwright's *Bill of Rights and Liberties*. They complied with Hunt's ban on simultaneous meetings on 1 November, but shortly thereafter divisions developed over the use of the mass platform. The intricacies of these disputes are impossible to follow, but certain points can be established.[163] The question of simultaneous meetings often divided what the magistrates described as the 'higher radicals' from the 'lower radicals', but even the most militant remained attached to Hunt, the people's champion—some believed that the letter denouncing the 1 November plan had not been written by Hunt but by the 'higher radicals' in the *Manchester Observer* office.[164]

In Lancashire, W. C. Walker, 'the Thistlewood of this part', tried to inject a strong anti-Hunt tone in his role as secretary to the Ultra Union Society which broke away from the Patriotic Union Society after the cancellation of the 1 November meetings, but he was a highly dubious

---

[161] See the declarations issued by the Birmingham Union Society, HO, 42/195, the Warwick Union Society, the Wolverhampton Union Society, and the Committee of the Coseley Union, HO, 42/198. *Birmingham Meeting . . . to take into consideration the late unhappy transactions at Manchester* (Manchester, 1819). See also, *Fourteen Anti-Reform Pamphlets published at Birmingham, 1819*, bound in one volume in the Goldsmiths' Library.

[162] *Full Account of the General Meeting of the Inhabitants of Newcastle-upon-Tyne* (Newcastle, 1819). Mayor of Newcastle, 9 and 12 Oct., HO, 42/196. There is a wealth of north-eastern material in *Political Tracts 1819*. See also, N. McCord, 'Tyneside Discontents and Peterloo', *Northern History*, ii (1967), 91–111.

[163] For a lengthier analysis, see Belchem, thesis, 110–44.

[164] Norris, 19 Oct., HO, 42/197, and 1 Dec. HO, 42/200.

figure, almost certainly an informer.[165] After attending the Smithfield meeting on 24 November, where he joined Thistlewood in execrating Hunt, he returned to Manchester by way of Nottingham to attend a secret delegate meeting, full details of which were subsequently made available to Colonel Fletcher.[166] The delgates were asked to endorse Thistlewood's new provincial-based plan for simultaneous meetings to coincide with the introduction of repressive legislation: most of the delegates still looked to Hunt for leadership and trusted that he would chair the meeting which would be 'the signal for all other meetings'. According to 'Alpha', the date was fixed for 13 December, and the meetings were a cover for insurrection.[167] On the basis of this information, the authorities decided to assert themselves. Byng was ordered to cancel all leave and his troops were put on extra duty. In the face of this show of force by the authorities, the radicals abandoned their meetings, much to the dismay of the militants.[168] At Birmingham the 'junior classes' of the Union Society were furious when Edmonds and the 'higher classes' decided to call off the meeting because of the large military presence in the town. That night they posted the town with inflammatory placards in anticipation of encouraging news from Manchester:

> BRITONS arise, and yet be free
> Defend your rights and liberty!
> Boroughmongers long have shar'd the spoil
> The working class shares all the toil;
> Now, or never, strike the blow
> Exert yourselves and crush the foe!!![169]

In Manchester the arguments over 13 December were particularly bitter, although secretary Walker was conveniently 'out of the way' at this time. Following the great Huntite gathering at Habergham Eves on 15 November (12,000–30,000), the leading Lancashire radicals had all agreed to take to the platform to protest at the introduction of repressive

[165] Norris, 30 Oct., HO, 42/197, enclosing a militant anti-Hunt posting-bill by Walker, supporting 1 Nov. meetings. For 'sailor-boy' Walker's dubious role, see Belchem 'Henry Hunt' (1978), 764.

[166] Informers' reports in HO, 42/199, in particular 'BC', 26 Nov. which suggests that Bentham provided Thistlewood with the money for Walker's travelling expenses.

[167] 'Alpha's' report, enclosed in Fletcher, 2 Dec., HO, 42/200. For the delegate meeting, and the links between Thistlewood, Walker and the anti-Hunt radicals in the north, see Prothero, *Artisans and Politics*, 124–6.

[168] Norris, 6–12 Dec., Hulton, 9 Dec., and Byng, 2–12 Dec., HO, 42/200. Hobhouse to Byng, 7 Dec., HO, 79/4.

[169] Bedford and Price, 13 Dec., Deputy Postmaster, 14 Dec., enclosing the posting-bill, 'An Address from the Members of the Birmingham Union Society', and Price, 24 Dec., HO, 42/201.

[170] *MO*, 20 Nov. Norris, 16 Nov., and Fletcher, 17 Nov., HO, 42/198.

legislation,[170] but as 13 December approached, Wroe and the 'higher radicals' of the *Manchester Observer* argued that all meetings should be abandoned for fear of violent consequences. As suspicions grew about a 'spy-system', most radicals were prepared to follow this advice, but the very vehemence and persistence with which the 'higher radicals' argued their case indicates that there was still considerable support for simultaneous meetings—the *Manchester Observer* even criticized Hunt for taking to the platform at Smithfield.[171] On 13 December, Hunt issued an 'Address to the Radical Reformers' in which he explained his conduct over the Six Acts and his refusal to co-operate with Burdett and the Whigs; detailed his progress in the courts where he had been beset with every 'disheartening impediment' that could be thrown in his way; and implored the radicals to concentrate their efforts on abstinence from excisable goods, a policy strongly endorsed by Cobbett, just returned from America.[172]

The introduction of repression forced the movement underground, and plans for a physical move were soon under discussion, particularly in Yorkshire which took the lead in the 'general rising' of 1820. In the West Riding, the split between the 'higher' and the 'lower' radicals had taken a somewhat different form: here the rank and file rebelled against the whiggish proclivities of the official leadership. The local leaders unashamedly toadied to the Whig worthies as soon as they stood forward for an inquiry into Peterloo. Members of the Leeds Radical Committee, acting under instructions from Baines, provided the necessary muscle to dislodge Mitchell from the platform at the county meeting in October when he tried to raise the issue of reform, to which Wooler, to his discredit, turned a blind eye.[173]

For his subsequent attacks on Dickenson, Willan and the other leaders who persisted in fêting the likes of Fitzwilliam and Milton, Mitchell suffered worse indignities, on one occasion being ducked in a canal.[174] At the Huddersfield meeting on 8 November (8,000–10,000) Dickenson announced that he would settle for less than Cartwright's *Bill*, but his heretical advocacy of household suffrage and triennial parliaments was too much for the crowd: on their way home the rank and file demonstrated their feelings with a discharge of pistols.[175] When the Yorkshire radicals met at Leeds on 9 December to protest at the Six Acts, the crowd rejected the petition presented by the leaders in favour of an emotive remonstrance recommending arming, moved by Brayshaw.[176] The introduction of the Six

[171] *MO*, 4–18 Dec. Fletcher, 11 Dec., Chippendale, Sharp, and Norris, 12 Dec., HO, 42/200.
[172] *MO*, 18 Dec. Hunt chaired the dinners at the Crown and Anchor on 4 Dec. to welcome Cobbett back, and on 13 Dec. to promote the abstinence campaign, *BD*, 8 and 15 Dec.
[173] Deputy Postmaster, York, 14 Oct., HO, 42/196. *MO*, 16 Oct. *London Alfred*, 3 Nov.
[174] *Blanketteer*, 23 Oct.–20 Nov.
[175] Horton, 11 Nov., HO, 42/198. *MO*, 20 Nov.   [176] *Leeds Mercury*, 11 Dec.

Acts, coming on top of the backsliding of some of the leadership, led many Yorkshire radicals to contemplate a physical move, for which they were trained by local war veterans, but the origins of the rising are difficult to unravel, particularly as they were to become a matter of heated controversy when Brayshaw led the attack on Hunt and the GNU in 1822.[177] Links with other areas were quickly established but, as so often in underground activity, proved tenuous, unreliable or positively dangerous, the strongest ties being with those places where economic distress was most severe, in this instance, the weaving districts of Glasgow and Carlisle. The 'general strike' in the west of Scotland is perhaps the best-known aspect of the 'rising', but Scottish nationalist historians have claimed this for their own.[178] The numbers involved in the English 'risings' at Huddersfield on the night of 31 March–1 April, and at Grange Moor on 11 April were far less impressive, but this attempt at a general rising was more significant in its way than the better-known events of the futile Cato Street 'conspiracy'. What is important here, and the point which most impressed the local authorities at the time, was that the 'rising' followed immediately on news of Hunt's conviction at York. The West Riding insurrectionists marched behind banners proclaiming 'Hunt the Intrepid Champion of the Rights and Liberties of the People'.[179] In Lancashire, too, the ultra-radicals still looked to Hunt for leadership. At the time of the general rising, all the leading Lancashire militants, including Naaman Carter, the indiscreet pike-maker, and the weaver James Lang, Walker's successor as secretary of the Ultra Union Society, were still being held by the authorities on summary committal following their arrest in the December clamp-down. When finally released, Lang and his colleague the shoemaker Richard Johnson, attended a meeting at Flixton to discuss the failure of the Huddersfield rising, at which they expressed their regret that they had not moved much earlier, noting that the original 1 November plan was 'well laid, and that *that* time was more favourable than any before or since'. But even so, they did not criticize Hunt, whose leadership they regarded as indispensable. Johnson wished that Hunt had 'made a stand' at the Preston election or on return from his trial at York when 'millions would have volunteered to crown his head . . . By commenting on these things I wish you to perceive that we must have some Popular Character of Weight and

---

[177] 'Statement of Joseph Brayshaw', *Republican*, 4 Oct. 1822.

[178] P. B. Ellis and S. M. A'Ghobhainn, *The Scottish Insurrection of 1820* (London, 1970).

[179] Haigh Allen, 30 Mar., and A. Campbell, 31 Mar., HO, 40/11. Chippendale, Haigh Allen, and Horton, 1 Apr.; 'Examinations and Depositions Relative to April 11'; examinations of Joshua Hirst, 3 Apr., and James Palmer, 30 Apr., HO, 40/12. Voluntary examination of Thomas Ferrymond, Mar. 1821, HO, 40/16. TS, 11/1055/4673. F. K. Donnelly, 'The General Rising of 1820: A Study of Social Conflict in the Industrial Revolution', unpublished Ph.D. thesis, University of Sheffield, 1975.

Influence to head us . . . This would stamp Revolution on the People's Hearts'.[180]

After Peterloo the weaknesses of popular contitutionalism were clearly revealed. The collapse of the radical challenge should be attributed less to the flaws in Hunt's character and leadership than to the nature of the radicalism he represented so well. Obsessed by legitimacy, the radicals failed to coerce the Government: forcible intimidation proved to be an idle threat, and the threshold of violence was not crossed by the non-represented millions who looked instead to the courts and public opinion. Furthermore, this respect for public attitudes had been accompanied by some backsliding to the Whigs, previously condemned for their repudiation of the mass platform: the only meeting held on 13 December was at North Shields where the radicals met to praise Lambton, Grey's son-in-law, for his exposure in the Commons of the alarmist fallacies in the 'Papers Relative to the Internal State of the Country', the pretext for the introduction of the Six Acts.[181] The strategy and ideology of the mass platform had been found wanting, but with Hunt elevated to martyrdom by his imprisonment, critics of the radicalism he personified so well were to find it impossible to dislodge him and redirect radical endeavour.

[180] Norris, 23 and 27 Dec., HO, 42/201. Norris, 12 Apr., and Fletcher, 13 and 19 Apr., and 25 May, HO, 40/12–13.
[181] W. Richardson, 14 Dec., HO, 42/201. *MO*, 8 and 15 Jan. 1820.

5

The Revision of Radicalism

FOLLOWING the collapse of mass platform endeavour, the working-class radical movement was particularly prone to divisive 'revisions'. Each defeat was followed by a post-mortem, as it were, a period of critical self-analysis and internecine argument as conflicting conclusions were drawn from the failure and dramatic decline of mass agitation. The history of the Chartist movement provides the best-known examples of this sequence of insurgency, defeat, introspection, dissension and revision, but the discussions which followed the collapse of the mobilization of 1819 were every bit as important, raising fundamental questions about the meaning of radicalism and the nature of protest. Once the significance of the controversies of 1820–2 is appreciated, it is possible to place Hunt's rather loathsome behaviour in its proper context. Regarding himself as the greatest martyr of the post-war campaign, Hunt behaved with insufferable vanity and self-pity during his imprisonment when he was under considerable psychological strain, but this interminable concentration on self, offensive as it sounds to the modern ear, must be read for the most part as political rhetoric. Self-promotion, a necessary part of the old tactic of 'consistency by contrast', reached new levels of self-adulation as the martyred Hunt deliberately personalized issues in order to vindicate the ways and means of popular radicalism and thereby upohold the democratic constitutional cause against moderate opportunism on the one hand and ideological extremism on the other. His egotistical prison writings, so readily dismissed as the demented outpourings of a blasted demagogue, are among his most important contributions to the radical movement. Personalities intrude at every point, but behind the contumely and obloquy were vital arguments about ideology, strategy and organization. His heated dispute with Carlile touched upon many issues of the utmost importance regarding the role of ideology in protest movements. Which mattered more: ideological purity or maximum popular participation? individual mental emancipation and counter-culture or mass agitation and political challenge? Here, indeed, was a precursor of many later debates in the labour movement about the difficulty of aligning ideological commitment and popular involvement. The controversies over strategy also have a familiar ring about them. In these years of despondency, Hunt upheld a strong fundamentalist line and censured all those he suspected of gradualism and compromise, including Cobbett, his quondam political mentor, who deserted his popular audience to offer his talents to the landed interest, trusting to exploit their grievances and clout to secure some measure of reform, political or financial. While Cobbett, the pragmatist, turned to the farmers, and Carlile, the ideologue, imposed his sectarian creed on the diminutive, self-improving zetetic societies, Hunt, the popular leader, tried to revitalize the radical challenge through popular organization based on the collective strength of the northern working class. Ridiculed by Carlile, ignored by Cobbett, Hunt's Great Northern Union pointed the way forward to the great Chartist challenge.

I. THE 'CAPTIVE OF ILCHESTER'

Hunt's earlier experience of prison had not prepared him for the full horrors of the unreformed penal system in an isolated county gaol. During his sojourn in the King's Bench in London he had enjoyed comfortable accommodation, good company, intelligent political debate, and the run of the key. At Ilchester he suffered considerable physical discomfort, unnatural solitude and confinement, petty tyranny and injustice, all of which told on his bodily and mental health. But even in these adverse conditions, Hunt proved an indefatigable agitator: as a result of his 'gaol politics' the governor was dismissed and convicted and the gaol itself condemned for demolition. In the history of prison reform, Hunt deserves an honourable mention.

Hunt's campaign for reform developed out of his struggle to secure his own 'political status'. He arrived at Ilchester expecting to be 'treated as other prisoners committed for political offences were treated'. To his horror, he found himself subjected to conditions which, he complained, 'more than QUADRUPLES the severity of the sentence passed upon me'. Ilchester gaol was a most insanitary place, poorly built in low-lying position by the river. The physical discomfort of confinement in a room which was 'alternately the atmosphere of an oven and a well' was much aggravated by the tyranny exercised by Bridle, the governor, a *'Hulk educated Monster'*. Worst of all was the political vindictiveness displayed by the 'moral gentry of Somersetshire', the visiting magistrates and other local minions of the 'Pitt System', who delighted in wreaking vengeance on such a troublesome freeholder of the county, by denying him the company of those who were nearest and dearest to him, his mistress and his ward, his beloved Mrs Vince and the devoted Miss Gray.[1] Throughout his imprisonment, Hunt fought a running battle with the authorities to establish his right as a 'political' prisoner to receive these female visitors in his room. It was an

[1] *TRR*, 28 Aug., 25 Sept. 1820, and 8 Apr. 1822. Manchester Central Library, Archives Dept: Manuscript journal kept during Hunt's imprisonment in Ilchester Gaol, ff. 76–7.

issue which also brought him into conflict with the social conservatism of some of the radicals. Bamford, convicted with Hunt at York, took a particularly prudish line. He refused to send Hunt an affidavit detailing the cosy arrangements at Lincoln gaol where his wife actually lived and lodged with him, because 'he could not but be sensible—though Hunt's self-love, which he was constantly disclaiming—blinded him to it—of the difference betwixt a man being indulged with the company of his own wife and being indulged with the company of another man's wife'. It was on this point that Hunt and Bamford parted company: Bamford, one of Hunt's most fervent supporters in 1819, became his most virulent critic when he published his autobiography many years later.[2]

Mrs Vince's company mattered a great deal to Hunt. Over the years, their relationship had been the target of incessant scurrilous attack, but it was their very happiness and stability together which provided him with the necessary equanimity to withstand the pressures and flak of political controversy and public notoriety. Without her steadying influence, Hunt seemed unable to stand back from political contention and keep his public life in proper perspective. Mrs Vince, it would appear, provided the balance that was lacking in his turbulent personality.[3] Denied her company, Hunt began to display symptoms of paranoia in prison. Other factors contributed to what Bamford disparagingly described as Hunt's 'derangement' at this time.[4] An outcast from respectable reform circles, Hunt had long been used to taking his own counsel—'I have, ever since March 1817, for the last four years, been accustomed to rely *entirely upon my own opinion*, never having had *one Friend*, whose judgement and principles I could depend upon, that I could consult'[5]—but he had never experienced such physical isolation. As a popular agitator he had always been near to events and greatly enjoyed the close contact with his supporters. Ilchester was removed from the centre of politics and far away from his followers in London and the north. Visits were few and political discussion limited. It was this distance, this physical isolation, as well as his frequent separation from Mrs Vince, which distorted his judgement and led him to exaggerate his own importance.

Soon after Mrs Vince and Miss Gray arrived at Ilchester from Sussex, the chairman of the magistrates issued an order prohibiting all females

[2] Bamford, 346–9.

[3] Glimpses of Hunt's domestic life and dependence on Mrs Vince can be obtained from his letters to Bryant over the years, in Lancashire Record Office: Hunt Correspondence, DDX/113; see, for example, the letter of 21 Dec. 1817 inviting Bryant to spend Christmas with them and 'join in the laugh at the past and present folly of mankind, and anticipate the prospect of better feeling amongst them'. See also Bamford's morally censorious description of 'Mr. Hunt and Family', 228–9.

[4] Ibid., 346–7.

[5] John Rylands Library: English MS 378/1029, Hunt to W. Shepherd, 16 Mar. 1822.

from visiting Hunt in his private room except his wife and children. All other female visitors were to be received at the double-grating in the felons' conversation-room or cage where 'felons, convicts, and prisoners, charged with, and convicted of, unnatural crimes, beastiality [sic], and murder, see and meet their associates'. Hunt refused to subject Mrs Vince and Miss Gray to such 'abhorrent and disgusting conditions', and protested strongly against being placed on a level with the felons. As all channels of complaint within the county appeared to be blocked, he wrote to Sidmouth and Justice Bayley, demanding their assistance in securing the privileges enjoyed in other gaols by his co-defendants, Johnson, Bamford and Healey. He then applied to the Court of King's Bench and obtained a rule against the sheriff and the gaoler of 'Ilchester Bastile', as he now called it, 'to shew cause why he should not be treated in the mode in which it has been usual to treat prisoners confined there for misdemeanour'. This prompted Sir Charles Bampfylde, the high sheriff, to visit the gaol and rescind the order and various other restrictions. Bampfylde, it transpired, had been kept in ignorance of Hunt's complaints by the magistrates and the 'Wells junto of perpetual under-sheriffs'.[6] Delighted by the outcome of Bampfylde's visit, Hunt withdrew his application to the King's Bench, a costly procedure and an expensive mistake since Bampfylde's term of office came to an end shortly afterwards, and his successor refused to over-rule Dr Colston and the visiting magistrates when they reimposed the restrictions on female visitors.[7] Hunt was enraged, but he directed his anger into a sustained campaign for reform throughout the prison. For some while he had kept notes of the various indignities and injustices he had suffered: now he started an inquiry into the treatment of all the prisoners—'when I found that every species of unmanly and vindictive treatment was inflicted upon *me*, who had in some measure the power of exposing and making public the conduct of the petty tyrants, I began to reflect what must be their treatment of poor prisoners who had no means of making their complaints known'. Hunt, Bridle rued, began to 'revolutionize the gaol'.[8] To publicize his disturbing findings he took two important steps: he instituted a petition campaign on behalf of the most unjustly treated inmates, which caused a considerable stir in the Commons and led to the appointment of a special commission;[9] and he published a sensational

[6] Hunt, 'Manuscript journal', ff. 50–69, and 113–50. University of Chicago: MS 563, Hunt Correspondence and Papers, item 27, Hunt to Davenport, 19 Sept. 1820. *BD*, 22 and 29 Nov. 1820, which prints Hunt's affidavit. *TRR*, 21 Oct. 1820–22 Feb. 1821.

[7] Hunt, 'Manuscript journal', f. 160. *TRR*, 22 Feb. and 26 July 1821.

[8] *TRR*, 11 Apr. 1821. W. Bridle, *Letter to the very noble, and most mighty, the aristocracy of England* (London, 1836), 17. See also his *Narrative of the rise and progress of the improvements effected in His Majesty's gaol at Ilchester* (Bath, 1822).

[9] *TRR*, 11 Apr. 1821 and 25 Mar. 1822. Ald. Wood presented the first petitions, 9 Mar. 1821, see *PD*, 2nd series, iv, 1170–2, and, v, 156–63 for the appointment of the commission.

pamphlet, *A Peep into a Prison*, in which he described the evils of 'Ilchester Bastile' in the most lurid detail.[10] Every aspect of the prison and its administration incurred his wrath: the insanitary location and buildings; the polluted water supply; the inadequate medical and washing facilities; the excessive punishment and torture inflicted by the corrupt, lecherous and sadistic governor; the inattention to the proper classification of inmates which explained the 'lamentable and disgraceful state of irreligion, immorality and irregularity'; and the invidious visiting arrangements which led to the most disgusting scenes in the general wards where poor debtors were not allowed to retire in private with their wives. 'If all the fire of Heaven had not been spent on Sodom and Gomorrah as an example to future ages,' Hunt declared, 'some portion of it would certainly have rained into this gulph of iniquity.' On receipt of his copy of the pamphlet, Hanning, the new sheriff, immediately ordered a magistrates' inquiry.[11] For the next three months, Hunt spent every minute of his time preparing, presenting and publishing his evidence to the magistrates' inquiry and the parliamentary special commission. The sheriff and magistrates restricted their attention to his charges against Bridle, among which were gross neglect of duty, inflicting torture by placing blisters on prisoners' shaven heads, and fornication with female prisoners whose illegitimate offspring were 'supported at the county expense'. Hunt's examination of witnesses and accounts lasted fourteen days, after which Bridle declined to present any defence as he wished to reserve his case for the forthcoming special commission.[12] The commission was conducted with exemplary thoroughness, sitting for eight or more hours a day, six days a week, from 24 May to 2 July. Hunt opened his case against Bridle on 26 May, and when he concluded his evidence on 13 June, he had examined over seventy witnesses in meticulous detail. Throughout the remaining sessions he subjected every defence witness to a rigorous cross-examination. All this evidence, together with the damning reports presented by Dr Kinglake and other medical experts, were carefully recorded by H. B. Shillibeer, a Taunton land surveyor who served as Hunt's clerk. A full-scale account of the 'Investigation into the Abuses of Ilchester Gaol' was then sent to Dolby to publish in cheap serial form.[13] 'The developement [sic] of the atrocities committed here', Hunt predicted in one of his *Addresses* to the radicals, 'will lead to a general investigation into all gaols of the Kingdom; but

[10] H. Hunt, *A Peep into a Prison* (London, 1821). This prompted other pamphlets, including *Visits to a Prison; A Peep at the Prisoners* (Ilminster, 1821).

[11] *TRR*, 5 May 1821.

[12] *TRR*, 5 and 26 May 1821. 'Ilchester Gaol, Somerset: Copies of Reports of the High Sheriff and Magistrates', *Parliamentary Papers*, 1822 (Irish University Press rpt.: Prisons, ix).

[13] 'Ilchester Gaol: Report of the Commissioners on the state of the Gaol' and 'Appendix to the above Report', ibid. *Investigation at Ilchester Gaol . . . with an address to his Majesty, King George the Fourth, by Henry Hunt* (London, 1821). *TRR*, 24 Aug. 1821.

unless there be a *Hunt* in every gaol, to attend the investigation, I fear we shall never come at any thing like the truth.'[14] The investigation into Ilchester gaol revealed the best and the worst in Hunt. He was unremitting in his labours and was put to considerable expense, but he never underestimated his contribution to prison reform and expected commensurate public recognition and approval.

Soon after the hearings, the sheriff decided to discharge Bridle. With the appointment of a new governor and officers, conditions in Ilchester improved considerably.[15] Hunt was again allowed the company of Mrs Vince and Miss Gray, and the poor prisoners were freed from torture and abuse. 'There is not one prisoner suffering torture of any sort . . . straight jackets, blisters for punishment, thumb screws, gags, and neck irons are all abolished', Hunt reported, adding with characteristic vanity that he cherished the 'sweet and delightful thought of having accomplished this at my own personal risk, and by my own personal exertions, and at my own expense'.[16] But conditions soon deteriorated. Six floods in six weeks heralded the onset of winter, during which time the rheumatic Hunt was afforded some protection against the damp by his 'radical flannel', a much-valued present from the Rochdale weavers.[17] Then the vengeful magistrates struck again. At the Quarter Sessions at Wells in January 1822 they issued new orders, apparently endorsed by Justice Best, which subjected Hunt to the rules 'intended only for felons'. No visitors, male or female, were to be allowed in his private room: all his visitors were to be seen at the double-grating in the felons' cage. Hunt regarded this as a 'total prohibition' and remonstrated against his 'solitary confinement'. He sent letters of protest to Bayley and to Robert Peel, the new Home Secretary, and his son Thomas made an application to the King's Bench, presenting affidavits from his father's doctor and lawyer who had been denied private access to his room.[18] Hunt's health, physical and mental, deteriorated at this point. The new regulations, following in the wake of an attempt to confiscate his Somerset estate, angered him to the point of paranoia. 'They have not the Souls to forgive the exposures I have made', he explained to Davenport, his old legal assistant:

They do not forget the Two Bristol Elections & the public meetings I have carried in this County . . . Was there ever a man so persecuted under such circumstances

---

[14] *TRR*, 9 July 1821.
[15] University of Chicago: MS 563, Hunt Correspondence and Papers, item 37, Hunt to Davenport, 21 Dec. 1821. Hunt's letter to Mr Baron Graham in Hunt, *Investigations at Ilchester Gaol*.
[16] *TRR*, 9 Oct., 24 Dec. 1821, and 11 Feb. 1822.
[17] *TRR*, 10 Dec.–23 Jan. 1822.
[18] *TRR*, 23 Jan.–25 Feb. 1822.

since the days of Jesus Christ and the Jews—in fact the Jews were more merciful to Jesus Christ than these infernal Wretches are to me.[19]

This was Hunt's nadir. Personal welfare took precedence over political principle as he accepted help and succour from any quarter, including moderate reformers and the renegade Burdett. Throughout 'liberal' circles there was now a general feeling that Hunt was more sinned against than sinning, and his 'gaol politics' were supported by those who had previously repudiated his mass radicalism. The parliamentary Radicals were particularly prominent in the campaign of protest against his 'solitary confinement', but this was not the first time they had offered their support. They had taken Hunt's side in his long-running legal battle with the Exchequer over the sale and manufacture of his famous 'Breakfast Powder'. Hunt started manufacturing this powder, a cheap substitute for highly-taxed imported coffee, based on a special method of preparing and roasting English rye, towards the end of 1819 as part of his policy of abstinence from excisable goods. The Excise soon intervened however, and took possession of his manufactory together with half a ton of the stock. Hunt decided to try the question in the courts and instituted proceedings against the officers. His conviction at York prevented him from taking the matter any further, at which point the Attorney-General announced that an action would be brought against Hunt himself in the Court of Exchequer. Denied a writ of habeas corpus, Hunt was unable to leave Ilchester and was fined £200 in his absence when the case was finally heard in London.[20] The judgement disturbed the parliamentary Radicals who believed that the Commissioners of Excise had overstepped their competence and trespassed upon Parliament's jealously-preserved right of deciding what articles should or should not be taxed. Sir Robert Wilson took a particular interest in the case, and as a result of his applications it seemed as if the Government would remit the fine.[21] But here Hunt's success in his 'gaol politics' gold against him. As soon as the special commission left Ilchester, he was informed by Broderip, the under-sheriff, that he had received 'a *process from the Exchequer* to seize me and my property for the penalties of £200 for making Breakfast Powder'.[22] At this time, Hunt was rather hard-pressed financially—on top of his many other legal bills, the Ilchester investigations had cost him over £300 out of his own pocket. Short of ready

---

[19] University of Chicago: MS 563, Hunt Correspondence and Papers, item 89, Hunt to Davenport, 'Tuesday 19th Day Solitary'.

[20] *BD*, 2 and 23 Feb. 1820. *TRR*, 22 Feb. 1821. He distributed the powder to the prisoners and visiting magistrates, see 'Manuscript journal', ff. 17, 22 and 30.

[21] University of Chicago: MS 563, Hunt Correspondence and Papers, items 29, 30 and 36, Sir R. Wilson to Hunt, 1 and 15 Mar., and 4 July 1821, and item 32, J. Hume to Hunt, 3 Apr. 1821.

[22] *TRR*, 26 July 1821.

cash, he arranged that the under-sheriff should collect the fine by distraining upon his tenants at Glastonbury for the rents due to him. The malicious Broderip, it seems, did not abide by the terms of the agreement—'this worthy gave my tenants notice not to pay me any more rent, but never took the slightest means of recovering it himself'. In January 1822, shortly before the imposition of the 'solitary confinement' regulations, Broderip informed Hunt that he had 'an EXTENT from the Crown, with orders to take my *person*, to seize and sell the manor and estate at Glastonbury'. Hunt promptly paid the fine, thereby precluding the plans of Broderip and other 'harpies' of the Government to 'rob and plunder me of my property . . . to sell my manor and estates, worth even in these times *many thousand pounds*, to pay a penalty of *two hundred pounds*'.[23] Once again, Wilson and other Radical MPs took up his case. Within a few months new legislation was introduced permitting the manufacture of 'breakfast powder', and Wilson encouraged Hunt to claim back his £200 fine. When he finally left Ilchester to take over the supervision of his roasted grain manufactory, he was still awaiting restitution.[24]

Encouraged by the support he had received from the parliamentary Radicals over his breakfast powder, Hunt decided to seek their assistance in a petitioning campaign to protest at his 'solitary confinement'. In his *Addresses*, he assured the radicals that no sacrifice of principle was involved in petitioning Parliament through the good offices of these moderate reformers:

We have not altered our opinions or our principles; but if they are *come up to our mark*, and allow the justice of our claims, let us in God's name, not draw back or stand still, but let us *one and all* hold out the olive branch of union, and receive them into our ranks with confidence and liberality. Try them, on my lads, with your *Petitions for the Captive*; demand that justice be done him.[25]

The ensuing campaign was a well co-ordinated operation. The Radical MPs briefed themselves very thoroughly: before presenting the petitions, Hume, Bennet and Hobhouse wrote separately to the 'Captive of Ilchester' for the very latest details of his unjust persecution.[26] Through Dolby's offices every MP was sent a printed copy of the petitions together with a suitable selection of Hunt's prison writings, including the *Peep*, his

[23] *TRR*, 24 Dec. 1821 and 12 Jan. 1822 Hunt hoped the profits from the powder would cover his other legal bills, see his letter to Wolstenholme, enclosed in Fletcher 27 Dec. 1820, HO, 40/15.

[24] University of Chicago: MS 563, Hunt Correspondence and Papers, item 45, Landsdowne to Hunt, 8 May, items 46, 48, 50 and 52, Sir R. Wilson to Hunt, 5, 28 June, 9 July and 3 Aug. 1822. *TRR*, 10 June, 14, 23 July and 29 Oct. 1822. Hunt brought a successful libel action against a newspaper which defamed the powder, see Osborne, 'Henry Hunt, 1815–1830', 192.

[25] *TRR*, 25 Feb. 1822.

[26] University of Chicago: MS 563, Hunt Correspondence and Papers, items 38–41, letters from Hume, 29 Jan., H. G. Bennet, 20 Feb., J. Hume, 22 Feb., and Hobhouse, 23 Feb. 1822.

correspondence with Peel and Bayley, and the relevant sections of his *Memoirs*.[27] Dolby also arranged for the parliamentary distribution of a special edition of a series of letters written by William Shepherd, the prominent unitarian, first published in the *Liverpool Mercury*, organ of the Burdettite Concentric Society, in which he discussed 'Mr. Hunt's unjust and cruel Imprisonment, his undaunted and humane exertions in effecting a Reformation in the Prison, in spite of all that Clerical Justices and their Understrappers could do to prevent it; and the cruel and unmanly Insults which he is now doomed to endure from those who are smarting at the exposure of their corrupt and cruel conduct'.[28] The campaign gathered further momentum when Burdett intervened and demanded Hunt's immediate release, on the grounds that his sentence was 'more severe than any which had been promulgated since the infamous time of the Stuarts . . . The sentence pronounced upon Mr. Hunt seemed not to have been applied to the offence, but to the individual—(*Hear.*) It was not an act of justice, but of vengeance.—(*Hear, hear.*) It was a paying off of old scores.' Not surprisingly, at this defence Hunt immediately jettisoned his stock-in-trade denunciation of Burdett and indulged in the most fulsome and obsequious adulation.[29]

The transfiguring of Burdett is the least attractive feature of Hunt's later prison writings, so much of which had been directed against this shoy-hoy reformer, and 'enemy to the People'.[30] Throughout his *Memoirs* it was Burdett's past cowardice, indolence and apostasy which provided the standard for his 'consistency by contrast'. In his *Addresses to the Radical Reformers*, he brought the diatribe up to date with a critical commentary on Burdett's 'temporizing conduct' and *rapprochement* with the Whigs. Burdett's postponement and final mishandling of the motion for an inquiry into Peterloo angered him intensely since he still believed that a proper investigation would vindicate the radicals and carry their cause. So strongly did he feel on this point that he adopted a special calendar: his second *Address* was dated 'Ilchester Bastile the 12th day of the 2nd year after the MANCHESTER MASSACRE, without enquiry', and a similar format was maintained in the following forty-odd issues. Hunt disapproved too of the way in which the wealthy Burdett succeeded in postponing the legal proceedings over his famous letter to the Westminster electors denouncing the massacre. Burdett, indeed, lost interest in Peterloo as soon as the

[27] John Rylands Library: English MS 378/1029, Hunt to W. Shepherd, 16 Mar. 1822.
[28] W. Shepherd, *Three Letters originally published in the Liverpool Mercury, with the introductory observations of the editor of that truly independent and liberal journal, on the subject of the Ilchester Gaol Investigation* (London, 1822).
[29] *PD*, 2nd series, vi, 151–9. *TRR*, 11 Feb. 1822. University of Chicago: MS 563, Hunt Correspondence and Papers, items 33 and 42, W. Shepherd to Hunt, 13 May 1821 and 25 Feb. 1822.
[30] Hunt to Saxton, 21 Oct. 1820, HO, 40/14.

Queen's Affair came to the fore and opened up the possibility of effective co-operation with the parliamentary opposition and the city reformers. When he was eventually convicted for the letter, Hunt refused to extend him any sympathy, noting that a three months' sojourn in the King's Bench in London was a suitable sham sentence for a sham reformer. Right until the moment Burdett spoke so eloquently on his behalf, Hunt continued on the attack, ridiculing his poor performance in the Commons by contrast with the industry and effectiveness of Hume and the Radical MPs.[31] Hunt's volte-face was thus sudden, transparent and distasteful. His fawning praise knew no bounds when Burdett announced his intention to move for the remission of his sentence and paid the 'Captive of Ilchester' a personal visit.[32] Burdett's present conduct, the obsequious Hunt proclaimed, 'convinces me that I must have been greatly deceived and mistaken in him'. In a quite remarkable reversal, he eulogized Burdett's 'truly great mind and innate nobleness of character' and condemned his own 'over-zealous mania' in advocating radical reform:

I was actuated, perhaps by an over zeal in the cause of Liberty, which frequently impels men to attack and quarrel with its best friends merely because they do not feel and act with the same warmth . . . because they do not fall into their particular views upon the subject, forgetting that the true spirit of Liberty entitles every man to think and act for himself, without being suspected either of desertion or apostasy. I fear that in my ardent pursuit of this great cause of Reform, I have been too prone to fall into this error.[33]

This recantation, a pathetic piece of self-interested temporizing, was Hunt's one and only lapse during his lengthy and hard fought career of uncompromising radical agitation. As he prepared to enter his third year of imprisonment in 'Ilchester Bastile' he welcomed sympathy and succour from any quarter. His obsequiousness towards Burdett proved a temporary aberration which came to an abrupt end when he returned to active politics on his release. But he did not forsake his essential radical spirit even while he panegyrized Burdett. Hunt had looked to the parliamentary Radicals for support in his campaign to end his 'solitary confinement'; he had no prior knowledge of Burdett's intention to move for his immediate release, a course he had never suggested himself; indeed, he went to great lengths to explain to his supporters that he was not really interested in remission. 'I have made up my mind', he wrote privately to William Shepherd, 'not to accept any thing short of a FREE PARDON':

I solemnly declare that I will accept of nothing less than that . . . The next Seven Months will soon pass away & I will not compromise one tittle of my Consistency.

---

[31] *TRR*, 1 July, 10, 23 Dec. 1820, 23 Jan., 10, 22 Feb., and 26 May 1821.
[32] Patterson, ii, 542–3.
[33] *TRR*, 24 Apr. 1822.

Perhaps you will blame me & call this obstinacy, but I must follow my own course in this respect.[34]

'I ask not—I want no mercy', he announced in his *Addresses* as the campaign for his remission gathered momentum, 'I demand justice, and *I do not wish one jot of my sentence abated*—I would rather rot in gaol . . . than sue for mercy; not I, indeed; I demand justice—justice upon the heads of the guilty murderers and their abettors.'[35] In the event, by the time Burdett's motion was debated, and was lost by 223 votes to 84, Hunt's situation in Ilchester gaol had improved considerably.[36] Thanks to the protests of the local reformers and ratepayers, the petitions of the northern radicals, and the parliamentary support of the Radical MPs, his 'solitary confinement' had been brought to an end, and visitors were freely admitted to his room. Much heartened by this success, Hunt thanked those who had helped his cause, assuring them that he would never cease in his endeavours to obtain 'a full, fair, and equal representation . . . upon the constitutional basis of ANNUAL PARLIAMENTS, UNIVERSAL SUFFRAGE and VOTE BY BALLOT.'[37] There were more victories to come. The commissioners' report created quite a stir when it was finally published. With Bennet and the other parliamentary Radicals pushing hard on the issue, the Government announced that Ilchester gaol was to be demolished and that Bridle was to be prosecuted. Hunt recorded all this with immense self-satisfaction and considerable self-congratulation.[38] Had he been in Parliament, he wrote to Shepherd, he would have used the commissioners' report to 'make such an impression upon the Country as should induce the people to demand with one voice a general & strict enquiry into the proceedings of every Gaol in England'.[39] In his gaol politics, as in his political activities generally, Hunt's inordinate concentration on self was in the best interests of a wider cause.

2. HUNT AND THE GREAT NORTHERN UNION

Hunt trusted that his success in gaol politics would strengthen his position within the radical movement during the period of critical self-analysis. His battles with the prison authorities were recited in full detail in his prison writings because they complemented his earlier platform credentials for leadership. But he took matters to quite absurd and reprehensible lengths.

[34] John Rylands Library: English MSS 378/1029, Hunt to W. Shepherd, 16 Mar. 1822.

[35] *TRR*, 11, 25 Mar., and 8 Apr. 1822.

[36] *PD*, 2nd series, vii, 2–49.   [37] *TRR*, 11 and 25 Mar. 1822.

[38] University of Chicago: MS 563, Hunt Correspondence and Papers, item 43, H. G. Bennet to Hunt, 27 Feb. 1822. *TRR*, 14 May and 23 July 1822.

[39] John Rylands Library: English MS 378/1029, Hunt to W. Shepherd, 16 Mar. 1822.

His sufferings and victories in Ilchester were magnified out of all proportion—'Where is the man that can say he has accomplished so much for humanity as I have accomplished, even when I was in bondage, under lock and key, and in the power of the inhuman tyrant and oppressor.' At the same time, he belittled or dismissed the sufferings of other imprisoned radicals. He was almost scornful towards the other Peterloo prisoners and their 'mere nominal imprisonment', and regarded it as a matter of pride and honour that his sentence was 'the most vindictive that has ever been passed since the reign of the Stuarts'.[40] By denying martyrdom to all but himself, Hunt was able to keep control of popular radicalism.

In Ilchester gaol 'Orator' Hunt turned writer, journalist and autobiographer in order to remind the radicals of his claims on their support. As well as the special pamphlets dealing with the Ilchester investigation, he brought out his notoriously immodest and unreliable *Memoirs* in forty-six parts. Often inaccurate, sometimes implausible, the *Memoirs* should be read as an exercise in political propaganda: through their columns, Hunt kept in regular contact with the popular radicals, reminding them with cumulative force of his early victories over the serried ranks of loyalists, Whigs, renegades, moderate reformers and shoy-hoys. On the blue wrappers for each issue there were details of the 'Tribute of National Gratitude to Henry Hunt, Esq.', established after the trial at York to cover the expenses incurred in his 'legal contests with the perpetrators and abettors of the Manchester Massacre'. Here too there were advertisements for his breakfast powder, the consumption of which promised 'a real benefit both to the AGRICULTURAL AND MANUFACTURING INTERESTS; to the former it gives profitable employment, while, to the latter it is a Beverage the most salubrious and economical'; and for his latest product, Hunt's British Herb Tea, 'pleasant and salubrious, and not more than one third the expence of the corroding, debilitating, noxious TAXED FOREIGN TEA'.[41] Stitched together with his *Memoirs*, and distributed with them to agents in forty-five towns from Andover to York, were his *Addresses to the Radical Reformers*.[42] In this diary of 'gaol politics' and commentary on current affairs the martyred Hunt tried to preserve the spirit and programme of the post-war radical campaign by promoting a system of national organization, and condemning all advocates of opportunism or revisionism.

From the start Hunt doubted whether the radicals would be able to maintain their hard-won independence and democratic programme with-

---

[40] *TRR*, 24 Sept. 1821 and 11 Feb. 1822. See also his letter in Bamford, 326–8.

[41] See the loose copies of Hunt's *Memoirs* in the Working Class Movement Library, Manchester.

[42] All these items were published by Dolby who regarded Hunt as exemplary in all financial and business transactions, evidence which should be placed alongside the well-known charges of Bamford and Johnson, see Dolby, *Memoirs*, 110.

out his commanding presence. The Queen's Affair confirmed his fears. An old supporter of Caroline, Hunt welcomed the controversy and was generous in his praise of the queen who had certainly eclipsed his popularity—'The Queen the Brave and persecuted Queen has worked miracles . . . she has prepared the Publick to receive the fruits of *our Exertions*'—but he disapproved of the way the Burdettites, Whigs and city reformers were exploiting the affair to recapture popular favour. He wrote to Mathew Wolstenholme, the Bolton radical leader, warning of the dangers ahead should the radicals be 'seduced by the Whigs or any other persons to petition the Infamous House of Commons'.[43] 'These are strange times,' he noted in a letter to Saxton, the Manchester agent for his *Memoirs* and breafast powder, '*my fingers itch to be doing more than I can effect in a Prison*'.[44] Through his correspondence with these leading Lancashire radicals, Hunt developed his plans, later published in his *Addresses*, for a system of popular organization which would preserve the independence and integrity of democratic radicalism. His proposals were an interesting mixture of self-conceit and political realism: he relied on his personal popularity as the people's champion and martyr to introduce a regular form of organization.

From the outset, he thought in terms of the largest possible body, based on the familiar subscription fund principle. 'Follow the example of the Methodists,' he advised Wolstenholme, 'every man should subscribe ½ or 1*d*. per week'. The first requirement, however, was the appointment of trustworthy leaders. Here Hunt was able to indulge in some characteristic egotism as he discussed the merits required at national level. 'You must not expect every man to sacrifice himself as I have done for the Public . . . I do not hear of a Man of the least consequence that is fit for it in London', he warned Saxton:

You ought to know the difficulties I have had to contend with amongst those with whom I have associated with Politically. I know no Man in England who is worth £500 a year that is an open friend to universal suffrage; with the exception of Major Cartwright & Sir Charles Wolseley. You know that I have never given up this point; if I would do that now I might be at liberty and in Parliament if I pleased; but I care not how the people behave to me and how they neglect me. I will never for one moment give up this point as long as I live.

Behind the bombast, vanity, and delusion, there was some political sense: in order to ensure incorruptibility and principle, the leadership had to be drawn from the ranks of gentlemen of independent means.[45] Much the same applied at local level: here Hunt looked to 'respectable tradesmen' to

---

[43] Hunt to Wolstenholme, Oct. 1820, enclosed in Fletcher, 27 Dec. 1820, HO, 40/15.

[44] Hunt to Saxton, 12 Oct. 1820, enclosed in Fletcher, 27 Dec. 1820, HO, 40/15.

[45] See the important analysis of O'Connor's gentlemanly status in Epstein, 92–3.

take the lead and manage the fund since they were unlikely to abscond, had sufficient time to devote to organizational matters, and were relatively free from economic persecution for their radical views, particularly if the local radicals practised 'exclusive dealing'. Such independent tradesmen, indeed, continued to play an important role in nineteenth-century radical organization: it was they who provided a network of premises, communication centres and meeting places for the working-class Chartists.[46] It was with the best intentions for the radical movement that Hunt announced his plan to establish a list of suitable tradesmen in each locality, but the scheme has been ridiculed or ignored by historians because of the showy nature of its presentation.

The much maligned 'knighthood' scheme[47] was made public during Saxton's visit to the 'Captive of Ilchester', when he came to present the Peterloo anniversary address signed by over 120,000 radicals. Hunt made the most of Saxton's visit, his first chance to discuss politics with one of his close supporters. 'I would give any thing to see you', he wrote to Saxton when the visit was first mooted: 'I have so much to say and so much to hear that cannot be conveyed in a letter, *never mind my sufferings . . .*'.[48] On arrival, Saxton was invested with a 'knighthood' according to the order of '*St. Henry* of Ilchester'. Such plagiarism of the distinctions employed by legitimate authority had a long popular history. The outcast queen had established her own order of 'St. Caroline of Jerusalem', an example which the Taunton radicals advised Hunt to follow so that he could reward all true radicals who came to visit him in Ilchester gaol. Through such familiar ritual and mummery, Hunt hoped to effect a wider purpose, the establishment of a 'sincere and efficient union', a permanent radical organization based around respectable and reliable local leaders or 'confidants'. Accordingly, he called for meetings to be held throughout the north at which the radicals were to elect these trustworthy leaders upon whom he would then confer 'the diploma of the order of the Cross of Ilchester'. The purpose of the exercise, a preliminary stage in his plans for permanent organization, was to provide 'a rallying point for all true radicals' at a time when the place-hunting Whigs and their Burdettite allies had seized the initiative over the Queen's Affair. It is easy to ridicule the scheme and censure Hunt's egotism, but the 'order of the Cross of Ilchester', together with the adoption of the white hat as the official radical symbol, was an important political gesture, an assertion of radical independence as the Whigs, stirred by the explosion of public discontent at

---

[46] D. Thompson, 152–72.
[47] See the scornful accounts in Bamford, 346–7; Huish, ii, 438; and Kent, 280.
[48] Hunt to Saxton, 12 Oct. 1820, enclosed in Fletcher, 27 Dec. 1820, HO, 40/15.

the ministers' treatment of the queen, started moving rapidly along the road to becoming a popular party.[49]

The knighthood scheme failed to rally the radicals, and the launching of the popular organization was perforce postponed. The Queen's Affair, an important boost to reform morale after the introduction of the Six Acts, brought an unwelcome division in radical ranks, and led Hunt away from organizational planning into heated ideological controversy. Many radicals welcomed the leadership of the Whigs and their renewed interest in reform: others turned away from constitutionalism in disgust and called for a republican revision. Flushed with victory in the Queen's Affair, Russell and the Whig reformers saw the chance of 'renewing the old and natural alliance between the Whigs and the people and weakening the influence of the Radicals with the latter.'[50] With the leadership's approval, Russell's reform proposals and Lambton's 'radical' bill were given another airing.[51] The Whigs, Hunt commented scathingly, had come up to Burdett's position, 'a week's march in the rear of the real Reformers'.[52] Some radicals, however, fell back from the front and talked of petitioning in support of Lambton's bill. Such desertion scandalized the ultra-radical delegates who met at Stockport in March 1821 and called for a new advance: in the name of the reformers of Yorkshire, Lancashire, Derby and Cheshire, they issued a republican declaration, insisting that the immediate priority was 'framing a National Constitution'.[53] This Paineite pronouncement was the work of Joseph Brayshaw, whose radicalism had previously been expressed in the most orthodox popular constitutional manner. It was the 'Queen's Affair' that converted him to republicanism, after an acrimonious clash with Baines and the 'Whig-gentry' at Leeds. When Baines hailed the withdrawal of the Bill of Pains and Penalties as a victory for 'our glorious constitution', Brayshaw retorted that the Queen's triumph was to be attributed 'entirely to the exertions of the people, aided by the public press, without being in the least indebted to any Constitution or laws existing in the country.' The laws of the land, he continued, were a mass of contradictory, vile and absurd rubbish: the much-vaunted Constitution was a nonentity. Thereafter Brayshaw headed a republican faction at Leeds which refused to accept any reform short of a written, republican constitution, in line with the policy recommended in Richard Carlile's *New Year Address to the Reformers* (1821).[54] Brayshaw's March declaration,

---

[49] *TRR*, 17 Nov. 1820 and 10 Feb. 1821.   [50] Quoted in Halevy, 104.
[51] Mitchell, 'The Whigs and Parliamentary Reform', 32–4.   [52] *TRR*, 11 Apr. 1821.
[53] R. Carlile, *An effort to set at rest some little disputes and misunderstandings* (London, 1821), 18–19. L. E. to Byng, 28 Mar. 1821, HO, 40/16 ff. 395–8.
[54] Brayshaw's letter, *MO*, 18 Nov. 1820. 'Whig management at Leeds', *BD*, 20 Dec. 1820. R. Carlile, *A New Year's Address to the Reformers of Great Britain* (London, 1821); and *Address to the Reformers of Great Britain*, 3 Mar. 1821.

apparently ratified by the other delegates at Stockport, was sent unsigned to Hunt and Wooler, who both declined to publish it. Hunt took a strong objection to the 'insufferable presumption' of the declaration, a veritable catechism of Paineite republican principles, 'a very different ground from that which the Reformers had always taken and publicly expressed'. He considered it 'downright tyranny and the greatest impudence' for the committee of delegates 'chosen by God knows who, and coming from God knows where . . . to pretend to say what shall and shall not be the Constitution or laws by which the whole shall be governed . . . this is one of the most sweeping acts of *despotism* that ever emanated from the brain of mortal man'. As in the past, he refused to have radicalism identified with republicanism or any other 'ism':

Let us have a House of Commons fairly chosen by the people, and then my worthies of the Committee, you may, if you please, submit to those representatives, the propositions contained in your declaration . . . Let us stick to the principle of Universal Suffrage and Vote by Ballot, by which to obtain an honest Parliament, and they will secure to us every blessing that Freedom can desire, or ought to enjoy.[55]

It was this decree which brought Carlile storming on to the scene.

In his prison cell at Dorchester, Carlile had spent much time ruminating on the failure of the post-war campaign. His disenchantment with the mass platform ran deep because he had entertained such high hopes of a successful confrontation with the authorities, particularly in the 'crisis' after Peterloo. With that opportunity squandered, he started to think in terms of a completely different approach to radical protest. Mass support, he believed, would not return until the next crisis, the timing of which depended upon 'the workings of our grand ally the Boroughmongers' debt, and the exchange of bank-notes for gold': in the interim, the radicals should concentrate on putting their ideological house in order. This meant the repudiation of popular constitutionalism and the adoption of rational republicanism. Thus he came forward to defend Brayshaw's 'extreme' declaration against Hunt's populist animadversions. 'If Mr. Brayshaw stood alone with his Declaration,' he proclaimed defiantly, 'I would defend it for the principle and sentiment it declares which are strictly in unison with my own.' By refusing to accept the principles of the declaration, Hunt and his supporters had shown themselves to be no better than 'the Wilkites, Pittites, Foxites, Burkites, and Burdettites'. In a devastating critique of bogus reform endeavour from the days of Wilkes to the 'Queen's Affair', Carlile demonstrated how 'great men' and mere political slogans had always taken precedence over principle and programme. The

---

[55] *TRR*, 25 Mar. and 11 Apr. 1821. See also *BD* 4 and 18 Apr. 1821.

name of Henry Hunt, he concluded, should not be 'the talisman for reform':

The Writings of Thomas Paine, alone, form a standard for any thing worthy of being called Radical Reform. They are not Radical Reformers who do not come up to the whole of the political principles of Thomas Paine . . . There can be no Radical Reform short of what is commonly called a Republican form of Government . . . The advocates of universal suffrage, who talk about their affection and esteem for royal families, and titled legislators, and certain priests and religions, are deeply tinged either with timidity or hypocrisy and corruption . . . Below the principles of Thomas Paine there can be nothing but sham-fighting with the enemies of the liberties of mankind.

After the controversy provoked by Brayshaw's declaration, Carlile now realized the 'necessity of holding up these principles as a test for the honesty of every public or private advocate of Radical Reform . . . I will divide the country, or all who call themselves Reformers, upon these principles'.[56] This defiant challenge was laid down just at the time when Hunt finally published his plans for a permanent popular radical organization to be known as the Great Northern Union.

The details of the GNU were announced to the Manchester radicals on the second anniversary of Peterloo when Shillibeer read out an address from Hunt recommending a national radical organization based on Methodist lines, 'a SUBSTANTIAL, a PERMANENT, and consequently an IRRESISTIBLE, INVINCIBLE *UNION* OF THE RADICAL REFORMERS OF THE NORTH, which will soon extend to the utmost corners of the kingdom'. In accordance with the popular, post-war subscription schemes, Hunt suggested that they should 'instantly begin to enrol names (the *grand object*) to subscribe one *penny* per week, to raise a FUND to enable the RADICAL OPERATIVES of the NORTH, to send ONE *Representative of their own* into the corrupt Senate'. He recommended the formation of a central committee at Manchester to assist every town in the north in establishing their own committees. These local committees would then divide their districts into sections under the leadership of a 'centurion' and five 'trusty men' drawn, like the 'knights', from the ranks of the radical tradesmen, the only traders with whom the people should deal—members of the union were enjoined 'not to lay out *one penny* of their money with any one unless he be a MEMBER OF THE UNION'. Each trusty man was to be responsible for a class of twenty—later changed to ten—'brothers', who were to subscribe a penny a week, while 3*d*. was expected from the trusty men and 6*d*. from the centurions. Within a year, Hunt calculated, the subscriptions of 100,000 brothers alone would amount to nearly £22,000, 'enough to purchase seats

---

[56] R. Carlile, *A New Year's Address to the Reformers of Great Britain* (London, 1821); *Address to the Reformers of Great Britain*, 3 Mar. and 24 June, 1821; and *An effort* (1821).

for five Radical Members, even if they were obtained at the Borough-mongers' price'. The Manchester radicals immediately adopted the scheme, and the new central committee proposed that the fund should first be used to secure Hunt's election at Preston, 'a talisman to throw open every city and borough in the kingdom'.[57] With the backing of the *Black Dwarf* and the specially revived *Manchester Observer*, a joint venture of Wooler and Saxton, the new union started well. Meetings were held in Nottingham, Leeds, Bolton, Blackburn, Barnsley, Royton, and Stockport to establish branches, and central committees were soon formed at Taunton, Newcastle and Leeds. When the radicals met to celebrate Hunt's birthday in November, it was clear that most localities highly approved of the GNU, particularly as it held out the promise of seeing their champion returned to Parliament.[58] Some radicals, however, questioned the ethics of the operation, since it appeared that the union was to indulge in 'boroughmongering' by purchasing seats.[59] '*All* means are fair against those who stop at no principle themselves', Wooler assured his readers, but when pressed on the same point Hunt insisted that no perjury or bribery was intended—'the sole object was, to devote the subscriptions towards paying the unavoidable expenses necessarily incurred to support a popular candidate at a contested election'.[60] Hunt was only too painfully aware how hefty these costs could be: at the top of his list of expenses incurred between his conviction at York and his liberation in October 1822, some £1,580 in all, was the sum of £470 which he had finally been compelled to pay the high-bailiff of Westminster for his share of the hustings expenses.[61] A more serious objection to the GNU was the fear that scarce resources would be diverted away from the relief funds for their imprisoned colleagues.[62] As prisoners themselves, Hunt and Wooler were sympathetic to the argument, and they applauded the policy followed at Birmingham and Coventry of '*first* relieving the wants of those who are suffering, and of forwarding the surplus, if any, to the funds of the Northern Union'.[63] In some areas, subscriptions were disappointingly low, not because of competition with relief funds, but because of the dishonest behaviour of patriots who had benefited from earlier collections. At Stockport, for example, there was a marked reluctance to contribute to any new subscription scheme since Bagguley 'went off with monies from Stockport and Macclesfield'.[64]

[57] *TRR*, 24 Aug. and 24 Sept. 1821. *BD*, 19 Sept., 10 Oct., and 7 Nov. 1821.

[58] *Wooler's British Gazette and MO* 25 Aug.–17 Nov. 1821. *BD*, 14 Nov. 1821. *TRR*, 24 Nov. 1821.

[59] R. Carlile, *Address to the Reformers of Great Britain*, 13 Oct. 1821.

[60] *BD*, 7 Nov. 1821. *TRR*, 12 Jan. 1822.   [61] *TRR*, 29 Oct. 1822.

[62] *BD*, 30 Jan. and 20 Feb. 1822, including the letter from the Nottingham Permanent Fund. *TRR*, 12 Jan. 1822.

[63] *BD*, 10 July 1822.   [64] Eckersley, 24 Jan. 1822, HO, 40/17 f. 39.

By the time of the first half-yearly meeting of the Manchester central committee, the GNU had made steady progress at a time when political excitement was low. Saxton reported that Manchester itself had despatched £40 to Sir Charles Wolseley, the union's esteemed treasurer and that branches had been established at Greenock, Carlisle, Preston, Blackburn, Bolton, Ashton-under-Lyne, Stockport, Leeds, Halifax, Bradford, Wakefield, Rochdale and other towns.[65] This solid but unspectacular beginning proved to be the high-point of the GNU. Ironically, Hunt must bear much of the blame for the failure to advance. His preoccupation with gaol politics during his 'solitary confinement' diverted attention and energies away from the promotion of the union.[66] Furthermore, the crude means by which he rallied support for his petitioning campaign, accentuating his own martyrdom by belittling the suffering of others, so antagonized the incarcerated Carlile that he redoubled his attacks on the GNU, using material provided by Brayshaw and the Leeds republicans to expose the new organization as 'a cheat that picks the pocket and corrupts the mind'.[67]

3. CARLILE AND RADICAL COUNTER-CULTURE

In his total repudiation of the GNU, Carlile, the sectarian ideologue, clashed head-on with Hunt, the great popular agitator, in a struggle concerning the very meaning and purpose of protest and reform. By promoting the GNU, Hunt was hoping to rouse flagging spirits and preserve some form of agitational framework. With its classes, sections and committees, accumulated funds and exclusive dealing, the GNU was designed to remind the people of their collective power. The borough-mongering plan, whilst giving the union popular appeal, was not Hunt's major concern: when taunted by Carlile, he readily renounced his 'well-earned' claim to be the first sponsored candidate.[68] What mattered to Hunt was collective unity and popular organization. 'There is public spirit enough in the country', he maintained, 'it only requires to be drawn together in one firm phalanx by one indissoluble Union.'[69] To this end, he exploited his 'charismatic' appeal to promote a regular form of organization, just as his successor, Feargus O'Connor, was to do in the age of the Chartists.[70] His plans for the GNU were announced on the anniversary of Peterloo, an occasion of the deepest reverence and respect, when nine Mancunian children were christened 'Henry Hunt' by the Revd J.

---

[65] *BD*, 30 Jan. 1822.
[66] See reports of Fletcher, Eckersley and Chippendale, Feb.–Mar. 1822, HO, 40/17.
[67] *Republican*, 20 Sept. 1822.
[68] *TRR*, 23 Jan. and 10 Aug. 1822.
[69] *TRR*, 24 Sept. 1821.   [70] Epstein, 93.

Scholefield.[71] The celebrations of his birthday in November provided the opportunity to 'cement the UNION of the real Radical Reformers'.[72] Hunt never missed the chance of using his personal popularity for the good of the cause. When he received various gifts on his birthday, including a particularly fine counterpane from the Bolton weavers, he decided—funds permitting—to mount a collection of these presents in London to be known as 'Hunt's Radical Museum', an institution 'dedicated to the industrious and enlightened Radicals of England, Scotland and Ireland . . . The Radicals have almost all honoured me with the title of the Champion of their political rights; I now voluntarily offer myself as the Champion of their *talent*, their *skill*, and their *industry*.' The museum would provide 'an ocular demonstration that all the wealth of the nation consists of the labour and talent of the useful or working classes; and that all the luxuries which the wealthy enjoy are produced by these useful classes, which they insolently call the "lower orders"'. Furthermore, the museum would assist organization and communication by providing a venue 'where the Radicals from all parts of the Kingdom may be sure to meet each other when they are in the metropolis'.[73]

From his prison cell, then, Hunt tried hard to rally the 'ragged radicals' and make them appreciate their collective strength. All the time he was busy planning for the next great radical mobilization, hoping to have '100,000 Radicals united and co-operating together, with eighty thousand pounds at their disposal', ready to take full advantage of the inevitable cataclysmic financial crisis which 'the debt and Mr. Peel's Bill must naturally produce'.[74] He refused to sit back and wait upon events: all his efforts were directed towards organization so that the mass platform could be reactivated with maximum speed and effect.

Carlile, by contrast, had lost all enthusiasm for agitation and mobilization. He was no longer interested in numbers and 'forcible intimidation'. His concern was to strengthen the quality, commitment and ideological rigour of the individual reformer, and purge the movement of its constitutional claptrap. Carlile's analysis of the failure of the post-war platform led him away from 'instrumental' towards 'expressive' politics, that is to say his radicalism became value-oriented rather than gaol-oriented: the defence of principle, the purity of ideology mattered most.[75] Where Hunt, the agitator, chafed at his confinement, Carlile, the purist, appreciated what he called 'the advantages of prison'. In Dorchester gaol he subjected himself to a rigorous regime of 'temperance by example': self-discipline, physical

[71] *Wooler's British Gazette and MO*, 25 Aug. 1821.
[72] *TRR*, 24 Sept. and 24 Nov. 1821.
[73] *TRR*, 24 Nov. 1821 and 22 June 1822.   [74] *TRR*, 24 Sept. 1821.
[75] For 'expressive' and 'instrumental' politics, see Wilson, 14–29; and Parkin, *Middle Class Radicalism*, 34–40.

puritanism, moral improvement and self-education, in the quest for a 'second birth of mind'.[76] As the complete reformer, political and religious, rational and ascetic, physical and moral, Carlile repudiated the ideological laxity, mere sloganizing, empty bluster, and personalized leadership of Hunt's agitational radicalism. Throughout his political career, Hunt had been 'nothing more than a little before the most forward, in what has been called the popular cause'; he had 'never yet rested upon any sound and definite principles'; he specialized in 'courting the prejudice of bigotry and superstition as a matter of popular applause and personal profit'. His latest ploy, the GNU, was 'one of the greatest humbugs that ever was attempted upon a cheated and deluded people'.[77] Instead of providing a forum for the necessary training in Paineite principles, Hunt was trying to mount another 'show' assisted by one or two others who persisted in putting names before principle:

Come, all good people, look at them and shout as nothing else is required from you but to pay your weekly pennies to support our show; which if you will do, you shall be excused from all further struggle from your liberties, as some half dozen of us, like the Catholic Priests, will take the burthen upon ourselves so as you support us well with your pay.[78]

The columns of the *Republican* were thrown open to those who disapproved of the diversion of funds away from the incarcerated victims whose numbers were now swollen by Carlile's family and shopmen who joined him, willingly or otherwise, in his struggle for the right to publish Paineite and other freethought material.[79] As further ammunition against the GNU, Carlile decided to chronicle the various disputes at Leeds which Hunt, Saxton and Wooler had chosen to ignore.

From the outset there had been arguments over the new union at Leeds,[80] but the contention became particularly heated when the radicals met to vote an address to Sir Charles Wolseley, recently released from prison and newly-appointed trustee and treasurer of the GNU.[81] Wolseley, the address proclaimed, had 'exhibited to the world the uncommon spectacle of rank, riches and talent, combating in defence of the people'. Brayshaw was appalled by this fawning tone, this 'compromise on the part of the Radical Reformers with the Aristocracy, on the subject of rank, rights, titles and privileges; a falling back which more than one of the persons who call themselves leaders of the Radical Reformers begin to exhibit'. He then deprecated the constitutional language of the address, reminding the radicals that the supposedly glorious struggles of the past were simply 'quarrels about dividing the spoil':

---

[76] Wiener, 55–75.   [77] *Republican*, 1 Mar. and 10 May 1822.
[78] *Republican*, 7 June 1822.   [79] Wiener, 76–100.
[80] *TRR*, 9 Oct. 1821 and 11 Feb. 1822.   [81] *BD*, 19 Dec. 1821.

The allusion to the British Constitution is an allusion to a phantom . . . The liberty of the people at large must not be founded on contests like those of our ancestors . . . their future liberty must arise from the progress of reason and philosophy.

The meeting came to a stormy conclusion after Brayshaw had been denounced as a 'visionary'. The address was amended to exclude any reference to Wolseley's rank, but the chairman decided to delay its presentation until a large subscription for the GNU was forthcoming, trusting that this would mitigate its disrespectful tone. This prompted Brayshaw to convene another meeting to censure the local leadership whose conduct was 'an insult to those who voted the Address, because most of those who voted for it decidedly disapprove of the principles on which the "Great Northern Union" is founded'. The GNU, he explained, was inconsistent with the principles of Paine and had no appeal for those who looked to the Stockport declaration as their creed. After the local leaders appealed to Wolseley for support, Brayshaw called a further meeting and heightened his attacks on the GNU, but the Leeds branch continued to contribute to the fund.[82]

While he gave national publicity and support to the Leeds republicans, Carlile criticized Brayshaw, a member of the Freethinking Christians, as 'but half a Reformer'.[83] An unerring ideologue, Carlile demanded strict adhesion to the Paineite formulary, religious and political, a complete identification with 'the Reformer of Priestcraft, as well as Kingcraft'.[84] In rediscovering Paine for the nineteenth century, and in highlighting the infidel mission, Carlile, it has been suggested, provided the radical movement with its nearest approximation to a 'counter culture' or counter-hegemonic ideology.[85] But in the process, he displayed the all too familiar weaknesses of the 'ideological' type of protest leader. His dictatorial, doctrinal pronouncements, as he reserved for himself alone the right of guardianship and reinterpretation of Paineite orthodoxy, divided the faithful and antagonized all the rest: they provoked schisms among the votaries in the free-thinking, self-improving zetetic societies;[86] and gave offence to the wider radical audience, where protest drew its strength from popular eclecticism and libertarianism. This explains why Carlile won so few radicals away from the GNU. Hunt was able to retaliate by attacking

[82] The meetings held between Dec. 1821 and Mar. 1822 were reprinted in full in *Republican*, 19 Apr.–10 May 1822. Carlile delayed publication because he intended to bring out a pamphlet about the controversy. See also *BD*, 22 May 1822.

[83] Carlile, *An effort*, 13.

[84] Carlile, *Address to the Reformers*, 13 Oct. 1821.

[85] G. A. Williams's introduction to E. Royle (ed.), *The Infidel Tradition* (London, 1976), x.

[86] For an excellent analysis of the zetetic movement, see I. McCalman, 'Popular Radicalism and Freethought in early nineteenth-century England', unpublished MA thesis, Australian National University, 1977, chs. 3 and 4.

his adversary's 'intolerant and bigotted dictation', in particular his injunction that 'no Reform can be of service till "*all religion* is destroyed"'. Hunt, of course, had a much better grasp than Carlile of popular attitudes and beliefs, political and religious. Infidelism, he realized, was not only anathema to middle-class juries but also an outrage upon popular feelings. 'I believe the great mass of the Reformers are religious,' he averred, 'but I hope they are neither bigotted nor under the influence of priestcraft.' Hunt articulated a popular, unsophisticated religious libertarianism:

I will, as long as I live, contend for the justice of placing all religions upon the same footing, and to establish full political liberty. I abhor priestcraft as much as the great Reformer, Christ did; I abhor all intolerance; I would have every one worship his Maker in his own way, and I shall certainly never trouble myself whether Mr. Carlile worships God or mammon. But I protest in my own name, and in the name of all the Reformers I ever knew, against the intolerant and bigotted dictation of Mr. Carlile.[87]

By such means Hunt was able to parry Carlile's criticism of the GNU, and retain the support of the great majority of the northern radicals. There were some defections: at Bolton, a small group of Carlile's followers decided to break away completely from the local branch of the GNU,[88] but elsewhere there was little dissension between radicals and republicans. Eclecticism was the norm in the localities, except at Leeds where Brayshaw pursued an exclusive Paineite line with renewed vigour after he had relinquished 'every system of religion'. He was called to account by the Christian Reformers at a series of meetings where fists started flying. Then came the inevitable charges of financial duplicity. Finally, he resolved to break his silence over the events of 1819–20 and issued a statement in which he accused the Leeds radical leaders of being 'the framers of the plot known by the name of the April Fool Plot, which produced the transportings of Yorkshire; the hangings, the beheadings, and the banishments of Scotland'.[89]

Commenting on Brayshaw's revelations, Carlile restated his reasons for demanding a thorough revision of radical endeavour. In the months after Peterloo, he admitted, he had considered that physical force was 'practicable': on reflection, he was glad that it had proved 'an opportunity lost':

There had never yet been any thing like a knowledge and a union upon sound political principles in this country; and until this can be effected, all attempts to reform had better be deferred. When the political principles laid down by Thomas

---

[87] *TRR*, 11 Mar. 1822.   [88] *TRR*, 25 May 1822.

[89] Brayshaw's letter to the Freethinking Christians, *Republican*, 21 June 1822. For his subsequent battles with the Christian Reformers, see *BD*, 10 July, and *Republican*, 26 July, 30 Aug. and 4 Oct. 1822.

Paine are well understood by the great body of the people, every thing that is necessary to put them in practice will suggest itself . . .[90]

To spread these principles and 'extend popular knowledge', he looked to the 'multiplication of reason' through a rational-republican press, free of 'delusion, error and falsehood'. There was no need for bombastic platform oratory, silly subscription schemes, or grandiose organizations like the GNU. When accused by Hunt of being 'a persecuted bookseller, but not a persecuted Reformer', Carlile replied that pamplet-vending alone was 'destined to work the great necessary moral and political change among mankind—The Printing Press may be strictly denominated a Multiplication Table, as applicable to the mind of man'.[91]

There was a fundamental difference of approach then, between Carlile, the sectarian ideologue, who looked to rational propaganda and individual ideological commitment, and Hunt, the popular agitator, who worked hard to preserve some form of mass involvement and organization within a popular constitutional framework. The points at issue, of course, were all but obscured by personal polemics. At the time of his 'solitary confine-ment', Hunt lashed out at Carlile, accusing him of running away at Peterloo and making money out of his politics and religion. Carlile, he insisted, deserved no sympathy for his lengthy confinement in Dorchester gaol:

. . . his cannot be fairly called a political offence, his was for maintaining, publishing, and selling theological opinions in opposition to the Christian religion . . . His, I always thought, a very different trade from mine; he was in the way always of *making money* by his politics as well as his religion—I always *spent money* in every political move that I ever made in my life.[92]

To refute Hunt's charges and debunk his leadership, Carlile enlisted the services of Joseph Johnson, who proceeded to draw up an itemized bill of the sums either appropriated or owed by the reprehensible individual 'who has so arrogantly called himself the Champion of Reform'.[93] Hunt, it must be admitted, did not provide a satisfactory explanation for every sum mentioned by Johnson, but Johnson, 'one of your mushroom Reformers who figured for a very short time upon the political scene in 1818 and 1819' was no more convincing in his reply to Hunt's counter-charges. The tool of both Carlile and Cobbett, Johnson was roundly condemned in the north once Hunt published the details of his treacherous negotiations with the Manchester magistrates immediately after Peterloo.[94] The events of 16

---

[90] *Republican*, 4 Oct. 1822.

[91] *Republican*, 1 Mar. 1822. *TRR*, 11 Feb. and 11 Mar. 1822.   [92] *TRR*, 11 Feb. 1822.

[93] *Republican*, 1 Mar., 12 Apr., 31 May and 14 June 1822. Johnson, *Letter*.

[94] *TRR*, 25 May, 24 Aug. and 9 Sept. 1822. J. Johnson, *Second Letter to Henry Hunt Esq.* (Manchester, 1822).

August were themselves the subject of bitter controversy. Hunt tried to discredit Carlile by accusing him of running away from St Peter's Field at the first sign of danger. His brief appearance on the platform, moreover, for which Johnson and others were responsible, had unfortunately allowed the authorities to stigmatize the radicals as Godless atheists and punish them accordingly. Johnson replied by reminding Hunt that the defendants had been convicted because of the 'very stupid resolutions' he had brought with him from Smithfield; and Carlile threw the charge of cowardice back in Hunt's face. He had refused to allow the people to come armed, and had thus permitted a massacre instead of leading a revolution: 'A better leader would have led to very different results. The disposition of the Reformers of Lancashire at that moment was for something more than clamouring "Hunt for ever" and being clamoured to with similar nonsense.'[95]

Carlile's recoil from the mass platform, and his proscription of the GNU, developed into a passionate hatred of Hunt and a near psychopathic suspicion of political organization, in which there was 'nothing but *nameism* . . . nothing but trick and trifling, ignorance, impudence and pomposity'.[96] Carlile and Hunt were never reconciled and there were to be some curious clashes in the future when Carlile, the republican ultra-radical, defended the compromises of the Catholic Emancipation settlement and the gradualism of the Reform Bill against Hunt's radical fundamentalism! At the time, Hunt retained the affections of the radicals, and the GNU withstood Carlile's rational-republican critique and Johnson's aspersions. Far more damaging, was the spread of indifference and apathy as the workers entered a period of comparative prosperity, enjoying cheaper commodities while the agricultural interest suffered considerable distress. 'The property refused to co-operate with the numbers of the country, in the contests of 1816, 1817, 1818, and 1819; because the system had not then reached the landed interest', Wooler explained in the *Black Dwarf*: 'Now the numbers hesitate to co-operate with the property, because the system, in its progression, has reached the landed interest, and released commerce and manufactures from a great part of its pressure.'[97] As Hunt tried to adjust to the altered economic circumstances, he found himself at odds with his old friend and mentor, William Cobbett, the self-professed champion of the distressed agriculturists.

[95] *TRR*, 11 Feb., 11 Mar., 24 Apr. and 14 May 1822, including the correspondence between Robert Wilde and Carlile. Johnson, *Letter*, 11. *Republican*, 1 Mar., 12 Apr., and 31 May 1822.
[96] *Prompter*, 3 Sept. 1831.
[97] *BD*, 29 Jan. 1823.

4. COBBETT'S DESERTION

When Cobbett returned from America in November 1819, within a week or so of Carlile's conviction for reprinting the *Age of Reason*, it appeared that he too was a disciple of Paine, whose bones he brought back with him. Cobbett, however, took care to dissociate himself from deism while he paid homage to the prescient author of *The Decline and Fall of the English System of Finance*.[98] Paine's financial predictions, Cobbett believed, were about to come true: the funding system was on the point of collapse, and a revolution in government was bound to follow. The rapid deflation consequent upon Peel's Act confirmed the prognosis. Much as he preferred gold to paper, Cobbett realized that Peel's Act would add immensely to the real burden of the national debt as the country returned to bullionism. By the beginning of 1821, he was offering to submit himself for broiling on a gridiron should Parliament succeed in carrying through with the Act without defaulting on the debt. By this time too, agricultural distress was deep and widespread, the result of falling prices and heavy taxes. Cobbett turned to the landed interest to campaign for what he called an 'equitable adjustment', a legalized reduction of all obligations—the national debt, leases, mortgages and other contracts—to meet the new price level, so that the burdens on one side and the benefits on the other would be approximately the same as they had been before the Government began its deflationary policy. According to his latest biographer, Cobbett concentrated all his energies on the agriculturists not because he believed they were particularly deserving, but because he regarded them as a means of gaining his objectives; he wished to exploit their political clout.[99]

Hunt's approach to these matters was very different. An agitator by nature, he had never agreed with Cobbett's assertion that reform could not occur until the funding system collapsed. The champion of the people, he was dismayed to find Cobbett 'too busily employed with the farmers and fundholders to notice the Radicals'.[100] Cobbett, he regretted, had deserted the popular cause to champion the interests of those who had displayed 'neither pity nor mercy to the Radicals, to the poor weavers and spinners, and mechanics, when they were in distress in consequence of the high price of provisions, they then laughed in their sleeves, and pocketed the cash'. Having suffered more than most from the loyalist prejudice and bigotry of the farmers and landowners, Hunt deprecated their newly-vaunted 'radicalism' which consisted 'not of principle, but of *empty pockets* and *no rents*'. Furthermore, he thought Cobbett was most unwise to 'shift our

---

[98] Hunt attended Carlile's trial, but repudiated deism at the dinner to welcome back Cobbett, see *BD*, 8 Dec. 1819, and *Republican*, 12 Apr. 1822.

[99] Spater, ii, 410–14.   [100] *TRR*, 24 Dec. 1821.

ground' by placing such emphasis on the 'equitable adjustment' and the reduction of interest on the national debt. The radicals, he believed, should still demand universal suffrage as the first priority, and thereby compel the boroughmongers to pay off the infamous debt. To start by reducing the interest was to begin at the wrong end: in the interests of the poor, reform must come first—'A Reformed House of Commons would not reduce the interest of the widow and the orphan, who have got their all in the funds, one shilling, till they have made the Boroughmongers DISGORGE those immense sums of which they have plundered the country.'[101]

This important contrast of approach was aggravated by personal considerations. Immured in gaol, Hunt was piqued both by Cobbett's success on the county platform and his failure to report on developments in 'Ilchester Bastile'. When Cobbett extolled the virtues of Sir Thomas Lethbridge, one of the county members for Somerset, and a vociferous parliamentry spokesman for the aggrieved agriculturists, Hunt was roused to fury. 'We know Sir Thomas of old,' the 'Captive of Ilchester' expostulated, 'and we shall not so easily be made to forget, that he has not only been a staunch supporter of that system which has reduced the country to its present state, but that he has been a persecutor of the Reformers.' It was old 'Leather-breeches' in fact who had publicly defended Bridle and the tyrannical Ilchester regime![102] Hunt's gaol politics, indeed, had hardened his radical instincts and led him to repudiate Cobbett's opportunistic intervention in county politics. While Cobbett toured the country, proselytizing amongst the ranks of the politically influential on the county platform in the hope of galvanizing the major landowners and county members, Hunt used 'Ilchester Bastile' as a base from which to radicalize county politics in Somerset, by mobilizing the small freeholders against the corrupt practices of the county establishment and the sitting MPs, Lethbridge and Dickinson.

It was *within* the county that Hunt sought an 'equitable adjustment' as he protested against the high county rate and the inflated salaries enjoyed by the surveyors, treasurers, clerks of the peace, 'perpetual' under-sheriffs and the like. As he predicted, the findings of the Ilchester investigation eventuated in a substantial reduction in the county rate, 'a saving on this SINK OF INFAMY alone of £2,000 a year'.[103] The delighted ratepayers then followed his advice and organized themselves as an independent electoral force to fight local corruption and extravagance. They succeeded in electing an independent candidate as coroner despite the 'Magisterial

---

[101] *TRR*, 22 June and 14 July 1822.   [102] *TRR*, 22 June and 23 July 1822.
[103] *TRR*, 5 May, 9 July, 9 Oct. 1821 and 22 June 1822. Hunt's letter 'To the Sheriff, Magistrates, Freeholders and County-Rate-Payers, of the County of Somerset', in *Investigations at Ilchester Gaol*.

dictation' exercised in favour of Lethbridge's nominee.[104] On the strength of this success, a permanent freeholders' union was formed under the leadership of Oliver Hayward and the Revd Henry Cresswell, two of Hunt's staunchest supporters in the county. Following Hunt's advice again, the union began a major registration campaign, hoping to increase the number of independent voters on the roll, and thereby 'emancipate the county'—Hunt offered to grant a freehold lease and hence the vote to those who had made encroachments upon the waste lands in the manor of Glastonbury.[105] According to Wooler, it was Hunt's success in mobilizing the freeholders which explained why he was treated so badly in prison and subjected to solitary confinement. Lethbridge and Dickinson were 'the secret authors' of this unjust treatment because they feared 'the *opposition* which Mr. Hunt is likely to awaken in the country . . . Freeholders' clubs, of various denominations, but uniting for the same purpose, of emancipating the county from the grasp of the minions of the Pitt System, have been formed at his request, and under his advice.'[106]

Hunt, then, was hoping to polarize and radicalize county politics, whilst Cobbett was seeking simply to exploit the financial grievances of the landed interest. Hunt's main target was not Lethbridge, but his colleague, Dickinson, the 'worthy Grenvillite Whig'. Dickinson, Hunt reported, enjoyed 'a very considerable plunder of the public money': every year he received some £2,000 clear profit from the duties charged by the Flat-Holm Lighthouse, for which he paid the Government an annual rent of £10. Furthermore, as chairman of the county magistrates and colonel of the East Somerset Yeomanry, he had 'feathered his nest pretty warmly', supervising the corruption which cost the ratepayers so dear. As one of his constituents, Hunt called upon Dickinson to provide a correct account of his receipts and disbursements for his various offices. This was the beginning of a sustained campaign on Hunt's release to reduce the rate still further, render all officials accountable, unseat Dickinson, and secure the return of an independent member for the county, 'totally unconnected with the Magistracy'.[107]

On his release and return to active politics, Hunt tried to offer a radical alternative to Cobbett's pragmatism, thereby clarifying the important differences between the two, previously somewhat obscured by personal obloquy and abuse. They had been on bad terms with each other almost from the moment of Cobbett's return from America. Disappointed by his reception, Cobbett treated his former colleagues rather coolly, including, his daughter noted, 'our friend Chasse [Hunt]; Papa begins to be sick of him and to find out that he is envious as well as the rest'.[108] Cobbett,

---

[104] *TRR*, 10 Dec. 1821.			[105] *TRR*, 12 Jan. 1822.
[106] *BD*, 27 Feb. 1822.			[107] *TRR*, 12, 23 Jan. and 10 June 1822.
[108] Anne Cobbett, 24 Dec. 1819, quoted in Spater, ii, 388.

however, was in need of his friends: on leaving the celebration dinner at
the Crown and Anchor he was arrested for debt and had to be bailed out by
Dolby and Hunt, who later accused him of trying to bilk his bail and cheat
his creditors.[109] Other factors explain their deteriorating relationship. In
the *Register*, Cobbett took little notice of the legal campaign over Peterloo:
Bamford noted that he was so jealous of Hunt's popularity that he chose to
'neutralize his powerful pen on the subject of the Manchester meeting, and
the extraordinary proceedings at York'.[110] To make matters worse, he
opened the columns of his short-lived daily venture, the *Evening Post*, to
one of Hunt's old Bristol antagonists, James Mills, who repeated his
allegations, first expressed in the *Examiner*, that Hunt had a 'government
protection' in his pocket at Peterloo. Sir Charles Wolseley rushed to
Hunt's defence, but Cobbett allowed the mendacious Mills the last word in
the controversy, much to Hunt's fury.[111] Then came Cobbett's admission
during the legal actions brought by Cleary and Wright that he had written
the famous letter denouncing 'one *Hunt*, the Bristol man . . . he rides
about the country with a whore, the wife of another man, having deserted
his own'. While Cobbett may have forgotten the letter, his wife had never
come to terms with Hunt's open relationship with Mrs Vince, and always
disapproved of her husband associating with such an adulterer and inviting
him to Botley. Hunt now repaid this inhospitality by publicly ridiculing her
poor housekeeping and inability to keep servants.[112] At this point, Cobbett
and Hunt seem to have broken completely; much to Dolby's annoyance,
Cobbett abruptly terminated the arrangement by which Hunt's publications
were distributed along with his *Register*.[113] Thereafter, Hunt's prison
writings regularly catalogued Cobbett's many acts of envy, malice and
meanness, including his recent derision of the gift of half a ton of breakfast
powder to the starving Irish as 'impudent, bragging "charity"'.[114]

Hunt and Cobbett were never fully reconciled. There was no ideological
issue at stake here: Hunt's only complaint against Cobbett's political
writings was that they taught their enemies too much, enabling the
boroughmongers 'to avoid those errors and those difficulties which they
would inevitably have fallen into'![115] The dispute was over strategy and

[109] *TRR*, 23 Jan. 1822. H. Hunt, *The Preston Cock's Reply to the Kensington Dunghill*
(London, 1831), 3–6.
[110] Bamford, 315 and 328, where he reprints Hunt's letter, 24 May 1820, complaining of
Cobbett's 'worse than neglect in not noticing the trial at York'.
[111] Mills's letters in *Examiner*, 14 Feb. and *Cobbett's Evening Post*, 17 Feb. Hunt's letter in
ibid., 14 Feb.; and 'Sir Charles Wolseley and Mr. Mills', *Examiner*, 6 Mar. 1820. Adelphi
University and Nuffield College: Cobbett Papers, Cobbett to Hunt, 24 and 25 Feb. 1820.
TRR, 23 July 1822.
[112] Spater, ii, 427–8. Hunt, *Memoirs*, iii, 21 and 30.
[113] See notes by Dolby at end of *TRR*, 24 Apr. and 22 June 1822.
[114] *TRR*, 23 July and 10 Aug. 1822. *The Times*, 4 Sept. 1822.
[115] *TRR*, 23 July 1822

tactics. Where Hunt was a radical fundamentalist, Cobbett was a pragmatic reformer, prepared to co-operate with those within the political nation in the interest of financial and/or gradualist political reform. During the Queen's Affair, he had managed to straddle two audiences, as it were, the politically influential and the people on the streets: his success here undoubtedly evoked some jealousy in the imprisoned Hunt. After this, however, he ignored the people in order to capitalize on the grievances of the landed interest, just as he was later to concentrate his efforts on the manufacturers and the middle classes when they acquired an interest in reform at the end of the decade. Such tactical expediency, sensible as it may appear, undermined Hunt's efforts to mobilize the people and develop a strong radical challenge. Cobbett gave the most extensive coverage to the plight of the agricultural interest and their moderate reform programmes, but he never reported (or encouraged) the progress of the GNU. Like Carlile, Hunt's other main antagonist, he had no time for radical organization, for the hard slog of mobilizing the people into an effective mass force. Rather than rebuild the popular movement from below, he preferred to throw in his lot with the class or interest that felt most aggrieved at the time. Several years later, this opportunist frame of mind, led Cobbett to defend the Whig Reform Bill against Hunt's radical opposition. The overwhelming problems and enmity which Hunt encountered during the Reform Bill agitation can be traced back to the controversies in the early 1820s with Cobbett, the opportunist, and Carlile, the ideologue.

5. LIBERATION

The celebrations which marked Hunt's release at the end of October 1822 testified to the decline in radical support and activity now that the people were 'much engrossed by the Engagement of the Blessings of Peace and Plenty'.[116] Hunt tried to make the most of the occasion, emerging from 'Ilchester Bastile' in suitably flamboyant manner, sporting the Argyle tartan cloak which the reformers of Greenock had presented to his 'Radical Museum', and proudly displaying the gold medal and chain which the female reformers of Leeds had given him after his trial at York. He lost no time in returning to active agitation. At the celebrations in Ilchester and the neighbouring towns, he started campaigning for a radical initiative in the county which would eschew a narrow concentration on agricultural distress. In his speech from his barouche outside the inn where breakfast was to be taken, he stressed the need for unity in the pursuit of radical reform:

[116] Chippendale, 14 Mar. 1822, HO, 40/17.

The object of the present government is to set the labourer against the farmer . . . for each class to press the other to the ground . . . I would caution both the labourer and the farmer against the consequences of such mutual discord—it is both of your interests to resist this snare, and you can do so by taking one course, and only one; which is to join the manufacturing interests in seeking a reform in the representation of all Englishmen.

At the breakfast, he was presented with a silver flagon and salver from the grateful ratepayers, who were delighted when he produced a specially prepared requisition for a county meeting to petition for redress and reform. After the breakfast, there was a triumphal procession through the county to Glastonbury where he held a court leet, followed by a public dinner at which he drummed up support for the county meeting. The Six Acts, he regretted, had curtailed all other avenues of protest, but by taking to the county platform the radicals would soon 'make the *namby pamby* politicians quake'.[117]

Throughout the country there were bonfires, dinners and processions to celebrate his release. There were festivities in southern market towns like Petersfield, and in the fenlands at Holbeach, Spalding, Glinton, Outwell, and Tydd St Mary, but most of the celebrations were in the industrial districts.[118] Full details of the festivities at North Shields, South Shields, Widdrington and Newcastle, where the Winlanton iron-workers' band was in attendance, were reverentially recorded in the first issue of the new monthly magazine published by the central committee of the GNU at Newcastle, the one area where the union was still quite strong.[119] In Yorkshire there were celebrations in Leeds, Holbeck, Hull, Skipton, Bradford, Huddersfield, Wakefield and Halifax; in Lancashire and the north-west at Manchester, Rochdale, Ashton-under-Lyne, Bolton, Padiham, Blackburn, Darwen, Oldham, Hollinwood, Royton, Bent Green, New Mills, and Carlisle; in the midlands at Nottingham and Coventry; and in Scotland at Glasgow and Greenock. In all, Hunt received about a hundred addresses of congratulation from radical groups up and down the country.[120] But these numerous festivities simply confirmed Hunt's enduring popularity with the radical stalwarts: his release did not occasion a great display of numerical force; it was celebrated by the faithful few in each locality. At Manchester, Norris dismissed the constables early, and reported to Peel that the evening had 'put a complete extinguisher upon Mr. Hunt and his followers here for the present'.[121]

---

[117] *BD*, 6 Nov. 1822. Huish, ii, 443–9. Town Clerk, Glastonbury, 31 Oct. 1822, HO, 40/17.
[118] *BD*, 6 and 13 Nov. *TRR*, 6 Dec. 1822.
[119] *Northern Reformers' Monthly Magazine*, Jan. 1823. For the origins of this GNU journal, see *BD*, 18 Sept. 1822. There are several items on the GNU in the north-east in *Political Tracts 1822–23*, a volume of press cuttings and pamphlets in the British Library.
[120] *TRR*, 6 Dec. 1822. [121] Norris, 30 Oct. 1822, HO, 40/17.

Hunt's 'triumphal' entry into London on 11 November also attested to the decline in popular support for radicalism. He claimed that some half a million lined the streets, but this was a gross exaggeration: the occasion was but a mere shadow of the events of September 1819.[122] Although the numbers were disappointing, the London festivities served a useful purpose by strengthening Hunt's links with the organized workers. The procession was arranged by a trades' committee led by William Washington and drawn from members of the Mechanics Union, which had co-ordinated the impressive trades' demonstrations in support of the Queen and in honour of the two workmen killed in the heroic struggle for control of the streets during her funeral cortège. The Queen's white flag was duly striped with green to welcome the 'Captive of Ilchester', and individual trade societies were invited to take their 'proper rank' in the procession alongside their fellow mechanics. Speaking after Gast had delivered the address of welcome, Hunt made a point of identifying the radical programme with the interets and needs of these 'labouring classes'. The true radical, he explained, was 'an honest man—a man who wishes to possess and to enjoy the fruits of his labour; and at the same time is determined to resist the attempt to take away from him any portion of them, for the purpose of lavishing it in the support of the lazy, the idle, the indolent, the profligate, and the corrupt (*Cheers*)'. All the old oratorical devices were then given another airing as he reaffirmed his leadership:

Have I ever done any thing for myself? ('*No, no; you have lost a good deal.*') Have I ever deceived my fellow-countrymen? ('*No, no; never.*') No! nor I never will:—in the face of God, and of you all, I solemnly declare I never will. (*Loud and repeated cheers.*)

On his release from prison, Hunt stuck fast to his radical colours despite, it would seem, the temptation to withdraw. During the heated disputes over the Reform Bill a decade later, he alleged repeatedly that the Whigs had tried to buy him off as soon as he was at liberty with Sir Charles Wolseley acting as intermediary. "'You see," said he, "it's of no use to fight for the people; they won't protect you from being sent to gaol." I said "thank God, I have a small patrimony left, a hand to work, if necessary, for my support, and a heart to spurn such a thing."' Wolseley vehemently denied that any such conversation had occurred, but he declined to discuss the issue with Hunt face to face.[123] Whatever the truth, there can be no doubt of Hunt's parlous financial position at the time of his release. The 'Tribute of National Gratitude' covered only a fraction of the expenses he

---

[122] This account is based on: 'Proceedings of Mr. Hunt's Committee', HO, 40/17; Peel to Lord Mayor, 9 Nov., HO, 41/126; *BD*, 13 Nov., and *TRR*, 6 Dec. 1822.

[123] See Hunt's speeches in *Penny Papers*, 23 Apr. and *Preston Chronicle*, 12 Nov., and Wolseley's letters in *CPR*, 23 Apr., and *Ballot*, 13 Nov. 1831.

had incurred since his conviction,[124] and his patrimony was quite insufficient to provide for Mrs Vince and Miss Gray as well as himself. Despite his whole-hearted commitment to radicalism and the people, boldly proclaimed on his 'triumphal' return to London, he was forced to spend most of his time not on the platform but in his roasted-grain manufactory. Thanks to his indefatigable energy, however, and recharged by his liberation, Hunt the businessman was soon enjoying some of the prosperity which had steadily undermined the post-war radical movement.

---

[124] The sum of £913.14*s*.11½*d*. was acknowledged on the wrapper of the 42nd issue of his *Memoirs*, 14 Sept. 1822.

6

Reform in the 1820s

In the annals of pre-Chartist working-class history, the 1820s generally feature as the crucial period of intellectual advance. Agitation was at its nadir, but theorizing flourished, preparing the way for the maturation of class consciousness in a movement geared to the grievances and needs of the new industrial workers.[1] The old preoccupation with political corruption was cast aside in favour of a 'new ideology' based on the labour theory of value: the old *petit-bourgeois* emphasis upon the state and taxation was superseded by a more class-based conception of exploitation within the economic process itself. Such a distinction between politics and economics, *petit-bourgeois* perspectives and working-class consciousness, the old ideology and the new, distorts the reality of the radical challenge in the first half of the nineteenth century: it overlooks the working-class character of the post-war movement; exaggerates the role of theorists and ideologues; and obscures the fundamental continuity of radical language, ideology and endeavour from Hunt at Spa Fields to O'Connor on Kennington Common.

By 1819 the radical movement derived its vigour and character from the prominence accorded to working-class interests and working-class pride. It was precisely because popular radicalism was so working-class in tone and perspective that the movement proved so impervious not only to the economic and political liberalism of the 1820s, but also to the anti-political and anti-class prescriptions of Owen and other expositors of the labour theory of value. At the popular level, there was no room for the exclusive spirit of the theorists, and no need to choose between political reform and economic and social reform, the rights of man and the rights of labour, as if they were competing ends. Popular radicalism displayed remarkable eclecticism and continuity: the 'new ideology' did not displace the old attitudes, concepts and aims: it reinforced them. The radicals persisted in explaining the essential division in society and the process of exploitation in political terms. Just as the funding-system had been built on the base of political monopoly so it was political power that underpinned the capitalist system and denied the worker his natural rights, the full fruits of his labour. The 'new ideology' simply extended the ranks of radical demonology: alongside the fundholders, sinecurists, pensioners and other tax-gorgers, there now sat the capitalists, parasitic middlemen whose privileged and

[1] Thompson, *Making*, ch. 16. Hollis, chs. 6 and 7.

tyrannical position of unequal exchange stemmed from the monopoly of political and legal power possessed by the propertied governing classes. The fundamental radical demand, whether voiced by Hunt or O'Connor, and whether directed against the tax eaters and/or the capitalists, was always the same: an end to the system which left labour unprotected and at the mercy of those who monopolized the state and the law.[2]

Hunt had no difficulty in coming to terms with the new ideology of the 1820s. His radical programme, so well attuned to popular attitudes and needs, absorbed the rights of labour, the new formulations of the time-honoured labour theory of value, just as readily as it had earlier subsumed the rights of man. In these unfavourable years, he worked particularly hard to keep the radical programme in the public eye, intervening in constitutional extra-parliamentary politics wherever he could in the hope of reactivating the independent radical platform around the contentious issues of the day. Throughout these efforts there was little evidence of the egotism that had bedevilled his politics in the unnatural isolation of 'Ilchester Bastile'. Happily domiciled in Stamford Street with Mrs Vince and Miss Gray, Hunt proved a worthy champion of the people's cause, fighting a wide-ranging battle for radical reform and democratic accountability at every level of the unreformed political system. Business provided another outlet for his natural vigour. The former gentleman farmer became a successful entrepreneur, manufacturing and marketing an extraordinary range of products, but true to character, he was a difficult business partner and a ready litigant. His commercial success owed much to his political notoriety, a reciprocal relationship which provided him with the financial wherewithal to campaign on such a broad front in so many different arenas in the 1820s. His persistence finally paid off. By the end of the decade, the problems of 'cash, corn, and catholics' had transformed the pattern of parliamentary politics, and reform came to the top of the agenda. Thus having kept the radical cause alive throughout the 1820s, he provided the rallying point for those who eschewed the new liberalism and moderate reform, and sought to secure working-class interests by demanding the full radical programme.

I. RADICAL BUSINESSMAN

After his release from prison, Hunt found that he could no longer rely on his patrimony and remaining landed holdings for a comfortable existence for himself, Mrs Vince and Miss Gray. Accordingly, he devoted his considerable energies to a number of business ventures, starting with his

---

[2] Stedman Jones, 'Rethinking Chartism', draws attention to the continuity and limitations of 'proletarian theory' during this period.

famous breakfast powder. Here, of course, business and politics combined: the roasted grain was designed both to boost the domestic agricultural economy at a time of depression, and to provide the poor radicals with a cheap, healthy alternative to highly-taxed, imported coffee. The protracted legal struggles with the Exchequer added to the fame of the product, and the business expanded rapidly after Hunt's release, when he took up residence at 36 Stamford Street, a stone's throw away from his factory and furnaces in Broadwall, Blackfriars.[3] He was later to diversify quite considerably, but he continued to produce his breakfast powder: in 1832 it was advertised as the best, cheapest and surest means of avoiding infection by cholera morbus, quite the 'most salubrious and nourishing Beverage that can be substituted for the use of TEA AND COFFEE, which are always exciting, and frequently the most irritating to the Stomach and Bowels'.[4] For a short while in the early 1820s he also marketed his British herb tea, 'a judicious mixture of the most wholesome, nutritious, and grateful Aromatic Herbs',[5] but his biggest business success was in a different field altogether, the manufacture and sale of his 'matchless' blacking.

From the Post Office and trade directories, it would seem that Hunt started manufacturing shoe-blacking in 1825.[6] It was an immediate success, enjoying much free publicity from satirists, cartoonists, playwrights, hecklers, and political opponents, none of whom could resist cheap jokes and gibes about Hunt 'the Blacking Man'.[7] Hunt welcomed his new sobriquet, particularly as it was so good for business and made his 'matchless' a household name, but he refused to allow anyone to score political points at his expense or denigrate his social status. Following some derogatory comments in the Commons, Alexander Baring received a complimentary bottle of 'matchless' in gratitude for the free publicity, together with a curt note, assuring him that the 'Blacking Man' would prove 'quite as good and efficient a Member of the Community, (whether within or without the Walls of Parliament) as the *Loanmonger* or the *Stockjobber*'.[8] Similarly, Hunt did not object to the various theatrical representations of himself and his 'matchless' until politics were involved. He was so delighted by the prominence of his product in the pantomime at

---

[3] T. Allen, *History and Antiquities of the Parish of Lambeth* (London, 1826), 319.

[4] *PMG*, 21 Jan. 1832. See also *AHH* (13), 9 Jan. 1832.

[5] See the advertisements for his breakfast powder and tea on the blue wrappers of his *Memoirs*.

[6] I am grateful for the assistance of Mr D. R. Webb of the Bishopsgate Institute in locating information about Hunt's business activities.

[7] See, for example, M. D. George, *Catalogue of Political and Personal Satires* (vols. x and xi, London, 1952–4), x, nos. 15124, 15150, 15422, and innumerable items in vol. xi (1828–32); and Hunt, *Deep Mourning. Wig v. Blackball* (London, 1828).

[8] Stevens-Cox Collection: Hunt to Baring, 14 Feb. 1826. See also *CPR*, 9 May 1829 and 18 Dec. 1830.

the Drury Lane Theatre that he sent the manager a set of genuine labels to stick on the props, but he disapproved strongly of the farce at the Royal Coburg, 'London Characters', and protested to the management about their 'gross breach of common decency, after the promise made me through your Prompter that nothing *political* should be introduced amongst the other ridiculous matter that had been written to misrepresent my character'.[9] Hunt, incidentally, was a great lover of the stage. He attended the theatre regularly in London, and made special visits whenever he was in the northern towns. Much to his delight, his ward, Miss Gray, chose to take up a career on the boards,[10] and he was quite disgusted when the Quakers refused to attend a public meeting to set up a subscription fund for the sufferers and bereaved after the tragedy at the Brunswick Theatre where the roof had collapsed in the middle of a performance.[11]

Thanks to his political notoriety, Hunt's blacking business prospered: one advertisement in 1829 claimed that the 'matchless' was available at 6,000 outlets in London.[12] Business and politics were seldom kept separate. The vans which distributed the blacking were put to a variety of political purposes over the years, serving as hustings at meetings, floats at processions, and transport for poor electors; even the labels on the bottles carried a political message in the 1830s when, to prevent fraud, they were embossed with the slogan 'Equal Laws, Equal Rights, Annual Parliaments, Universal Suffrage, and the Ballot'.[13] As the business flourished, Hunt developed a subsidiary line, his 'easy-flowing, never-fading, writing ink', much praised and favoured by radical publishers like Henry Hetherington.[14] His next step was to venture into the continental market in partnership with Sir Charles Wolseley and another friend, 'Frederick Slade.[15] In October 1828 an agreement was signed by which the profits from the manufacture and sale of '*Cirage Anglais*' were to be split twelve ways, four parts to Hunt, who 'brings into the Partnership his knowledge in point of fabrication and his two brevets of innovation', two parts to his son, Henry, and the remainder to the partners who were to provide the first 50,000 francs capital for the factory in Paris—three parts to Slade, two to Wolseley, and one to Eyre, who was to manage the concern along with

[9] Stevens-Cox Collection: Hunt to Winston, 3 Jan. 1826. University of Chicago: MS 563, Hunt Correspondence and Papers, items 60 and 61, correspondence between Hunt and S. B. Davidge and Co., 7 and 12 Dec. 1825.

[10] Ibid., item 59, Hunt to Davenport, 3 July 1825.

[11] *TFP*, 8 Mar. 1828.

[12] Stevens-Cox Collection: H. Hunt jun. to Hunt, 19 July 1829.

[13] *Destructive*, 9 Feb. 1833.

[14] Ibid., 13 July 1833.

[15] University of Chicago: MS 563, Hunt Correspondence and Papers, item 70, draft agreement between Hunt, Wolseley and Slade, 17 July 1828.

Henry Hunt junior.[16] From this arrangement Hunt hoped to clear £1,000 a
year for himself and provide some gainful employment for his son, recently
returned from Illinois.[17] Things went badly from the start, and the young
Hunt found fault with every aspect of the business: the formula produced
blacking of poor quality; the English bottles took too long to arrive and
were far too expensive; the French workers were loathsome ('I hate
frenchmen in general', he confided to his father); and as for the partners,
Eyre was an 'old woman', and Wolseley too fickle and meddlesome.[18]
Slade tried to sort things out, but further arguments developed when Hunt
senior presented the partners with hefty bills for the supply of bottles,
labels, and the like, his trouble-shooting trips to Paris, and the losses he
had incurred by sending out three of his best workmen from Blackfriars.[19]
The partners registered their objection by withholding the salary to Hunt's
son. Since his father refused to undertake the payment, Hunt junior threw
in his lot with the partners who now decided to remove Hunt from the
business altogether, by dissolving the partnership on a majority vote and
then starting up on their own again. Hunt, they maintained, had been
treated far too generously in the original agreement, particularly as his
patents were useless and his name was not the sales asset in France that it
had proved to be in England.[20] After a lengthy legal process, Hunt was
finally awarded 5,000 francs compensation with costs.[21] By this time,
however, the new partnership was in serious financial difficulties, and in
August 1830 Hunt's son decided to flee Paris, taking with him the cash in
hand and the English workers.[22] This led to an interlocking series of legal
actions. First, there was the partners' appeal to the Cour Royale against
the arbitration award;[23] then there was their claim for compensation
against Hunt's son;[24] and finally, there was another action relating to the
original partnership in which Wolseley, Slade and Eyre accused Hunt of
contaminating the blacking with beer and the ink with urine.[25] In each

[16] Stevens-Cox Collection: Agreement, 20 Oct. 1828, copies in English and French. There
are three bound volumes of several hundred manuscript items in this private collection
relating to Hunt's business activities in France: the following references are to this collection
unless otherwise stated.
[17] Hunt to Moore (his attorney in Paris), 7 Oct. 1829.
[18] H. Hunt jun. to Hunt, 10, 17 Nov., 25 Dec. 1828, 8 Jan. and 11 Mar. 1829.
[19] Slade to Hunt, 6 Feb. and 3 Mar.; Eyre to Hunt, 16 May; H. Hunt jun. to Hunt, 23 May;
and Hunt to Moore, 15 Sept. 1829.
[20] H. Hunt jun. to Hunt, 18 Aug.; Moore to Hunt, 28 Sept.; and Hunt to Moore, 7 Oct.
1829.
[21] Hunt to Moore, 10 Jan. 1830; Moore to Hunt, 26 Oct., 23 Nov., 7 Dec. 1829, 21, 28 May
1830; Thomas to Moore on the 'jugement arbitral', 16 July 1830.
[22] Lancashire Record Office: Hunt Correspondence, DDX/113, Hunt to Moore, 19 Aug.
1830.
[23] Hunt to Moore, 11 Oct., and Moore to Hunt, 15 Oct. 1830.
[24] Tribunal of Commerce, 4 Nov. 1830.
[25] Moore to Hunt, 28 Jan. 1831.

instance, Hunt emerged triumphant: the partners lost their appeal and the contamination case, and, hard as they tried, they failed to implicate Hunt in his son's flight.[26] At first Hunt regretted the dispute with Wolseley who, he informed his attorney, had been 'very kind to me and twice visited me when I was in prison'. But as the legal actions dragged on and arguments developed over the Reform Bill, Hunt finally instructed that no quarter should be given to the 'Blaguard Wolseley'.[27] In the end, he was advised by his attorney to accept a compromise settlement offered by Wolseley and the other partners.[28]

Undeterred by the failure of the blacking venture, Hunt tried to introduce a different type of product into the French market, his patent composition fuel. In May 1830 he purchased five patents for this artificial coal which he intended to sell in France, 'where fuel is so scarce and so dear'. As the July revolution caused a crisis in business confidence, he was unable to attract any financial backers, but he hoped to turn the political situation to his advantage. Addresses of congratulation to Lafayette and the people of Paris from radical groups in London were forwarded with details of the new product which brought to complete perfection 'the art of manufacturing a cheap, a wholesome, a beautiful substitute for that first necessary of human life *Fuel*'.[29]

For the domestic market, Hunt introduced another, more expensive product, his patent waterproof composition, 'one of the most useful inventions that ever was offered to the public', Cobbett admitted. Available in shilling bottles from all the usual outlets, including the new Westminster Co-operative Trading Association, it was 'warranted to keep one person's Boots or Shoes dry for a year'.[30] Despite the quite remarkable expansion of his business interests, Hunt managed to preserve his close links with the agricultural community. He regularly toured the west country where he had seventy-three agents handling yet another of his products, annatto, a dye used for colouring cheese.[31] In his last years, most of his business was conducted in these familiar parts, the one steady market after his other sales collapsed in consequence of his unpopular stance over

---

[26] Moore to Hunt, 21 Mar., 27 May, and 15 July 1831. In England, Hunt also won an action against a supplier of defective bottles for his blacking, see *WFP*, 30 Oct. 1830.

[27] Hunt to Moore, 8 Dec. 1830, 2 Feb., 17 Aug., and 15 Nov. 1831.

[28] Moore to Hunt, 29 Aug., 7 Oct., 25 and 28 Nov. 1831.

[29] Moore to Hunt, 28 May, 15 Oct. 1830, and 3 Oct. 1831. Hunt to Moore, 11 Oct. 1830 and 28 Oct. 1831. University of Chicago: MS 563, Hunt Correspondence and Papers, item 75, agreement between Sunderland, Tachariah and Hunt, 15 May 1830; and item 78, Hunt to Lafayette, 1 Sept. 1831.

[30] *CPR*, 25 July, and *WFP*, 21 Nov. 1829. Stevens-Cox Collection: Hunt to the editor of the *Mirror*, 17 Aug. 1829.

[31] See the account of his Nov. 1830 trip in *PD*, 3rd series, ii, 249–50.

the Reform Bill.[32] Hunt's uncompromising radicalism finally cost him
dearly.

2. COUNTY POLITICS

Business kept Hunt in London for much of the time, but he remained an
active—and unwelcome—participant in Somerset county politics, heading
the challenge against the corrupt county establishment. Soon after his
release from gaol, he returned from London to attend the two county
meetings at Wells in January 1823. This was the time when Cobbett and the
Whigs were making all the running in distressed agricultural areas, but
Hunt stood forward to propound a radical programme designed not for the
aggrieved landed interest but for the lower orders, the poor ratepayers,
small farmers, and labourers.

   The persistence of agricultural distress in the early 1820s produced a
strong demand for reform in the counties. Agriculturists now blamed
internal underconsumption rather than foreign competition for the chronic
low prices: instead of lobbying for higher protection, they condemned the
Government for its high taxes and deflationary currency policy which cut
into consumer spending and stifled demand.[33] This was the point of entry
for the Whigs to promote a programme of moderate reform and
retrenchment. In Yorkshire there was talk of reviving the famous
'association' movement of the late eighteenth century: a committee of
leading Whigs and landowners, chaired by Walter Fawkes, tried to co-
ordinate a campaign of county meetings for reform in the opening months
of 1823.[34] Disheartened radicals like Wooler bitterly regretted that Fawkes
and his kind had not taken this step back in 1819 'when the PEOPLE were so
ready and eager to have seconded it to advantage. It is unfortunate that the
"natural leaders" of the people, and the people have never moved together
or acted in concert.'[35] But the Whigs and the natural leaders did not have
the stage completely to themselves. Cobbett entered the '*deadly dispute*
between the *Land* and the *Funds*', and enjoyed considerable success on the
county platform. At the famous Norfolk meeting on 3 January, he outbid
the Whigs, and carried a petition embodying his 'equitable adjustment' in
its most radical form.[36] Several of Cobbett's proposals were included in the
petition Hunt presented to the meeting at Wells on 21 January, but there
was a marked difference of emphasis. Cobbett's radicalism was financial
and geared to the grievances of a specific interest: in his framework,

---

[32] *Midland Representative*, 12 May 1832, and *Destructive*, 9 Mar. 1833, sadly report the
decline in Hunt's trade.
[33] Hilton, 130–65.   [34] Mitchell, *Whigs in Opposition*, 180–1.
[35] *BD*, 28 Aug. 1822.   [36] *CPR*, 11 and 25 Jan. 1823.

parliamentary reform had been reduced almost to an incidental, the details and terms of which were of little importance so long as it would facilitate the liquidation of the national debt and the equitable adjustment of 'all debts and contracts between man and man'. Hunt, by contrast, remained doggedly political in his radicalism. With his country roots, he sympathized with the farmers in their distress, but he took to the county platform *faute de mieux* to raise the people's banner of universal suffrage, annual parliaments and the ballot.

Hunt, then, made use of the Somerset meetings on agricultural distress to expound the merits of radicalism and continue his campaign against the corrupt county establishment. A few days before the first meeting, he sent Dickinson a letter informing him that he intended to ask for a full public statement of his various salaries, fees, and perquisites.[37] He kept to his word, and a much embarrassed Dickinson was forced to make a brief exculpatory statement to the meeting. Then came the major argument over the type of petition to be adopted. Here too, Hunt championed the interests of the ratepayers and freeholders in the audience against the landowning dignitaries on the platform. The county notables proposed that they should ask Parliament simply to adopt 'such measures as may alleviate the existing and accumulating distress of the Landed Interest, from the unequal and severe burthens under which they now suffer'. Hunt ridiculed their 'milk and water petition' which left the root of the evil untouched, and introduced a petition of his own, insisting on the need for radical reform in Parliament and the county, whereupon the sheriff tried to rule him out of order on the grounds that any discussion of reform must be deferred to a specific meeting on the subject. Hunt, however, refused to be silenced. 'Let us have no Petition at all unless we have a Petition for Reform', he appealed to the audience: 'You must decide and not the Sheriff, whether that subject is relevant or not.' After much argument, he agreed to drop the clauses relating to reform when the sheriff consented to a county meeting on the subject in seven days' time. His duly shortened, Cobbett-like petition was then carried with acclamation, but the sheriff refused to append his official signature, which prompted Hunt to move a vote of censure against him as the meeting ended amidst considerable confusion.[38]

Battle was resumed the following week when Sandford and the Whigs tried to bring Somerset into line with the Yorkshire, county-based campaign for 'a speedy and effectual reform in the Commons' House of Parliament'. Disapproving of such vague generalities, Hunt called for the adoption of the full radical programme, and secured the support of the audience by asking them whether they wished to be 'half-free or free

[37] Somerset Record Office: DD/DN 282, Hunt to Dickinson, 18 Jan. 1823.
[38] *Taunton Courier*, 22 Jan., and *BD*, 5 Feb. 1823.

altogether?—(Cries of "Free altogether, to be sure!")'. Sandford then tried
to discredit Hunt's democratic radicalism by dragging up some details of
his 'fierce ultra loyalist' past, but he was soon shouted down by the
independent freeholders. Dickinson fared little better, and Hunt's radical
petition was carried by an overwhelming majority, although the sheriff
once again withheld his official signature.[39]

Hunt was to be denied any further success at the expense of the Whigs
and the agricultural interest. The county meetings came to an abrupt end
as farming prices began to improve, and the return to specie, now eased by
the Small Notes Act, no longer compelled the agriculturists to demand
economy and reform. Hunt, then, had to wait until the general election of
1826 before he could challenge the Somerset establishment on their own
ground again. As there were so many old scores to settle, the election was a
remarkably bitter contest.[40] Hunt took to the hustings to expose the sitting
members who had persecuted him in 'Ilchester Bastile', defrauded the
ratepayers in collusion with the magistrates and the venal county
treasurer,[41] and ignored their constituents by failing to support the radical
petitions adopted in January 1823. Dickinson and Lethbridge, angered by
the cost and inconvenience of a contested election, decided to silence Hunt
once and for all: acting in unison, they calumniated him unmercifully on
the hustings, and mobilized all their influence to inflict a humiliating defeat
on him at the polls. The independent vote which Hunt had been cultivating
for so long, collapsed in the face of the 'influence and intimidations'
exercised by every magistrate, clergyman, attorney, and newspaper
proprietor in the county. His 'radical' election principles did not help
matters as he refused to spend any money to secure his return, not even on
travel expenses for his supporters, although this would have been a
legitimate use for the remaining balance of the GNU funds, according to
Wolseley, the treasurer.[42] All that Hunt would offer by way of transport
were his uncomfortable blacking vans which he had brought down specially
from London. In a final effort to rally support, he returned to his old
stamping-ground, the Bristol Exchange, where he mounted the pedestal
again to canvass Somerset freeholders resident in the city. Here, in front of
crowds of 10,000–12,000, he spelt out the simple economic and social
philosophy that underpinned his uncompromising political radicalism:

[39] *Taunton Courier*, 29 Jan., and *BD*, 5 Feb. 1823.

[40] This account is based on: *Taunton Courier*, 21 June–5 July; *The Times*, 17 June–1 July;
and *TN*, 18 June–2 July 1826.

[41] Hunt had recently undertaken a major study of the county finances which led him to a
very different conclusion from Dickinson's select committee of inquiry, see University of
Chicago: MS 563, Hunt Correspondence and Papers, item 58, Hunt to the Chairman of the
Select Committee on the County Rates, 18 Mar. 1825.

[42] Ibid., items 64 and 68, Wolseley to Hunt, 30 Oct. 1826 and 17 Feb. 1828, in which there
are intriguing references to GNU funds and the purchase of muskets.

I have had all the magistrates, all the parsons against me, because they all know that my exertions tend to check the impetuous growth of their wealth upon the vitals of the hard-working poor . . . I am an enemy to the injustice that naturally arises from the system on which they act, which extends itself through all the branches of the community. (Loud cheers.) I am an enemy to corn laws, to game laws, and to all laws that mark a degrading contrast between the lazy and the industrious . . . There must be high and low, rich and poor; but the honest hard-working man ought to have all the conveniences of life, and some of its comforts. (Cheers.).[43]

The trip to Bristol did little to boost his vote and for once, he did not object when the election was closed early. There were ugly scenes, however, after the results were announced—Dickinson 1,812, Lethbridge 1,719, and Hunt 309—when Hayward and Cresswell had to be physically restrained from coming to blows with Lethbridge who continued to decry the 'dishonest' electors who had voted for Hunt. Throughout the campaign Lethbridge's behaviour had been quite contemptible: even *The Times* reporter admitted that Hunt was a model of dignity and restraint by comparison. In Lethbridge's eyes, Hunt stood condemned as a man of no family, education, property or morals, a troublesome and convicted radical, an interfering, insubordinate tradesman, a manufacturer of blacking, who had the audacity to offer himself for a respectable county constituency. For all his experience in the rough and tumble of election politics, Hunt was clearly distressed by such persistent vilification, but as he took his leave of Somerset politics he retained his sense of humour and political showmanship, now allied, of course, with his sound business acumen:

As for himself, he should go home and attend to his blacking. (Laughter). To shew that he had no animosity remaining, he should now make the other two candidates a present of a bottle of his best blacking . . . He had thought of sending for another, but as they had split votes, why they might as well split the bottle of 'matchless' between them. (Gt. laughter).

Despite his concentration on business and residence in London, Hunt maintained his special interest in agricultural matters and county politics. He still hoped to split the landed interest, by isolating the landowning establishment and radicalizing the farmers and labourers, prior to their joining the workers and manufacturing interest in an overwhelming challenge from without. The Government's decision to relax the Corn Laws in 1826, following the sequence of financial crisis, manufacturing depression, and industrial riots, offered an opportunity to promote the much-desired juncture. As the protectionists prepared to defend their cause, Hunt arrived unannounced at a 'snug' meeting of prominent

---

[43] *The Times*, 27 June, and *Bristol Gazette*, 29 June 1826.

landowners and farmers at the George Inn, Andover, in September, and promptly subverted the proceedings by rehearsing the familiar figures about the prosperity of the landowners and the immiseration of the farmers and poor labourers, a polarization aggravated by the operation of the Corn Law, 'a tax to support the landlord upon the vitals of the tenant, who is in turn compelled to take the sweat of the poor labourer for little or nothing'. The discomfited protectionists tried to call him to order as he demanded the total repeal of the corn laws and game laws, the reduction of rents and taxes, and the introduction of radical reform, for which purpose the farmers and labourers should join together, shun the landlords, and unite with the manufacturing interest, thereby preventing the Government from 'knocking one head against the other'. In a final effort to rescue the situation, the protectionist organizers tried to restrict the right of voting, but Hunt defeated this stratagem and his petition was carried, condemning the corn laws *in toto*.[44]

Hunt's celebrated triumph over the landowners boosted his popularity in the city, and he was received with 'undivided applause' at a special Common Hall convention on the Corn Law issue in October—'he should certainly go home, suspecting his own principles', he quipped, unless he were to 'regain his character and obtain a few hisses'.[45] 'What!! *really not one hiss*', Wolseley wrote from Brussels: 'Why surely the tide must be turning! Well I am very glad to find it, as you are popular, do your best to continue so; you have a fine chance before you, for your Sir Francis's etc. etc. etc. are now become so contemptible, that you may have it all to yourself.'[46] Hunt certainly tried to make the most of the opportunity. In his speech to the livery, he developed a wide political theme tracing the corn laws back to the 'Pitt system which has demoralized the whole nation, from head to foot, from the highest to the lowest'. 'No real good would emanate to this country', he concluded, 'without a thorough alteration in the whole system, and he hoped to see the day when the stone figure to which he pointed (Mr. Pitt) would be removed from Guildhall and taken into the public streets and Macadamised'.[47] But the popularity and rhetorical licence which Hunt enjoyed over the Corn Law did not extend to other issues. Time after time in the 1820s, he clashed with the Waithmanite reformers in the city and the Burdettite 'liberals' in popular Westminster. There was a new arena of conflict too, now that he was permanently based in south London: the Surrey county meeting where he came up against the 'saints'.

Hunt made his first appearance on the Surrey county platform at Epsom

---

[44] *TN*, 1 Oct., and *CPR*, 7 Oct. 1826.   [45] *The Times*, 20 Oct. 1826.

[46] University of Chicago: MS 563, Hunt Correspondence and Papers, item 64, Wolseley to Hunt, 30 Oct. 1826.

[47] See also his speech to the Common Hall on 29 Sept., *The Times*, 30 Sept. 1826.

in 1826 when he proved himself to be 'a very troublesome character'. The meeting was called to petition for the abolition of negro slavery, an issue later raised in the Somerset election when Hunt, the much-abused 'blacking man', reminded the voters that Dickinson derived considerable profits 'from an article of a much blacker dye (mingled cheers and hisses)—the bl——y West India blacking . . . The bread this man eats, the drink he drinks, the clothes he wears, are all steeped in the blood of his fellow-creatures. (Expressions of horror and hisses and applause inter-mixed).'[48] At Epsom, Hunt's target was not the rapacious slave-owners like Dickinson, but the 'saints', the hypocritical abolitionists. Public apathy towards abolition, he explained, 'arose not from any feeling towards the encouragement of slavery, but from the fact that those gentlemen called saints . . . were to be found voting in the House of Commons for the taxes, and for all the other measures which distressed the people. (Cheers)'. They should concentrate their attention on this domestic misery, he continued, since distress was not 'the lash of God' but the direct consequence of 'mal-administration of government'. At this point the sheriff tried to call him to order, but Hunt persisted in his attack on the double standards of the saints who overlooked the plight of 'at least 5,000,000 of paupers who were worse fed than the dray-horses of Mr. Barclay', and condoned at their own county quarter sessions punishments more cruel and severe than any inflicted on the colonial slave.[49] When distress intensified in the autumn of 1829, he returned to Epsom to attend a meeting of the Surrey Anti-Slavery Society in the vain hope of persuading them to reverse their priorities.[50] In the county politics of the 1820s, as on the mass platform in the post-war years, Hunt always championed the rights and interests of the unrep-resented poor.

3. CITY POLITICS

As his business developed in the 1820s, most of Hunt's political energies were centred on London where he took a prominent and contentious part in the popular politics of the city, Westminster, and the Borough. He re-entered city politics in 1824 when Waithman, his old enemy, was lord mayor, and political excitement was low. Within Hunt's radical perspective, this was just the time for some internal reform of the city's administration. Here, too, he championed the commonalty, the rate-paying livery, against the establishment, the corrupt corporation. At the Common Hall in June,

[48] *The Times*, 17 June 1826.
[49] *TN*, 12 Mar. 1826. For Hunt's opposition to the recently introduced treadmill, see 'Brixton Purgatory' in George, x, no. 14406.
[50] *Leeds Patriot*, 5 Dec. 1829.

he carried a resolution calling for the city's accounts to be published and distributed to all 12,000 or so liverymen. Waithman refused to do anything about it since the livery had no funds to cover the cost.[51] But Hunt would not let the matter drop, and for the next couple of years he battled on to have his resolution carried into practice. He spoke particularly strongly on the subject at the Common Hall in June 1827:

No funds! . . . there were funds, in fact, to be found for every thing except for the publication of accounts, with the items of which it was absolutely necessary that every member of the Livery should be acquainted . . . there was enough of cash for gormandizing, for guttling and guzzling, (loud laughter), for treating emperors and kings, for stuffing themselves (loud laughter), and for carrying some home in their pockets too (more laughter).

In what was to prove a most unwise attempt to silence such criticisms, Stevens, a non-radical liveryman, nominated Hunt for the post of auditor, to which he was duly elected by an overwhelming show of hands.[52]

From his new vantage ground, Hunt campaigned vigorously for reform, retrenchment, and accountability. All the city officers—elected, venal, and professional—came under his critical scrutiny in the course of the next two years. He objected to the system whereby the lord mayor—who enjoyed an annual income of more than twice that of the president of the USA!—was chosen by 'rotation', thereby reducing the livery to mere fools in the electoral process.[53] He denounced the various abuses connected with the annual election of sheriffs, in particular 'the practice of nominating persons as Sheriffs for the purpose of extracting fines'.[54] In alliance with Charles Pearson, his legal friend, he campaigned for reform in the office of secondary or under-sheriff, an office sold by the corporation for '*ten thousand pounds* and upwards, thus empowering, nay sanctioning, one of their officers to *oppress*, *plunder*, and *rob*, any and every unfortunate Citizen who had the misfortune of being arrested in the City, by the *exaction of extortionate and illegal fees*, to double the amount the law permitted'.[55] The recorder and the other legal officers also attracted his censure because of their inflated salaries, innumerable perquisites, and expensive feasts at the Old Bailey where they indulged in a 'profusion of hock, of champagne, and other stimulating wines', before taking their places in court to administer justice.[56] Hunt's own incorruptibility was

---

[51] *The Times*, 24 June and 29 Sept. 1824.
[52] *The Times*, 26 June; *CPR*, 30 June; and *TN*, 1 July 1827.
[53] *The Times*, 30 Sept. 1828 and 25 June 1829.   [54] *TN*, 8 July 1827.
[55] *The Times*, 20 Dec. 1827 and 25 June 1828. Hunt's address 'To the Public-Spirited Inhabitants of the Ward of Farringdon Without', 29 Nov. 1828, in *Collection of Particulars Relative to the Election of Common Council-Men for the Ward of Farringdon Without in the year 1828* (London, 1829), 1–5.
[56] *The Times*, 25 June and 30 Sept. 1828.

never in doubt as he exposed the 'gross and disgraceful system of feasting' that prevailed in the city, financed out of funds intended for the poor and needy:

He would never eat venison and turtle, or drink Burgundy and Champagne out of Orphan Funds—(A few hisses from the Platform, and loud cheers from the body of the Hall.) It might be displeasing, but he would speak out.—(Bravo Hunt.) If he drank such Champagne, it would not exhilirate him, as he should imagine he should not forget he was drinking the tears of the orphan and the widow.—(Cheers.)[57]

True to the last, he refused to hold the traditional retirement dinner at the city's expense when he completed his term of office in 1829: instead he applied for the money to which he was entitled to be distributed to the widows of the poor freemen. When the chamberlain informed him that payment could only be made for 'eating and drinking purposes', he proposed to 'call together 400 widows of freemen, and give them a dinner of roast beef, plum pudding, and a pint of ale each'. No money was forthcoming for such a humble feast, however, even after he applied to the lord mayor for a warrant against the chamberlain.[58]

Hunt's sensational revelations about 'guzzlings and gormandizing' attracted much publicity. 'I have long been writing about *tax-eaters*, who have very unreasonable appetites', Cobbett remarked as he listed some of Hunt's early findings about the misappropiation of city funds, 'but I have now got to do with *alms-eaters* who seem to have appetites still more unreasonable'.[59] Convinced that much corruption and maladministration remained to be exposed, Hunt decided to seek election to the Common Council, the 'Little House of Commons', which had refused him access to their accounts and records. Having hastily complied with the residence qualifications, he offered himself for election to the resident freemen of Farringdon Without in December 1827, but he finished at the bottom of the poll.[60] The following year he was far better prepared for the contest. Once again he stood for election in order to get at the books and fulfil his responsibilities to the rate-paying liverymen as city auditor, although there is some evidence in Wolseley's correspondence to suggest that he had higher ambitions, that he was planning a political career based on the city, and was looking beyond election to the Common Council to becoming sheriff and finally one of the city's MPs.[61] Davenport, his old Bristol assistant, was

---

[57] *TN*, 8 July 1827. [58] *The Times*, 25 June, 30 Sept., and *WFP*, 3 Oct. 1829.

[59] *CPR*, 10 May 1828, which includes Hunt's letter 'To the Liverymen, Freeholders and Inhabitant Householders', an interim report of his findings and the obstacles he had encountered.

[60] *Collection of Particulars relative to the Election . . . Farringdon Without*, iii–vii. University of Chicago: MS 563, Hunt Correspondence and Papers, item 67, Hunt to Davenport, 23 Dec. 1827.

[61] Ibid., item 68, Wolseley to Hunt, 17 Feb. 1828.

brought into the campaign and a committee was appointed to arrange 'a simultaneous Canvass'.[62] Cobbett lent him his full support and offered to stand on the same ticket, a well-meaning gesture no doubt, but the prospect of a Hunt–Cobbett alliance only served to rally ministerialists, Whigs, and reformers to unite and resist the radical challenge by fair means or foul. The Tories led the way with a series of posting-bills enjoining the electors to ask themselves whether Hunt and Cobbett were 'such persons as you would like to introduce into the society of your Wives and Daughters? Would you present them as proper examples to your Servants and Apprentices? Would you place them in a situation to be mixed with the Magistrates and Members of the Corporate Body of the first City in the World?' Cobbett soon withdrew but the calumny continued, portraying Hunt as 'a shameless, an open, and avowed adulterer . . . the very reverse of every thing that is good, virtuous and consistent'.[63] At the wardmote Hunt protested about these scurrilous attacks, but Waithman, the chairman, afforded him no protection from the scandalous misrepresentation of his private life and political principles which, it was claimed, threatened 'the total destruction of the privileges of the city'. Thus mistreated, he finished at the bottom of the poll again, but he refused to retract any of his charges against the corporation; for good measure, he listed some further examples of corrupt malpractice, implicating none other than Waithman, 'their worthy Alderman, the ultra Whig'. Waithman lost his temper and in an impassioned speech from the chair castigated Hunt's meddlesome and pernicious political career. Hunt challenged him to repeat his words on some other occasion when he would not have 'the protection of the gown'; Cobbett was so disgusted by Waithman's partisan outburst that he devoted the next issues of the *Register* to an exposé of 'Signor Waithman' the 'haberdasher Alderman' and renegade reformer. Defeated and abused, Hunt took his leave of Farringdon determined 'not to expend another shilling in the public cause . . . He might have realised a considerable property, if he had devoted that time to private pursuits which he had devoted to the Public'.[64] But this was not the end of his career in city politics. Within a few months of his drubbing at Farringdon, he scored some notable victories over the city's 'jobbers', and was soon to lead the livery towards the radical programme.

His first success came in June 1829 when he petitioned the Lords in protest at the corporation's application for financial assistance with the approaches to the new London bridge. He advised the Lords 'not to

[62] Ibid., item 71, Hunt to Davenport, 5 Dec. 1828; see also Stevens-Cox Collection, H. Hunt jun. to Hunt, 25 Dec. 1828.

[63] *CPR*, 6 Dec. 1828. *Collection of Particulars relative to the Election . . . Farringdon Without*, 5–52.

[64] Ibid., 53–125. *CPR*, 27 Dec. 1828–10 Jan. 1829. *WFP*, 10 Jan. 1829.

continue the tax upon coals, nor to advance the Corporation any of the public money, but to make them pay the expenses out of their own enormous estates'. The Lords appointed a committee to investigate the matter, and compelled the recalcitrant Common Council to produce their accounts. Hunt prepared a dossier of damning evidence to present to the committee, but a compromise agreement was reached before he was called. Financial assistance was provided, but the corporation had to hand over the management of the entire concern to the Treasury. 'The whole *job*' Hunt reported triumphantly, was to be 'taken out of the hands of the corrupt *City Jobbers*'.[65] A week later he presented his final report to the Common Hall as senior auditor, and succeeded in carrying resolutions which compelled the chamberlain and others to keep receipts for every transaction and produce their accounts in adequate time and detail for a full scrutiny by the auditors. Furthermore, steps were now being taken for a major reform in the secondaries office.[66]

When distress intensified in 1830, the livery turned to their recently retired radical auditor for a lead, and rejected the more cautious policies of the established leaders. Hunt's new popularity and authority in the city was made dramatically apparent in February when he took over the proceedings at a meeting of merchants, ship-owners, manufacturers and traders, convened by Waithman to petition for a parliamentary inquiry into distress. Waithman tried to restrict the discussion to the need for tax reform, currency changes and other minor adjustments, but Hunt unfurled the radical banner. Distress, he insisted, 'originated in the long, bloody, and extravagant wars waged and carried on against the liberties of the people of America and of France'; amelioration could not be effected 'till there is a real, effectual, and radical reform in the Commons House of Parliament (Enthusiastic and long-continued cheering)'.[67] After this success, he requisitioned a Common Hall to discuss distress, and encountered no opposition when he introduced a string of resolutions calling for radical reform. Waithman and the Whigs tried to throw cold water on the day's proceedings by reminding the livery that there was 'no probability of the question of reform being carried, or even arising soon'.[68] Here, of course, they were quite mistaken: events were moving quickly at this stage, much to Hunt's advantage. His radical proposals were adopted by the livery when the Common Hall met in July to pass an address to the new King on the throne, but the Government refused to allow its

[65] Hunt's letter to the liverymen in *CPR*, 27 June 1829. *PD*, 2nd series, xxi, 1545–49, and 1559–65. George, xi, no. 15783.
[66] *CPR*, 4 July, and *The Times*, 25 June and 30 Sept. 1829.
[67] *WFP*, 27 Feb. 1830.
[68] Corporation of London Records Office: Common Hall Book, x, 263. *The Times*, 6 Apr. 1830.

presentation.[69] At the next Common Hall on Michaelmas Day, he was loudly cheered as he denounced the monarch's 'secret counsellors' who had denied the livery their traditional rights, but he was ruled out of order by the new lord mayor when he tried to move a vote of censure upon the ministers, using the very words of a resolution carried during John Wilkes's mayoralty in 1774.[70] Thereafter, Hunt concentrated his efforts on opposing the proposed 'grand civic feast' on lord mayor's day to which the new King and his ministers were specially invited. In October, he wrote to the King, explaining that the cost of the feast would not come out of the pockets of those who had invited him—'they will extract it from those funds which belong to the whole of the commonalty of the citizens of London, the Lord Mayor and Common Councilmen being merely the trustees to watch over and to direct the proper application of the said funds, for the benefit of the citizens at large, any part of which being applied to the purpose of giving your Majesty and your family a dinner, will be a gross, an illegal, and a wanton misapplication of the same'.[71] As the day approached, Wellington and Peel were forced to cancel the visit, a humiliating decision which tore away their last shred of prestige.[72] After Wellington's astonishing declaration against reform on 2 November, the city was no safe place for the ministers, but the cancellation must be explained as much in terms of Hunt's persistence as of Wellington's indiscretion. It was Hunt who had made the city a bastion of radicalism with his great campaign against the corrupt corporation: his long struggle for retrenchment and accountability reached a suitable climax when it precipitated the downfall of Wellington and the advent of a reform ministry.

From his base in Stamford Street, Hunt, the city radical, was also very active in vestry politics south of the river, taking a prominent part in the campaign for parish reform which spread through the London area in the late 1820s.[73] At the parish meeting in Christchurch, Surrey, on Easter Tuesday 1829, Hunt and the radicals caught the 'high party' unawares. They challenged every major item of expenditure and succeeded in getting themselves elected to various parish offices on a show of hands.[74] As auditor, Hunt found himself 'like "a cat in hell without claws"', since the select vestry obstructed him at every turn, but he was able to undertake some historical research along the earlier Bristol lines, and produced a

[69] *WFP*, 31 July 1830.   [70] *WFP*, 2 Oct. 1830.

[71] Hunt's letter, 21 Oct. 1830, was printed in several pamphlet forms by Chubb, see *The King's answer to Cobbett's letter on the present state of England; and Hunt's letter to His Majesty, and every particular of the intended Grand Royal Civic Feast* (London, 1830); and *Hunt's Letter to the King, Peel's Letter to the Lord Mayor. Disappointment of the Grand Civic Feast. With every particular of Hunt's Lecture at the Rotunda; and all the news of the day* (London, 1830).

[72] M. Brock, *The Great Reform Act* (London, 1973), 117–29.

[73] Prothero, *Artisans and Politics*, 272–3.   [74] *WFP*, 25 Apr. 1829.

pamphlet which demonstrated that by proper management, the funds arising from the charities of the parish would be 'nearly, if not quite sufficient, to pay all the expences of Church and Poor'.[75] On the eve of the next parish meeting, he called a public meeting at which a committee was formed to promote the interests of the poor parishioners and ratepayers, and thereby ensure that 'those who were in office would do their duty (hear), and perform public offices upon a public principle, and not be guilty of the abuses which existed'. This time the high party were prepared for the challenge. When Hunt's nominees won the show of hands, the rector ruled that parish officers must be elected by a poll on the same property-based lines as the select vestry, which duly ensured, the *Weekly Free Press* reported, that 'those who have so long had the distribution of the loaves and fishes . . . carried the day'.[76] A few months later, however, the high party welcomed the support of the radicals in the campaign against the cost of the new metropolitan police whose presence contributed so much to the tension on the streets of London in the autumn of 1830. The vestry arranged a special parish meeting at which it was agreed that Hunt should draw up a petition to the King praying him to 'exert his power with his Ministers to make them abolish the Police System'. Staunchly opposed as he was to the new police, Hunt could not resist the opportunity of attacking the 'gross mismangement that existed under the old system' when policing was the responsibility of 'a snug little parish party'.[77]

Hunt's efforts for parish reform won him much applause in neighbouring Lambeth, where he had once served on the vestry.[78] When the radical challenge was contained in Christchurch, the Borough radicals formed the powerful Lambeth Parochial Association, leading members of which were among Hunt's strongest supporters in his efforts to widen the reform issue and initiate a popular movement for radical parliamentary reform.[79] Hunt's presence made south London a radical stronghold.

4. POPULAR WESTMINSTER

While battling for reform in the city and the Borough, Hunt moved further apart from the leading metropolitan reformers, the now fashionable Westminster 'liberals'. In the 1820s 'liberal' opinion flourished: Burdett and

[75] H. Hunt, *A brief history of the Parish of Christ Church in the County of Surrey, with its public charities* (London, 1830).

[76] *WFP*, 17 Apr. 1830. See also 'A Parishioner of Christ Church' in *BD*, 11 Nov. 1818, protesting at the electoral procedure under the Sturges Bourne Act.

[77] *WFP*, 11–25 Sept. 1830.

[78] Records in the Minet Library list Hunt as a vestry member in 1826.

[79] See Grady's speech at the first anniversary dinner, *Ballot*, 3 July, and *Political Letter*, 9 July 1831.

Hobhouse were soon integrated into the mainstream of parliamentary liberalism, joining the reforming Whigs in the constitutional opposition.[80] Throughout the decade, Hunt stood forward to expose the double standards concealed behind the internationalist and progressive image of the new liberalism: by the end of the 1820s, it was clear that radicalism and liberalism were divided by an unbridgeable chasm. Under Hunt's leadership, radicalism remained well attuned to popular attitudes and grievances, deeply concerned with the welfare of the common people, and resolutely committed to the struggle for political power. Liberalism, by contrast, had no patience with old notions about political and economic justice: it was a proudly progressive creed at odds with every aspect of popular experience and culture.

Hunt's first clash with the liberals was over foreign affairs, the lodestone of the English liberal conscience. He was a most unwelcome participant at an illustrious meeting in the London Tavern in June 1823 chaired by Lord Erskine to protest at the despatch of French troops to Spain. When he rose to harangue the assembled dignitaries and liberals, he was rudely interrupted by Hobhouse who accused him of throwing the 'torch of discord' among the reformers wherever he went. Hunt, however, refused to be silenced: he reminded the meeting that the Spanish were 'only fighting for that cause for only begging for which the Manchester people were put to death'; he then proposed that a circular letter should be sent to all persons 'receiving emolument from the Government'—including, of course, certain members of the Hobhouse family—entreating them to make a special subscription to the Spanish cause.[81] Hunt delighted in this moral victory, which he recounted in heroic detail to the Birmingham radicals at a public dinner in his honour shortly afterwards. 'It was among those gentry that his presence always threw the torch of discord', he reported triumphantly, 'and I trust that amongst such I shall always throw that much feared torch.'[82]

Hunt was soon joined in his condemnation of the liberals by Cobbett, who remained a good populist radical at heart.[83] They clashed with the Westminster liberals over many issues in the 1820s, the most important of which was Catholic emancipation and the plight of the Irish. Here the difference between liberalism and radicalism was particularly marked. The liberals were concerned with civil rights, or more specifically, the removal of those civil disabilities which hindered the professional careers of middle-class Catholics. Hunt, Cobbett and the radicals were moved by the dire distress of the Irish poor, and campaigned for economic and social

---

[80] Thomas, *Philosophic Radicals*, 194.

[81] *BD*, 18 June, and *CPR*, 21 June 1823.   [82] *BD*, 23 July 1823.

[83] For Cobbett's anti-liberal attitude to Spain, see H. Weisser, *British working-class movements and Europe 1815–48* (Manchester, 1975), 22–3.

amelioration as well as the recognition of the political rights of all, Prostestant and Catholic, rich and poor.

To Hunt and Cobbett, Catholic emancipation was merely the starting-point for tackling the Irish problem, a necessary preliminary as it were to the really important reforms: the disestablishment of the Church, the abolition of tithes, and the introduction of a proper poor law system financed by the landowners. By itself, the elimination of civil disabilities would benefit only the middle classes, not the starving Irish poor, whose desperate plight, Cobbett noted, was completely overlooked by those 'buttonless hypocrites', Wilberforce and the 'saints', and by the liberals who preferred to sympathize with affluent Spaniards, Neapolitans and Greeks.[84] Throughout the ranks of the radical movement and the trades there was much concern for the Irish poor in the 1820s, as these were the years when immigration developed apace following the collapse of Irish proto-industrialization into de-industrialization.[85] Ireland, the *Trades' Free Press* reported, 'innundates us with her miserable poor to gradually push tens of thousands "from their stools" . . . multitudes are daily poured upon our shores ready to invade the work of every labourer and operative'. But the trades and the radicals refused to fan any anti-Irish feeling or raise the old cry of 'No Popery' again. Instead of ostracizing the immigrants, they promoted working-class support for Catholic emancipation and a wide-ranging programme of reforms in Ireland which would 'provide employment at home to those hordes of human beings who now seek it at any price abroad'.[86] At the same time, the radicals hoped to incorporate the Irish, resident and immigrant alike, in the popular challenge for democratic rights throughout the united kingdom. Hunt led the way here, adding Catholic emancipation to the radical programme at Smithfield in 1819, whence he issued his *Address from the People of Great Britain to the People of Ireland*, recommending 'Political Union in the cause of Universal Civil and Religious Liberty'. From his cell at Ilchester, he advised his Catholic friends in the north of England to subscribe to W. E. Andrews's *Catholic Advocate*, a paper he greatly admired as it embodied 'the true Radical spirit of civil and religious liberty'. At this time, he entertained high hopes of a powerful radical–Irish alliance since Daniel O'Connell had apparently accepted the Smithfield 'olive branch': the Irish leader, Hunt enthused, had resolved 'no more to petition an *unreformed Parliament* for Catholic emancipation; but to join, heart in hand, with the people of England, and demand Reform'.[87] Such hopes were sadly dashed in 1825.

---

[84] *CPR*, 21 June 1823 and 3 Jan. 1824. Spater, ii, 465–6.

[85] B. Collins, 'Proto-industrialization and pre-Famine emigration', *Social History,* vii (1982), 127–46.

[86] *TFP*, 29 July 1827.   [87] *TRR*, 23 Dec. 1820, 23 Jan. and 10 Feb. 1821.

Hunt and Cobbett were scandalized by the Emancipation Bill which Burdett presented that year, the terms of which had been previously agreed with O'Connell. To facilitate its passage through Parliament, the Bill incorporated the infamous 'wings': state payment of the Catholic clergy, and the disfranchisement of the forty-shilling freeholders. There were ugly scenes when Hunt arrived at a Westminster public meeting, convened to petition for the repeal of the House and Window Tax, and proceeded to inveigh against the proposed new tax 'to pay the Roman Catholic Priests of Ireland, as a bribe to induce them tamely and basely to submit to the treasonable disfranchisement of half a million of their countrymen, the 40 shilling freeholders'. He refused to be called to order, and came under heavy attack: in the end he was escorted to safety by a group of his supporters.[88] He then tried to rally opposition to the Bill by organizing a public dinner for John Lawless, editor of the *Irishman* and stern critic of the 'wings', but the attendance was disappointing.[89] After the Bill was defeated in the Lords, the 'wings' notwithstanding, he endeavoured to call O'Connell to account at a meeting of the English Catholic Association, but he was ruled out of order by the Duke of Norfolk as soon as he mentioned reform.[90] In his *Register*, Cobbett echoed Hunt's strictures and ridiculed the 'Big O' quite unmercifully, noting how easily O'Connell had been duped by Burdett, old 'Sir Glory', because of his '*inordinate vanity* . . . the great bait was, a *seat in parliament*, of which he was *sure*, if the Emancipation Bill passed'.[91]

While there was little to separate Hunt and Cobbett in their attacks on Burdett and O'Connell, they were still on bad terms with each other. There were two long-standing points of contention, both relating to money matters. The first stemmed from Cobbett's success in Norfolk in 1823, and his standing with the landed interest. Sir Thomas Beevor, a prominent Norfolk landowner, was so impressed by Cobbett's financial nostrums that he proposed to open a fund to secure a parliamentary seat for him. A public meeting was advertised for this purpose in March 1824, but as there was no immediate prospect of an election it was decided to postpone the proceedings until a more opportune occasion.[92] At the peak of the financial panic in December 1825 Beevor announced that the meeting would be held at the Freemasons' Tavern in February. The venue proved far too small, and there was much criticism by Hunt and others of the poor arrangements. When the crowded meeting adjourned to Lincoln's Inn Fields, Hunt announced his readiness to subscribe to the fund, but criticized the 'bigoted disciples of Mr. Cobbett' for their exclusive concentration on financial reform, and called upon Cobbett to reassure the subscribers by

[88] *CPR*, 2 Apr. 1825.   [89] *CPR*, 16 Apr. 1825.
[90] J. A. Reynolds, *The Catholic Emancipation Crisis in Ireland, 1823–29* (Yale, 1954), 131.
[91] *CPR*, 23 July–24 Sept. 1825.   [92] *CPR*, 10 Jan. and 21 Feb. 1824.

restating his 1806 Honiton pledge not to take a farthing of the public money. A heated dispute ensued, as Cobbett took great exception to this thinly-veiled attack on his financial probity, and refused to comply with Hunt's demand.[93] In the end, some £1,700 was raised, which was used to finance Cobbett's campaign at Preston in 1826, where he finished at the bottom of the poll, condemned by the 'Testimonial of Henry Hunt, Esq.'—a long list of charges about his disreputable financial past, patched together by his opponents from Hunt's writings of the early 1820s.[94]

Money matters were at the centre of the second long-standing point of contention: the management of the fund for James Byrne, an unfortunate Irish Catholic who had been imprisoned and publicly whipped back in 1811 for making a charge of indecent assault against the Protestant Bishop of Clogher. Some eleven years later, the Bishop was caught all too literally with his pants down, and as a consequence there was a wave of public sympathy for the much abused Byrne.[95] In London, Cobbett was particularly active in his behalf, although the management of the subscription was in the hands of Parkins, a former sheriff of the city, and a friend of Hunt. A number of legal actions began when Byrne, encouraged by Cobbett, accused Parkins of withholding some of the funds. After the first trial at which he was ordered to pay nearly £200 to Byrne, Parkins wrote to Hunt for evidence which could be used against 'Squire' Cobbett, including the details of his long outstanding debt to Burdett, his 'famous *equitable* adjustment with the Foxhunting Baronet'.[96] When Parkins secured a new trial in April 1825, Hunt testified that Byrne had spoken to him in glowing terms of Parkins and in condemnation of Cobbett. Byrne, who was not in court, later swore an affidavit that he had never spoken to Hunt 'disrespectfully or injuriously of Mr. Cobbett; and that, if he had done so, he would be guilty of the blackest ingratitude'.[97] At this stage Hunt would have been well advised to let the matter drop, although there were some grounds for believing that the affidavit had been penned by one of Cobbett's sons. As it was, he rashly decided to sue Cobbett for libel for printing Byrne's affidavit in the *Register*. The ill-considered case was finally tried in February 1826, in the wake of the dispute at Lincoln's Inn Fields, and the jury had no hesitation in finding for Cobbett. At this point relations between Hunt and Cobbett were at their nadir.[98] A year later,

---

[93] *CPR*, 11 Feb.; *TN*, 12 Feb. 1826; and George, x, no. 15124.

[94] Spater, ii, 457–63. Lancashire Record Office: *Addresses, Squibs, etc. at Preston Election, 1826* (n.p., n.d.), 87–8.

[95] *TRR*, 10 Aug., and *CPR*, 12 Oct. 1822.

[96] *CPR*, 21 Feb. and 28 Aug. 1824. University of Chicago: MS 563, Hunt Correspondence and Papers, item 56, Parkins to Hunt, 29 Mar. 1824.

[97] *CPR*, 23 Apr. and 14 May 1825.

[98] *CPR*, 25 Feb., 4 and 18 Mar. 1826. Nuffield College: Cobbett Papers, Faithfull MSS, box xi, Hunt versus Cobbett, 1826.

however, they buried their differences to unite against the old enemy, Burdett and the Westminster reformers.

What brought Hunt and Cobbett together in 1827 was Burdett's decision to support Canning's premiership and endorse 'Liberal Toryism'. Disgusted that Burdett had chosen to stick his knees into Canning's back on the treasury benches, Hunt and Cobbett sent a joint letter to the *Morning Herald*, giving notice that they would attend the annual 'purity of election' dinner when they would demand a full explanation of this 'settled design' to betray the people and 'barter the remnant of their liberties for the gratification of the vanity, or pecuniary interest, of those who have heretofore professed themselves to be the most zealous defenders of those rights'.[99] Before battle was joined at the Crown and Anchor, they scored an early victory on the streets of Westminster when they gained control of an open-air meeting called to congratulate the King on his appointment of Canning: speaking from one of the blacking vans, they carried an amendment regretting that the King had chosen a prime minister who had 'declared his decided and never-ceasing hostility to that great measure, Parliamentary Reform, which we deem absolutely necessary to our restoration to real freedom and happiness'.[100] At the Crown and Anchor a few days later, it was a very different story. The Rump were firmly in control, and Burdett was loudly cheered as he praised Canning and his government, 'a Ministry of more talent, of more credit, of more liberal principles'. Hunt was heckled and jeered when he tried to remind Burdett and the Whigs in attendance, that Canning was 'notoriously one of the most inveterate enemies of Reform'. 'Without reform', he asserted defiantly, 'any other measures were a mere farce—a mere delusion'. Cobbett adopted a more personal approach and raised objections when toasts were proposed to Burdett and Hobhouse, the 'Don' and 'little Sancho'. At this point Hobhouse and the stewards advanced towards Cobbett and Hunt, flailing their seven-foot long 'wands', whereupon the quick-thinking Hunt 'made a *chevaux de frieze* with the chairs turned upside down'. In the ensuing mêlée, tables collapsed and windows were broken. Some semblance of order was restored after Burdett and the Whigs had left the room, when Wooler took the chair, Hunt having refused to 'disgrace himself by sitting in a chair that had been sitten in by Sir Francis Burdett'.[101]

The 'purity of election' dinner became an annual battleground for radicals and liberals. The 1828 dinner was a relatively quiet affair. Circumstances had altered considerably: Wellington was prime minister and Burdett, Cobbett noted, was keen to 'get back against amongst the democracy'. This prompted Hunt to remind the gathering that 'the Sir F.

---

[99] *CPR*, 12 May 1827, reprints the letter. [100] *CPR*, 19 May 1827.
[101] *CPR*, 26 May; *TN*, 27 May 1827; Patterson, ii, 560–3; and George, x, no. 15422.

Burdett of 1828 was not the Sir F. Burdett of 1807 (Uproar). He was no longer the advocate of universal suffrage, as he then was; and when a million and a half of persons had petitioned Parliament to that effect, he had refused to make a motion on the subject'.[102] As the 1829 dinner approached, both sides prepared for all-out conflict. Catholic emancipation was at the centre of the dispute, as the Westminster reformers openly approved of the recent settlement which sacrificed the rights of the forty-shilling freeholders. But there were several other issues which divided the radicals from the liberals, the most important of which was Warburton's 'Dead-Body Bill'.

Amidst the furore caused by the Burke and Hare murders, the Benthamite Henry Warburton brought forward a Bill which sought to remedy the deficiency of cadavers for dissection and teaching purposes, by sending the surgeons the bodies of paupers dying unclaimed in workhouses and hospitals. Such a utilitarian solution to the pressing needs of science was much applauded by the liberals and 'advanced' radicals like Carlile, but it horrified the popular radicals like Hunt and Cobbett who were joined in opposition by many old Tories. Here was an issue which adumbrated the divisions over the new Poor Law in the 1830s when class resentment was reinforced by Tory paternalism. For all its efficiency and rationality, Warburton's Bill was a blatant piece of discrimination against the poor, offending deeply-held popular attitudes towards death, burial and the human body: it condemned the poor, Hunt and Cobbett protested, 'to undergo the degradation which our forefathers allotted as part of the sentence of the murderer'. Hunt and Cobbett campaigned vigorously against the Bill, upholding the interests of the 'worn-out and afflicted labourer or artisan': a couple of days before the Westminster dinner they sent a joint petition to the Lords where the Bill was defeated, although this was by no means the end of the matter.[103] Hunt arrived at the Crown and Anchor with a long list of questions on the Dead-Body Bill, the disfranchisement of the Irish freeholders and various other issues. But it was Hobhouse who took command of the proceedings. In a powerful and witty speech, he defended the Irish disfranchisement 'for the sake of the good which accompanied it', and looked forward to the day when Hunt and Cobbett would 'do credit to a scientific dissection, and afford us an example calculated to enlighten and illustrate us in a physical, if not in a moral, point of view. (Cheers and laughter)'. At this point, Hunt and Cobbett beat a hasty retreat, a wise decision since the Rump had packed the Crown and Anchor with 'hired ruffians'.[104]

[102] *CPR*, 31 May, and *TFP*, 31 May 1828.

[103] See Ruth Richardson's forthcoming study of *Death, Dissection and the Destitute. Lion*, 20 Mar. and 22 May; and *CPR*, 30 May and 6 June 1829.

[104] Hobhouse, *The Speech of John Cam Hobhouse . . . at the Purity of Election Dinner* (London, 1829). *CPR*, 30 May 1829.

It was the final parting of the ways. Radicals and liberals took their separate paths at the very time when parliamentary reform was placed on the agenda of 'high politics'. At the beginning of June, the Marquis of Blandford, spokesman for the outraged ultra Tories, incensed by Catholic Emancipation, announced his intention to introduce a motion for 'radical' reform. Hunt was delighted that the subject was to be discussed in Parliament again: he had become very critical of Burdett and Hobhouse for their indolence in this respect. The Westminster liberals, however, saw things very differently, and refused to give the proposed measure any support. Hobhouse, indeed, stated his preference for the unreformed system, since reform at the hands of the ultra Tories would jeopardize the recent, all-important triumphs of liberalism from religious liberty to freer trade.[105]

5. RADICAL ORGANIZATION

Hard-fought as his struggles were in county, city, parish and Westminster politics, Hunt's main hopes centred on the revival of the independent radical platform. Thanks to his efforts, radical organization was re-established in the late 1820s around the issue of civil and religious liberty. In the process, Hunt and his colleagues displayed a remarkable ambivalence towards O'Connell and the Catholic Emancipation settlement. At first they felt nothing but anger at O'Connell's apostasy and abandonment of the poor freeholders, but they soon came to envy his reputation as the great 'liberator' who had forced the Government to yield. O'Connell's leadership, Hunt finally came to believe, offered the best hope of securing mass support for the radical programme.

(i) Friends of Civil and Religious Liberty

Following the ignominious failure of the Emancipation Bill of 1825, a group of London-based Irish Catholics joined together as the Friends of Civil and Religious Liberty to promote a radical alternative, a composite programme of religious liberty, radical reform, wholesale retrenchment, and an equitable adjustment of the national debt. The society was steered in this direction by three of Hunt's closest colleagues in the following years: John Grady, an attorney's clerk and leading Lambeth radical; Daniel French, barrister and distinguished Latin scholar, whom Brougham denied a chair at the University of London; and Emmanuel Dias Santos, prominent parish reformer and envoy to the people of Paris in 1830. Their position was not seriously challenged until O'Connell's sensational by-election victory

[105] *CPR*, 13 June 1829.

at Clare in 1828 when the society was riven with dispute between radicals and Catholics, the supporters of Hunt and the followers of O'Connell.[106]

At first, the radicals claimed O'Connell's famous victory as their own: he had stood not only as a Catholic but also as a radical pledged to church reform, retrenchment, and 'every measure favourable to Radical Reform in the Representative System'. The experience of 1825 notwithstanding, Hunt and the radicals decided to take him at and hold him to his word. The Friends of Civil and Religious Liberty, which previously had concentrated on tract distribution, arranged a series of public meetings to 'take into consideration the necessary steps for the promotion of those principles upon which Daniel O'Connell, Esq. offered himself for the Representation of the County of Clare'. Hunt, the main speaker at the first meeting, expressed his delight that O'Connell had finally come to recognize the all-important truth—'that there was no chance of obtaining emancipation or the redress of any other grievance, without first obtaining a *Radical Reform. (Great cheering)*'. 'We will not now suspect him of shifting or shuffling or deserting the cause of Radical Reform', he continued, 'because he is now nailed, (*applause*), solemnly pledged, nailed to the cause of Radical Reform (*three rounds of applause*)'.[107]

It soon became clear that O'Connell had no intention of sticking to his radical election pledges. Following the advice of the Whigs and liberals, he did not present himself at Westminster to demand his seat, but remained in Ireland where his speeches studiously excluded any reference to the term 'radical' and called instead for 'constitutional' reform. This convinced Hunt that O'Connell had turned 'apostate to the principles of Radical Reform' and was trying to conciliate the aristocracy.[108] O'Connell resented the charge: he restated his commitment to universal suffrage, biennial parliaments and the ballot, but reserved the right to support gradualist initiatives; he also made it clear that he regarded parliamentary reform as the means to a far more important end, a full reform 'in the theory and practice of our laws . . . This is my ambition—the great and darling object of my life—to be the practical patron of a Code'.[109] Hunt interpreted this as an abjuration of the Clare declaration, and so at the next meeting of the Friends of Civil and Religious Liberty he opposed the adoption of a vote of thanks to O'Connell. This caused a sensation and the chairman wisely adjourned the proceedings there and then. At the next

[106] *Account of the meeting of the Friends of Civil and Religious Liberty . . . 12th of Feb. 1827* (London, 1827). *TFP*, 16 Sept. 1827. Prothero, *Artisans and Politics*, 143, traces the 'Friends' back to the Queen's Affair.
[107] *TFP*, 26 July, and *CPR*, 26 July and 2 Aug. 1828. Cobbett doubted O'Connell's sincerity, see Adelphi University and Nuffield College: Cobbett Papers, Cobbett to Hunt, 6 July 1828.
[108] 'Mr. Hunt to "The Member for Clare"', *CPR*, 30 Aug. 1828. Reynolds, 132–3.
[109] 'Mr. O'Connell's Political Creed', *WFP*, 20 Sept. 1828.

meeting, Murphy and the Catholics insisted that the vote of thanks be carried, while French and the radicals argued that it should be suspended until O'Connell had 'redeemed his pledge by taking his seat in Parliament'.[110] The matter had still not been settled when another controversy developed at the London dinner in honour of Richard Sheil, O'Connell's closest colleague. Here Hunt was called to account for his conduct at the recent Penenden Heath meeting, the most important of the monster meetings arranged by the Brunswickers or 'High Court' party to protest against any concession to O'Connell and the Catholic Association.

Hunt and Cobbett had attended the Penenden Heath meeting in October in the hope of taking over the proceedings from Lord Winchilsea and the Brunswickers. The Catholics, too, planned to subvert the meeting and arrived in great force, marshalled, Cobbett noted, by 'the *Liberals* or *Whigs* or *Non-descripts*'. Considerable confusion ensued when Hunt and Cobbett apparently joined the Brunswickers in outmanœuvering the liberals, but were then denied the opportunity of putting their own radical petition for the abolition of the accursed tithe system as 'the very best and only means to uphold the Church Establishment for any length of time'. Matters had become so confused that most people had little idea what they were being asked to vote for, and in the end it was far from clear whether the meeting had decided for or against emancipation.[111] At Sheil's dinner, Hunt admitted that he had opposed the liberals and the Brunswickers, but insisted that he had 'never uttered one word that was hostile to the Catholics of Ireland'. He then, however, confessed to considerable reservations about a Catholic relief bill which would 'bring about an union between the Irish and the English Aristocracy, and somewhat damp the seeds of liberty which were now so glowing in the breasts of some gentlemen (cries of No, no), so they would no longer, as now, be agitators . . . the success of the Catholic cause might be the means of retarding the great question he had always advocated (cries of No, no)'.[112]

Hunt's radical position attracted little support in the Irish camp. 'Honest' Jack Lawless, his ally in 1825, but now O'Connell's dutiful lieutenant and Catholic rent-collector in Ulster, turned against him and accused him of hostility to Catholic claims. In a strongly-worded rejoinder, Hunt tried to recall Lawless to his radical past and reminded him of the need for a thorough-going radical approach to the Irish problem. 'You know, as well as I do,' he concluded, 'that Catholic Emancipation, unless it

---

[110] *WFP*, 11 and 18 Oct. 1828.

[111] *WFP*, 25 Oct.; *CPR*, 1 Nov. 1828; and G. Machin, *The Catholic Question in English Politics 1820 to 1830* (Oxford, 1964), 140–2. Hunt later succeeded in carrying a similar radical amendment at a Brunswick meeting in Westminster, which was promptly dissolved by the chairman, see *CPR*, 21 Feb., and *Lion*, 20 Feb. 1829.

[112] *WFP*, 8 Nov. 1828.

be accompanied by a Radical Reform of the Parliament, will never relieve the poor people of Ireland from the dreadful evils inflicted upon them by the cursed tithe system; and that without the abolition of *tithes*, and the introduction of the *Poor Laws*, the people will remain in a state of comparative wretchedness and want, in spite of Emancipation.'[113]

The public meetings of the Friends of Civil and Religious Liberty seem to have come to an end at this point, with the radicals and the Catholics hopelessly divided. Hunt and French turned to the British Catholic Association to argue their radical case, but their intervention was most unwelcome and served little purpose.[114] In February 1829, Wellington's government at last broke their silence since the Clare election, and announced their intention to introduce an Emancipation Bill. While the details were awaited, O'Connell started making all the right radical noises again, prompting Hunt to offer reconciliation and support. At the annual dinner of the East London Catholic Association on 25 February, he proposed the toast to O'Connell's health, to which the Irishman replied with a radical speech, imploring the Government 'not to mar the measure, by the destruction of the forty shilling freeholders . . . as he had erred once in respect to the forty shilling freeholders, he would in future endeavour to preserve them at the expense of his life'.[115] Within a few days, Hunt was forced to throw these words back in O'Connell's face. To his amazement, O'Connell and his allies seemed prepared to accept the Government's Bill which raised the franchise to £10. He issued a desperate appeal to O'Connell to shun the heartless liberals and make a radical stand against the Bill:

. . . in the name of the Reformers of England, who are ready to stand by you; also in the name of the brave, honest, virtuous, public-spirited, and about-to-be sacrificed forty-shilling freeholders of Ireland, I implore you either at once to take your seat in the House of Commons, where you may defend and protect them, or instantly return to Ireland, and rouse them (ere it be too late) to make every legal exertion to save themselves and the country from inevitable destruction.

But O'Connell ignored Hunt's letter, and continued to offer no more than token opposition to the disfranchisement of the freeholders.[116]

Disgusted by O'Connell's apostasy, Hunt turned to the Brunswickers again. He attended a county meeting in Surrey convened to petition the Lords and the King against the Catholic Relief Bill which had already completed its passage through the Commons. Without much success, he tried to turn the discussion to the need for parliamentary reform, since it

---

[113] "'Honest Jack Lawless'", *CPR*, 29 Nov. 1828.
[114] *WFP*, 15 Nov. 1828 and 24 Jan. 1829.   [115] *WFP*, 28 Feb. 1829.
[116] *CPR*, 14 Mar. 1829, includes Hunt's letter to O'Connell; see also, his letter to Lawless, *Leeds Patriot*, 28 Mar. 1829.

had proved 'vain for the people to petition the House of Commons, as it is at present constituted, as the members of that House do not represent the voice and feelings of the majority of the people'.[117] He failed to find a seconder, but this was the line of argument appropriated by Blandford and the ultra-Tory reformers once Catholic Emancipation passed into law. Parliament, Blandford regretted, had acted neither as conservative oligarchy nor as democratic assembly: it had failed to maintain the Anglican character of the state and to represent the real opinion of the nation. The Catholic Settlement was the most dramatic demonstration of the undue and corrupt influence wielded by the executive, for which the only remedy was 'radical' parliamentary reform.[118]

The prospects for reform improved considerably in the wake of the Catholic Emancipation settlement. The disenchanted ultra-Tories were the first in the field. Drawing upon the old country party programmes of the past, Blandford and his colleagues called for the abolition of the rotten boroughs and various other reforms to restore the landed interest to their rightful influence, and thereby curb the executive and guarantee the independence and purity of Parliament. Following on their heels, came the Whig reformers who trusted that parliamentary reform would now be recognized as the party's defining issue. The various schemes abandoned in the prosperity of the mid-1820s were thus picked up again, with Russell and others advocating the incorporation of new commercial and manufacturing interests to make Parliament more representative. These parliamentary initiatives were accompanied by a new interest in reform amongst the middle class as prosperity came to an abrupt end in 1829, the worst year in Professor Rostow's famous chart of 'social tension'. In the large provincial towns, Whigs, Liberals and Tories all came together in support of reform once the local businessmen recognized that their economic interests required direct representation.[119] It was against this blackcloth of growing interest in parliamentary reform, that the radical members of the Friends of Civil and Religious Liberty, much angered by the Catholic Emancipation settlement, regrouped as the Friends of Radical Reform, better-known by their later name, the Radical Reform Association.

(ii) Radical Reform Association

The initiative for a new radical venture came from Hunt and Cobbett, in what was to prove their last major exercise in political co-operation. 'There must, very soon be a *stir* of some sort', Cobbett predicted in a letter to

---

[117] *WFP*, 28 Mar. 1829.

[118] N. Gash, *Aristocracy and People* (London, 1979), 142.

[119] Cannon, 191–7. A. Briggs, 'The Background of the Parliamentary Reform Movement in Three English Cities (1830–2)', *Cambridge Historical Journal*, x (1950–2), 293–7. W. W. Rostow, *British Economy of the Nineteenth Century* (Oxford, 1948), 123–5.

Hunt in June 1829, 'and, I think we should now put ourselves forward, and *take the lead* in pointing out what ought to be done':

. . . we should put forth a DECLARATION TO THE REFORMERS, stating to them 1. the situation of affairs; 2. the views that these new reformers have, or are likely to have; 3. showing them how they would be cheated by schemes like that of Ld. J. Russell; 4. calling on them to listen to nobody who is not for *Universal Suffrage*, *Annual Parliaments*, and *Vote* by *Ballot*; 5. and proving, that any thing short of this would only *enable the aristocracy to rob the fundholders*, to keep their own pensions and their army, and *to continue to oppress the people for ever*.[120]

Their joint declaration, appropriately published on 4 July, was a strident statement of uncompromising radicalism, warning the people 'not to be deluded by the words "moderate reform"':

Listen not to those who may tell you, that it is better to *get a little* than to get nothing; and that tell you, in the old adage, that *half a loaf is better than no bread*; in this case half a loaf *is no bread*: it is worse than no bread; it can only deceive, only enthral; only prolong your degradation.[121]

A few days later, Hunt chaired the opening meeting of the Friends of Radical Reform, and roundly condemned the new reform proposals of Russell and Blandford, regretting that the latter had issued a press statement explaining that 'on the subject of Universal Suffrage and voting by Ballot he differed as widely from the declaration of Messrs Cobbett and Hunt as the poles were asunder'. Whether patronized by Whig or Tory, the schemes to give seats to a restricted electorate in the large unrepresented towns meant 'placing power in the hands of some great Cotton Lords, iron Lords, etc': they were therefore of no benefit to the people, Hunt insisted. The Friends of Radical Reform, he declared, would demand universal suffrage, the only way to ensure freedom 'for every class and every sect'. Cobbett spoke in similar vein, and the meeting called for a 'General Union of the People', a national campaign for radical reform to secure the labouring classes their 'undoubted right—the ample reward of labour'.[122]

   This was an encouraging start but further progress was impeded by Cobbett. Ever since the post-war years he had been suspicious of political organizations and had accorded primacy to currency matters rather than parliamentary reform. It proved impossible for him to lay aside his prejudices and reverse his priorities. After the first meeting, he wrote anxiously to Hunt expressing his concern about infiltration by republicans

[120] Adelphi University and Nuffield College: Cobbett Papers, Cobbett to Hunt, 15 June 1829.
[121] W. Cobbett and H. Hunt, 'To the Reformers of the Whole Kingdom', *CPR*, 11 July 1829.
[122] *WFP*, 18 July, and *CPR*, 18 and 25 July 1829.

and infidels who would alienate respectable supporters.[123] Several steps
were taken to allay his 'entryist' fears, including new restrictions on the
right of admission and speaking, introduced at the second meeting in
August, when Hunt deliberately emphasized the constitutional nature of
the new society—'It should not go forth to the world that we wish for the
spoliation of property—(No, we do not); but that we earnestly wish for a
reform of Parliament.'[124] But Cobbett remained ill at ease, his anxiety
aggravated by certain personal factors. In August his sons were arrested
for an assault on French, who had offered a sensational explanation for the
well-known unhappiness in the Cobbett household. Cobbett, he implied,
had engaged in 'unnatural propensities' with Charles Riley, his secretary,
much to the disgust of his wife who had been driven to attempt suicide.
French's innuendoes, Cobbett's latest biographer maintains, were pure
fiction, but the marriage was in dire straits at this time. Whatever the truth
of the matter, it is most significant that Nancy Cobbett's suicide attempt
and estrangement from her husband dated back to May 1827 when she was
furious with him for resuming his friendship with Hunt and accompanying
him to the Westminster dinner.[125] With more than a whiff of scandal in the
air, there was a huge crowd at the next meeting of the RRA in September:
2,000 people packed into the Mechanics Institute, and there were another
3,000 outside. No personal issues were raised, but the meeting marked the
parting of the ways for Hunt and Cobbett. Their speeches were markedly
different in content and tone. Hunt took pride in the radical programme
and its history, and condemned all moderate reformers. The plans of
Russell and Blandford, he repeated, 'will only benefit the rich and
powerful in the towns, without investing the laborious classes with the
elective franchise'. 'We will not agree to accept a moderate reform in
satisfaction of our claims', he proudly maintained, pledging his continuing
commitment to the historic programme adopted at Spa Fields. Cobbett, by
contrast, warned of the danger from extremist ultra-radicals, from those
who 'go beyond radical reform, who wish a new government—or a republic
as they call it'. 'If we leave in the minds of the middle class of this country,
that we have lurking in our minds motives and intentions of this
description', he warned, 'we shall never, by our exertions, at all promote,
but shall retard, and, perhaps, ruin, the cause of radical reform.' The
audience grew impatient as he proceeded with a lengthy diatribe against
American republicanism, and in the end he was ruled out of time by Hunt
from the chair. The next day he resigned from the RRA on the spurious

[123] Adelphi University and Nuffield College: Cobbett Papers, Cobbett to Hunt, 16 and 18
July 1829.
[124] *WFP*, 8 Aug. 1829.
[125] Spater, ii, 518–19, and 616 n. 49. Osborne, 'Henry Hunt, 1815–1830', 192. *CPR*, 3 Oct.
1829. D. French, *French versus Cobbett* (London, 1829).

ground that French had spoken in favour of republicanism and *'universal confusion'*. Cobbett's version of events, Grady and the committee of the RRA subsequently reported, was a *'deliberate* falsehood': French had said no such thing in the few minutes left him after Cobbett's inordinately long and splenetic speech.[126]

Cobbett took his leave of the RRA to tour the country, lecturing at a shilling a head to merchants, traders and farmers on the accuracy of his financial predictions, offering himself as the 'rallying-point of all those who detested the paper system'. This time, Cobbett believed, the feast of the gridiron really was at hand: with the Small Notes Act at an end, the distress of 1829 could not be 'changed into prosperity' as the distress of 1822 had been.[127] In a reprise of the earlier arguments, Hunt condemned Cobbett's narrow preoccupation with currency matters: at the regular fortnightly or monthly meetings of the RRA he continually ridiculed 'Doctor' Cobbett's quack remedy for distress. Cobbett, he regretted, 'only looked at the surface of the disease he did not probe it to the core': he had 'altogether lost sight of radical reform':

Doctor Cobbett, indeed, had plainly said, that the only cause of the distress was the alteration that had been made in the currency. That was a little strange, to be sure, for when he (Mr. Hunt) used to converse with the doctor, some twenty years since, that was before any alteration that had been made in the currency, they were unanimously of the opinion that the cause of the distress was the cursed Pitt system—the war against liberty in France and America—that had done all the mischief . . . The alteration of the currency was only a part of the Pitt system . . . The radicals, therefore, should take care that they were not led away by false doctors or false doctrines.[128]

Cobbett, however, continued on his individual path, opposed to all organized endeavour, even the new Birmingham Political Union with its concentration on currency reform. The only way forward, Cobbett opined, was his own return to Parliament, whence he could address the whole nation. While Hunt persisted with the RRA, patiently building up mass pressure from without, Cobbett, the self-proclaimed 'teacher of the nation', started touting for contributions to purchase himself a parliamentary seat.[129]

After Cobbett withdrew from the RRA, the society came under attack from Hunt's other old adversary, Richard Carlile. Still the ultra-radical Paineite ideologue, Carlile was now the apologist of gradualism and economic individualism. Thus he opposed the 'radical mania' embodied in the RRA because it both checked the 'mental progress of those who would

[126] *WFP*, 12 and 26 Sept., and *CPR*, 12 and 19 Sept. 1829.
[127] *CPR*, 10 Oct. 1829 and 9 Jan. 1830.
[128] *WFP*, 24 Oct., 12 and 26 Dec. 1829.
[129] *CPR*, 27 Feb. and 10 Apr. 1830.

be usefully travelling farther' and undermined the labours of practicable reformers like O'Connell, whose flexibility he greatly admired. Hunt, he feared, was using the RRA to 'play over again the tricks and games of 1816, 17, 18 and 19': by condemning everything but his own shibboleth, he effectively prevented any reform. 'I think it better to reform practically and effectually the smallest twig of the tree', Carlile opined, 'than to talk, and do nothing but talk, about reforming down to the root.'[130] When he started attending RRA meetings in the autumn, Carlile found the society 'contemptibly devoid of intellect and useful purpose', as bad if not worse than the BAPCK. He soon decided to shun all contact with these 'addressing reformers, these shallow pretenders, politically to instruct and direct others', when the RRA adopted an address to the people which sought to mobilize the masses by rehearsing all the 'trash' about glorious ancestors and constitutional rights. Hunt and the RRA, Carlile concluded, stood on a par with the Whigs for their lack of principle and practicality— 'Thomas Paine has drawn up a political alphabet for them; but they are either too corrupt to look at it, or too dull to learn it'. From this point, Carlile advised the true reformers to have nothing more to do with 'any sect, party, or society, instituted for any purpose whatever. I carry the principle even to trade societies, and think them injurious to the general interests of the trades.'[131] Individualist to the core, he returned to the 'march of infidelity', the great mission which required self-discipline, self-education, and self-improvement: '*You cannot be free, you can find no reform, until you begin it with yourselves* . . . abstain from gin and the gin-shop, from ale and the ale-house, from gospel and the gospel-shop, from sin and silly salvation'.[132] Carlile, the ideologue and infidel, the advocate of birth control and supporter of the 'Dead-Body Bill', the critic of co-operation and disciple of economic individualism, stood widely divorced from popular radicalism, culture and experience. The economic distress of the time, he maintained, was not caused by taxes and bad laws but by the people themselves through their bad and improvident habits and 'excess of their numbers in relation to the supply of labour that can employ them'.[133]

Against the attacks of Cobbett and Carlile, Hunt successfully steered the RRA into the mainstream of popular radical attitudes and beliefs. Moderate reform was repudiated, and no discussion was allowed of anything beyond the radical programme, whether republicanism, infidelism, Spenceanism or whatever. 'All what the radicals required', Hunt repeatedly emphasized, 'was a reformed parliament which would act for the benefit of the people . . . It was said that property should be

---

[130] *Lion*, 4 Jan., 7 and 14 Nov. 1828, and 6 Mar., 17 and 24 July 1829.

[131] *Lion*, 9–23 Oct. 1829.

[132] *Lion*, 24 July 1829.

[133] See the series on the 'Currency Mania', *Lion*, 13 Nov.–11 Dec. 1829.

represented; so he said, for labour was the property of the people.'[134] But despite its simple message and its specially prepared constitutional address to the people, the RRA failed to attract mass support in the country, even though distress was reaching catastrophic levels: a heart-rending survey of twelve parishes in the Huddersfield woollen area, much quoted at RRA meetings in London, revealed that over 13,000 people had to subsist on 2½d. a day.[135] By the end of 1829 only two provincial associations had been formed, one at Paisley, and the other at Leeds, where the local supporters of Carlile, now led by John Smithson, caused considerable difficulties.[136] Hunt still awaited the revival of the mass platform.

(iii) Metropolitan Political Union

Disheartened by the slow progress of the RRA, Hunt welcomed the formation of the Birmingham Political Union (BPU) in January 1830 and its plan for 'a great National Union of the middling and lower classes of Englishmen, for the purpose of obtaining such an *effectual* reform in the Commons . . . as will restore and secure to the people the right of electing their own representatives'. Here, he believed, was a useful model for mass pressure from without, and he wanted to adopt the scheme in London without delay, 'keeping strictly, for the sake of union, to the words as well as the sense of the people of Birmingham':

We, the Radical Reform Association, in our Address to the People of the United Kingdom, laid down the great and unerring principles of Radical Reform and National Union. The people of Birmingham, in endeavouring to give those principles practical effect, have in no instance departed from their genuine purity. It is true they have substituted the word effectual for radical; but, my friends, we will neither quarrel nor cavil with them on this distinction without a difference, for whatever is effectual must be radical!!—The reformers of Birmingham have cast the die—they have set in motion this great, national, practical, political engine . . . Let our exertions be to promote and to concentrate Union;—let no consideration induce us to endanger Union, by departing one iota from the Birmingham plan, either in theory or practice.

Benjamin Warden, John Grady and others advocated a more cautious approach, and wanted to wait and see whether the assorted currency reformers, ultra-Tories and parliamentary reformers who had come together in Birmingham would actually commit themselves to the full radical programme. Hunt, however, pressed on with his plans for a great mass meeting in London to launch the new metropolitan union: to allay the

---

[134] *WFP*, 26 Sept. 1829.
[135] *WFP*, 24 Oct. and 26 Dec. 1829; see also, *Leeds Patriot*, 19 Dec. 1829.
[136] *WFP*, 9 Jan. 1830. *Leeds Patriot*, 19, 26 Sept., 3 Oct. and 26 Dec. 1829.

remaining doubts he suggested that the RRA should continue in being as a radical watchdog over the new union.[137]

In the hope of attracting the biggest possible crowds he invited O'Connell to take the chair on 8 March. 'I heretofore had my doubts of him', he freely admitted to the RRA, 'but they are now entirely removed by his appearance in the House of Commons, and his avowal there that he was a radical reformer.'[138] For once, O'Connell did not disappoint him. He introduced himself to the crowds of at least 20,000 in the grounds of the Eagle Tavern as 'a radical reformer of the abuses of the law' who wanted to open the courts to the poor 'for the poor wanted law, as well as the rich, perhaps much more . . . But he could not expect those reforms carried, until the House of Commons was reformed, and made what it really ought to be—the people's house'. He then pledged himself to universal suffrage and the ballot, and recommended the radicals to follow the example of the people of Ireland who had conquered the hero of Waterloo by 'moral force', through a united campaign of 'constitutional and peaceful resistance'. A petition for 'real Radical Reform' was then adopted, together with a number of resolutions, previously carried at the RRA, tracing distress back to 'the long, sanguinary, extravagant, and unnecessary wars'. The meeting then proceeded to adopt the Birmingham model of organization, including the appointment of a 36-member political council to head the 'General Political Union between the middling and labouring Classes of the People of the Metropolis'. Thus, it was to further the cause of radicalism, not currency reform or moderate parliamentary reform, that the MPU was formed. Hunt, appointed treasurer of the new union, was delighted with the day's events. As in the old days on the mass platform, he spoke at some length about his dedication and now gaol-tested consistency, but this time he offered his services as follower not leader, since a member of Parliament had at last mounted the platform to pledge commitment to the radical programme:

Formerly, whenever a great multitude of people were to be assembled, he (Mr. Hunt) was generally called upon to preside, and upon no occasion, when in health, had he ever failed to do so. Then, however, it used to be, 'Oh, it is one of Hunt's Meetings'—(*a laugh*)—'one of Hunt's nobs' . . . It was all Hunt then, but why was it so? Because men of talent, and of consequence, and of power, never offered to come forward (*Cheers*). They would find in him, however, no feeling of petty jealousy, for he would be as anxious to work under Mr. O'Connell as he was ever

---

[137] Hunt's letter to 1 Feb. RRA meeting, and his speeches to 15 Feb. RRA meeting and 24 Feb. planning meeting for the MPU, *WFP*, 6, 20 and 27 Feb. 1830. On the origins of the BPU, see C. Flick, *The Birmingham Political Union* (Folkestone, 1978), ch. 1.
[138] *WFP*, 6 Mar. 1830.

anxious that others would work under him; and as long as he had health he would never cease to advocate the rights of the people.[139]

With the formation of the MPU, Hunt's persistent if not entirely selfless efforts to promote mass organization and the radical cause appeared to have paid off at last.

[139] *WFP*, 13 Mar. 1830. BL Add. MSS 27822 (Place papers), ff. 11–14, *Authorised Copy of the Resolutions adopted at the Great Public Meeting, consisting of 30,000 people . . . for forming a Metropolitan Political Union, for the recovery and protection of public rights.*

7

1830 and the Development of Radicalism

THROUGH the MPU and other platforms, Hunt tried extremely hard to initiate a national campaign for radical reform in 1830, but he failed to elicit a mass response. In the north, the people were slow to respond to his lead, and his successes were confined to those Lancashire textile towns with which he had enjoyed a special affinity since Peterloo. In London, his efforts were hindered by personal and ideological rivalries and antagonisms which became more intense with the heightening of political excitement in the summer and autumn. The excitement died away after the appointment of a reform-pledged Whig ministry in November, but it was at this late stage that Hunt's radical challenge received its greatest boost, his sensational electoral victory at Preston.

I. THE EARLY MONTHS

In the hope of activating a mass campaign, Hunt missed no opportunity to promote the radical cause. At an anti-capital punishment meeting in January, for example, he 'worked in the old story or corollary to everything—that a man ought not to be hanged, unless he consented to the law by his representative'.[1] On the traditional extra-parliamentary circuit, his oft-repeated arguments acquired a new respectability and a wider audience as distress broadened its impact and persisted into spring. His radical programme was carried without opposition at a Surrey county meeting in March, and, as already noted, at the Common Hall a fortnight later.[2] There were encouraging signs too that radicalism was gaining support among 'non political' labour organizations and social reform groups. The stone-masons were the first of the distressed trades to petition for radical reform, and the BAPCK included radical reform in its demands when the co-operators met to petition Parliament in April for effective action to alleviate the unremitting distress.[3] A few days later, Robert Owen, practitioner of the a-political 'science of society', apostle of rational religion, and prophet of the gerontocratic new moral world, called a public meeting to discuss the urgent need for 'a change of system from the

---

[1] *Carlile's Journal*, 21 Jan.
[2] *WFP*, 20 Mar., and *The Times*, 6 Apr.   [3] *WFP*, 3 and 10 Apr.

individual competitive to the co-operative', but the audience voted in favour of Hunt's amendment for immediate radical reform.[4] Other debating victories followed, of which the most hard-fought was the radicals' triumph over the liberals and middle-class reformers in the midst of their preparations for the summer general election, on the accession of the new King. To promote the cause of moderate reform, a talented array of liberals, Westminster reformers, and Radical MPs assembled at the Freemasons' Tavern to institute a parliamentary reform association, precursor of the Parliamentary Candidate Society. For most of the proceedings, Hunt was muzzled by some strict chairing, but he was finally allowed to address the floor when he called upon the new association to adopt the programme and principles of the MPU, by now the sworn radical opponent of the BPU which had committed itself officially to Blandford's household suffrage bill. True reformers, he insisted, repudiated any connection with moderate reformers like the BPU, whose 'mode of proceeding would exclude two-thirds of the people of England . . . until it could be proved that nature had affixed a damning mark upon the brow of any one class of Englishmen, he should contend that none should be excluded'. Burdett tried to regain control of the meeting by reminding the audience that he was 'a sincere friend of reform to the fullest extent, but he objected to all bullying and bustling upon the subject . . . he was willing for the present to take all that he could possibly get, however little it might be, as a most desirable boon'. But it was Hunt's uncompromising radicalism that won the day. Manfully supported by Hetherington and others, he emerged triumphant from an unholy row on the platform, and carried his specially-prepared, highly subversive amendment to the very first proposition of the 'Parliamentary Reform Association'. In place of the original words which called simply for an extension of the franchise, the meeting resolved:

That all plans for reform which do not embrace universal suffrage, with the protection of the ballot, are unjust in principle, will prove to be inefficient and delusive in practice, and are calculated hopelessly to prolong the slavery and degradation of the intelligent and industrious workmen of the United Kingdom.[5]

It was a classic statement of the radical rejection of moderate reform, the position to which Hunt adhered so loyally throughout the Reform Bill agitation.

Such victories over the opposition were good for publicity and morale, but did little to enlist mass support. Here, of course, Hunt's hopes were pinned on the MPU, and its radical watchdog, the RRA. He chaired the weekly council meetings of the MPU at the Globe Tavern, and encouraged the union to go into open rivalry with the renegade BPU for the allegiance of the provincial reformers. Thus, when the BPU adopted Blandford's Bill

---

[4] *WFP*, 17 Apr.   [5] *CPR*, 31 July.

and issued a declaration repudiating universal suffrage, the MPU drew up a rival declaration stressing the urgency, constitutionalism, and indivisibility of the full radical programme.[6] The council followed this up with an 'Appeal to the People', explaining that their aim was to 'raise the *productive classes* to their just and constitutional rank in the State . . . we want to requite the *productive classes* for their labour, and to give them the opportunity, by political representation, of protecting themselves in the enjoyment of it'.[7] At the next general meeting of the MPU, held in Carlile's Rotunda, it was agreed to follow Hunt's suggestion and launch a national campaign on the basis of these radical demands and principles.[8] In some parts of the country there was a good response. The Leeds RRA provided a strong lead in Yorkshire, and had already recommended the general adoption of the rules and resolutions of the MPU 'to unite all the friends of effectual and radical reform'. After a mass meeting on Hunslet Moor, a radical union on MPU lines was established in Leeds itself, and similar bodies were formed at Keighley, Morley and Almondbury (Huddersfield).[9] Elsewhere apathy prevailed. Reporting back to the RRA on his business trips to the west country, Hunt noted that distress had reached terrible levels, but he had found that those who complained loudest that there was 'no money, no trade, and no confidence between man and man . . . sat grumbling at their own fire-sides; there was no excitement, no meetings, and no union amongst them'.[10] 'Notwithstanding the sufferings of the productive classes, and the general decrepitude of the nation . . . there is no stirring voice abroad', the RRA committee recorded with disappointment and incredulity in its first annual report: 'a political stillness, so unusual and so unnatural, now pervades the land'. The annual general meeting in the Rotunda in July, chaired by Hunt, looked forward to a more promising future for the RRA: subscriptions were reduced; another Irish radical, Bronterre O'Brien, joined the ranks and delivered an impressive maiden speech; and energies were concentrated on the forthcoming general election, with all available funds being allocated to Hunt's campaign at Preston.[11] Before news reached London of the sensational events in Paris and the overthrow of the Bourbons, Hunt had already set off to canvass the popular vote in Preston where something akin to the radical goal of universal suffrage was already in operation: all males over twenty-one, free from pauperism and crime, and with six months' residence were entitled to vote.

[6] See the weekly reports in *WFP*, 20 Mar.–8 May.
[7] *WFP*, 15 May.
[8] *WFP*, 10 July. O'Connell took the chair; the attendance was nearly 3,000.
[9] *Leeds Patriot*, 10 Apr., 8, 15 May, and 5 June.
[10] *WFP*, 20 Feb.
[11] *WFP*, 17 July. A special subscription fund for the Preston election was opened at the next RRA meeting, *WFP*, 7 Aug.

2. THE JULY REVOLUTION AND THE REVIVAL OF THE PLATFORM

News of the July Revolution had little effect on the general election, but provided a great boost to radical morale. As excitement began to mount, political discussion became more contentious, particularly in London, where the invigorated MPU persisted with its strict constitutionalism to the disapproval of ultra-radicals. Veteran republicans like Gale Jones—Cobbett's *bête noire* from his brief RRA days—favoured a much more militant course. Revolutionary France, he proclaimed, was 'at once our example and our reproach . . . France has done what Englishmen only talked about'.[12] Jones's unrestrained republican rhetoric led to his expulsion from the MPU, along with Robert Taylor, the infidel missionary, who promptly registered his protest at the narrow-mindedness of the 'petty-fogging tyrants' on the Catholic-dominated MPU council. Carlile spoke up for Jones and Taylor, his close colleague, and issued a 'Declaration of Political Principles in England, arising out of the new and most glorious revolution in France', which dismissed the MPU by stressing that there were 'no political societies in France—none are required. None are required in England for the carrying on of any useful purpose.'[13] Cobbett returned to the radical fold to extol the events in France, 'a revolution made by the *industrious classes*, and by the working part of those classes . . . This is no "*Glorious Revolution*" effected by the holders of Church and Crown, and by a *Dutch army*!' But he refused to have anything to do with the MPU despite the purge of republicans and infidels. He took a resolutely individual path, organizing his own public dinner to congratulate the people of Paris, and delivering a series of eleven lectures at the Rotunda on the French revolution and the English boroughmongers.[14] At the same time he drew up his 'Manifesto of the Industrious Classes', a lengthy petition to the King, detailing the ravages of distress, the terrible consequence of 'the whole of the laws passed within the last forty years . . . one unbroken series of endeavours to enrich and to augment the power of the aristocracy, and to impoverish and depress the labouring part of the people'. Later, he produced his 'Plan of Parliamentary Reform', which explained how the constitutional system of universal suffrage, annual parliaments and the ballot could be put into practice: it soon became the standard radical text on the subject.[15]

[12] *WFP*, 14 Aug.

[13] *WFP*, 21 Aug., includes the correspondence between Taylor and Dias Santos, secretary of the MPU, and Carlile's 'Declaration'. See also, HO, 64/11 ff. 214–15; and Lovett, 46.

[14] *CPR*, 14 and 21 Aug. W. Cobbett, *Eleven Lectures on the French and Belgian Revolutions, and English Boroughmongering* (London, 1830).

[15] *CPR*, 18 Sept. and 30 Oct.

Up in the north Hunt followed a very different course in order to maximize the impact of the heartening news from abroad: ideological controversy and individual initiatives were eschewed as he tried to prepare the way for a revival of the mass platform and the GNU. Timely as it was, his trip to the north proved rather dispiriting, revealing the insuperable difficulties of mobilizing the masses. The Preston election itself was a bitterly disappointing and disheartening experience, which made him regret not standing for a London seat as he had originally intended. He had been enticed north by the irresistible offer of an election free of all expenses, and the alluring prospect of a Tory-radical alliance against the hateful Whigs. The old coalition between the Tory corporation and the Whig Derby family, which had controlled the Preston electorate for so long, had finally come to an end in 1826, when the Whigs had taken both seats. Disgruntled Tories, still seething at these events, offered the local radical committee funds and support if they could persuade Hunt to stand against the Whigs, a task they accomplished by sending him his travelling expenses in advance together with an unqualified assurance that he would be free of all costs.[16]

On arrival, Hunt soon discovered that he had been given a false impression of his chances. The new system of polling in district booths put him at a hopeless disadvantage since his Whig rival, the Hon. Edward Stanley, had '60 land-sharks, called lawyers, to direct his voters to their respective booths . . . his (Mr. Hunt's) men had to find their way as well as they could, and were accordingly driven from one to another, and some of them could not get to vote at all'. Then the Tories reneged on their promises, financial and electoral, as soon as they heard him declare on the hustings that he wanted to 'stop the plundering system altogether, in order that the people might retain the fruits of their earnings'. Confronted by such honest radicalism, they immediately ordered their workmen to vote for Stanley and joined the Whigs in a lavish exercise in traditional bribery and corruption. The taps were opened on Saturday night and beer continued to flow free for the rest of the weekend. This ensured that on Monday, Stanley overtook the Liverpool lawyer John Wood, the unobjectionable liberal candidate, and acquired a commanding lead over Hunt who left town in disgust: the final figures were Stanley 2,996, Wood 2,489, and Hunt 1,308. The only bright spot in the whole of the proceedings was the discipline and support of the 300 or so members of the 'black fleet', the local aristocracy of labour, implacable radicals who marched to the polls behind their band and radical banners to vote *en bloc* for Hunt, their champion. These 'ingenious and clever workmen', the *Preston Chronicle*

---

[16] Hunt's correspondence with the Preston radicals, *Preston Chronicle*, 31 July; his speech on the hustings, 31 July, ibid., 7 Aug.; and at the Common Hall, *WFP*, 31 July. Proctor, 130–7.

explained, were so well paid and independent that they were able to 'spurn all attempts to win their votes by liquor, or other bribes; or to gain them by the undue interference of those to whom the men give their labour for their wages'.[17]

The disillusionment of the election notwithstanding, Hunt decided to remain in the north-west in the hope of harnessing the enthusiasm generated by the news from France. Here he worked in close alliance with two heroes of the post-war campaign who had recently settled in Preston: John Johnston, the former Manchester tailor, Hampden Club delegate and triumvir of the Blanketeers; and Joseph Mitchell, the Liverpool draper turned Union Society missionary and radical journalist, the unwitting and exonerated travelling companion of the infamous Oliver. These esteemed veterans, now respectively chairman and secretary of the Preston radical committee, encouraged Hunt to delay his return south in order to tour the region, promoting their plans for a new campaign of mass pressure from without, centred on Preston and based on a revival of the GNU. Bruised by his electoral defeat, Hunt did not underestimate the difficulties of the task: the radicals, he now realized, had to contend with the forces of drink, religion, ignorance and indifference. Admonition and censure replaced the usual rhetoric of mutual flattery during his speechifying tour of the north-west.

The series of speeches, meetings and dinners began in Preston itself, to which Hunt returned once the shameful election was over. Large crowds lined the streets to welcome him back from Liverpool, and he was drawn in procession to the Black Bull Inn where the radicals had arranged a public dinner to announce the revival of the GNU. In his harsh address to the crowds outside, Hunt lamented the decline of 'Proud Preston' into 'drunken Preston': 'There was no other place in England, Scotland, or Ireland, where the people had the same power as they had in this town . . . Though they had the power, they had not the will—a little money, a little fear, and not a little drink, prevented them from doing their duty.' Preston was a sad example of the evils of universal suffrage without the ballot, he admonished the diners, a sorry contrast with Paris where the people were 'falling at the point of the bayonet in support of those rights which the Preston electors were abandoning and abusing'.[18] He repeated these strictures to other audiences on his tour, sadly recording that his trips back and forth from Preston to Liverpool had left him convinced that the English were too entrammelled by liquor and priestcraft to fight for their rights and enjoy their liberty like the French. Whilst in Paris on business, he had found the people merry and dancing: they were no longer humbugged by priests, and enjoyed their Sundays and leisure time in

---

[17] *Preston Chronicle*, 7 Aug. Proctor, 137–41.   [18] *Preston Chronicle*, 14 Aug.

rational pursuits. Lancashire presented a very different picture: here the people were 'all priest and parson ridden', everybody looked 'sheepish and melancholy', drunkenness was endemic, and the churches were crowded. Priestcraft and drunkenness, he regretted, went hand-in-hand and led to political slavery. 'The influence of the Priests over the minds of the electors of Preston, and of Stanley's beer over their heads had caused his defeat', he reported to the Bolton radicals, noting that he had 'certainly seen fifty times more drunkenness in England than in France, and yet there was in appearance fifty times as much religion in this country'.[19]

Whilst Hunt persisted with these animadversions on the besotted and deluded Lancastrians, he took heart from the welcome he received in radical Blackburn, Bolton and Manchester, old strongholds from the Peterloo days. Numbers fell far short of the multitudes that had honoured him in 1819, but the crowds were large and enthusiastic. Over 10,000 people crowded into Market Street Lane, Blackburn to hear his address from the Castle Inn. At Bolton, centre of the muslin weaving trade, he was led into town by a great procession headed by a band and three radical flags which, the local press reported, had 'scarcely ever seen the light since the passing of the Six Acts'.[20] The climax of the tour was the anniversary address on the hallowed ground of Peterloo, which attracted a crowd of between 40,000–50,000, although Hunt, with characteristic exaggeration, claimed a six-figure attendance.[21] All his speeches were suitably revivalist in tone as he updated his record of consistency, commitment, and leadership. 'Although it is now eleven years since you saw me', he began his Peterloo speech, 'did you ever hear of me deserting my colours? Did you ever hear of me deserting the cause of the people, even when confined in a gaol. (Loud cries of "we never did.") I know you have not, and you never will. ("Bravo Hunt").' Then came the familiar and simple radical message, traditionally phrased and still directed against the boroughmongering aristocracy:

Gentlemen, I always was of opinion that there must be some mismanagement in the affairs of the country, where the labouring man cannot, by incessant toil from Monday morning to Saturday night, provide himself and family, not merely with the necessaries, but a portion of the luxuries of life. This is your situation, and I attribute the cause to the great landed aristocrats, the peers of parliament, who make laws, in which the people have no other voice than to obey.

He then turned to agitational matters and warned the radicals against the hollow and hypocritical BPU, before giving his blessing to the revival of the GNU, the details of which were expounded by Johnston and Mitchell. On only one occasion was there any suggestion of the kind of ideological

---

[19] *Bolton Chronicle*, 14 Aug.   [20] Ibid.
[21] Ibid., 21 Aug., and *Preston Chronicle*, 21 Aug.

strife which beset metropolitan radicalism at this time. From the chair at the dinner after the Peterloo meeting, Hunt cut short an argument about Paine's religious views, much to the annoyance of Doherty, the spinners' leader, and Detroisier and Prentice, the main antagonists. Convinced that Prentice and the other middle-class reformers were out to trap him into appearing an infidel, Hunt, the critic of northern priestcraft, carefully avoided any reference to Paine's theological views while he dutifully praised *The Rights of Man*. 'He was as religious as any of them, not excepting Mr. Prentice (Laughter)', he declared, repeating the libertarian creed he had avowed at Owen's contentious meeting in April:

Freedom of conscience, (and to let people think as they liked in these matters, without interfering with them) was his religion . . . the man who either on his pillow, or in the closet secretly offered up his thanks to the supreme being, for blessings received, was a truly religious man.[22]

Hunt's brief tour of the north-west prepared the way for a mass petitioning campaign for radical reform. The first issue of *The Crisis, or Star to the Great Northern Union*, appeared on 28 August, published 'by order of the Committee of the Preston and other branches of the great Northern Union'. In its columns, Mitchell, the editor, called for mass meetings throughout the north to raise subscriptions, form branches of the GNU, adopt petitions to the new King, and appoint deputies to take the petitions to London where they would all meet together to 'discuss modes of proceeding to recover their rights'. Preston led the way with a mass meeting in Chadwick's Orchard on 8 September, the first such meeting in the town for fourteen years. Mitchell was appointed to take the petition to London and Johnston was chosen as missionary to tour the north promoting the GNU. An adulatory address to Hunt was adopted, inviting him to assume his rightful role as their honoured 'leader and adviser', a post which included the treasureship of the revived GNU with its special fund for a 'people's press'.[23] Hunt's reply, suitably overblown in its rhetoric, pretensions and confirmatory record of his credentials, gave details of his current efforts to extend the petitioning/addressing campaign and establish a national framework. On return to London, his first task had been to canvass support for Thomas Wakley, the radical surgeon, in the election for Middlesex coroner, but he was now busy arranging a meeting of the middle and working classes of the capital on 27 September to adopt addresses to the King and their heroic counterparts in Paris. 'Our meeting on Kennington Common will be stupendous,' he assured the northern

[22] Mitchell's letter to Prentice, *Crisis*, 28 Aug. Kirby and Musson, 424. At Owen's meeting on distress, Hunt protested that 'had he not previously heard of the object of the meeting, he should have thought they had met to settle some theorem in theology', *WFP*, 17 Apr.

[23] *Crisis*, 28 Aug. and 11 Sept.

radicals, 'we will give you the tone—get meetings all over the north for the same day, for the same purpose, and send delegates from each place to proceed to Paris, and to present addresses to our King before the Parliament meets.'[24]

These hopes for a great platform campaign were quite unrealistic. The Kennington Common meeting, the first open-air demonstration in London since the July Revolution, was marred by division and bad organization. Hunt could no longer rely on the talents of the 'revolutionary party' to arrange a mass display of strength. Old confrontationalists like Blandford and Preston, who had recently regrouped as the 'Committee of Observation' in the wake of events in France, refused to have anything to do with the meeting. 'In the most of the persons I associate with', the Government's informer reported, 'there is no notice taken of it for we have long thought nothing of Hunt or his proceedings, we know too that his Meeting is got up by the members of the Reform Association and with it we in no wise agree.'[25] On the day, there was an inordinate delay while a set of railings was removed to allow Hunt and the speakers to enter the ground in a blacking van specially bedecked with a tricolour awning, patriotic flags and a *bonnet rouge*. The crowds were small, perhaps 10,000 at the height of the proceedings when Hunt spoke with considerable energy 'of the importance of the working classes, upon whose exertions all the best interests of the community depended', and called for a national campaign of petitions to the King. Most people drifted away, however, before Lovett and Cleave finished reading the prolix addresses which Hunt was asked to present to the King and the people of Paris.[26]

In the north-west, the campaign was for the most part restricted to those areas where Hunt had recently evangelized, and there was little evidence of any breakthrough to mass support. There were some additions to the radical cause. The meeting at Carlisle, where the weavers and master-manufacturers had recently clashed when they met to discuss the formation of a political union on BPU lines, was probably the most successful of the petitioning meetings. Addressing the crowd of 4,000 or so on the Sands on 21 September, John Dixon warned of the dangers of middle-class reform:

Those sordid wretches who cried out for the representation of property would leave the largest class, the labourers, the only really productive class, wholly unrepresented,—and throw them for a redress of their grievances upon a House of Commons elected by their masters, probably their oppressors. (Cheers). Oh, no, such a Reform would be useless . . .

After Johnston, the Preston missionary, addressed the meeting, the

[24] Johnston read out Hunt's reply at a meeting in Carlisle, *Carlisle Journal*, 25 Sept. For Wakley's unsuccessful campaign, see *WFP*, 25 Sept.

[25] HO, 64/11 ff. 165–6. The informer was probably Abel Hall.   [26] *WFP*, 2 Oct.

Carlisle radicals agreed to subscribe to *The Crisis*, join the GNU, and send their petition via Mitchell and Hunt to the King. The proceedings came to a fitting conclusion when Johnston put the question: 'Do you agree to ask Mr. Hunt to place himself at the head of the reformers of the North?—(A general shout—Yes, we do).'[27]

Elsewhere there was less enthusiasm for the petitioning/addressing campaign, even on the radical Manchester–Preston axis. There was a poor attendance at Chadwick's Orchard, Preston on 27 September, the only meeting in the north held to coincide with Hunt's Kennington Common demonstration.[28] Some momentum developed, however, over the next few weeks as the new parliamentary session approached. The Middleton radicals adopted an address to the King at a mass meeting in the market place on 4 October, when the hallowed veterans, Fitton and Knight, were the main speakers.[29] The Bolton Political Union, recently radicalized to conform with the MPU, passed a similar address at a crowded meeting in the local theatre on 19 October.[30] Around this time too, radicals at Chorley formed a political union and started collecting subscriptions for the GNU together with signatures for an address to the King.[31] Across the Pennines, in the woollen district, the Almondbury Political Union, a staunchly Huntite body in close contact with the Preston radicals, seems to have been the only group to join the campaign. The council drew up an address to Hunt, 'respectfully requesting him to become leader and adviser of the Almondbury Political Union', and drafted a petition for him to present to the King, which was duly ratified at a mass meeting of 2,000 or so on 23 October.[32]

By this time political excitement was running high in London in response to the Belgian revolution, the persistence of distress, the spread of rural incendiarism in nearby Kent, the appearance of the new metropolitan police, and the publication of the first unstamped papers by Hetherington and Carpenter.[33] As he rallied the MPU and RRA behind the campaign of addresses and petitions to the King, Hunt's speeches caught the new mood and were among the most republican he ever made—they were later quoted against him in the Commons. Under his chairmanship, the council of the MPU issued a new 'Appeal to the People' which hinted at the desirability of a constituent assembly to frame a proper written constitution, but stressed that the immediate need was for the people to 'universally and (if possible) SIMULTANEOUSLY petition the King himself, imploring that his Majesty will be graciously pleased to recommend in his message to both

[27] *Carlisle Journal*, 11 and 25 Sept.
[28] *Preston Chronicle*, 2 Oct.
[29] Ibid., 9 Oct.   [30] *Bolton Chronicle*, 23 Oct.
[31] Ibid., 9 Oct.   [32] *Leeds Patriot*, 2 and 30 Oct.
[33] BL Add. MSS 27789 (Place papers) ff. 168–86.

Houses of the new Parliament, a RADICAL REFORM'.[34] 'Give the people of
England a House of Commons chosen by themselves,' he declared from
the chair at the MPU public meeting later that week to address the
Belgians, 'and he would be for the system of Kings, Lords and Commons;
but should the people of this country ever be so oppressed as to make
resistance a duty, and he should survive the struggle, he would be a
republican.'[35] The new militant tone was evident too in his speeches to the
RRA which began a series of eight weekly meetings at the Rotunda,
starting on 25 October with a discussion of the evils of military flogging,
which prompted him to express his hope of seeing the time 'when a
standing army would be abolished, and the country have a National Guard
(*loud applause, cheers, and cries of bravo*!)'. He chaired the next weekly
meeting when a manifesto was issued, advising the people not only to
petition the King but also to prepare 'a plan of mutual protection' should
radical reform not be forthcoming.[36] Two days later, on 3 November, he
attended the King's levee and presented a sackful of petitions and
addresses from Preston, Carlisle, Bolton, Middleton, London and elsewhere. By now, political excitement had reached fever pitch, following
Wellington's declaration against reform and the King's speech on the
opening of Parliament which, the Blackburn radicals regretted, 'rendered
his Majesty unworthy of the confidence of the labouring classes'.[37] Hunt
seemed well placed to exploit such public anger and discontent.

3. THE ADVENT OF THE WHIGS; 'CAPTAIN SWING'; AND THE PRESTON BY-ELECTION

The Government's declaration against reform inflamed political passions in
London, particularly as the ministers had also glossed over the severity of
distress and were apparently preparing for war to assist the Dutch against
the new Belgian and French regimes. As the date of the King's visit
approached, nightly riots and clashes with the new police developed in the
city, and huge crowds attended the meetings at the Rotunda, proudly
described by Carlile in his new unstamped paper, the *Prompter*, as the
'birth-place of mind and the focus of virtuous public excitement'.[38] Many
of those who flocked to the Blackfriars Road, however, were simply
looking for 'trouble', the most common form of metropolitan protest. On 8

[34] *An Appeal to the People of England, by the Council of the Metropolitan Political Union;
signed H. Hunt, chairman* (London, 1830).
[35] *Carpenter's Political Letters*, 21 Oct. *PD*, 3rd series, iii, 858–9. *Republican*, 3 Apr. 1831.
[36] Ibid., 29 Oct. and 6 Nov.
[37] *Preston Chronicle*, 13 Nov. George, xi, no. 16399.
[38] *Carpenter's Political Letters*, 6 Nov.; *Penny Papers*, 31 Oct., 2, 5 and 8 Nov.; *Prompter*,
13 Nov.; and Prothero, *Artisans and Politics*, 277–8.

November, when Hunt and the RRA held their weekly meeting, the Rotunda was packed to capacity, and a crowd of over 2,000 was left outside where they were addressed by Carpenter, Cleave and others, and, at the end of a long evening, by Hunt himself, who advised them to 'follow his example, to give three cheers for reform, and then go to their beds as he intended'. But as soon as Hunt left, trouble developed: a tricolour was unfurled and a cry of 'Now for the West-end' was instantly raised. A crowd of 1,500 crossed the bridges shouting 'Reform', 'Down with the Police', 'No Peel', 'No Wellington', and fought a pitched battle with the police which lasted until two in the morning.[39] The next evening there were a number of similar incidents as 'mobs' crossed over Blackfriars Bridge at regular intervals, but a major confrontation was averted because the royal visit had been cancelled and the police were on full alert. According to Place, the Government abandoned the visit because the police had information that Hunt 'was to lead 20,000 men from the Surrey side of the Thames over Black Friars Bridge to Ludgate Hill to pay their respects to the King, and to let him hear the sentiments of the people. That Hunt could collect and lead twice that number I have no doubt, but I do not believe that any such a procession would have taken place.'[40] When Hunt went to Union Hall on 11 November to inquire about a charge erroneously linking his young friend Lyne, secretary of the Christchurch ratepayers, with the mysterious 'Captain Swing' fires in Kent, he was severely reprimanded by the magistrates for his speeches at the Rotunda, the principal cause, they opined, of all the riots and violence. In reply, Hunt denied any responsibility for recent events: he not only denounced the rioters but also disclaimed any connection with the trading orators of the Rotunda, Cobbett and the 'Atheists', Carlile, Gale Jones and 'the Devil's Chaplain, as Mr. Christian Evidence Taylor was called', all of whom 'pocketed the whole of the receipts of their nights of speechifying'. After this disturbing interview with the magistrates, he went to see the lord mayor and then Peel to reassure himself that there was no warrant out for his arrest.[41]

The events of early November highlighted the weaknesses of London radicalism. Popular support was spasmodic, dependent upon political excitement rather than economic fluctuations: the crowds declined and the riots died away once Wellington resigned on 16 November. The leadership was particularly prone to division and dispute, ideological, tactical, and personal. The contention displayed over the July Revolution returned with

---

[39] *Hunt's Letter to the King . . . with every particular of Hunt's Lecture at the Rotunda; and all the news of the day* (London, 1830); *The Times*, 9 and 12 Nov.; *WFP*, 13 Nov.; and *Carpenter's Political Letters*, 11 Nov.

[40] *WFP*, 13 Nov. BL Add. MSS 35148 (Place papers), ff. 69–70, Place to Hobhouse, 8 Nov.

[41] *The Times*, 12–15 Nov. including the correspondence between the misreported Hunt and the aggrieved Taylor. *WFP*, 20 Nov. See also, *CPR*, 12 Mar. 1831.

a vengeance in the wake of Hunt's gratuitous disparagement of the Rotundanists at Union Hall, thereby precluding the development of a united radical stand towards the new Whig administration and its reform proposals. All the 'ultras'—republicans, infidels, old confrontationalists and new radical co-operators—rallied to the support of Carlile and his Rotunda colleagues against Hunt's 'bad moral and tyrannical spirit'. The Government informer hastened to enroll in the anti-Hunt ranks—'Grady, Hetherington, Cleave and Thompson having taken Hunt's side of the affair and all the rest against it and finding that the most likely to be desperate side was of my old acquaintance I took that side also.' Battle was joined at the next meeting of the RRA at the Rotunda, for which Lovett and Watson, the co-operator, marshalled a strong contingent of anti-Hunt forces. On arrival, Hunt objected to the tricolour which had been suspended over the platform by 'some persons unconnected with the persons on the stage'. 'The greatest confusion here was manifested', the informer reported, 'by cries of down with the flag, No. No, hissings, hootings oh you Coward, no blacking puffs, go to Union Hall . . . and a thousand noises of all sorts which lasted at least an hour'. This was merely a preliminary skirmish. Fists started flying when Hunt objected to Carlile's unbridled strictures in the *Prompter* and repaid him in kind, raking up all the old charges about the coward who had fled the field at Peterloo to 'come off to London to make money of the News'. When Carlile stood up to defend himself, the informer continued, 'the Row became so great that nobody could be heard and the abuse between him and Hunt became nearly to a fight. We surrounded Carlile and the Mob rushed on to the Hustings and a general fight took place in the midst of which Hunt stole away.'[42]

In his lecture a few days later, Gale Jones challenged Hunt to show his face at the Rotunda again and 'argue the proofs of his denouncement of them', but by this time Hunt had left for the west country on a business trip, stopping off to attend a meeting on negro slavery at Rowland Hill's chapel where his 'political abuse was much reprobated by the persons assembled and he was not allowed much chance of proceeding'.[43] Thereafter excitement died away and the attendances at the Rotunda were to take a dip, but the divisions between the leaders widened. In early December, the informer sent in a lengthy report of the 'disunion existing among the Committee of the Reform Association by Lovett, Cleave, Watson and Millard, who are accused of going too far in their principles for Grady, Fitzgerald and others, the former being advocates of Republicanism and Atheism, the latter being Catholics and Christians and Reformers.'[44]

[42] HO, 64/11 ff. 119–21. *Prompter*, 13 and 20 Nov.
[43] HO 64/11 ff. 98 and 126. *Prompter* 20 Nov.   [44] HO 64/11 f. 151.

Thus the political excitement of the autumn, which ended with the appointment of a Whig ministry pledged to peace, retrenchment and reform, left Hunt dependent for support on the loyal group of radicals who had followed him from the Friends of Civil and Religious Liberty into the RRA and then the MPU. Most of the metropolitan ideologues and activists were strongly opposed to him, although Hetherington's *Penny Papers*, soon to become the celebrated *Poor Man's Guardian*, looked to him to head a national convention to secure a proper radical reform bill.[45] Outside London, however, Hunt was held in much higher esteem. During his west country tour, he was welcomed as a conciliator in towns torn by 'Captain Swing' riots, and his popularity in the north was dramatically underlined by his sensational election victory at Preston in December.

Loyalists and alarmists were quick to point out the remarkable coincidence between the spread of the 'Captain Swing' riots and the route of Hunt's business trip. Hunt's name, indeed cropped up everywhere, as many riot-captains adopted it as their own. The Government, however, was reliably informed from the Rotunda that Hunt and the radicals had 'nothing to do with these proceedings and though Hunt has been in the Country it is own business totally unconnected among them'.[46] Hunt, in fact, tried to do all he could to prevent the spread of violence, until he became so disgusted with the behaviour of the farmers and the authorities that he refused to offer his services as conciliator and arbitrator. His most successful intervention was at Overton, scene of the first major rioting in Hampshire. First the farmers and then the labourers called upon him to mediate, the latter, he noted with pride, 'grounded their request on the recollection of the excellent treatment of his own workmen, when he was a resident in that neighbourhood.' He drew up an agreement that was so satisfactory to all concerned that the labourers immediately returned to work, much to the relief of the shopkeepers and magistrates, who had been 'closely immured for the two previous days, during which their services were so much required'.[47] The riots confirmed his long-held fears about the disastrous impact of the funding-system on rural society: in order to pay the fundholders the Government had to 'apply a screw' to the landowners who in turn 'screwed down' the farmers; 'these applied the screw with double force, and all joining together, screwed the poor labourer, who had been screwed so long and so tight, that the labourers had now been under the necessity, having no other alternative but starvation, to endeavour to screw some portion of their hard earnings back again'.[48] After Overton and the wage riots, Hunt's route took him to Andover and Salisbury where

[45] *Penny Papers* 20 Nov.
[46] Hobsbawm and Rudé, 184–6. HO 64/11 f. 130.
[47] *The Times* 22 Nov.; *Carpenter's Political Letters* 25 Nov.; and *PD*, 3rd series, ii, 250–3.
[48] *Preston Chronicle* 18 Dec.

violence soon ensued and the threshing machines were destroyed. For this unfortunate turn of events, he blamed the incompetent local authorities and the irresponsible farmers, who had distributed money and liquor, encouraging their men to "'Smash away, let us all be on all equality'".[49] He then travelled further west, away from the main centres of disturbance, and was staying in Somerset when he received the remarkable news that he had been put in nomination at the Preston by-election and stood in the lead after the first day's polling. He immediately set off for Bristol to catch the Manchester mail and head north.

The Preston radicals decided to nominate Hunt after they had quizzed Stanley, the newly-appointed chief secretary for Ireland, about the reform intentions of the Whigs. When the new minister presented himself for re-election, Johnston demanded to know whether he would support the ballot and the immediate abolition of the Corn Law. Stanley made it absolutely clear that he had no such intentions, and added that he had no reason to believe that the ballot 'forms any part of the reform under consideration (Clamour).' Dismayed by this reply, the radicals decided to run the risk of nominating Hunt, even though there were considerable expenses outstanding from the last contest, after which Hunt had vowed never to return to contest the seat unless he found himself placed at the head of the poll.[50] Much had been learnt from the disastrous summer election, and the radical vote was now far better organized. There was close co-operation between the radicals and the spinners, typical of the coalescence of political and industrial protest in the north-west at this time. The Grand General Union was preparing for a major turn-out, and the election coincided with the famous Ashton-Stalybridge strike, where the carrying of tricolours and radical rhetoric of the strike leaders seriously alarmed the authorities.[51] The Preston spinners, the lowest paid and most oppressed of their trade in Lancashire, held a series of meetings at which they decided 'not to submit to any dictation from their masters, as to the exercise of their elective franchise',[52] and their trade union pooled resources with the radical committee to set up a fund to aid those thrown out of work for voting according to their conscience.[53] There were other, more technical reasons which explained the dramatic improvement in the radical poll. Mitchell had persuaded the new Tory mayor to abolish the system of district voting which had so suited Stanley and his army of lawyers: the free-for-all

---

[49] *The Times* 23 Nov.; *PD*, 3rd series, ii, 253–5; and Hobsbawm and Rudé 91–8. Significantly, the most bloody of the Wiltshire riots took place at Pyt House, the estate of Hunt's old adversary, John Benett.

[50] *CPR*, 18 Dec.; Mitchell's letter, *Preston Chronicle* 20 Nov., and Hunt's speech on arrival, ibid. 18 Dec.

[51] Foster, 6 Dec., HO 40/26/1 ff. 161–3. Kirby and Musson, ch. 5; and R. Sykes 'Early Chartism and Trade Unionism in South-East Lancashire' in Epstein and Thompson, 165–7.

[52] *Preston Chronicle*, 11 Dec.   [53] Mitchell's speech, *CPR*, 18 Dec.

method of polling more than redressed the balance in favour of the radical crowd.[54] Stanley's largesse fell way below expectations as he faced a second contest within a matter of months: the taps were kept shut and his supporters were offered no more than a five shilling ticket for refreshment after they had polled.[55] After the end of the first day's polling on 8 December, the absent Hunt had a commanding lead with 1,204 votes to Stanley's 791. By the time he arrived in town, late at night on 13 December, his position was unassailable. On the hustings the next day, he expressed his surprise and delight at this unexpected turn of events, and reassured those who had voted for him that 'none of them would be hurt, they would be under the protection of the Trades' Union, now established in London, Bristol, Manchester, and other places'. Much of his speech was directed against the Whigs and their false promise of reform. Stanley, he noted, had 'let the cat out of the bag': his answers to Johnston confirmed that the ministers 'intended to do nothing . . . He, Henry Hunt, believed, all that could be done, without the vote by ballot, and a repeal of the corn laws, to be a mere nothing—all trash . . . Reform, indeed! he was old enough to recollect the jockeys when they were in office before, in 1806 and 1807.' To achieve real reform—to rid the system of Stanley and his class, the 'overruling aristocracy'—would require a great campaign by the people which he would be proud to co-ordinate from the Commons where he would 'apply such a lever to the system, as would produce an effect (Much cheering)':

As much as any man could do, he would attempt to do, in behalf of the poor, the honest, and the industrious who live by the sweat of their brow . . . It was the voice of the people that would produce reform, and he hoped to be favoured by their petitions which would, by him, never be slighted; from every town and village he would make their prayers heard, in spite of all the means that might be taken to the contrary.[56]

When the final figures were declared on 15 December—Hunt 3,730, Stanley 3,392—Stanley tried to overturn the result by demanding a full scrutiny, a bare-faced attempt, Hunt protested, to 'put down the people by the means of money and insolence'. The radicals organized a mass protest meeting in Lune Street and launched a national appeal for funds to counter Stanley's plan to bear them down *with such heavy expenses, as he believes, we are not able to sustain*. When the scrutiny got under way, they took to the streets to display their strength and register their anger: every night there were processions with lighted tar-barrels, music and flags to Hunt's lodgings where he addressed the crowds from the window. Much to the relief of the local authorities, Stanley suddenly decided to abandon the

---

[54] Proctor, 142–3. Grimshaw 5 Jan. 1831. HO 52/13 ff. 221–2.
[55] *Preston Chronicle*, 11 Dec.   [56] Ibid. 18 Dec.

scrutiny on 23 December, and Hunt was at last declared duly elected.[57] He remained in Preston over Christmas, spending Boxing Day visiting his principal supporters, the poor weavers who worked fourteen hours a day but earned only 4/6d. a week.[58] Members of the spinners' union and the radical committee organized the traditional 'riding' of the successful candidate, which took place on 27 December, a bitterly cold and snowy day, but with at least 16,000 people joining in the festivities according to the report in Doherty's new paper, the *Voice of the People*. Hunt took his leave of the cheering crowds, assuring them that he would convey 'the wishes and wants of the whole of the industrious classes of the country to parliament; and as Daniel O'Connell, the only honest man in parliament, is the member for all Ireland, so I shall be the representative of the great mass of the industrious population of this country, to advocate their interests, and to regain and maintain for them their rights'.[59]

The next few days were a happy round of triumphal processions, speeches, dinners and theatre visits as the 'man of the people' made his way slowly back through the radical heartland to Manchester, stopping at Blackburn, Bolton and Oldham to drum up support for a new petitioning campaign—'he had often recomended them to discontinue petitioning the House of Commons, as they pay no attention to them; but he would ask them to try once more, now that they had got Henry Hunt into the House (Laughter and great cheering)'.[60] On new year's day he arrived in Manchester where spirits were low after the failure of the turn-out on 27 December. The magistrates described Hunt's visit as a failure too, but press and broadsheet reports suggest otherwise. A large procession accompanied him down the Oldham Road to the site of Peterloo where thousands more were waiting, many of whom had come into town 'from all parts of the country'. His speech exemplified the new class emphasis in his radical language as he stressed that his 'principal duty at present led him to advocate the cause of the labouring classes . . . He was convinced the working classes wanted support, and they must be supported. He stood there as the advocate of their rights, and hoped their voices would ultimately prevail.' At the dinner afterwards, he patched up the differences with Doherty over the Paine affair in August, and then set off for London,

[57] Ibid. 24 Dec. *CPR*, 25 Dec. Phillips to Bouverie, 22 Dec., and to Messrs. Gorst and Birchall, 30 Dec., HO, 41/9 ff. 154–5, and 230–1. Bouverie, 24 Dec., HO, 40/26/2.

[58] *Penny Papers*, 21 Jan. 1831. The ratio of weavers who voted for Hunt in Dec. 1830—6 to 1—is the highest occupational voting ratio recorded in John Vincent's study of *Pollbooks: How Victorians Voted* (Cambridge, 1968), 24 and 160–2. Mechanics and spinners supported Hunt by a lower ratio, 2 to 1.

[59] *Voice of the People*, 1 Jan. 1831. *Preston Chronicle*, 1 Jan. 1831, estimated the crowds at 9,000; *Penny Papers*, 31 Dec., claimed 40,000–50,000.

[60] *Bolton Chronicle*, 31 Dec. *Penny Papers*, 8 Jan. 1831. Ratcliffe, 4 Jan. 1831, HO, 52/13 ff. 227–8.

accompanied by Mitchell, proud representative of the brave electors of Preston who had 'returned the champion of the people to parliament'.[61] They were warmly applauded as they passed through the west midlands: after a public breakfast at Wolverhampton, they dined at Birmingham with the council of the BPU, and made arrangements for celebratory medals to be struck for each of the 3,730 electors; at Coventry, their last stop, Hunt addressed a crowd of over 3,000 in Broad-gate.[62]

After the cordiality and festivities of the provinces, Hunt encountered the rivalries and antagonisms of the metropolis again when he tried to arrange a triumphal public return to the capital. He was forced to abandon plans for a public dinner when the hard-pressed RRA objected to the expense—they were in a rather embarrassing financial position after Carlile had upped the rent at the Rotunda before refusing them the use of the premises altogether. The proposed procession, the Government informer predicted, would be no more than 'a Monday's Mob' since the 'Radical Committee', the BAPCK, and Carlile's party all refused to participate in this 'overpowering instance of personal vanity', as the *Weekly Free Press* described it. On the day it was not a bad show, although the weather was most unkind. A crowd estimated at 6,000–15,000 braved the rain to hear Hunt's address on Islington Green, where the procession assembled. As in 1822, certain trades' groups were to the fore, although the carpenters and others were absent because of misleading placards. Pride of place, of course, went to Hunt and Mitchell in their barouchette, drawn by four grey horses, with the post boys in pink satin jackets. They were cheered by decent sized crowds as they made their way across the city to Stamford Street, where Hunt closed the proceedings with the assurance that he was 'just the same unflinching, uncompromising man as he had showed himself to be, during a twenty-five years' struggle in the cause of the people. (Cheers.) He had made no one promise before he came into Parliament, that he would not sedulously endeavour to redeem. (Cheers.)'.[63]

A week later, Wakley chaired a meeting at the London Tavern to congratulate the Preston electors and raise a subscription to help with the outstanding expenses. It was a great radical occasion. Bronterre O'Brien set the tone when he moved a vote of thanks to the electors of Preston who had returned Hunt, 'the uncompromising and fearless advocate of the people's rights and liberties', and spurned a Whig minister, the representative of 'a faction unexampled for hypocrisy and rapacity in the annals of

---

[61] Foster, 27 and 30 Dec., HO, 40/26/2, and 1 and 5 Jan. 1831, HO, 52/13 ff. 417, and 423–4. Manchester Central Library: 'Speech of H. Hunt Esqr. M. P.', broadsheet. *Voice of the People*, 8 Jan. 1831. Kirby and Musson, 424.

[62] *Penny Papers*, 8 Jan., *Bolton Chronicle*, 15 Jan., and *Voice of the People*, 15 Jan. 1831.

[63] HO, 64/11 ff. 169 and 171. WFP, 15 Jan.; *Penny Papers*, 15 Jan.; and *Carpenter's Political Letters*, 13 Jan. 1831.

political tergiversation'. Grady explained how the victory would facilitate a new campaign for radical reform based on the parliamentary office which Hunt, in imitation of O'Connell, intended to establish with a full-time clerk, funds permitting. The office, 'a receptacle for the complaint of every man in the community', would co-ordinate the radical challenge by arranging public meetings, collecting petitions, and forming a 'bond of union among Reformers'.[64] Before Hunt took his seat in the Commons on 3 February between Hume and Warburton, there were several signs that his election had generated a new demand for the radical programme. Radical activists disrupted the anniversary dinner of the BPU on 25 January;[65] radical petitions, the first of many, were adopted at mass meetings at Ashton, Butterworth and Oldham;[66] and, most important of all, a new type of organization had come into being in New Cross, Manchester, a 'Political Union of the Working Classes', committed to opposing anything less than the full Huntite radical programme.[67] Just as the Whigs were about to unveil their reform bill, Hunt seemed to have achieved the elusive breakthrough for the radical cause.

[64] Ibid., 21 Jan.; *Penny Papers*, 21 Jan. 1831; and HO, 64/11 ff. 235–6, and 64/12 f. 197.
[65] *Carpenter's Political Letters*, 25 Jan. 1831.
[66] *Voice of the People*, 29 Jan. and 5 Feb. 1831. In February, similar meetings were held in Stockport, Great Horton, Lees, Elland and Keighley.
[67] Ibid., 29 Jan. 1831. Kirby and Musson, 424. R. A. Sykes, 'Popular Politics and Trade Unionism in South-East Lancashire, 1829–42', unpublished Ph.D. thesis, Manchester University, 1982, 367.

8

Hunt, Working-Class Radicalism
and the Reform Bill

BY the end of 1830 Hunt had achieved some success with his unstinting efforts to mobilize the people and reactivate the radical challenge. In the next eighteen months or so, he faced a far more difficult task—upholding the radical programme against the overwhelming popularity of the Whig Reform Bill, the 'Bill of Bills'.[1] He could not counteract the hegemonic forces promoting moderate reform in the early 1830s, but his thankless efforts to preserve the independence and integrity of popular radicalism proved to be his greatest contribution to the making of the English working class. His objections to the Bill lacked any intellectual or ideological rigour, but his basic fundamentalist criticisms were addressed with particular force and relevance to the northern working class. Here he laid the foundations for the Chartist movement, his true memorial.

Chartism derived its vigour and assertive working-class independence from a powerful myth: the pervasive belief that the people had been deliberately deluded by the Whigs and manipulated by the middle-class reformers during the Reform Bill agitation. Having been encouraged by the Whigs to expect benefits for themselves, they had then been mobilized as a 'reserve army' by the self-interested middle-class reformers to ensure the Bill's passage. Shorn of its conspiratorial overtones, the myth accurately reflected the dramatic change in popular attitudes to the Bill from initial enthusiasm to eventual disillusionment. During the agitation of 1831–2, the people supported the Bill without question or waver. In a mood of collective self-deception, they chose to ignore Hunt's criticisms and forewarnings, and shouted him down as a Tory. Within the ranks of radicalism itself, he was condemned by gradualists and confrontationalists alike. Gradualists were delighted by the extensive nature of the Bill. This was where the Whigs displayed their shrewd sense of self-preservation: Grey and his colleagues wisely calculated that the best way to conserve the traditional political order was to produce a thorough, once and for all, measure of reform, a bold approach which had the added short-term advantage of confounding the radicals and converting many of them into proselytes of the Bill. Having expected so much less, most radicals extolled

[1] *CPR*, 19 Mar. 1831.

the Whig measure, believing that it left the full radical programme no more than an easy instalment away. The confrontationalists were attracted less by the Bill than by the militant extra-parliamentary posture of its middle-class supporters. At decisive moments in the Reform Bill agitation, the middle-class reformers kept the Whigs up to the mark by implementing their 'art of revolution', summoning up the spectre of uncontrollable popular fury should the Bill be dropped or diluted. The success of the 'brickbat argument', the middle-class version of 'collective bargaining by riot', depended on the willingness of the working class to do the rioting for them.[2] The ultra-radicals were quick to respond, and joined the middle-class reformers in their militant plans and talk, trusting that a real revolutionary confrontation would ensue. A staunch critic of the Whigs and the middle-class political unions, Hunt stood apart from the popular enthusiasm of the day, refusing to join in the clamour for a Bill which offered nothing to the working class. At the time, some loyal radicals and desperate handloom-weavers in the north supported his stand: a few years later, vast numbers of the working class, their expectations thwarted and dashed, belatedly recognized the wisdom of his opposition to the Bill.

I. THE 'BILL OF BILLS'

By proposing the wholesale abolition of the rotten boroughs and the enfranchisement of all the large towns, the Whig Reform Bill far exceeded expectations and was greeted with great enthusiasm in the radical press where the limitations of the £10 franchise were quite overlooked. Among the most fulsome in their praise were Hunt's old adversaries, Cobbett, the pragmatist, and Carlile, the republican idealist-cum-practicable politician. Under the heading 'My Triumph', Cobbett preducted that the Bill, 'the thing we have been labouring for, for many years', would go down in history as '"THE REFORM," as the change made in the time of Henry VIII is called "THE REFORMATION," and as that made in 1688 is called "THE REVOLUTION"'.[3] Proclaiming himself '*a Ministerial Man*', Carlile welcomed the Bill as a major exercise in practical politics, precipitated by the dramatic progress of his propagandism of the principles of Paine and the religion of Mirabaud. 'Other Radical Reformers', he noted, 'may quarrel with it, because it does not echo their parrot-cries . . . I take this bill as an earnest of Radical Reform in the House of Commons, and as a pledge of Radical Reform in the affairs of the country.'[4] Such optimism pervaded the radical press. William Carpenter, the diligent reporter of the RRA and MPU, was the most eloquent exponent of the instalment thesis of reform.

[2] Thomis and Holt, 85–99.   [3] *CPR*, 5–19 Mar. 1831.
[4] *Prompter*, 5 Mar. 1831.

He enjoined the radicals not to criticize the Bill or impede its progress because it was 'well understood by all, that the present measure will not be a final, but only a preparatory one; that is, a sort of provisional settling of the constitution, until the nation finds itself in a condition to make the final perfect settlement'.[5] Thomas Wakley, editor of the *Ballot*, advised the radicals to support the Bill 'because we see in it the certain, the well-set, machinery for ultimately obtaining for the people that only security for real freedom—THE RIGHT OF SELF-GOVERNMENT'.[6] In the *Voice of the People*, John Doherty, the spinners' leader turned radical journalist, rallied the north behind the cry 'the bill, the whole bill, and nothing but the bill'.[7]

There were only two papers that criticized the Bill and drew attention to its limitations: John Foster's *Leeds Patriot* cautioned its readers amongst the labouring classes against 'too sanguine expectations of its results';[8] Henry Hetherington's *Penny Papers* condemned it outright since it would actually delay any progress towards equal political rights. Under Thomas Mayhew's editorship the *Penny Papers* stood forward as the 'Poor Man's Guardian' to challenge the foolish enthusiasm for the Bill. 'The greatest enemies the people have are these "middling classes"', Mayhew warned, direfully predicting that the newly enfranchised middlemen and shop-keepers would establish the £10 suffrage as 'the low water mark upon the scale of privilege'. The people, Mayhew regretted, were 'too ignorant to form a correct opinion for themselves; they only call for a change, because their animal feelings tell them that a change is necessary . . . they want an adviser—they want a *Guardian*; we, for want of a better, have elected ourselves into that situation; and we, in their name, assert our unqualified disapprobation of the proposed measure'.[9]

Hunt's own position towards the Bill was confused and confusing at first. To Cobbett's anger, he refused to support it without reservation: to Mayhew's consternation, he refused to oppose it outright. As he sat attentively through the parliamentary debates, he struggled to come to terms with the ambivalent nature of the Bill, and the glaring discrepancy between the Government's intentions and the people's expectations.[10] He was as surprised as anyone by the extensive nature of the Bill, much of which he openly applauded. Schedules A and B spelt out the abolition of the rotten boroughs, the surrender of corporate rights, and an end to the 'comfortable feasts on which corporators have so long fattened'. But while the Bill was a death blow to certain aspects of the old system—and for this reason alone he always voted for it in the Commons—there was nothing in the Whig proposals to justify all the public enthusiasm and eager

---

[5] *Carpenter's Political Letters*, 11 Mar. 1831.   [6] *Ballot*, 6 Mar. 1831.
[7] *Voice of the People*, 2 Apr. 1831.   [8] *Leeds Patriot*, 12 Mar. 1831.
[9] *Penny Papers*, 4, 12 and 18 Mar. 1831.
[10] See his speeches, 1–11 Mar. 1831, *PD*, 3rd series, ii, 1208–17, iii, 18–19, 341, and 372–3.

expectation of progressive reform. In the Commons he heard the Whigs present the Bill as a carefully designed 'final' measure, which specifically incorporated the middle class and permanently excluded the working class. The people, Hunt later complained, 'had been grossly deceived in the Reform Bill':

The lying press had deceived them, or they would know that Lord John Russell, Lord Althorpe, and others of the ministry, had never pretended that this bill was to give any substantial benefits to the working classes; they had all along declared that they had proposed it as a means of cementing the tottering institutions of the country, by giving to a large portion of the middle class the right of exercising the elective franchise. It was their agents and the public press out of doors that had said otherwise, and endeavoured to make the nation believe that it would benefit the mass of the people . . . .[11]

Hunt's first response to the Bill in the Commons revealed considerable confusion in his mind as he was caught unawares by the extent of the measure and its popularity. He tried to reconcile the criteria of the reforming Whigs with an amended version of the radical programme, drawn from his recent experience at Preston where he had come to appreciate the importance of the aristocracy of labour and the imperative need for the ballot. Speaking after Macaulay's paeans to the respectable middle class, he drew attention to the claims and character of the respectable working class:

He was told that £10 was the proper qualification, but he thought that the best vote was that which came from the industrious artificer or manufacturer, who earned from 30s. to £3 a week . . . He did not wish the rabble, as the hon. Member called them to have votes; but he did wish that those who paid a rent of from £3 a year up to £10, the men who were the sinews and nerves of the country, should not be excluded.

He tried to rally support for what he called the Preston-type of universal suffrage, a franchise which excluded all paupers and criminals but otherwise recognized the 'principle of an equality of political rights . . . that all who paid taxes should have a vote'.[12] In the absence of any response, he turned his attention to the ballot, the *sine qua non* of his radicalism after his experience at Preston. The Bill, he insisted, required the protection of the ballot if it were to be of any use, but here too he failed to elicit any support in Parliament or the country. The nation, he discovered, was enraptured with the Bill just as it stood. Reform groups retracted the radical petitions they had previously sent him, and pledged their unqualified approval of the ministerial measure.[13] The livery, so radical in 1830, refused to endorse his criticisms, and greeted the Bill with

[11] *PMG*, 3 Nov. 1832.   [12] *PD*, 3rd series, ii, 1212–14, and iii, 81.
[13] *PD*, 3rd series, ii, 1215–17, iii, 250, 372–3, 450, and 919–21.

ecstatic enthusiasm: the Common Hall on 7 March was an occasion of great celebration, at which Hunt's call for the ballot was considered quite out of place.[14] In Somerset he was ruled firmly out of order when he tried to bring in the ballot at a county meeting to adopt a petition 'expressive of entire approbation of the Reform Bill'.[15] From Somerset, he set off north to Preston, where his faith in radicalism and the people was restored, and his critique of the Bill acquired a new clarity and a sharper social edge.

Confused and conciliatory as Hunt's early comments on the Bill were, they infuriated Cobbett who immediately accused the 'Preston Cock' of colluding with the Tories to destroy the Bill. Cobbett, indeed, took exception to Hunt's first and rather tortuous Commons' speech on the Bill in which he had given the measure his begrudging support but raised the possibility of a popular 're-action' against it since he questioned 'how the great mass of the people could be called on to come forward to support a Reform, from the benefits of which they were to be excluded, and which was intended for those above them?'[16] This was enough to convince Cobbett that Hunt intended 'to *furnish the strongest of all argument to the opponents of the measure*, and thereby to cause one of two things, the *rejection of all reform*, or the *producing of a convulsive revolution.*' Determined to discredit Hunt before he could do any real damage to the Bill, Cobbett addressed a vitriolic warning letter to the people of Preston, thereby initiating a controversy which kept the antagonists apart for the rest of their lives. Underlying the political difference of opinion was the familiar clash of personalities, aggravated by Cobbett's ill-concealed envy of Hunt's seat in the Commons. Every aspect of Hunt's conduct since his victory at Preston was subjected to critical scrutiny, censure and ridicule: the 'idle parade all the way from Preston to London'; the needless expense and mock-heroics of the medal scheme; the jobbery of the proposed parliamentary office; and above all, the abysmal performance in the Commons, scene of 'the hackerings, the stammerings, the bogglings, the blunderings, and the cowering downs of this famous Cock'.[17] Hunt, it is true, was less effective in Parliament than on the platform but what Cobbett overlooked were the obstacles and opposition he encountered as he laboured to fulfill his onerous responsibility as the people's representative. Whenever he raised controversial issues or spoke at any length, members conspired to drown him out. 'Let the people of England know, that when he wished to protect them from oppression, he was to be coughed down', he protested at the end of his somewhat discursive but stirring speech on his first major motion, calling for an amnesty for the agricultural rioters convicted by the Special Commissions. He battled

[14] *CPR*, 12 Mar. 1831.　　　[15] Taunton Courier, 30 Mar. 1831.
[16] *PD*, 3rd series, ii, 1208–17.
[17] 'To the People of Preston', *CPR*, 12 Mar. 1831.

against similar, well-orchestrated obstruction during the presentation of petitions, a duty he took extremely seriously, much to the annoyance of the impatient House. In all his parliamentary duties, Hunt was remarkably diligent, at the cost of his health. He found the late hours particularly disagreeable and within a fortnight of taking his seat he was taken ill in the chamber, with a bad attack of rheumatism. 'It is a devil of a life', he reported back to his Preston constituents: 'I must attend at the house by nine o'clock in the morning if I intend to get any business done, and stay there till three the next morning, and have the misery to listen to some sham debate.' When he tried to persuade the House not to proceed to new business after midnight, he failed to find a seconder.[18]

In his riposte to Cobbett, *The Preston Cock's Reply to the Kensington Dunghill*, Hunt defended his parliamentary conduct with great vigour, and reprinted a petition he had recently presented from some of Cobbett's labourers claiming that their employer operated a scandalous form of truck system. Naturally, he rehearsed the full catalogue of Cobbett's other misdeeds over the years, including French's sensational allegations, but most of the pamphlet was given over to a full and correct report of his first Commons speech on the Reform Bill, which, he claimed, had been wilfully misreported in the press. With the record set straight, he left it to his constituents to decide whether he had said 'one thing at Preston and another in the House of Commons'.[19]

2. 'RE-ACTION' IN THE NORTH

During the Easter recess, Hunt set off for Preston, intending to distribute the 3,730 victory medals, a pleasure he had to forgo because of difficulties with the manufacturer in the midlands who demanded payment of the £250 or so still outstanding. When he stopped at Darlaston, however, he found that the local radicals were dissatisfied with the Bill, and he decided to continue on to Preston to sound out popular feelings there. His own attitude to the Bill had hardened, following the polemic with Cobbett, and he wanted to be sure that he could rely on the support of his constituents. 'The whole country is going mad about it', he reported to the crowds assembled outside his Preston lodgings, 'if I speak against it, I may stand a chance of getting my brains knocked out . . . I cannot conscientiously say I

[18] *PD*, 3rd series, ii, 246–72, 366, 535–8, 547, and 821–4; *Voice of the People*, 26 Feb.; and *Preston Chronicle*, 9 Apr. 1831. On one occasion, he produced some lozenges which he offered to the coughing members; he later made it a point of principle to divide the House on every question when members tried to cough him down, *PD*, 3rd series, iii, 920 and iv, 985. See also, J. W. Osborne, 'Henry Hunt's Career in Parliament', *Historian*, xxxix (1976), 24–39.

[19] Hunt, *Preston Cock's Reply*. *PD*, 3rd series, iii, 579–82.

approve of the measure, nor am I bold enough to stand in the face of all the country to oppose it . . . Now let me ask you—because I have come to be instructed by you—my duty.'[20] The speech, specially repeated in the evening for the benefit of the factory workers, marked the start of Hunt's tireless campaign to generate the 're-action' he had predicted. Much that was said became part of his standard routine over the next year or so as he tried to dispel the enthusiasm for the Bill and rally the working class for a comprehensive radical alternative. First there was a set of telling figures to demonstrate the limitations and inconsistencies of the Bill, 'a *mixty-maxty hodge-podge*':

ministers propose to give the right of voting to something short of *one* million, and leave the *seven* millions unrepresented. They say they are mixing up property and population together. There is one million that it may be reasonably estimated possess £150 per annum each: thus their annual income is 150 millions. With regard to the remaining seven millions, the highest of their earnings will not exceed a pound per week, and the lowest about four shillings, or parish allowance; which, being averaged, will be twelve shillings per week, for seven millions of the people; this is 218 millions or thereabouts per annum. So that one million of the people, and 150 millions in property, are all that is represented; while 7 millions of the people, and 218 millions in property have no representatives at all: so much for the amalgamating of persons and property together.[21]

After presenting these figures, he posed the crucial question of whether the Bill should be supported by the excluded seven millions, into whose ranks, he regretted, the poor electors of Preston were doomed to fall as 'the object of this bill is to take away the rights of the labourer, and give them to the middle class'. 'The reform bill is not going to give you anything', he asserted: 'Ministers do not pretend that it will do you any good. There will be neither cheaper bread, beer, nor clothing. No, but they say it will satisfy you.' At this point he called for a show of hands to see whether the people really were satisfied with the Bill and if they approved or disapproved of his conduct. The response was suitably reassuring: the mass meeting, the one form of universal suffrage without the ballot to which Hunt never objected, was a welcome refuge for the leader of democratic radicalism.

Whilst the crowds plumped for Hunt and radical reform, some of the local leaders in the north-west openly approved of gradualism and the Bill. In Preston, the leadership was split in two by the Whig proposals. Mitchell adopted a position of outright opposition, based on the fear that the Bill

---

[20] *Preston Chronicle*, 9 Apr. 1831 for an extensive report of Hunt's visit. For Darlaston, see *PD*, 3rd series, iii, 1503–7.

[21] Hunt first used these figures in the Commons on 24 Mar., *PD*, 3rd series, iii, 919–21. A correspondent to *Penny Papers*, 29 Apr. 1831, complained that Hunt 'has made the income of the labouring class full one-third more than what it really is, and the income of the upper orders less than one-half of what it is'.

with its uniform £10 franchise would disfranchise the poor Preston electors. Johnston, by contrast, subscribed to the instalment thesis, and welcomed the Bill as 'part payment' after which 'it would be the more easy to obtain the rest'. For this 'improper view of the measure', Johnston was publicly criticized by Hunt who explained that 'instead of being an instalment of so much in the pound, it would prove to be an actual bankruptcy and a final dividend'.[22] The next day, Hunt went to Bolton, where William Naisby, the veteran radical leader and former local secretary of the GNU, shared Johnston's gradualist views and had organized a petition in support of the Bill. 'I see you are all running mad for the Reform Bill', Hunt chided the crowds in his speech from the Swan Hotel. 'But what good do you expect to result from it? Oh, it was to be a *liberal* measure; it certainly was all very good, very *liberal*; but *would it get the people something more to eat*? (No, no).'[23] Later that afternoon he addressed huge crowds at Peterloo— according to the local press some 50,000–70,000 gathered behind the band and banners of the Manchester Political Union of the Working Classes— and roundly condemned the Bill, its supporters and promoters, whose evil intention was 'to give what they call the middle classes, which amount to about a million of people, a share in the representation, in order that they may join the higher classes to keep seven millions of the lower classes down—(Hear and shame)'. A barrage of rhetorical questions forced the point home:

Do they propose to lessen the taxes? Do they propose to keep their hands out of our pockets? To give us cheaper bread, cheaper meat, cheaper clothing, to work us fewer hours, or to give us better wages?—(Cries of no, no.) Then how the devil are you interested, pray?[24]

On his return to London, Hunt promptly reported to the Commons that 'a great re-action had taken place in the public mind on the subject of the Bill':

The country had now had time for reflection, and there was a re-action of opinion (*Cheers from the Opposition.*) Notwithstanding those cheers from those who he knew would not support his view of the Bill, he would state what he knew to be the fact as to the opinion of the people . . . the people thought they were deluded by it. They thought that they should have got something for themselves by it . . . They said that they would much rather see their Representatives chosen by the gentry

---

[22] *Preston Chronicle*, 9 Apr. 1831.

[23] *Bolton Chronicle*, 9 Apr.; and *CPR*, 16 Apr. 1831. For an excellent analysis of the popularity of the Bill in south-east Lancashire, particularly with the local leaders, see Sykes, 'Popular Politics', 362–6.

[24] *Penny Papers*, 15 and 23 Apr. 1831, reprinted several Manchester press reports. Bawtry, 7 Apr. 1831, HO, 40/29/1 ff. 42–3, put the attendance at 6,000.

and the higher classes of society than by that class which was immediately above themselves.[25]

After this speech, several thousand free copies of which were printed and distributed by the Tories,[26] Hunt was ostracized and condemned by the entire reform establishment, and most of his erstwhile radical supporters. O'Connell led the Radical MPs in an orchestrated attack on the 'oracle of the Tories', accusing Hunt of selling himself to the Tory opposition, a charge amplified by the Whig-liberal press.[27] In the radical press, he was reviled, execrated, and damned as 'the Liar'. Cobbett challenged every detail of the alleged 're-action', and printed letters from Archibald Prentice, Richard Potter and other prominent middle-class reformers in the north-west, repudiating Hunt's 'infamous falsehoods' and attesting to the overwhelming popular support for the Bill in Manchester and throughout Lancashire; for good measure, he enlisted the services of Sir Charles Wolseley, Hunt's estranged and embittered business partner.[28] Carlile particularly disapproved of Hunt's spurious 'clamour about the working man', and read him a lesson in political economy, reminding him that prices, wages and the like were determined by market forces, not by politics and the law. Hunt, he concluded, was a malignant wretch, 'the great marplot of improvement and progressive Reform'.[29] Other radical publicists joined the attack, some with more venom than others. John Doherty simply pointed out that as far as the northern radicals were concerned, Hunt's comments in the Commons were 'grossly untrue . . . the bill, *as far as it goes*, has THEIR UNDIVIDED SUPPORT'.[30] William Carpenter showed much less restraint: he worked himself up into a fury with Hunt's 'peculiar infirmity of mind', 'extreme of vanity', and 'egotistical pertinacity'. The leading proponent of gradualism, Carpenter repudiated Hunt's analysis of social antagonism, and waxed lyrical about the 'identification of interests and sympathy subsisting between the labouring classes and the shopkeepers'.[31] The *Leeds Patriot* was the only paper to defend Hunt without reservation.[32] The *Penny Papers* welcomed the 're-action', but could not understand why Hunt was still prepared to

---

[25] *PD*, 3rd series, iii, 1245–6.   [26] Proctor, 147.

[27] *PD*, 3rd series, iii, 1349–58. See the various press cuttings in PC, set 17, i; and *CPR*, 11 June 1831, for Hunt's counter-attack, accusing O'Connell of 'trafficking for a place under the Government'. As Hunt and O'Connell became implacable opponents, Hunt was approached for help by a destitute woman who claimed to have been seduced and abandoned with child by O'Connell, see University of Chicago: MS 563, Hunt Correspondence and Papers, item 77, Hunt to O'Connell, 25 Nov., and 79, 81 and 82, letters from Ellen Courtenay, 7, 16 and 28 Dec. 1831.

[28] *CPR*, 23 Apr. 1831. Wolseley vehemently denied that he had tried to bribe Hunt into the Whig camp in 1822.

[29] *Prompter*, 16 Apr. 1831.   [30] *Voice of the People*, 16 Apr. 1831.

[31] *Carpenter's Political Letters*, 16 Apr. 1831.   [32] *Leeds Patriot*, 23 Apr.–14 May 1831.

vote for the Bill in the Commons—'we still must own ourselves dissatisfied with our friend HUNT's reasons for approving of and supporting a measure which he himself considers, and so ably proves, will effectually answer its intended object, that is, of ever excluding the poor people from their rights.'[33]

From this point on, Hunt followed a clear, consistent path in the Commons: 'he voted for the disfranchisement of the rotten boroughs', he later explained to radical audiences, 'and he also protested at making all England a rotten borough (laughter and applause)'.[34] He refused to join O'Connell, Hume and the Radical MPs in praising the Bill as 'an unmixed good' and a 'great national bo-o-n': as a radical, he 'opposed, or rather exposed the Bill, because it did not come up to any of the points he had advocated'. He regularly warned the gradualists of the folly of their position:

> . . . the Ministers had from the first moment, declared the Bill to be final, and as the people had in all parts of the kingdom petitioned for the Bill, the whole Bill, and nothing but the Bill, if they or he for them, should ask for more, the Government would say, 'No, this is not fair; the bargain was, that you should be satisfied with the measure we gave you, and you shall have no more'.

Finally, he decided to move an amendment during the committee stage to exempt all those excluded from the franchise from paying taxes or serving in the militia.[35] But just at this point, the Government was defeated on Gascoyne's amendment, and a general election was called, courtesy of the 'Patriot King'.

3. THE GENERAL ELECTION OF 1831, THE NORTHERN DEPUTIES AND RADICAL OPPOSITION TO THE BILL

While the political nation prepared to endorse the Bill in what was a referendum rather than a traditional general election, Hunt hurried back to Preston, escorted by Fitzgerald, his parliamentary clerk, to defend his seat and reinforce his radical links with the northern workers. Enthusiastic crowds welcomed him back to the north-west and his re-election campaign was supported by radical leaders throughout the region, including veterans like John Knight of the Oldham radicals, and George Cheetham of the Stockport Political Union, together with an important new figure, Edward Curran, leader of the once prosperous silk-weavers, co-ordinator of joint weavers activity, and chairman of the Political Union established by the Working Classes of Manchester and Salford.[36] The London press, implacably

[33] *Penny Papers*, 23 Apr. 1831.   [34] *PMG*, 3 Nov. 1832.
[35] *PD*, 3rd series, iii, 1503–9 and 1665–7.
[36] *Penny Papers*, 29 Apr., 7 and 13 May 1831.

opposed to Hunt's radical stand in the north, tried to write off any suggestion of popular support by starting a rumour that he had been burnt in effigy on the very field of Peterloo, but the ploy rebounded. After Hunt had addressed the cheering Manchester crowds, it was the effigies of Richard Potter and Hugh Birley, local protagonists of the Bill, that were burnt back to back. Potter, Hunt had been informed by a deputation from the 'Trades Union', was responsible for all the calumnies heaped on him in the north. Birley, of course, was the infamous captain of the yeomanry at Peterloo, whose sights were now set on one of the new Manchester seats, the prospect of which, Hunt opined, was reason enough to oppose the Bill! Local and radical demonology was part of Hunt's stock-in-trade in the north, a useful tool with which to dispel any lingering enthusiasm for the Bill. The working class, he insisted, could not possibly benefit from a measure supported by the likes of the notorious Captain Fletcher of Bolton, let alone blood-stained Parson Hay of Rochdale and his accomplices, 'Polly' Hulton and Captain Birley.[37]

After all the criticism and contumely he had endured, Hunt was delighted by his reception in the north. 'The lies in the Newspapers had very little effect here but the moment I set foot in Lancashire it all vanished like a chaff before the Wind', he wrote to his old friend Bryant:

I got to Manchester Sunday Night & before I was there half an hour I got a deputation from the *Manchester Political Union* to attend a meeting of several Hundred of them which was got up at short Notice, where they passed an unanimous Vote of thanks to me for the whole of my Parliamentary exertions, and gave the *lie direct* to the assertions of Mr. Ric[d] Potter—Next morning at 8 o'clock upwards of 20,000 persons came spontaneously to the front of my Lodgings where I addressed them an Hour & put the question fairly if any one of them objected to any part of my Parliamentary Conduct—Not one Hand held up—Vice Versa—20,000 the same at Bolton and when I entered Preston never before was there greater enthusiasm.[38]

For the next few days, he delighted the Preston crowds with his animadversions on the Bill, while the Whigs, the reformers, and the Parliamentary Candidate Society tried to find someone to run against him. Stanley preferred the security of Windsor, Potter was already committed at Wigan, and Swainson, the most likely local manufacturer, refused to stand once it was clear that the election was to be conducted 'in the same manner as the last'. Eventually the reform camp persuaded Colonel De Lacy Evans to come and offer himself, but he soon quit Preston when the electors of Rye pressed their prior claim to his services. Hunt was thus returned

[37] *Voice of the People*, 30 Apr.; *Preston Chronicle*, 9 and 30 Apr.; and *CPR*, 30 Apr. 1831, which reprints the *Morning Chronicle* effigy-burning article.

[38] Lancashire Record Office: Hunt Correspondence, DDX/113, Hunt to Bryant, 26 Apr. 1831. See also, *Bolton Chronicle*, 30 Apr. 1831.

unopposed, along with Wood, who displeased the crowds by his ardent support of the Bill and Warburton's latest 'dead-body' proposals. In a victory address, the Preston radical committee assured the 'seven millions' that Hunt would 'fearlessly and zealously maintain and defend the just rights, of not only a *part*, but the *whole people*'.[39]

Hunt's re-election at Preston took the 're-action' a stage further: he went on the counter-offensive against the Bill and the campaign for a radical alternative began in earnest. Supporters of the Bill, radical and liberal, were roundly condemned as he returned in triumph to Manchester, reminding the enthusiastic crowds *en route* that he was 'the only man in public that has stood up for the interest of the working classes'. At Blackburn, he clashed with George Dewhurst, who persisted in defending the Bill as a stepping-stone and insisted on his right to differ from Hunt who was 'too stiff and formal in his principles'. At Bolton, where he was welcomed by crowds of over 15,000, his speech was delayed by a physical altercation with the reporter of the liberal *Bolton Chronicle*. Poor old Naisby was given another ticking off when he admitted that he 'would take a part rather than have nothing', and Hunt picked on a suitable image to clinch the argument with the crowds. 'If a person were to offer you half a glass of ale', he suggested, 'you'd take that, I suppose, rather than have nothing? (yes, yes.) Aye, but suppose there was a dose of arsenic in it, would you take it then? (no, no!)'. When he arrived in Manchester to speak on the hallowed ground of Peterloo, it was Doherty who incurred his wrath since his paper, 'established with the money of the labouring classes', had belied its title: it had not 'spoken "the voice of the people" in its censures of him'.[40] After a friendly reception at Stockport, he set off south to Somerset to nominate Thomas Northmore for the county seat. Here, however, he was greeted rather differently: the 'Liar', Cobbett and Wakley gleefully reported, was heckled off the hustings as a Tory and turncoat, and pelted with rotten oranges as he withdrew.[41]

Back in London, he kept up the counter-attack on the Bill and started campaigning for its radical amendment. In the name of 'justice to myself and to the deluded and deceived public', he filed a number of libel actions against *The Times* and other pro-Bill papers which had misrepresented his reception in the radical north. At the same time, he strengthened his links with Hetherington, Foster and the anti-Bill, radical press. He wrote a public letter in praise of the *Penny Papers*, which now defended and applauded him without reservation, and opened its columns to his supporters in the north-west, proudly printing their radical addresses,

[39] *Preston Chronicle*, 30 Apr.; *Penny Papers*, 7 May 1831; and Proctor, 148–9.
[40] *Bolton Chronicle*, 7 May; *Voice of the People*, 30 Apr. 1831; and Kirby and Musson, 426.
[41] *Penny Papers*, 7 May; *Ballot*, 15 May; and *CPR*, 21 May 1831.

reports and letters.[42] He struck up a personal correspondence with Foster of the *Leeds Patriot*, thanking him for his backing 'throughout this *trying period of delusion*'. 'As long as I have health and strength I will never cease to advocate the rights of the useful, the labouring Classes of the Community', he assured Foster, 'as long as my Heart tells me that this course is the just and right course so long shall I continue that course in spite of calumnies, persecution, & oppression. Surely, surely the people will not be deluded forever.'[43] With Foster's assistance Hunt hoped to consolidate his position in the north and carry the fundamentalist message across the Pennines. There were some encouraging signs here—after his re-election he received addresses of congratulation from radicals at Huddersfield and Elland, but the Carlilites at Leeds had caused trouble when James Mann and the radicals met to celebrate the Preston victory and condemn the Bill. On Mann's advice, Hunt drew up an 'Address to the Radical Reformers of Lancashire and Yorkshire', a damning critique of the Bill specially penned for 'the millions of the working classes who are to be totally excluded by the intended *Whig* measure of reform, from having any share in choosing those representatives who ought to be the guardians of their rights, and who are to have the making of the laws by which their property, their lives, and their liberties are to be disposed of'. The address, sent to Foster for publication, was the clarion call for radicals to mobilize and demand their just rights. It led to a major petitioning-cum-convention exercise by which the Huntites of the north sought to enforce the radical amendment of the Whig Reform Bill.[44]

Emboldened by Hunt's address, the radicals of the north gained control of Doherty's petition and delegate scheme, initially designed to prevent the Whigs from dropping or weakening the Bill. According to Doherty's plan, each town was to send two delegates to London, armed with loyal addresses to the King and petitions to the new Parliament, recommending the Preston-type suffrage as the uniform franchise for the Bill. 'Would not our demanding the larger sum induce the debtor to think he would be fortunate if he could escape with paying the sum at first required?', Doherty asked, not concealing his satisfaction with the Whig Bill. He was closely questioned on the point by radicals at public meetings in Stockport, Bolton, and Preston, and in Manchester the Political Union of the Working Classes decided to implement their own radical version of the scheme.[45] They arranged a regional meeting of delegates from Lancashire,

---

[42] *Penny Papers*, 13 May 1831, including Hunt's letter to 'The Poor Man's Guardian'.

[43] Bodleian Library: Montagu MSS, Autograph Letters, iii, ff. 298–301, Hunt to Foster, 17 May 1831. Lancashire Record Office: Hunt Correspondence, DDX/113, Hunt to Foster, 17 June 1831.

[44] *Leeds Patriot*, 21 May and 4 June; and *Voice of the People*, 14 May 1831.

[45] Ibid., 7–28 May 1831.

Yorkshire and Cheshire, at which it was agreed that every city, town and hamlet should hold public meetings and elect deputies to take petitions demanding the full radical programme to London, where they were to sit during the progress of the Bill through Parliament, receive communications from their respective constituents, and 'forward to the utmost of their power the great principle of Universal Suffrage, Annual Parliaments and Vote by Ballot.' Before dispersing, the Manchester regional delegates passed a series of resolutions extolling Hunt, and quoting verbatim from his recent address to condemn the Bill, the Whigs, and the middle-class reformers.[46]

Over the next few weeks several public meetings were held to put the scheme into operation, but once again the mobilization was restricted to traditional strongholds. At the Manchester meeting on 13 June, chaired by Lee, an operative weaver, Doherty and Prentice attended to counsel caution and moderation, but the crowd, a disappointing gathering of 3,000 or so, voted in favour of a strongly-worded radical petition calling for reform on the lines of Cartwright's famous *Bill of Rights and Liberties*.[47] A week later, Brooks and Curran were elected by ballot to be the Manchester deputies: they were the first to set off for London where they hoped to be joined by forty-odd colleagues from the north.[48] Other towns, however, found they could not afford the expense of sending two deputies and elected only one—George Meikle was chosen at Blackburn, Smedley at Macclesfield (an important silk-weaving centre), Joseph Harrison at Stockport, and another post-war veteran, William Fitton, at Oldham. According to informers' reports, Leeds, Lees, Huddersfield and Chorley intended to elect deputies when funds permitted. In some towns, such as Bradford where Peter Bussey, the future Chartist leader, was one of the main speakers, public meetings were held and radical petitions adopted, but no deputies were appointed.[49]

The northern deputies expected to join forces with the new National Union of the Working Classes in London to mount an effective radical opposition to the Bill under Hunt's parliamentary leadership.[50] To their dismay, they found the NUWC rather indifferent towards both Hunt and the Bill. The NUWC had developed out of the Metropolitan Trades Union, formed by the Argyle Arms carpenters in the early spring, to embrace the 'new ideology' of the BAPCK and the general unionism of the

[46] Foster's reports and enclosures, HO, 52/13 ff. 422, 438 and 447.
[47] *Voice of the People*, 18 June 1831.   [48] HO, 52/13 ff. 447 and 449.
[49] *Voice of the People*, 18 June–2 July; *Leeds Patriot*, 11 June 1831; and HO, 52/13 f. 448. Sykes, 'Popular Politics', 367, maintains that the indifferent response to the delegate scheme illustrated the continuing popular inclination to back the Bill, and the tactically impossible position of the radicals who wanted to press for full radical reform but without harming the Bill's progress.
[50] See Mitchell's letter, *Penny Papers*, 4 June 1831.

National Association for the Protection of Labour in the north. From the start, the new union recognized the importance of political demands and action, realizing that 'the Working Classes of Great Britain and Ireland must obtain their rights *as men*, before they can possess their rights *as workmen*, or enjoy the produce of their own labour'. In May the title NUWC was adopted, and a comprehensive programme outlined 'to obtain for every working man, unrestricted by unjust and partial laws, the full value of his labour, and the free disposal of the produce of his labour'. By the early summer, when the first northern deputies arrived in town, the NUWC had become, as Iorwerth Prothero notes, *the* ultra-radical organization in London: it had absorbed British Co-operators, Rotundan-ists, parish radicals, Irish, Deists and members of the RRA and MPU, both of which seem to have terminated amidst the disunion in London at the end of 1830. But opposition to the Bill was not one of its priorities.[51]

The northern deputies tried to rally their London comrades to the task at hand. At the NUWC meeting on 22 June, Hetherington introduced Brooks and Curran, 'the delegated voice of 20,000 men, who are determined to be free'. They reported on the progress of the radical campaign in the north, and predicted that there would soon be 200 delegates in London, supporters of Hunt to a man.[52] At the next weekly meeting of the NUWC, at which Joseph Harrison, the venerable Stockport delegate was honoured with the chair, Brooks chided the London radicals for their quiescence and complacency. 'No doubt the Bill might pass with all plausible appearances of benefit in London', he observed, 'where every house would have a rental of £10; but he would caution them as to how it would affect Manchester, where the landlords must have their rents *weekly*'.[53] By way of contrition, the NUWC agreed to arrange a public meeting in London, and to send an address of thanks to Hunt, a proposal seconded by Meikle, the Blackburn delegate who called upon the people to assist Hunt—'the only man who had the decency and honesty to advocate the people's rights'—with petitions and remonstrances, since 'the opinions and desires of the working classes must be constantly forced upon the attention of the house'.[54]

The northern deputies failed to stir the London radicals into concerted action against the Bill. The public meeting in Portman Market was a one-

<hr>

[51] *Penny Papers*, 29 Apr. 1831; BL Add. MSS 27822 (Place papers), f. 37, *Rules of the National Union of the Working Classes*; and Prothero, *Artisans and Politics*, 268–71 and 281–3.

[52] *Penny Papers*, 24 June; and *Political Letter*, 25 June 1831.

[53] *Penny Papers*, 2 July 1831.

[54] *PMG*, 9 July 1831, which also includes details of the abortive Million Shilling Fund, launched in Manchester as a grateful tribute for Hunt's 'honest and indefatigable exertions in support of the rights and liberties of the people at large'. For Hunt's reply to the NUWC address, see *PMG*, 16 July 1831.

off affair, and the attendance was far from impressive, although it was enthusiastically supported by old confrontationalists like Benbow.[55] The northerners could not counteract the divisions and rivalries which dogged metropolitan radicalism: an informer reported that they were 'much disappointed at finding Hunt so little thought of and so little unanimity among the Reformers'. Harrison, Brooks, Fitton and other deputies left the Rotunda in disgust when Jones, Cleave and Hibbert 'denounced Hunt for his conduct to them and as unfit to be thought much of by the people. Hibbert said he might be very well to these persons as delegates to present petitions and so on, but they had done with him'. Hunt's popularity was probably at its nadir in London as a result of his regular repudiation of the Rotundanists and hostility to the Bill in the Commons. 'There has been no Meetings of any person in Hunt's favour', the informer observed, looking back over the last few months, 'but a total disunion among the reformers and since he has, as many consider, acted wrong and is suspected of being "bought over by the Tories" a great deal more disunion exists and he has lost much of his popularity even among the people.'[56]

The northern deputies were unable to rouse their London comrades, but some important links were forged between London and the north, chiefly through Benbow and Hetherington, who welcomed the deputies, supported their campaign against the Bill, and shared their high regard of Hunt, who proved most attentive to the deputies while they were in town: they used his house in Stamford Street as their meeting-place, and he arranged parliamentary visits and private interviews for them with various ministers and Radical MPs. He tried to make the most of the petitions they brought with them, which he presented to the House as decisive proof of the popular 're-action', of working-class dissatisfaction with the reintroduced Bill. But he was forced to withdraw the Stockport petition because of its intemperate tone, and the debate on the important Manchester petition, with its 20,000 signatures, soon descended into a slanging match as he came under fire from O'Connell, Hume and the other 'pseudo Reformers'. By the end of July, with nothing to show for their efforts, most of the deputies had left London to return to the north.[57]

It is generally maintained that political excitement died away in the summer as the Commons went into committee to consider the Bill, a process which took forty days to complete. But it was during this period of relative quiet that Hunt and the northern working-class radicals, seemingly undeterred by the failure of the delegate scheme, strengthened their resolve to oppose the Bill and demand a radical alternative. Thus, when

---

[55] *Political Letter*, 16 July; and *PMG*, 16 July 1831.

[56] HO, 64/11 ff. 333–6. Soon after taking his seat, Hunt had disclaimed all connection with the Rotundanists, see *PD*, 3rd series, ii, 343–4.

[57] HO, 64/11 ff. 333–6; *PMG*, 16 July 1831; and *PD*, 3rd series, iv, 578–80 and 954–66.

the Bill was finally rejected by the Lords in the autumn, they stood apart from the riots, violence and sudden explosion of anger, and tried to promote a new mass movement for the radical programme.

Hard-line opposition to the Bill developed apace in the north-west in the summer, following the return of the deputies, visits by Hetherington and Benbow,[58] and a purge of the moderate leaders. The anniversary of Peterloo provided an opportunity for a great display of radical strength. The Manchester and Salford Political Union of the Working Classes organized a huge procession from New Cross to St Peter's Field, several thousand strong, many of them arrayed 'in the chief articles of funeral costume'. On the hallowed ground, Curran read out a suitably melodramatic address from Hunt 'To the Brave but Persecuted Men of Manchester', enjoining the working classes to '*speak out* . . . put their shoulders to the political wheel and rescue the just rights of the people':

Shall the expiring groans of those martyrs who have suffered military execution and death in the holy struggle for equal *political rights*,—shall the heaving sighs,—shall the deep aspiration,—shall the just curses of those which have filled the cold and damp cells—of those who have been immured in the tyrants' dungeons for standing up for the rights of *every Englishman* to exercise the elective franchise, be drowned in the senseless cry for *partial* suffrage?[59]

After the Peterloo demonstration there was a purge of the moderate leaders, with the Manchester Huntites acting as the guardians of the radical conscience. Their most dramatic intervention was at Preston where Mitchell, once Hunt's most trusted lieutenant, underwent a volte-face and was publicly exposed by Brooks and Curran. Somehow or other, they had come into possession of a private letter from Mitchell to Whittle, editor of the *Manchester Times*, denouncing Hunt and 'intimating a wish to have Mr. Cobbett in his place'. What prompted Mitchell to defect is difficult to establish. Money matters, of course, had something to do with it, and a heated controversy soon developed about Mitchell's probity and competence in handling Hunt's election expenses and the medal subscription. Simple jealousy seems to have been a factor too: Mitchell took umbrage at Fitzgerald's appointment as Hunt's parliamentary clerk and was furious when the Irishman started editing his letters and addresses from Preston before passing them on for publication in the *Penny Papers*. When challenged by Brooks and Curran, Mitchell openly admitted that he had 'gone off' Hunt, and listed a number of complaints against his parliamentary performance culled from Cobbett, Carlile and Carpenter, to which Brooks responded with 'a strong eulogium of the character and conduct of Mr. Hunt, describing his exertions in the House of Commons to be almost

---

[58] *Voice of the People*, 23 July 1831. HO 64/11 f. 369.
[59] *Voice of the People*, 20 Aug.; and *Radical*, 27 Aug. 1831.

Herculean'. Condemned by the Huntites, Mitchell became an apologist of gradualism and class alliance, joining Johnston and the town's leading liberals, Isaac Wilcockson of the *Preston Chronicle,* and Joseph Livesey, of temperance fame, in their paeans to the Bill and plans for joint celebrations of the rich and poor at the forthcoming coronation of the 'Patriot King'. The Preston radicals stuck firm to their radicalism and resolved to observe the coronation as a day of mourning. After Mitchell's desertion, indeed, Preston radicalism became more aggressively working-class in tone, with Joseph Hanson, weaver, and John Taylor, clogger, heading the radical challenge.[60]

In Parliament, Hunt kept in step with this hardening of attitudes in the north. Frustration and obstruction in the Commons reinforced his radicalism to the point at which he began to doubt whether he could continue voting for the Bill in the division lobbies. As the session continued, he became very critical of the general conduct of the Whigs. A victim of Peterloo, he was scandalized by their refusal to institute inquiries into the carnage at the Merthyr riots and the tithe massacres across the Irish Sea at Newtonbarry and Castlepollard.[61] As the 'Representative of all the unrepresented portion of the people', he was disgusted by their profligacy and broken promise of retrenchment: to his ire, Hume and the Radicals refused to vote with him on such matters for fear of offending the ministers and jeopardizing the Bill.[62] Frequently he found himself in a minority of one, as when he opposed an additional grant to Princess Victoria and was accused of lacking all decency. 'He wished he could take hon. Gentlemen down to the North of England', he retorted: 'He would take them to where the poor weavers of Lancashire were working without necessary clothing. Would that be called decent?'[63] Such basic social criticism, drawing upon his close ties with his northern constituents, pervaded his spirited denunciation of every item of lavish public expenditure. He had to be called to order when he inveighed against the salaries paid to Oxford professors out of the pockets of 'poor weavers and other labourers who were nearly starving . . . in order to provide a fund for the education of the sons of the rich'.[64] It was the protracted committee stage of the Bill, however, which left him with no illusions about the Whigs and their intentions. The factional nature of the measure was clearly revealed during the discussion of Schedules A and B: it was Tory boroughmongering only that was to be eradicated.[65] During the discussion

[60] *Preston Chronicle,* 27 Aug.–24 Sept. 1831.

[61] *PD,* 3rd series, iv, 204–5, 268–9, 274, 563, 586, and 1064–5. G. A. Williams, *The Merthyr Rising* (London, 1978), 166.

[62] *PD,* 3rd series, vi, 876, and his speech at Bolton, reported in *Bolton Chronicle,* 30 Apr. 1831.

[63] *PD,* 3rd series, v, 656–60.

[64] *PD,* 3rd series, iv, 983–5.   [65] *PD,* 3rd series, v, 506, 542, 570–2.

of the borough franchise he tried to amend the £10 franchise, which discriminated in favour of London where there were 'no houses under £10 per annum, while in the other towns of England, the average rents of the houses of the working classes were from £5 to £7'. In the interests of simplicity and uniformity, he moved an amendment for household or scot and lot suffrage—'that all housekeepers paying rates and taxes, as in Westminster, should be allowed to vote'. The franchise, he contended, 'ought to be extended much further; but he was content to give up a great deal in order to meet the wishes of those who did not go the full extent that he was prepared to go'. Even so, he found himself without a seconder as none of the Radical MPs was prepared to support his compromise proposal.[66] His next amendment was his long-delayed, well-advertised and uncompromising demand that 'all persons who shall be excluded from voting for Members of Parliament, shall be exempt from the payment of taxes and rates, and from serving in the militia'. It was immediately negatived.[67] His final amendment, the last item discussed in the committee stage, called for an escalating scale of fines and prison sentences for peers who persisted in interfering in elections: it too was negatived without a division after Russell had denounced it as the most 'monstrous and unjust' resolution every submitted to the consideration of the House.[68] Once the committee stage was over, Hunt went ahead with his long-prepared motion for the total repeal of the Corn Laws, which, he insisted, 'would afford greater relief to the labouring classes, than any other measure that could be adopted'. This involved him in another dispute with Hume and the Radicals who once again refused to support such an untimely initiative.[69] Much embittered by his experiences in the Commons during the summer, Hunt refused to enthuse about the Bill when it was presented for its third reading. He now freely admitted that 'he did not care whether the Bill was passed or not. He did not anticipate much good from it; whatever others might.' From the petitions he had received from 'most of the great towns in the north of England' it was clear that the people shared his view and regarded the Bill as 'a dead letter'. He closed the debate on the third reading by dismissing the alarmist predictions of riot and rebellion should the Bill be rejected by the Lords.[70]

In the north-west Hunt was proved correct. Elsewhere popular anger at the Bill's defeat in the Lords led to riots against the anti-reformers, but in Lancashire, where the radicals had been gaining in strength throughout the summer, popular indignation was expressed in a different way, through the

[66] *PD*, 3rd series, vi, 552–4.   [67] *PD*, 3rd series, vi, 686.

[68] *PD*, 3rd series, vi, 1226–8.

[69] *PD*, 3rd series, vii, 67–78, and the much fuller report in Fitzgerald's pamphlet, *To the Electors of Preston* (London, 1831).

[70] *PD*, 3rd series, vi, 871–2 and 1407, and vii, 462.

assertion of working-class radical independence and the rejection of middle-class political leadership. This was the moment of breakthrough to popular support for which the local radicals or Huntites, as they now proudly called themselves, had been striving for some months. When the Bill was first sent to the Lords, they had managed to disrupt the proceedings at middle-class meetings called to petition for the Bill's swift passage. Curran and Ashmore defiantly condemned the Bill and upheld the cause of working-class radicalism at the exclusive meeting in the Manchester Manor Court Room, deliberately held at a time when 'workmen could not, dare not, leave their employment to attend it, because, if they did, they would be "bagged"'.[71] At the meeting at Blackburn, an unnamed radical from Daisy Field 'got upon the hustings to oppose the proceedings, and embracing a variety of topics foreign to the purposes for which they met, condemned the use of machinery, etc. etc., and then denounced the supporters of the reform bill as enemies of the working classes and of their advocate, Mr. Hunt! and in supporting that measure, they were getting power into their own hands, more effectually to oppress the labouring man (loud cheers from the Huntites)'. This led to a local pamphlet war in which 'A Huntite' clashed with 'A Reformer', and implored the Blackburn radicals: 'Join not in the senseless and stupid cry of "the Bill, the Bill". Let your cry be OUR RIGHTS, OUR WHOLE RIGHTS, AND NOTHING BUT OUR RIGHTS.'[72] At the meeting in the Corn Exchange in Preston, there was uproar when Taylor, 'one of the lower orders', refused to withdraw an amendment for the full radical programme. When the middle-class Preston reformers re-assembled a fortnight later to protest at the Lords' rejection, the Huntites scored a famous victory and carried the radical amendment, a triumph also secured at Manchester at the open-air meeting in Camp Field, the largest meeting in the cotton district during the Reform Bill agitation, and at which the middle-class Reform Committee lost control of the proceedings to the Political Union of the Working Classes.[73] Here in the radical heartland, the people were wise to the 'brickbat argument': committed to the full programme of equal rights, they refused to serve as a reserve army for the middle-class reformers to intimidate the Lords and stiffen the Whigs. 'What the ten-pounders said about bloodshed and riot if the Bill did not pass, was nothing but a pack of heaped-up lies and faction', Taylor asserted at the Preston meeting: 'Would the lower orders favour such a measure? When they had nothing to

---

[71] *Voice of the People*, 24 Sept. 1831.

[72] *Bolton Chronicle*, 1 Oct. 1831. 'A Huntite', *Letter to the Working Classes of Blackburn* (Blackburn, 1831). 'A Reformer', *Letter to the Working Classes of Blackburn* (Blackburn, 1831).

[73] *Preston Chronicle*, 1 and 15 Oct. 1831. Sykes, 'Popular Politics', 368–9.

defend by supporting it, was it likely they would run the risk of being shot at, or hung, or transported, all for another man's gain? (Cheers).'

4. THE AUTUMN CRISIS

The north-west apart, news of the Lords' rejection of the Bill was greeted with violence and anger throughout the land, and there were serious riots in Derby and Nottingham. Hunt was shocked and horrified, incredulous of the irresponsibility displayed by the Government, the press and the middle-class reformers in condoning such violence and illegality. Through the hireling press, the Government had fermented the riots, 'the turbulence which it served their present purpose to permit'. The ministers too, had connived with the BPU and other middle-class reform groups in their plans to stop the payment of taxes and other illegal acts, well beyond anything contemplated by the poor working-class radicals who had been massacred at Peterloo.[74] With the Bill's supporters openly talking of simultaneous meetings and conventions, Hunt's radical mission acquired a new sense of urgency. The deluded people had not only to be won over from foolish enthusiasm for the Bill to uncompromising commitment to the radical programme: they had also to be persuaded not to fight other people's battles for them but to enrol in the ranks of their own independent organization.

The new campaign for independent radical organization began at the Rotunda on 10 October, at a meeting arranged by Fitzgerald and Dias Santos to receive a Huntite address from the radical reformers of Blackburn. The aim was to promote Hunt's leadership, revive the RRA and strengthen ties with the radicals in the north-west. There were powerful speeches by Grady, French, Fitzgerald and Dias Santos, but the usual problems prevented any positive, on-going action in London. Most of the crowd were simply looking for 'trouble': when Hunt left the meeting early to attend the Commons, large numbers followed him through the streets. Furthermore, personalities and finance intruded: Gale Jones was furious at having to give up the large theatre for the evening; and a wrangle over the takings led Carlile to rescind his agreement for the RRA to hire the Rotunda for the following three Wednesdays.[75] The next stage in the campaign proved far more successful. When Parliament was prorogued later that month, Hunt headed north to rally the workers and revive the GNU yet again.

To prepare the ground for his tour, he brought out a series of unstamped penny *Addresses* 'on the Measures of the Whig Ministers since they have

[74] *PD*, 3rd series, viii, 462–3, 634–9, and 702.
[75] *PMG*, 15 Oct.; Prompter, 15 Oct. 1831; and HO, 64/11 ff. 241–2, 423 and 429.

been in Place and Power'. It is these little-known unstamped papers, together with his northern speeches, which reveal something of the true importance of Hunt in labour history, the uncompromising, uncomplicated and undaunted radical who so impressed and inspired Feargus O'Connor. Battling against establishment propaganda and the hireling press, radical treachery and defection, popular ignorance, prejudice and delusion, Hunt laid the foundation for the great Chartist challenge as he directed his radical message specifically to working-class audiences in the north.

In the *Addresses*, so lively in style and coarse but effective in tone, he practised arguments for his northern meetings when he excoriated the Whigs and condemned the Bill at Macclesfield, Stockport, Manchester, Bolton, Blackburn, Preston, Leeds and Huddersfield. He drew particular attention to the factionalism of the Whigs and the chicanery of Russell, 'cunning little Isaac', who juggled with nomination boroughs and the like to ensure that the Whigs would 'retain the power which they have now got in their hands, and which they have been so for many years, longing for in vain'. 'There never was a greater falsehood, a greater cheat, or a greater fraud and delusion practised upon the people', he protested, as he denounced the disingenuous and partisan reform propaganda in the Whig-liberal press: 'The sole struggle is in my honest judgment, which of the Factions shall have the power to govern, to rule over and to Tax the people, the one, not the whit more inclined to give the People a fair representation than the other.'[76] The Bill was not only designed to strengthen the Whigs, but was also intended to reinforce the influence of the aristocracy, a point emphasized in the technical details of the Bill, although completely ignored by the press. Through the division of the counties, the composition of Schedule B, and the granting of the vote to copyholders, leaseholders and tenants-at-will, Russell had taken 'special care that the power and influence of the Peers, instead of being diminished in the House of Commons, should be frightfully increased'.[77] Criticism of the middle-class nature of the Bill, the exclusive £10 franchise, was now sharpened by some figures provided by Naisby, the local tax collector, which suggested that only one adult male in thirty would meet the qualification in Bolton. This was before any account was taken of the registration requirements, such an important aspect of the 'franchise factor'. Under the terms of the Bill, no man was entitled to be registered until he had paid up his rates, rents and taxes. 'This is a good tax gatherer's bill,' Hunt protested, 'because it will make the people pay up their taxes; it is a good landlord's bill, because it will make them pay their rents! and it is a good parish bill, because it will make them pay up their rates; but it is not a bill for the Working Classes.'[78] Such detailed exegesis of the Bill was

[76] *AHH* (1), 20 Oct. 1831.   [77] *AHH* (2), 27 Oct. 1831.
[78] *AHH* (5), 4–12 Nov. 1831.

always placed in the context of the misdeeds, broken promises and profligacy of the Grey administration and earlier Whig ministries, so that the northern workers were well placed to judge whether the Whigs deserved the confidence of the nation or were 'likely to carry into effect any Reform intended to benefit the Working Classes'.[79]

After exposing the Whigs, he rounded on the parliamentary Radicals, 'O'Connell, Hume and Co', who had 'abandoned the Rights of the Seven Millions' the moment the Whigs 'brought out their Plan'. 'Because I would not fall into their wake, and like them abandon my principles,' Hunt protested, 'they were not only the first to assail me, but they were the most ready to denounce me as an Enemy to all Reform'. What rankled here, of course, was the charge that he had sold himself to the Tories, a cowardly and malicious falsehood fabricated by O'Connell, 'the impudent Whig bully', and duly reiterated in the press day after day by the likes of 'trundle-belly' Barnes, editor of *The Times*. Hunt's best self-defence against such calumny was his old stand-by, consistency by contrast. 'Now my friends, let us look back to the years 1816, 17, 18 and 1819', he advised the readers of his second *Address*: 'Who were the Men, and where are they now, who stood forward with the people and demanded their whole Rights of the Parliament, in days when there was not only great odium cast upon all who professed themselves reformers, but when there was actual danger in being a Reformer, and attending the Meetings of the Reformers.' None of the Radical MPs—not to mention Russell and the ministers—could stand comparison with Hunt on this ground. Furthermore, the hireling papers which now extolled the Bill were the self-same papers that had condemned the post-war radicals:

These dirty knaves abuse me now, for the very same reason that they abused me in 1816, 1817, 1818 and 1819. They abused and vilified me then, because I was true to the people, they abuse, lie and misrepresent me now for the very same reason because I would not desert, abandon, and betray the rights of the working Classes in order to curry favour with the Whigs.[80]

His next target was the radical press, and those 'traitors to the cause of the Working Classes', Cobbett, Wakley and Carpenter. The moment the Whigs had come into place, these worthies had 'turned round, left the working classes, joined the Whigs, and almost foamed at the mouth, in

---

[79] *AHH* (1), 20 Oct. 1831, and (13), 9 Jan. 1832.

[80] *AHH* (2), 27 Oct. 1831. See also his private letter to his Blackburn friend, Gilbert Martin, 26 Oct. 1831, quoted in Huish, ii, 488: 'What motive could possibly induce me to stand up against all the hired press of England, but that of principle, that of consistency. How much easier would it have been for me to have swam down the tide of popularity, to have plunged into the ministerial stream, and to have obtained any thing that selfishness could have suggested if I would but have followed the example of Hume and O'Connell, and have deserted the radicals in the hour of need of of danger also.'

favour of the Whig humbug of a Reform Bill'. Wakley was the easiest to stigmatize: a '*Mushroom Reformer*', he was damned as the 'trickery Dead Body Bill Man' because of his connections with Warburton. Carpenter, who regularly rehashed all the post-war scurrility about Hunt's adultery, was dismissed as a 'tub-preacher' turned trading politician. The strongest denunciation was reserved for Cobbett, 'the prince of *Liars* of *The Register*'.[81] For a start, he was condemned by his own words as Hunt reprinted their joint declaration of 4 July 1829 repudiating any compromise with the moderate reformers.[82] Later issues of the *Addresses* were given over to an impassioned attack on 'Cobbett's Corn', his abortive attempt to introduce Indian corn or maize, which Hunt pronounced 'a total failure, and fraud upon the public, a downright imposition and a cheat from beginning to end'. Considering their origins, it was perhaps appropriate that Hunt and Cobbett were to be at their most acrimonious when questioning each other's agricultural knowledge and competence on the land.[83]

In his *Addresses* and northern speeches, Hunt freely availed himself of the opportunity to settle some personal scores and repay obloquy in kind. His main purpose, however, was to promote independent radical organization. He left for the north, after closing his third *Address* with an impassioned plea for radical unity:

UNITE. I call upon the lads of Lancashire—I call upon those of Yorkshire—I call upon those of Cheshire—to *unite*. Once more, *up* I say for the 'NORTHERN UNION.' Let us have in one month, a 'HUNDRED THOUSAND *men united*' in these three counties.[84]

As he journeyed to Preston, polling the crowds *en route* on their attitude to the Whigs and the rejected Bill, he called for the 're-formation of the great Northern Union'.[85] With organization, he believed, the radicals would be able to turn the crisis to their advantage: without organization he feared, the people would be duped by the Whigs, exploited by the middle-class reformers, or misled by republican revolutionaries. His fears were intensified when news reached him of the violent riots at Bristol, where, since his days in the city, the people had been 'duped, deceived, deluded and persuaded to abandon *Radicalism*, and to adopt *Whigism* [sic].' The middle-class reformers, of course, were quick to exploit the impact of these riots, and raised the spectre of widespread popular convulsion unless Parliament were promptly recalled and the Bill reintroduced. Hunt was outraged when *The Times* and other papers close to the Government

[81] *AHH* (3), 29 Oct. 1831.   [82] *AHH* (4), 3 Nov. 1831.
[83] *AHH* (8), 3 Dec., and (9), 11 Dec. 1831.   [84] *AHH* (3), 29 Oct. 1831.
[85] For Hunt's speeches *en route* to Preston, see *AHH* (4) and (5), 3, and 4–12 Nov.; *Bolton Chronicle*, 5 and 12 Nov.; and *Preston Chronicle*, 5 Nov. 1831.

sought to protect property and the Bill by advocating an armed middle-class national guard 'to compel the Lords at once to pass the Whig Bill and the working classes to put up with all future claims to exercise their just rights'. In league with the Whigs, the armed and enlisted middle-class reformers or 'conservative guards', were engaged in 'a conspiracy against the working classes to make them satisfied with low wages and high corn'. 'When the rich conspire to oppress the poor,' he advised his northern audiences, 'the poor ought to unite for self-preservation.' Through the new northern union, the working-class radicals would be able to protect their interests, thwart the Whigs and outmanœuvre the middle-class reformers, by giving the lie to the irresponsible and hypocritical political unions. He was particularly scornful of the 'rich men' on the council of the BPU, an organization 'fit for nothing but to create division, for how can men be expected to unite, when some have all and the others none'. He was critical too of the new National Political Union which 'professes, like the Birmingham Union, to amalgamate and to unite in one firm bond, the rights and interests of the middle and the working classes'. The NPU owed much to Francis Place who appreciated the urgent need for some new initiative in class co-operation to pre-empt a popular swing towards the NUWC at this critical juncture, although the indolent Burdett, the fourth-choice chairman, thought only in terms of supporting the King, his ministers, and their Bill. 'I am much mistaken if the working classes are not a little more alive to their own rights and liberties than Sir Francis Burdett, Bart., and Francis Place, Tailor, and Esq., will be disposed to admit', Hunt wrote: 'Let the two Francises look sharp about them, or these working classes will *make use of them*, instead of their *making use* of the working classes'.[86]

Hunt's promotion of independent radical organization during the autumn crisis, confirmed that his uncompromising and unsophisticated popular radicalism was essentially 'working class' in content, character and appeal. He took pride in addressing himself exclusively to working class audiences in the north, whose importance he acknowledged in the new title of his *Addresses*, now dedicated 'to the Radical Reformers of England, Ireland, and Scotland, *and particularly those of Cheshire, Lancashire, and Yorkshire*'. In the north, he delighted, the workers were not the dupes and tools of the Whigs and middle-class reformers. 'All is, and will be peace here!!!', he reported on arrival in Lancashire, 'I defy them to get up a *Whig riot* throughout the county.'[87] But he was worried that the northern radicals might be drawn into the path of dangerous extremism by the London ultra-radicals who hoped to exploit the crisis and precipitate a

[86] *AHH* (3), 29 Oct. 1831. BL Add. MSS 27791 (Place papers), part I, 'Historical Account of the National Political Union'. See also the press cuttings in PC, set 17, i, f. 249 on.
[87] *AHH* (4), 3 Nov. 1831.

revolutionary confrontation by convening simultaneous meetings and the like. In London, militant extra-parliamentary politics was the order of the day for a wide range of groups from supporters of the Government and the Bill through to republican revolutionaries, from practitioners of the 'art of revolution' to those who actually sought revolution. There was well-publicized talk of secret republican conventions and open popular arming—Carlile, whose new periodical, the *Union*, reported the proceedings of the NPU, tapped the market here with a special edition of Macerone's booklet on street-fighting against the troops; he even contemplated converting the Rotunda into a military school.[88] The NUWC planned a massive open-air demonstration for White Conduit House on 7 November when they hoped there would be simultaneous meetings throughout the north. At the meetings, the people were to be asked to adopt a militant declaration, unmistakably Paineite in tone, demanding the abolition of all hereditary privilege as well as the introduction of universal suffrage, annual parliaments, the ballot, and no property qualification for MPs, 'the only sure guarantees for the securing to us the proceeds of our labour'.[89] As he journeyed to Preston, Hunt warned of the danger and folly of the plan. Such a mobilization, he contended, was untimely and unwise: the priority was organization not agitation. He was suspicious of the patronage and motives of reformists like Carpenter and Wakley, who agreed to chair the London meeting, but it was the extremism of the declaration which worried him most. For tactical as much as ideological reasons he had always opposed programmes which went beyond traditional radical demands and the 'constitutional' idiom: he correctly predicted that the declaration would provide the Government with the pretext to ban the London demonstration.[90] The northern radicals felt the force of his arguments: they agreed to postpone their plans for simultaneous meetings and excise the contentious clause about hereditary privilege from the declaration. On the day, the authorities in the north-west still expected disturbances, particularly at Blackburn, where there had been much loose talk about an armed 'muster' on Blakely Moor, until the local Political Union issued a handbill reminding the people of the advice of their 'grey-headed Representative Henry Hunt Esq . . . that his party the True Radicals *always* keep the peace, and that he had *always* advised them so to

---

[88] BL Add. MSS 27791 (Place papers), f. 22; *Ballot*, 23 Oct.; *Union*, 26 Nov.; and *Prompter*, 12 Nov. 1831. See also, Prothero, *Artisans and Politics*, 286–9.

[89] *PMG*, 22 and 29 Oct. 1831. The northern meetings were to be arranged by Doherty, now a critic of the Bill.

[90] *AHH* (5), 4–12 Nov. 1831. See also the letters from the Preston radicals to the NUWC, censuring Wakley and Carpenter, and the London committee for 'failing to live up to their professions' on 7 Nov., *PMG*, 3, 10 and 31 Dec. 1831.

do'. All was quiet in Blackburn on 7 November, but in Preston there were turn-outs and riots as soon as Hunt left town early in the morning.[91]

The Preston riots followed in the wake of Hunt's most exciting visit to the town. He arrived on Guy Fawkes night in spectacular style, escorted by a band, 40 flags and banners, and a great procession, ablaze with light from 200 flambeaux and 30 tar barrels. 'Never before, I believe, was a Member of Parliament so caressed, by so very great a majority of his Constituents, as the *Member* of the *Working Classes* of Preston', he reported in his *Addresses*, touching a homely, paternalist chord: 'If I had been the father of the whole of them—the kind, considerate, and indulgent parent—it is impossible they could have received me with more affection, or with more enthusiasm.' In front of large crowds, some 5,000 strong, he kept to his election promise and offered to resign his seat if they were not 'perfectly satisfied' with his 'exertions in the House of Commons in favour of the Working Classes'. Having unanimously approved of his conduct, the crowds then registered their disdain for the Bill, lack of confidence in the Whigs, and utter contempt of the treacherous Mitchell and his ambitious accomplices, Cobbett and Wolseley, vain aspirants for the Preston seat. After this display of radical strength in the charged atmosphere of bonfire night it was hardly surprising that there were serious riots shortly afterwards, leading to twenty-five arrests and the billeting of troops in the town for the rest of the winter. But in their reports to the Home Office, the local authorities exonerated Hunt from any responsibility, and the local press praised Taylor and the other radical leaders for their desperate efforts to persuade the turn-out crowds to disperse by reminding them of Hunt's condemnation of the 7 November plan.[92]

Hunt left Preston early that morning to visit Yorkshire, whither he had been specially invited by Mann and the Leeds radicals to help them establish a 'Political Union of the working classes to obtain Universal Suffrage, Short Parliaments, and the vote by Ballot'. As he made his way to Leeds, 'the focus of *Whigism* [sic] and delusion in Yorkshire', he was warned by Foster and others of the dangers to his personal safety as Baines, the Whig 'liar of the North', had procured the services of Smithson and the 'Carlile gang' and was determined to 'Bristolize' Leeds should Hunt show his face in town. Undeterred, Hunt continued with the visit and addressed a crowd of 8,000–10,000 from the window of Scarborough's Hotel.[93] Midway through his speech, just as he reached the set-piece

[91] Magistrates of Blackburn, 9 Nov. 1831, HO, 52/13 ff. 292–7.
[92] *AHH* (5), 4–12 Nov.; *Preston Chronicle*, 12 Nov. 1831 and 7 Jan. 1832, for the legal proceedings against the rioters. Letters from the mayor and town clerk of Preston, 7–10 Nov., HO, 52/13 ff. 276–9, 283–7 and 310–11; and Melbourne to Derby, 12 and 22 Nov., HO, 41/10 ff. 385–6, and 422–5.
[93] For Hunt in Leeds, 8 Nov. 1831, see *Leeds Patriot*, 12 Nov.; *AHH* (5), 4–12 Nov. and

questions about the Bill, the Whigs and the working classes, he was rudely interrupted by Baines, who seized hold of his collar and tried to drag him away from the window. After a scuffle, Baines started to address the crowd from an adjoining window, but he was soon forced to withdraw by the jeers of the crowd. Hunt was then able to resume what was probably his best speech during the entire Reform Bill agitation. Here at Leeds, the climax of his northern tour, he merged leadership, programme and class interest together with considerable populist force, proudly portraying himself as 'John Bull's watchman'. 'I come here today to visit the Working Classes, and no other', he asserted, 'I profess only to represent the Working Classes of England in the House of Commons . . . I am determined the Working Classes shall have the reform they want, and by the living G—d I'll resign my trust before I desert my Constituents or the Working Classes of England. (Immense cheering)'. 'I am for all voting,' he continued, 'I am not for disfranching any man, but if any, it should be the rich man. (Hear, hear.) I say to the rich man—you have got money, you have got influence, you have friends to protect you; but the poor man has nothing on earth to protect him but his political rights.' Protected by the vote, the working man could be sure of a decent living according to the terms of his homely and familiar economic and social philosophy by which 'the industrious poor man, who works hard from Monday morning to Saturday night, ought, and would earn as much as should support his family, and have something to put by for old age or a wet day'. In Hunt's uncomplicated radical frame of mind, the well-being of the working class, as 'the people' had now become, depended upon democratic control of the state, to achieve which independent radical organization was an essential preliminary. Within a few days of his departure, a meeting of operatives was held at the Falstaff to form a union for 'the protection of the rights of the working classes', and the important Leeds Radical Reform Union came into being.[94] But in Yorkshire, independent working-class radicalism was complicated by the factory question and popular Tory paternalism as Asa Briggs demonstrated in his seminal article on the local background to parliamentary reform. Hunt responded very readily to these local circumstances and advised the Leeds radicals to support Sadler, Tory though he was, at the town's first election, as he was 'ten thousand times more disposed to assist the Working Classes than the briefless barrister Mr. Macauley (Cheers)'. In his speech at Huddersfield, centre of the small-scale fancy and narrow cloth

(6), 18 Nov.; Bawtry, 10 Nov., HO, 40/29/1 ff. 144–5; *PD*, 3rd series, ix, 86–8; and Bodleian Library: Montagu MSS, Autograph Letters, iii, ff. 300–1, Hunt to Foster, 21 Nov. 1831. A. S. Turberville, 'Leeds and parliamentary reform 1820–1832', *Thoresby Miscellany*, xii (1954), 45–6, misdates the meeting as 3 Nov.

[94] *Leeds Patriot*, 19 Nov. 1831.

trade, he made a special point of emphasizing his interest in the factory question, before taking his leave for London:

'He had personally visited the factories, and witnessed the sufferings of the over-worked children, and in his place in Parliament he had been the means of causing some hearts to feel.' 'But, my friends,' continued the hon. member, 'you never heard of this. No, no, my speeches on the subject were all suppressed through the villainy of the base metropolitan press . . . it would not do for the 'apostate Hunt' as the vulgar fellow Baines, of Leeds, calls me, to be too popular.'[95]

Hunt's northern tour and his penny *Addresses* failed in their main purpose: he was greeted with enthusiasm on both sides of the Pennines, where trade had still to recover from the downturn of 1829, but there was no mass revival of the GNU. The autumn 'crisis' did not lead to an independent radical initiative as he had wished, although opposition to the Whigs and the Bill was clearly quite strong in certain parts of the north. Once the 'crisis' was over, the familiar pattern was restored: London radicals were beset with internecine dispute, while the Huntites in the north grew in strength and resolve but failed to retain or attract popular support outside of the traditional radical strongholds.

In London political excitement died away when the Whigs agreed to reconvene Parliament and reintroduce the Bill. The NPU and the NUWC hastened to comply with new regulations restricting political organizations, but popular support declined and disputes recurred, in part the product of the rivalry of the two societies with their over-lapping memberships. Some leading radicals argued that it was quite consistent to support both the NPU and the NUWC—such was the case with William Carpenter who welcomed any exercise in cross-class endeavour, and stepped up his attacks on the fundamentalism and class exclusivism personified by Hunt, the 'Alpha and Omega' of the 'reforming anti-reformers . . . who tried to prop up their sinking popularity by affecting a zeal for the working class, and at the same time doing all in their power to injure the interests of that class'.[96] Hardliners like Benbow and his group shunned all links with the NPU, but much time and effort was wasted by others in vain attempts to capture the NPU for the democratic cause. Place ensured that most of the working-class seats on the council, a concession to radical pressure, went to harmless stooges, and an attempt to add Hunt's name to the council was given short shrift—Wakley announced that he would 'never form part of any Society to which Henry Hunt belonged—that heartless and cold-

---

[95] Briggs, 'Background of the Parliamentary Reform Movement', 309–15. *Leeds Patriot*, 12 Nov. 1831.

[96] *Carpenter's Political Magazine*, Jan. 1832. See also his weekly anti-Hunt letters in *Ballot*, 16 Oct.–20 Nov. 1831; and his *Address to the Working Classes on the Reform Bill* (London, 1831). Carpenter's attacks on Hunt were answered by Hetherington, 'Justitia' and others in *PMG*, 17 Dec. 1831–18 Feb. 1832.

blooded traitor'.[97] As well as the rivalry between the NPU and the NUWC, there were major disputes within the NUWC itself. Benbow's group was never reconciled to the decision to comply with the Government's ban on the 7 November demonstration, and remained committed to a confrontationalist stance. Later that month, the NUWC repudiated Benbow's 'mad plan' for a grand national holiday, whereby everyone should accumulate provisions for a week, go on strike for a month, elect a national convention and requisition food. There were divisions on ideology as well, in which Benbow was again at the centre of contention, fighting against the increasing influence of the Owenites in the NUWC, and promoting his own anti-Owenite co-operative society.[98]

In the north, radical opposition to the Bill remained undiminished, less effected by the decline in 'excitement' and untroubled by tactical or ideological disputes. But when the northern radicals decided to proceed with their amended version of the 7 November scheme, they were unable to mobilize the masses who had pledged their support in the immediate aftermath of the Lords' rejection. Once again, positive radical action was restricted to the old strongholds, handloom-weaving communities, and towns with a proud Peterloo connection. The initiative came from the depressed woollen centre of Huddersfield, that Huntite pocket of Yorkshire, when the General Committee of the Political Union and Operatives, headed by Joshua Hobson, later printer, publisher and editor of the great Chartist paper, the *Northern Star*, sent out a circular calling for a delegate meeting at Manchester 'to arrange a plan and frame general resolutions for a grand meeting all over Britain and Ireland, on the same day and hour'.[99] On 16 November, eighteen or nineteen delegates duly met, pledged themselves to the radical programme, and recommended 28 November as the date for simultaneous meetings 'to agree upon a declaration of Rights, also to choose Deputies who shall meet in some central town to form a National Convention . . . to draw up a Reform Bill . . . expressive of the just claims of the British Nation'.[100] On the day, however, only two meetings were held, at Manchester and Bolton. The Manchester meeting was poorly attended as the magistrates had instructed the factory owners to keep their workers locked in: thus a crowd of only 2,000, 'all operatives of the lowest class' assembled on Camp Field to listen to Curran, the veteran radical weaver Nathan Broadhurst, and William Ashmore, secretary of the New Cross Political Union.[101] The lock-in

[97] BL Add. MSS 27791 (Place papers), ff. 58–122.

[98] HO, 64/12 ff. 434–5. Prothero, *Artisans and Politics*, 289–90.

[99] *PMG*, 5 Nov.; and Holme, 5 Nov. 1831, HO, 52/13 ff. 272–3.

[100] Foster, 19 Nov. 1830, HO, 52/13 ff. 477–9. J. R. M. Butler, *The Passing of the Great Reform Bill* (London, 1914), 311–12, misdates the delegate meeting as 28 Nov.

[101] Foster, 24 and 28 Nov., HO, 52/13 ff. 480–1 and 488–9; Lt. Col. Shaw, 28 Nov., HO, 40/29/1 ff. 153–4; and *Preston Chronicle*, 3 Dec. 1831.

reflected the authorities' concern at the growing strength of the Huntites in Manchester and their determination to prevent any juncture of political agitation and industrial power. During the autumn crisis, the Manchester and Salford Political Union of the Working Classes had come into its own. Flushed with victory over the Reform Committee at Camp Field, the working-class radicals held nightly meetings in the streets of New Cross until Foster, the magistrate, sent in the troops.[102] Previously Foster had been preoccupied with industrial disturbances and militancy, with 'picquetting', strikes, the spread of general unionism and the National Association for the Protection of Labour. After the autumn his fears centred on political agitation and the rapid progress of the so-called 'lower political union' which, he reported at the end of November, had 27 lodges and some 4,000 fully paid-up members. It was to prevent these numbers rising still further that he advised the factory owners to keep their workers locked in during radical meetings.[103]

The attendance at Bolton on 28 November was smaller still, but the problem here was internal dissension. The decision to proceed with the simultaneous meeting plan split the Political Union, and finally prompted Naisby and others to resign. To make matters worse, John O'Brien, elected as the local delegate to the convention, turned out to be rather a rogue, subsequently exposed by the *Bolton Chronicle*.[104]

After these two rather unsuccessful meetings, it seems that plans for the convention proceeded in secret, much to the dismay of Benbow. 'Secrecy in political transactions is out of date', he cautioned Ashmore in a letter intercepted by the Post Office: 'I hate secrecy. I hate anything that the Enemies of the People might be able to torture into conspiracy . . . you know that I am not lukewarm, that I was always for bold measures. I am so still, but boldness must be tempered by prudence.'[105] Thereafter all is mystery and confusion, an insoluble enigma for the historian, making it impossible to establish the strength of radical feeling in the north and the extent of co-ordinated endeavour between the northern Huntites and Benbow's group in London. It is even possible that there were two conventions in Manchester, one public and the other secret. The report of the opening of the 'National Convention' in Manchester on 13 December in the *Poor Man's Guardian*, suggests a public affair, and was openly signed by William Jackson, president, and William Moreton, secretary.[106] But

[102] Foster, 10–19 Oct. 1831, HO, 52/13 ff. 454–70.
[103] See Foster's reports in HO, 40/27/3; and 9 Jan. and 27 Nov., 1831, HO, 52/13 ff. 425–7 and 482–7. Sykes 'Popular Politics', 372, maintains that numbers fell away after the autumn crisis.
[104] *Bolton Chronicle*, 3 Dec. 1831.
[105] Freeling, 19 Dec. 1831, HO, 64/16. See also Benbow's speech at NUWC, *PMG*, 24 Dec. 1831.
[106] *PMG*, 31 Dec. 1831.

this is the only report of the proceedings in the radical press, apart from a dismissive reference to 'a club at Manchester' calling itself 'a National Convention' in Lorymer's *Republican*, which had persistently recommended a council or convention of the unrepresented.[107] Other evidence indicates a secret gathering later in the month, following the election of delegates at meetings on 26 December.[108] From the intercepted correspondence with Benbow it would seem that Ashmore was the secretary and leader of this secret convention: through a private letter to Benbow, he asked the NUWC to send a delegate, a request they ignored 'as it was not addressed to the body and as our funds were not sufficient for our present purposes'.[109] O'Brien's reports on the 'Great National Convention' confirm the secrecy of the whole affair but refer to Ryelance as the president: the delegates, O'Brien recorded, were constantly on the move to avoid detection by the authorities. These reports, however, lost their credibility when the Bolton radicals learnt of Broadhurst's allegations that O'Brien had spent most of his time and their money at a house of 'ill-fame' in Manchester.[110] Then there is the problem of the number of delegates who attended. When they announced the scheme on 28 November, the Manchester radicals spoke in terms of a hundred or so—'in one hundred and four Towns there are Unions formed, from each of which one or two Delegates are to be sent to the National Convention'. O'Brien hit upon the figure of 103 in his report, but when challenged on the point, he spoke of meeting only eighteen or twenty. J. Hulme, former secretary of the Bolton Political Union, was convinced that the true number was no more than three![111]

Most puzzling of all, however, is the Reform Bill drawn up by the delegates, public or secret, numerous or exiguous. The convention was called to produce a radical alternative to the Reform Bill, and the intercepted correspondence in the Home Office papers suggests that the Manchester Huntites were hoping to link up with Benbow and the NUWC in a national campaign for this new radical bill. But the 'Manchester Reform Bill' fell short of expectations and was curtly dismissed by the NUWC and radical groups in the north. When the NUWC committee received their copy through another private letter from Ashmore to Benbow, James Osborne, the secretary, was instructed to write an official letter of censure to Ashmore, reminding him that it was NUWC policy 'never to correspond with any secret or private Society or Body of

---

[107] *Republican*, 17 Sept. 1831–Jan. 1832.

[108] For the Manchester meeting on 26 Dec., see *Preston Chronicle*, 31 Dec.; Foster, 26 Dec., HO, 52/13 ff. 492–3; and the Attorney-General's speech at the trial of Broadhurst, Curran, Ashmore and Gilchrist, *Bolton Chronicle*, 17 Mar. 1832.

[109] HO, 64/11 f. 460.

[110] *Bolton Chronicle*, 7 Jan., 4 Feb.–3 Mar. 1832.   [111] Ibid., 7 Jan. and 25 Feb. 1832.

individuals'. Significantly, Osborne sent a covering letter to Brooks and Curran, the former Manchester delegates to London, in which he put a friendly gloss on the affair and drew their attention to the 'one good way of effecting our object Developed in a plan of A National Holiday published by our Friend Benbow . . . you must study it as soon as possible'.[112] The 'Manchester Reform Bill' was discussed at a full meeting of the NUWC the following week when it was dismissed as 'a compilation of superfluities, inconsistencies, absurdities, and palpable contradictions'.[113] Similar criticisms were expressed in the north. The Bolton radicals regretted that the bill was 'as absurd as the conduct of those who framed it was fraudulent'; and the Preston radicals detected 'the handy-work of the treacherous Whigs' as the bill 'pretended to set out on the principle of Universal Suffrage, and at the same time disfranchised thousands of *tax-payers*'.[114] In February, the council of the Political Union of Chorlton Row and Hulme issued a statement disclaiming 'all and every part of the REFORM BILL, professing to be drawn up by a NATIONAL CONVENTION—otherwise called the MANCHESTER REFORM BILL. We deny its having any connection with the Radical Reformers of Manchester; they having had no knowledge of the *parties calling themselves* the NATIONAL CONVENTION;—and that the BILL has never received the sanction of the members of the Political Union of Manchester and Salford.'[115] This unequivocal disclaimer notwithstanding, the Manchester Huntites were closely involved with the bill. To circumvent the lock-in of the workers, they planned a number of Sunday public meetings in the new year at St George's Field, and intended to launch the series with a petition in favour of 'the Reform Bill, as drawn up by the National Convention, the Bill, the whole Bill, and nothing but the Bill'. The petition was duly adopted on 22 January, but most of the meeting was given over to more pressing matters, in particular the savage sentences recently inflicted on the Bristol and Nottingham rioters. There were impassioned speeches by Curran, Ashmore and Broadhurst, 'one of the foremost of the red hot radicals, a member of the Political Union of the Working Classes, and a leader of the gang styled the Hunt mob', at whose suggestion it was agreed that Hunt should be asked to present an address to the King calling for the reprieve of the condemned rioters. It was decided to meet again the following Sunday to receive the King's answer.[116]

Foster decided that drastic action was necessary to curb the radical threat, particularly as he had information about secret systems of

---

[112] HO, 64/12 f. 14; and HO, 52/18 ff. 58–60. Benbow's 'National Holiday' already had strong support in Huddersfield, see *PMG*, 10 and 17 Dec. 1831.

[113] *PMG*, 4 Feb. 1832.

[114] *Bolton Chronicle*, 25 Feb.; and *3730*, 28 Jan. 1832.   [115] *PMG*, 25 Feb. 1832.

[116] PC, set 17, ii, f. 99; Foster, 22 and 30 Jan., HO, 52/18 ff. 2, and 9–18; and *Bolton Chronicle*, 28 Jan. 1832.

organization, arming and night-drilling. The Home Office readily endorsed his view that the Sunday meetings were illegal and of a dangerous tendency. Bills were issued prohibiting the meeting on 29 January, when the military took possession of the ground and arrested Robert Gilchrist and seven others for assembling in defiance of the magistrates' ban. Foster was not satisfied with the haul and issued warrants against Ashmore, Broadhurst and Curran for their part in the previous meeting, soon after which they had left Manchester for London.[117] The arrival of these leading Manchester radicals in London naturally alarmed the authorities who feared some sinister link between the convention in the north and the NUWC in the capital. As it transpired, Ashmore, Broadhurst and Curran were not on any secret or political mission but had come to London as witnesses for Hunt in his successful action against *The Times* for its libellous misrepresentation of his reception in the north back in the spring of 1831. They were '*nearly constant in their attendance* on Hunt', the informer reported, until they were arrested and sent back north to stand trial with Gilchrist and the others.[118] Hunt immediately took up their case. In Parliament, he insisted that they had committed no offence at all by meeting on a Sunday, the only day they had at their own disposal, the day on which 'his Majesty's Privy Council was even in the habit of assembling for the despatch of business'. As the trial approached, he wrote to the new Preston unstamped paper, known as the *3730* in honour of the electors who had voted for him in December 1830, calling upon the Lancashire radicals to 'stand by Curran, Broadhurst and others. I believe they are persecuted solely because they have supported our principles, instead of those of the Whigs.' When Ashmore, Broadhurst, Curran and Gilchrist were convicted in March and sentenced to a year's imprisonment for unlawful assembly on the sabbath, he was determined they should not be neglected. He wrote regularly to them, and protested angrily when the prison authorities opened the correspondence; he also presented petitions criticizing their general ill-treatment in Lancaster Castle, but they received little succour from other radicals. In the hope of deriving some material benefit, they produced a pamphlet, *The Whigs, v. The People*, recording their trial, explaining their plight, chiding the neglectful radicals, and extolling Hunt for his spirited opposition to the Whigs and their 'mere humbug' Bill.[119]

The sorry fate of the imprisoned Manchester Huntites personified the

---

[117] Foster, 25, 29, 30 Jan. and 4 Feb., HO, 52/18 ff. 4–5, 9–11, 19–26, 29, and 39–41. *PMG*, 4 Feb. 1832.

[118] HO, 64/12 ff. 28–36, and 73. For the successful libel action, see *PMG*, 18 Feb. 1832.

[119] *PD*, 3rd series, x, 195–6 and xi, 944–7. *3730*, 25 Feb.–19 May 1832, includes weekly letters from the Lancaster prisoners. N. Broadhurst (ed.), *The Whigs, v. The People* (Preston, 1832).

failure of the radicals to mount an effective campaign for a radical alternative to the Bill. Active support for the radical cause was a fleeting occurrence during the Reform Bill agitation: on-going organization and agitation proved impossible to sustain against the enduring popular appeal of the Bill. Applauded by the crowds during the autumn crisis, Broadhurst and his colleagues were left isolated and impecunious in Lancaster gaol. The NUWC reognized their obligation to assist their northern comrades but their funds were severely depleted by the legal actions which followed in the wake of their only successful attempt at attracting popular support, the monster street procession in London on 21 March, the official day of fasting, prayer and humiliation, demanded by the 'saints' to appease the Almighty's wrath as the cholera outbreak reached epidemic proportions.[120] By early May, the Lancaster prisoners were utterly destitute, the subscriptions collected by a handful of faithful radical groups in Preston, Manchester, Leeds, Heywood and Clitheroe, having proved quite inadequate.[121] It was a sad end to the Huntite attempt to mount an independent radical initiative in the midst of the Reform Bill agitation.

5. 'THE POOR MAN'S PROTECTOR'

Back in Parliament, after his return from his autumn trip to the north, Hunt took little interest in the progress of the new Whig Bill, which he considered little better than its rejected predecessor.[122] As 'John Bull's watchman', he concentrated on matters of more immediate relevance to the welfare of the working class. The guardian of democratic radicalism, he was also the spokesman for an alternative political economy at odds with the *laissez-faire* prescriptions of the liberal supporters of the Reform Bill. His economic analysis was not particularly rigorous, but it underlined his commitment to the working class whether in the old trades or the new factories. He was particularly concerned with the plight of those in the 'luxury' trades whose livelihoods had been ruined by foreign competition, by a disingenuous system of free trade which 'allowed the importation of luxuries, such as were consumed by the rich, but which prohibited the necessaries of life, corn, from being imported without great restrictions'. He presented many petitions on behalf of workers in the glove and silk trade in his native west country and in the east end of London, where distress had reached crisis proportions in Bethnal Green and Spitalfields. As cholera approached, he repeatedly called on the Government to

---

[120] HO, 64/12 ff. 36–74. Prothero, *Artisans and Politics*, 291.

[121] 'Victims of Tyranny', *3730*, 19 May 1832.

[122] *PD*, 3rd series, ix, 545–6. For the benefit of the northern radicals he printed the new bill in full in *AHH* (10), 21 Dec. 1831.

intervene in the east end and assist the over-stretched parish authorities.[123] Alongside these efforts to protect poor handworkers, he campaigned for legislation to curb the 'pernicious system of overworking children', the 'horrible practice which had so long prevailed in exacting undue and severe labour from the children in the manufacturing districts of this country'. 'The question was not one of pounds, shillings, and pence', he declared, seconding the motion for the second reading of Sadler's Factories Regulation Bill, 'but whether the English people were to be worked beyond their powers of endurance'.[124]

Hunt's interventionist stance on such issues was much appreciated in the north, where the radicals were kept fully informed of events at Westminster by the *3730*. This Preston unstamped paper served as Hunt's principal means of communication after his *Addresses* came to an end in January. Each issue gave full reports of his speeches and printed his correspondence with petitioners and constituents, alongside letters, poems and songs lauding his conduct:

> Harry stands in St. Stephen's as bold as a hector,
> Beset on all sides by corruption's foul knaves,
> Who strive to put down the poor man's protector,
> When he speaks truth to those men who make you their slaves.[125]

In each issue too, there were articles and letters condemning Mitchell and Cobbett, who persisted in their efforts to discredit and unseat the paragon Hunt. Some complicated arguments were involved here, relating to disputes not only at Preston but also in Leeds where Tory radicalism, Carlilite infidelism and Mitchell's links with Oliver were issues of considerable contention. In the Commons, Hunt always supported Sadler, the prospective Tory candidate for Leeds, in his paternalist initiatives on factory reform and the Poor Law in Ireland, particularly when there was an opportunity to castigate their mutual opponents, Baines' middle-class liberals and Smithson's infidels. On one occasion when a Leeds petition was under discussion, he referred to Smithson as 'a notorious individual who has roasted the Bible'.[126] Convinced that Hunt and his cronies at Leeds had invented this tale of sacrilegious pyromania, Cobbett brought out a special edition of his *Twopenny Trash*, addressed to the people of Preston, in which he proceeded to expose Hunt, 'the FOOL-LIAR', who had slandered Smithson and renounced his belief in poor Mitchell's innocence. For good measure, he printed Smithson's version of events in Yorkshire after Peterloo and the Six Acts, a reprise of Brayshaw's damaging

---

[123] *PD*, 3rd series, ix, 86–8, 255, 590, 1088, x, 386, 390, 470–1, 582, 974–5, and 1038.

[124] *PD*, 3rd series, ix, 1093, x, 895, and xi, 398. Hunt made many other speeches protesting at factory conditions, child labour, the truck system and other abuses.

[125] 'A Song', *3730*, 3 Mar. 1832.   [126] *PD*, 3rd series, ix, 715 and x, 21–2.

allegations against Mann and the Leeds Huntites, and concluded the polemic with a wealth of documentary evidence attesting to the great success of his corn and farming methods, thereby refuting Hunt's continual and envious claims to the contrary. 'Your FOOL-LIAR seems to be upon a *perfect equality with the Negroes*', Cobbett concluded in a typical display of prejudice: 'He has all their *animal-cunning*; and all their disregard of truth'.[127] Farming matters apart, Cobbett had chosen his ground most unwisely. Smithson had indeed publicly burnt the Bible in Leeds. The new Leeds Radical Reform Union, headed by William Rider after Mann fell victim to cholera, rallied to Hunt's defence, and joined the Preston radicals in attacking Mitchell and demanding a full statement of the election accounts. Cobbett was denounced by radicals throughout the north, including Broadhurst and the Lancaster prisoners.[128]

Hunt's hold on the prized Preston seat was never seriously challenged by Cobbett and Mitchell. The poor electors were most appreciative of his close attention to their interests in the Commons, where he endeavoured to protect their rights against the reforming influence of the Bill. 'Here was a body of between 7,000 and 8,000 electors, who were totally free from any imputation, about to be Burked at once by the Bill, which was miscalled a Reform Bill', he protested during the committee stage when he moved an amendment that 'nothing in the present Bill do have any operation on the borough of Preston'. He was supported by only five MPs, from which number, John Wood, the liberal member for Preston, was conspicuously absent. 'All who voted with me to save Preston were rank Tories', he reported to the *3730*: 'The brave sons of Preston will not be disfranchised as long as they live in Preston. But no new constituents will be created unless they live in £10 houses. This much has been conceded to me . . . A pretty situation we, the people are in; the only chance of support that I have, is from a few of the Tories.'[129]

There were several issues of course on which Hunt stood far apart from the Tories. 'Issues' cut across the new, deceptively modern-looking two-party system in a most bewildering fashion in the early 1830s. Social reform and humanitarian causes were by no means the prerogative of Tory paternalists like Sadler. The campaign against military flogging, for example, was very much a crusade of the liberal left, as John Dinwiddy has recently shown.[130] In 1832 it was Hunt who took the lead on this issue, regularly taunting his old enemy Hobhouse, now 'liberal Secretary at War' for his failure to 'put a stop to this most inhuman custom'.[131] There was a

---

[127] *Twopenny Trash*, Apr. 1832. [128] *3730*, 14 Apr.–5 May, and 23 June 1832.
[129] *PD*, 3rd series, ix, 1222 and 1259–60. *3730*, 25 Feb. 1832.
[130] J. R. Dinwiddy, 'The early nineteenth-century campaign against flogging in the army', *English Historical Review*, xcvii (1982), 308–31.
[131] *PD*, 3rd series, x, 421–3, xi; 1221–34, and xiii, 874–97.

similar line-up when he brought forward his long-awaited motion for an inquiry into Peterloo. Once again, he was seconded and supported by Hume, Warburton and the parliamentary Radicals, but opposed by all others, a disappointing conclusion to what was perhaps his most carefully-prepared parliamentary endeavour.[132] On most other issues, however, Hunt stood firmly opposed to the parliamentary Radicals and found himself in alliance with Tories of the old school. This was certainly the case when Warburton introduced a cosmetically-revised version of his Dead-Body Bill. Hunt opposed it with all his might: when the House went into committee on the Bill, he announced that he had 'an Amendment on every clause. He detested the whole measure. He wished those rich Gentlemen, who talked about the poor, would give up their bodies. He would move, that every Gentleman who voted for the Bill, as well as all sinecurists, should be given up for dissection.' To Hunt, the *3730*, and radical groups in the north, the campaign against this hated Bill quite overshadowed events in the Lords where the Reform Bill was again under critical consideration.[133]

6. THE DAYS OF MAY

As in the autumn crisis of 1831, Hunt refused to join in the public clamour in support of the Whigs and the Bill when the Government resigned in May 1832, following their defeat in the Lords and the King's refusal to create new peers. He directed his anger at the deceitful Whigs who had 'led the people to believe that the King would sanction any measure, no matter what kind, to enable them to carry their measure'. Such was his disgust with the Whigs that he voted against the Address to the King, expressing the Commons' 'unaltered confidence' in Grey and his ministers and earnest desire for an 'unimpaired reform':

He believed that the people were anxious for Reform, but he believed that the great body of the well and sound thinking people of this country did not care one rush whether that Reform were carried by Whig or Tory. For his part, he could not place confidence in a Ministry which, out of office, inveighed against a standing army, but, in office, increased that standing army, not once, but twice, and never

---

[132] *PD*, 3rd series, xi, 251–85. For some while Hunt had been collecting material for the motion, and issuing strict instructions to radical groups about how to draft petitions acceptable to the Commons, see *AHH* (11) and (12), 28 and 31 Dec. 1831; *3730*, 3 Mar. 1820; and Lancashire Record Office: Hunt Correspondence, DDX/113, Hunt to J. Peck, 24 Feb., and Hunt to T. Wilde, 12 Mar. 1832. Manchester Central Library, Misc. 47: letter from Hunt to a radical leader in Hull, 23 Feb. 1832.

[133] From 15 Dec. 1831 Hunt made innumerable speeches against Warburton's Bill, see in particular, *PD*, 3rd series, ix, 582–3, 1276–7, x, 832–4, and xii, 309–22, 666–9 and 904. For letters, articles, meetings and petitions against the Bill, see *3730*, 31 Dec. 1831–3 Mar. 1832, and 22 Sept. 1832; and *Bolton Chronicle*, 11 Feb. 1832.

diminished it. Neither could he place his confidence in a Ministry which, while it expressed its sympathy for the Poles, actually paid money to Russia, which enabled that country to conquer and subdue the brave patriots of Poland. More than that, he could not place his confidence in a Ministry which had so grossly deceived the people, even upon the question of Reform.

He was soon forced to amend his view when the middle-class reformers started a run on the banks and prepared to transform their 'art of revolution' into physical reality to prevent Wellington from taking office. 'The feelings of the people were so worked up, and so excited,' he acknowledged, 'that no Administration could possibly be found, except the late Ministry, calculated to satisfy and tranquillize the country'.[134]

Many working-class radicals, long-standing critics of the Bill and its supporters, were swept along in this great display of extra-parliamentary strength, prompted into temporary alliance with the 'shopocrats' and middle-class reformers by what Edward Thompson has described as the well-nigh neolithic obstinacy with which Old Corruption resisted reform.[135] As in the autumn, the confrontationalists welcomed the crisis, believing that an armed clash was at hand, although the official policy of the NUWC was to 'stand at ease' and wait upon events. Amongst the working-class radicals generally, there was hope and expectation that something better than the Bill would emerge from it all.[136] Middle-class reformers were happy to foster the illusion to gain support. Preston is a good case in point. 'Instead of "the bill, the whole bill", our demand should now be—the bill, and a good deal more than the bill', Livesey proclaimed as he welcomed the working-class radicals to the meeting at the Corn Exchange, where the middle-class reformers brought forward a petition demanding the withholding of supplies and advocating household suffrage and the ballot. At the suggestion of Taylor, spokesman for the Huntites, they decided to go one stage further and substitute universal for household suffrage. The next day this radical petition was adopted at a large open-air meeting at Chadwick's Orchard, where Livesey, Segar and the other middle-class reformers joined in the cheers for Hunt and announced that the meeting would be reconvened in a week's time to establish a political union which would 'bring all classes into their ranks, and then bring about a thorough and radical reform'. The *3730* was delighted by this turn of events although before the paper could report the proceedings, Wellington had given up his attempt to form a ministry, the Whigs were back in power, and the Bill was secure. 'Will the middle classes, now that the Whig ministry are recalled, stick to the promises they have made to stand by the people?', the paper

[134] *PD*, 3rd series, xii, 862–4 and 971–2.
[135] Thompson, *Making*, 898.
[136] HO, 64/12 ff. 90–6; *PMG*, 12 and 19 May 1832; and Prothero, *Artisans and Politics*, 291–2.

wondered: 'If they do not, the curses—loud and deep—of their betrayed fellow-countrymen will deservedly light on their guilty heads.' The middle-class reformers, of course, immediately reneged on their radicalism, and cut a sorry figure when they attended the reconvened meeting at Chadwick's Orchard to form 'a Political Union of the Working and Middle Classes'. 'They actually appeared as if they were struck dumb, and seemed to have forgot all their fine promises, and their pretty posting bills with "Real Radical Reform!!" and "No More Division!!!" upon them', the *3730* reported angrily, 'they seemed totally unconscious of the petition which *they* had got up and signed, praying for the House of Commons to stop the Supplies until the people obtained Universal Suffrage, Annual Parliaments, and the Vote by Ballot'. It was agreed to adjourn the proceedings until 21 May when the middle-class reformers 'showed their zeal for the cause of a *real* reform by absenting themselves from the meeting!!'[137]

A similar sequence of events happened in towns and cities throughout the country as the middle-class reformers dropped their militancy and their radicalism the moment the Bill was safe.[138] This betrayal and the class hostility it engendered represent the real significance of the 'Days of May'. Historical debate has concentrated on the efficacy of extra-parliamentary pressure and its impact on Westminster: the aftermath in the localities has been unduly neglected. The myth of the Days of May, the pervasive belief that the people's will had prevailed, that the Lords had been beaten, the Tories thwarted, the Whigs recalled, and the Bill secured, through the sovereign force of public opinion, certainly provided the logic and inspiration for all subsequent extra-parliamentary agitations.[139] But it was the bitter disillusionment which followed in the wake of the events of May 1832 which gave the greatest of these agitations, the Chartist movement, its aggressive Huntite independence and working-class stance.

7. DEFEAT?

After the Reform Bill was finally passed, the indefatigable Hunt tried to protect working-class interests in a number of ways: in the Commons, he continued to serve as 'John Bull's watchman'; on the platform he lent his services to the NUWC, promoted new working-class radical organizations, and rallied support for the radical press; and on his various trips to the

---

[137] *Preston Chronicle*, 12–26 May; and *3730*, 19 and 26 May 1832.

[138] See, for example, the events at Bolton, Blackburn and Manchester reported in *Bolton Chronicle*, 19 May–2 June, and *Blackburn Gazette*, 16 and 23 May 1832.

[139] D. Fraser, 'The Agitation for Parliamentary Reform' in J. T. Ward (ed.), *Popular Movements c.1830–1850* (London, 1970), 46.

north he campaigned for a strong Radical representation in the first reformed Parliament.

'They might ask him what good he had done during the year and a half he had been in parliament?', he acknowledged in a speech at Manchester in the summer: 'It was true he had done very little; but he took credit for having consistently and fearlessly advocated the right of the working classes to earn not only the necessaries of life, but some of the comforts also—[Cheers].'[140] Every issue at Westminster, no matter how local or technical, came within his self-defined remit for the protection of the working class. His close attention to the Gravesend Pier Bill, for example, won him the public praise of the Thames watermen, further proof, the *3730* reported, 'that the exertions of our patriotic Representative are always employed on the side of the working classes'.[141] He tried hard to honour his pledge to present every petition sent to him, although such was his work-load that he seems to have read some of them rather cursorily before taking them to the Commons. In August, for example, he was taken to task by the editor of the *Cosmopolite* after presenting a petition from Mary Smith in favour of the 'rights of women'. This was one of Hunt's all too rare initiatives on female suffrage, an issue never mentioned by the various female reform societies which had inundated him with laudatory addresses over the years. The petition, however, had a sting in the tail. In the last paragraph, which Hunt admitted overlooking, the petitioner, 'a lady of rank and fortune', vilified the advocates of the rights of man, the followers of Tom Paine who were 'peculiarly prone to those execrable propensities which are cursed with a malignant hostility to the female sex'.[142] As the people's representative, Hunt was allowed no lapse from the utmost rectitude and incorruptibility by his radical supporters. He was given a particularly rough ride when he spoke in favour of the Speaker's pension. Hunt, it seems, genuinely admired the Speaker, who put in long hours at the House, spent every farthing of his salary in the performance of his office, and acted with exemplary impartiality, a point he much appreciated as he was treated most discourteously by the other members. 'Those who did exert themselves honestly in the public service ought to be well paid', Hunt insisted, assuring the northern radicals that he had 'never voted away a farthing of the public money, without thinking of the labour and the sufferings of the working classes':

He had done his duty on voting for the reduction of the army, the civil list, the pension list and other abuses, though he had stood alone, when the house was voting these extravagant items, which was paid by the poor Lancashire weavers

---

[140] *Bolton Chronicle*, 21 July 1832.   [141] *3730*, 8 Sept. 1832.
[142] *Cosmopolite*, 25 Aug. and 8 Sept. 1832. *PD*, 3rd series, xiv, 1086.

who were working fourteen hours a day. He was an enemy to the corrupt system, and he would not give the King any more to live upon than the President of the United States. He was so far a republican that he would try whether a king could not live on the same (cheers). He had said this in the house as well as here.[143]

In his view of his Herculean labours in the Commons—he spoke well over a thousand times during his brief parliamentary career—it was rather fitting that he had the satisfaction of 'giving the last kick to the last Borough-mongering Parliament', by counting out the House in the final debate in the unreformed Commons.[144]

In his last weeks at Westminster, he continued to work in close co-operation with the parliamentary Radicals in the 'liberal' campaigns against the taxes on knowledge, and against military flogging, a subject of much public interest following the Somerville *cause célèbre*.[145] To counter the decline in radical activity since the Days of May the NUWC decided to hold a public meeting on the flogging issue in July, and invited Hunt to take the chair, trusting that his name would pull in the crowds. Hunt was only too happy to oblige, and posted his blacking vans with placards advertising the meeting on Kennington Common. The attendance was encouraging—estimates varied from 3,000 to 40,000—and Hunt was in fine form, castigating Hobhouse, Burdett and the renegade Westminster reformers, censuring other absent liberals for their refusal to co-operate with the NUWC, and assuring the assembled crowds that he would 'monthly, weekly, nay daily if necessary, bring the subject before the House . . . I call upon you as the People of England to assist me (cries of we will, we will)'.[146] But the Kennington Common meeting did not presage a sustained revival of popular radicalism in London: as so often in the past, the crowds, passion, enthusiasm and excitement proved evanescent. The NUWC kept up its strength only by absorbing other unions,[147] and the general weakness of metropolitan radicalism was soon evinced by the parlous financial position of the *True Sun*, an ambitious attempt to provide a daily radical paper. In the autumn a general committee was formed, headed by Hunt and Dr Wade, the radical parson, to promote a subscription to rescue the ailing paper. The fund was launched at a meeting at the Crown and Anchor where Hunt reminded the radicals of their

---

[143] *PD*, 3rd series, xiv, 996; *Cosmopolite*, 4 Aug.; *PMG*, 4 Aug.; *Preston Chronicle*, 25 Aug.; and *Bolton Chronicle*, 18 Aug. 1832. See also his 'republican' speech during the discussion of the withholding of supplies in the Days of May, *PD*, 3rd series, xii, 1034.

[144] *PD*, 3rd series, xiv, 1412. Osborne, 'Henry Hunt's Career in Parliament', 24.

[145] *PD*, 3rd series, xiii, 645–6, 874–90, xiv, 34, 679–83, and 1325.

[146] HO, 64/12, ff. 110–14, 64/13, ff. 81–104, and 64/16 report by T. Hunter, 8 July 1832; and *PMG*, 14 July 1832.

[147] Prothero, *Artisans and Politics*, 293.

combined financial strength and their need for a paper 'identified with the best interests of the Working Classes'.[148]

Elsewhere in the country there were signs that working-class radicalism was growing in strength after the Days of May, proud of the new independence from the middle-class political unions whose hypocrisy stood exposed as the courts of revision set to work. Hunt's last major success on the platform was at Birmingham, proverbial centre of class alliance, where he was the main speaker at the inaugural meeting of the Midland Union of the Working Classes, an under-rated rival to the BPU. The best qualified leader to rally the disillusioned people to independent working-class organization, Hunt was appointed to head the NUWC deputation sent to the midlands in response to the joint invitation from the non-electors, the united trades, and the unemployed artisans, three disaffected working-class groups who found fault with Attwood and the 'tardy policy of the "parent union"'.[149] Torrential rain kept the crowds away and forced the venue to be transferred indoors from Newhall Hill, but Hunt was in fine form, insisting that he had been 'grossly maligned and misrepresented to the working classes, from the advocacy of whose cause he had never for one instant flinched'. Once again, consistency was his trump card:

. . . they would all remember that in 1817 he first publicly put forward at the Spafields meeting the three principles they were that day asserting, and had ever since advocated them. Knowing this, then, could they imagine that it was consistent or right for him to sit still in the House of Commons when he heard it asserted that this bill would satisfy the people, and that it was to be a final measure ('no,' 'no.') That then was the head and front of his offending.

In a melodramatic climax, he generously forgave the Birmingham radicals for being deceived in him by the lying press, and then blessed their new union, assuring them that he would 'always be ready to co-operate with them in endeavouring to forward the interests of the working classes (great applause and cries of "bravo," "bravo.")'.[150] Before he left Birmingham, he delivered a special lecture 'on the Conduct of the Whigs, to the working classes', the proceeds of which were donated to the new Midland Union. The lecture, which became part of his stock repertoire, struck a familiar theme, the collective strength of the working classes. True to his origins as an 'independent' reformer, he began by denouncing the complicity of the factions and cataloguing the profligacy of the Whigs. He then condemned the Reform Bill, which 'by bringing in the middle classes, was intended to

[148] *Report of the Proceedings at the Public Meeting of the Working Classes and Others . . . to support the people's daily press, The True Sun* (London, 1832), in HO, 64/18.
[149] HO, 64/12 ff. 152–62. *PMG*, 20 and 27 Oct. 1832. C. Behagg, 'An Alliance with the Middle Class: the Birmingham Political Union and Early Chartism' in Epstein and Thompson (eds.), 63–5.
[150] *PMG*, 3 Nov. 1832.

enable the Whigs to carry on the Government as nearly in the old way as possible'. Then came the crucial question—'whether any Reform will benefit the working classes that will not secure to them the fruits of their labour? ("No, no.")'. Finally, he called on the working class to unite and organize, and rehearsed the familiar but still impressive set of figures to demonstrate their collective financial power:

This was the moment when they should show the Aristocracy what power they had, but they must be united . . . supposing a million of the working classes were to subscribe a penny each, in a week the sum would amount to £4,166.13s.4d; in a month, to £16,663.13s.4d, and in a year to £200,000. And yet the Aristocracy dared to laugh at the weakness of the working classes, and at their poverty. (Great applause).[151]

After the Bill was passed, Hunt made three separate visits to Preston to prepare for the first election under the new system in December. On each occasion there were great meetings and processions as he travelled along the main radical artery from Manchester to Preston. An old-stager on the platform, he made the most of these displays, employing tried and tested rhetorical devices to reaffirm his special relationship with the northern workers. 'I must ask you why it is, that when I come to Blackburn, to Bolton, and to Manchester, that you turn out in such immense numbers, to honour me as you now do?' he began his speech at Blackburn in July: 'Is it because you have heard that I had advocated the cause of the rich against the rights and interests of the poor (No, no) or is it because I have exerted my humble efforts to maintain the rights of the poor against the oppression of the rich? (Loud cheering).'[152] The purpose of his first visit to Preston was to explain the new registration procedure. Huge crowds, some 20,000 strong, greeted him on his arrival at the end of race week, when all the factories were closed. Mitchell rather spoilt the celebrations, however, when he had the temerity to register his disapproval during the obligatory show of hands on the merits of Hunt's parliamentary conduct. He then entered Hunt's hotel room and tried to address the crowd from the other window, at which point, a press correspondent reported, 'Mr. H. let fly with his left, and would have planted a teazer on Mitchell's conk, but fortunately the bystanders interfered and prevented further mischief.' The next day, Mitchell brought Hunt before the magistrates who bound him over to keep the peace for twelve months.[153] On a later visit, Hunt paid the

---

[151] H. Hunt, *Lecture on the Conduct of the Whigs to the Working Classes, delivered at Lawrence Street Chapel, Birmingham, on Wednesday, October 31st, 1832* (London, 1832).

[152] *Blackburn Gazette*, 18 July 1832.

[153] *Preston Chronicle*, 14 July; *Bolton Chronicle*, 14 July 1832; and *The Demagogue; or 'Old Harry's' last speech and visit to his constituents* (Preston, 1832).

magistrates out of his own pocket, the outstanding hustings expenses for 1830, the source of so much contention with Mitchell.[154]

Hunt returned to Preston in August, immediately after the dissolution of the unreformed Parliament, in order to introduce Captain Forbes, 'a true British tar', who was to be his running mate at the forthcoming election, when they would stand on the principle that 'the honest labourer and mechanic should have the full reward of their industry'. Forbes, a distinguished war-time naval officer, had no political ambitions of his own, but was a great admirer of Hunt, to whom he offered his services at Preston on the understanding that he would second him without reservation on every issue in the Commons. Whilst in the north-west with Forbes, Hunt canvassed on behalf of radical candidates throughout the region: he went to Bury to support Edmund Grundy, the first witness for the defence at the Peterloo trial, and to Rochdale to promote James Taylor, 'a true radical reformer'; at Bolton he tried to persuade the elderly Naisby to stand against Colonel Torrens, 'a clever political economist, a thing he [Mr. Hunt] did not understand much about'.[155]

The next visit was in November, when he and Forbes attended the court of revision throughout the entire registration of voters, in order to keep an eye on Stanley's 'land-sharks' and safeguard the interests of the poor electors, particularly those 'imprisoned in the factories by their masters, who would not allow them to attend'. In the evenings they addressed the crowds from the windows of the Blackamoor's Head, and on the last night Hunt gave a special rendition of his lecture on the conduct of the Whigs at threepence-a-head, the proceeds going to the 'fund for supporting those persons who have been discharged, and may hereafter be discharged for voting agreeable to the dictates of their conscience'. To boost his election expenses fund, he repeated the lecture at the theatre at Blackburn on his way back to Manchester.[156]

After all this preparation, Hunt was to suffer a humiliating defeat at the general election in December. Writing shortly after the event, Huish hailed the defeat as Hunt's nemesis, a tribute to the wisdom of the people and the new reformed system, a judgment subsequently enshrined in liberal history.[157] Hunt, however, was not deserted by the working-class radicals. The support he secured against the overwhelming pressures of the reformed establishment formed the bedrock on which the Chartist movement was subsequently built. The Preston Political Union, proud of

[154] *Preston Chronicle*, 25 Aug. 1832.

[155] Ibid.; *3730*, 1 and 8 Sept.; and *Bolton Chronicle*, 18 Aug. and 1 Sept. 1832. Back in London, Hunt canvassed on behalf of Murray, the radical candidate in Southwark, PC, set 17, iii, f. 258.

[156] *Preston Chronicle*, 17 Nov.–1 Dec.; *3730*, 17 and 24 Nov.; *Blackburn Gazette*, 28 Nov.; and *PMG*, 8 Dec. 1832.

[157] Huish, ii, 485–7. Proctor, 151–4.

its working-class independence after the middle-class betrayal in the Days
of May, developed rapidly in the summer and autumn—by November
there were forty-nine branches in the town[158]—and campaigned hard to
secure Hunt's re-election. The Union tried its best to counter the
intimidation exercised by Hunt's opponents, the supporters of the revived
coalition between Whig and Tory, the Stanley interest and the Hesketh-
Fleetwood family. The main problem here, of course, was the power of the
millowners and their 'disgraceful system of compulsion'. As well as
building up a fund for the victims of the 'shameful and wanton tyranny
exercised by several Cotton Lords', the Union called upon the spinners,
that crucial group in the factory work-force, to use their industrial
muscle—'one single hours general resistance'—to prevent radicals being
thrown out of work and/or off the register.[159] While the Union relied on
the spinners against the millowners, the women came forward to put
pressure on the 'shopocrats', trusting to 'make this crawling, money-
hunting crew wince under exclusive dealing'. The female reformers of
Soapery supported Hunt by withdrawing their custom from all anti-radical
shopkeepers, those arrogant individuals who stood behind their counters
'decked out at the expense of our labour, like so many lords and ladies'.
The High Street branch of the Preston Female Association, the *3730*
reported, 'carry on exclusive dealing, aye to the very letter, even to the
mangle-man and baker'.[160] As the preparations for the general election
show so clearly, radical Preston was not the preserve of some isolated
vanguard, revolutionary in their consciousness and scornful of traditional
popular attitudes and beliefs. Working-class radicalism in Preston was
popular in tone, mood and programme, depending on community support
rather than ideological commitment.[161] Hunt struck just the right note with
his simple, democratic social and political philosophy of self-determination
and economic contentment, his 'God-like principle', as one Preston radical
described it, that every working man should have it in his power to earn
sufficient to keep his family comfortable and happy, and have something to
put by for a rainy day and old age.[162] In support of Hunt's democratic
radicalism the Preston radicals mobilized as best they could against what
they called 'the property-class: meaning they who possess a licence, or
right, by virtue of aristocratic law, to take whatever they may deem
sufficient for their maintenance from the labour of others'.[163] On the eve of
the election, the Union issued a last minute appeal for funds and support in

---

[158] *3730*, 17 Nov. 1832.   [159] *3730*, 17 Sept., 17, 24 Nov., and 8 Dec. 1832.
[160] *3730*, 1 Sept., 3, 17 Nov., 8 Dec. 1832 and 5 Jan. 1833.
[161] For comparison see Foster's work on Oldham, ch. 3. The Preston Political Union
wanted every street, alley and court to have its political class, see *3730*, 23 June 1832.
[162] 'Fire-Side Talk', *3730*, 31 Mar. 1832.   [163] *3730*, 3 Nov. 1832.

what had become 'a struggle of principle against wealth, power and tyranny':

Numbers are turned away from their employments, because the men are too noble and brave to sacrifice their principles to their inhuman masters. Numbers are receiving assistance weekly from the Political Union . . . the whole camp of our enemies are in motion, threats, intimidation, fraud, deceit and treachery, are put in requisition to break our impenetrable phalanx.[164]

Hunt's speech on nomination day was informed with a similar spirit of working-class pride. 'The contest', he predicted, 'would assuredly be between those "respectable parties" who lived upon the labour of the working class, and the working class themselves . . . he would give to Mr. Stanley and Mr. Fleetwood every parson, every lawyer, every magistrate, every master manufacturer, and every large shopkeeper, and he would take against them the working classes alone, and would secure a victory for their cause. (Loud cheers).' The speech proudly reflected his close identification with the interests of the northern working class, a relationship which had developed so strongly during his term as MP for Preston. This concern for the workers was not an expression of some backward-looking paternalism: the sufferings of the working class reinforced his commitment to political equality. He had no revolutionary blueprint to reorder the economic and social structure, but he was implacably opposed to the oppression, injustice and inequality of the existing system upheld by political monopoly. 'Cursed be the monsters, and cursed be the system that produces such effects upon the working classes', he fulminated as he addressed himself to the poor weavers, forced to work fourteen or sixteen hours a day to earn a miserable subsistence:

The system and their sufferings he had never ceased to urge upon the attention of the members of the house of commons. Some of those members had, he admitted, hearts to feel for the poor . . . and many would lend a hand to relieve the people, provided they could do so without giving them their political rights.—*Loud cheers.* The only thing they stuck at was giving them their political rights; giving a voice in the making of those laws which they were bound to obey.—*Cheers.*

He then turned to the terrible plight of the factory children as he ridiculed Fleetwood's vaunted concern for the education of the poor:

Mr. Fleetwood would, no doubt, support his own charity schools: he would have the children of the working classes to read all the pretty little books which he chose to put into their hands, but if he would give every man the just benefit of his labour, he would do better than this, for then the working man could do all this for himself—*Cheers* . . . of what use was it to give education to the children of the poor, while the poor are held as they are now . . . compelled from the condition of

[164] *3730*, 8 Dec. 1832.

their parents to work more hours than the sun shines.—*Cheers*. They have no time to read or to study, even if they were taught to read . . . if justice were done to the people they would have time, which they have not now. If justice were done the working man might earn a sufficient subsistence by four day's labour in the week, and he might then devote the other three days to reading and reflection.—*Cheers*.

After Hunt's poignant speech, the mayor called for a show of hands, which produced an emphatic victory for Hunt and Forbes. The election itself, however, was quite a different matter. The radicals could not match what the press euphemistically described as the 'electioneering tact' of the Stanley and Fleetwood interests: 'the orange and blue mutually combined', the *Preston Chronicle* reported, 'and, in addition to constables all provided with long or short stave, they had procured a posse of about forty rough brawny fellows, some of them from the country'. Confronted by this combined force, the Huntites were soon compelled to retreat from the Court House, the only one of the twenty or so polling booths which they had been able to claim as their own. There were more clashes later in the day as the Huntites tried to protect their voters and defend their new red flag. When the day's polling closed, Fleetwood and Stanley had a commanding lead over Hunt and Forbes—Crompton, the hapless independent liberal candidate had already withdrawn from the contest. Bruised and angry, the Huntites wrought their vengeance after dark, attacking the inns patronized by Stanley and Fleetwood, and then taking possession of the market place, until the mayor read the Riot Act and ordered in the military from Chorley. The next day the roughs of the orange and blue retaliated: the radical inns were attacked, the Riot Act read a second time, and the troops recalled. After this the radicals gave up the fight, and Hunt decided to leave town as there were fears for his safety. The final result was declared two days later: Fleetwood 3,372, H. T. Stanley 3,273, Hunt 2,054, Forbes 1,926, and Crompton 118.[165]

'Money, bribery, treating, intimidation, and hired bludgeon-men have prevailed', Hunt protested in his farewell address, 'and the working-classes of Preston must remain in the power of the Whig and Tory factions, till they have the protection of the ballot.' Self-praise and class-interest were characteristically interwoven in this valediction:

I know you will feel satisfied, my friends, that I have done every thing in my power to maintain, uphold, and secure your rights, but I have failed upon this occasion. I shall retire into private life with the reflection, that I have never, upon any occasion, flinched from performing my duty to you, and the whole of the working classes of the United Kingdom.[166]

As he headed for the south and retirement, he was greeted by large

[165] *Preston Chronicle*, 15 Dec.; and Mayor of Preston, 13 Dec., and Town Clerk, 17 Dec. 1832, HO, 52/18 ff. 114–19, and 139.   [166] *Preston Chronicle*, 22 Dec. 1832.

crowds, and capacity audiences attended special performances of his lecture at Manchester, Middleton, and Oldham.[167] By the end of 1832, working-class radicalism was already strong in the north-west, although it was as yet quite unequal to the power and force exerted against it by the new reformed order. Thanks to Hunt's defence of working-class interests in the Reform Bill agitation the foundations had been laid for the great Chartist challenge. The heroic Preston 'red caps', who had defied intimidation and voted for their champion, refused to give up the struggle:

> The 'Cotton Lords'! how flush'd they seem!
> They *taunt* us while they ROB!
> How impotently vain they deem
> The efforts of the 'MOB'!
> They jeeringly ask—'where is Hunt?'
> 'Our boasted bravery—where?'
> And think we 'pocket the affront'
> And *hopelessly* despair!![168]

---

[167] *PMG*, 29 Dec. 1832.

[168] 'A Republican Melody', *3730*, 5 Jan. 1833. For a stimulating study of the radicalizing and polarizing impact of the general election of 1832 in south-east Lancashire, see Sykes, 'Popular Politics', 379–94, where it is argued that 'the line from 1832 to Chartism was a very direct one indeed'.

Conclusion

AFTER his defeat at Preston, Hunt returned to London in poor health, financial difficulties, and low spirits. 'You and I of all Men now living are an example of disinterested patriotism, and a pretty reward we have had', he wrote to Foster of the *Leeds Patriot*, recently forced into bankruptcy:

The people of the Metropolis are like those in Leeds running after shadows and following blind guides. But let them go, they will have plenty of time to repent of not having listened to you and myself—almost their only true and steady friends during the most fearful times of Humbug.

Dispirited as he was, Hunt did not withdraw from radical politics, although as the months went by his deteriorating health led him to restrict his appearance on the extra-parliamentary platform. 'The infernal air and late Hours of the humbug and hypocritical reforming House of Commons have had such an effect upon my Constitution that I almost despair of recovering my usual good health and strength of Constitution', he informed Foster: 'However it is in vain to look back, and I must still struggle on.'[1]

For the next few months, he managed to continue the campaign for democratic radicalism, upholding the cause in new and traditional arenas of popular politics in London. He made several appearances at the Institution of the Working Classes, Theobalds Road: in January, for example, he chaired the public meeting convened by the NUWC to protest at Hetherington's second arrest, and began a series of three specially-extended lectures on the 'political tergiversation of the Whigs' and the 'atrocious proceedings of the late Election for Preston', a useful means of raising some money for his unpaid election expenses.[2] In January, too, he returned to his old stamping ground in city politics, the Guildhall, and addressed the new electors in a suitably self-righteous speech when they registered their dismay at the language of finality favoured by the Whigs during the general election. True to his uncompromising working-class radicalism, he refused to endorse the new campaign for the abolition of the house and window and assessed taxes launched by the disabused and angry city reformers.[3] He issued a cautionary address 'To the Unrepresented Seven Millions of Working Men of England, Ireland, and Scotland':

All sorts of attempts are about to be made to entrap you once more to aid and assist

[1] Stevens-Cox Collection: Hunt to Foster, 12 Feb. 1833.
[2] *PMG*, 19 and 26 Jan.; *Destructive*, 2 Feb. 1833; and PC, set 17, iv, f. 107, handbill advertising the lectures.
[3] *Morning Chronicle*, 22 Jan. 1833; and PC, set 17, iv, ff. 93–7.

the Middle Men and the Men of Property to relieve themselves from some of the burthens of taxation . . . my solemn belief is, that the millions will continue to suffer, they will never experience either relief or redress till the millions enjoy Equal Laws and Equal Rights.

Therefore, my advice is to the working, producing *Seven Millions*, never to join in any public meeting,—never to join in or sign any petition—that does not embrace a prayer for Annual Parliaments, Universal Suffrage, the Ballot, and an immediate repeal of the Starvation Act, called the Corn Bill.[4]

He also sent a letter to John Knight and the Oldham radicals, warning of the danger, and ridiculing the conduct and preoccupations of their new MP, William Cobbett who was content to expose 'the inequality of the Stamp Duties. Pshaw, what has that to do with relieving the poor or giving them political rights?'[5]

By the spring of 1833, feelings were running high against the 'Whig conservatives', and Hunt considered himself well and truly vindicated for his constant opposition to the ministers and their Reform Bill. The Irish Coercion Act, '"Lord" Grey and Co's Irish Murder-and-Bastille Bill', enraged working-class radicals and middle-class reformers alike, and efforts were made to rally the people against the 'base, bloody and brutal whigs'.[6] The BPU launched an abortive second campaign,[7] and the Irish-dominated NUWC finally went ahead with the endlessly discussed plans for a national convention, the traditional 'revolutionary' expedient. Hunt was not involved in these discussions, but he stood forward to head the protest against the Cold Bath Fields 'massacre', when the crowds at a meeting to take preparatory steps for the convention were brutally assaulted by the police, two of whom were killed in the process.[8] His campaign to bring the authorities to justice proved to be his last attempt to make concerted use of the various arenas of metropolitan extra-parliamentary politics, radical, reformist and official. Speaking from the chair at a crowded meeting in the National Exchange Bazaar, he reprobated the Whig ministers who had 'laid their forces in ambush for the purpose of rushing out in a body upon the people, and beating them to death'. 'What were the first fruits of the Reform Bill?', he continued in fine rhetorical form: 'An atrocious and unjustifiable Bill for Ireland.—(Loud hissing.) What were the second? The bloody massacre attempted in Cold-bath Fields—(Loud hissing).'[9] He spoke in similar terms to middle-class audiences at the meeting at the Crown and Anchor, convened by the NPU to protest at the violence of the police, and at the Common Hall in June,

---

[4] *PMG*, 9 Feb. 1833. | [5] *PMG*, 13 Apr. 1833.
[6] *Le Bonnet Rouge*, 23 Feb. and 30 Mar. 1833. For Hunt's strident opposition to the Act, see his letters in *Destructive*, 23 Mar. 1833.
[7] Flick, 102–10. [8] Prothero, *Artisans and Politics*, 293–6.
[9] *Destructive*, 1 June; and *Working Man's Friend*, 1 June 1833.

when he condemned the bloody Whigs for by-passing the sheriff and the city authorities.[10] After attending the inquest on Cully, one of the policemen, at which the jury returned the sensational verdict of justifiable homicide, he issued a rousing address 'To the Friends of Humanity and Justice, Male and Female, of the United Kingdom', advising them to be 'up and doing':

Let the people meet at all parts of the metropolis; let the people meet at Manchester, at Bolton, at Blackburn, at Preston; let them meet in every town and village in the north, in the south, in the east, and in the west; let all the people, male and female, do honour and justice to the brave jurymen of Calthorpe-street.[11]

As events turned out, the meeting at the National Exchange Bazaar was his last appearance on the radical platform in London, and it was therefore rather fitting that the proceedings closed with the presentation of a silver cup from the Female Union of Preston 'for his unwearied exertions in advocating the cause of liberty, and promoting the welfare of the labouring classes of the community'.[12]

During the remaining eighteen months or so of his life, Hunt participated in politics whenever business and health permitted. In the city he continued his campaign against the mismanagement of funds, the unaccountability of officers, and the undemocratic procedures by which aldermen were elected.[13] At the East Somerset county election in February 1834 he declined an invitation to stand because of lack of funds, but he took the opportunity to appear on the hustings and 'condemn the policy of the Whigs, and their pretended anxiety for the liberties and pockets of the people'.[14] Through the columns of Hetherington's publications, he kept in touch with the radicals of the north to whom he offered some timely advice when he replied to their votes of thanks and birthday addresses: they should shun all contact with the disillusioned middle-class reformers and parliamentary Radicals, and concentrate their efforts on the burgeoning trade union movement. 'Till the people obtain and enjoy their political rights,' he advised, 'they can have no better protection than that of forming themselves into one mighty legion, and let that legion be the Trades' Union'. As the Reform Bill had 'turned out just what I told the people it would before it passed into a law', he felt sure the Blackburn radicals and others would heed his words and thereby preserve their independence and integrity:

Let the people beware, I say of following the advice of those who were the foremost in persuading them that the Whig Reform Bill was intended to benefit the working

---

[10] *Destructive*, 8 June; and *Gauntlet*, 30 June 1833.   [11] *Destructive*, 25 May 1833.
[12] *PMG*, 1 June 1833, including Hunt's letter of thanks 'To the Female Reformers of Preston'.
[13] *Gauntlet*, 30 June; and *Destructive*, 5 Oct. 1833.   [14] *PMG*, 8 Feb. 1834.

classes. The paltry and hollow excuse that they were deceived themselves, is only an additional reason why they should never be trusted again as guides or leaders of the people.[15]

But while he remained a close and authoritative observer of the political scene, most of his remaining energies and funds were drained away by two long-running disputes: his libel action against the *True Sun*, and his protest against the cost, conduct and result of the Preston election.

Through his involvement in the rescue operation, Hunt became very critical of the management of the *True Sun* and disapproved in particular of Carpenter's increasing influence. Matters came to a head when the paper reprinted some libellous allegations from the anti-radical press about his conduct during the Preston election riots, without taking any trouble to contradict them. Not content with successful actions against the original sources, Hunt decided to sue the *True Sun*, with which he and his supporters, Hetherington and O'Brien, were constantly in conflict: the case was finally brought to court in December 1833 when he was awarded satisfactory damages of one farthing, together with costs.[16] His attempt to contest the Preston election ended far less happily. Realizing that it would be a costly business, he decided against an official appeal, and petitioned the Commons instead, demanding that the returning officer be brought before the bar of the House to explain his part in the 'hellish proceedings which took place at Preston during the last mock election'.[17] No notice was taken of the petition, and he was not in the best of health when he had the chance to restate his case some months later before a parliamentary committee, following Hume's motion for a return of all the expenses at the last contested elections. When his health improved he petitioned again, this time concentrating on the excessive and illegal cost of the election, at which point he suddenly found himself faced with an action brought by the Preston returning officer, seeking to recover 'what he calls my share of the expences that were incurred by him in order to extinguish the last remaining vestige of the freedom of election for that borough'.[18] The case was heard at Lancaster in March 1834, when the verdict went against Hunt to the sum of nearly £90 along with taxed costs of over £150.[19] Ill-health and financial stringency prevented his applying for a new trial on his return to London, but he protested strongly against the verdict and its consequences.

[15] Hunt's letters in *PMG*, 6, 23 and 30 Nov. 1833. *Destructive*, 23 Nov. 1833 has a lengthy account of the Hunt birthday festivities at Padiham.
[16] Hunt's letters in *PMG*, 26 Jan., *Destructive*, 23 Mar., 9 Nov. and 7 Dec. 1833. See also, Lancashire Record Office: Hunt Correspondence, DDX/113, Hunt to Bryant, 11 Feb. 1833; Stevens-Cox Collection: Hunt to Foster, 12 Feb. 1833; *Destructive*, 13, 20 July and 21 Dec. 1833; and *PMG*, 7 Dec. 1833, 4 and 25 Jan. 1834. The Library of Congress holds a pamphlet copy of the trial.
[17] *Destructive*, 23 Mar. 1833.   [18] Hunt's letter in *PMG*, 1 Mar. 1834.
[19] *Gauntlet*, 23 Mar. 1834. The Library of Congress holds a pamphlet copy of the trial.

From his sick bed be wrote to the electors of Preston, inveighing against 'corrupt judges' and 'packed juries of the middle tyrants' who were able to interpret the provisions of the 'precious "Reform Bill"' to suit their purposes and preserve their monopoly. Radical candidates like himeself, he regretted, were now financially debarred from popular elections: 'no man shall represent Preston', he fulminated, 'but one that can pay enormously for it'.[20] Much saddened by Hunt's withdrawal from electoral politics, the loyal radicals of the north mounted a subscription to cover his latest legal expenses. By August, the central committee at Preston had received some £80 or so, the largest contribution coming from Manchester where Edward Curran dutifully passed the box round after every meeting at the Temple of Liberty, Oldham Road, venue of heated discussions about the viability of the Regeneration Society and its plans for an eight-hour day.[21]

Despite his poor health at the time of the Lancaster trial, Hunt decided to undertake a brief speechifying tour before returning to London. He put in an appearance at Peterloo, but was forced to cut short his speech and retire to a convenient public house.[22] A week later, and still infirm, he paid his first visit to Ashton-under-Lyne, where he deplored the 'degrading apathy' of labouring men in his short speech to a mass meeting of 5,000 or so, and then assisted in the formation of a new radical committee at the dinner in his honour. The new committee, it was hoped, would 'rouse the people to a sense of their duty', and head a campaign for equal political rights, now that it was clear to all that the Reform Bill 'has not conferred, nor was ever intended to confer, any benefit upon the people'.[23] On return to London he was forced to take to his bed, but he still managed to write to the northern radicals, the 'Productive Classes of Lancashire', condemning the Reform Bill and the Lancaster verdict, and extolling the merits of trade unionism, the strength of which greatly impressed him during the protest campaign at the Dorchester sentences, the transportation of the Tolpuddle martyrs. There was a distinct note of optimism in his last general letter to his supporters in the north, an appeal to the northern radicals to join their unionized London comrades:

Let the working classes be but united and steady to their purpose, and their oppressors must give way. One of two things must follow. There are seven millions of men in the United Kingdom, who are rendered so many *political outlaws* by the Reform Bill; by the provisions of that act, they are to all intents and purposes so many political slaves. Therefore the Unionists say, you have deprived us of all share in making the laws, and we will make laws for ourselves, as far as the

[20] Hunt's letter 'To the Electors of Preston', *PMG*, 3 May 1834. See also Hunt's letters to Gilbert Martin, 15 Nov. and 16 Dec. 1834, quoted in Huish, ii, 491–2.
[21] *PMG*, 10, 24 May, 5 July and 16 Aug. 1834.
[22] *PMG*, 5 Apr. 1834.
[23] *PMG*, 12 Apr. 1834.

regulating the hours of our labour and the amount of our wages. Consequently, one of two things must happen, either the workmen must have *more wages* and *less work*, or an *equal share* in making the *laws* that are to regulate the measure of labour, wages, and profit.[24]

These confident words constitute a suitable epitaph: throughout his lengthy political career he had always advocated unity and organization; by the end of his active political life he stood firmly committed to a class-based radicalism, the working-class challenge for economic amelioration and equal political rights. Doubtless, he did not understand the full implications of the new proto-Marxist ideology of economic exploitation, or the syndicalist aspirations of some of the trade unionists, but he had carried traditional radicalism far beyond the confines of *petit-bourgeois* preoccupation with 'cheap government' into open hostility with the dominant creed and prevailing practice of *laissez-faire* politial economy. In aims and aspiration, language and methods, ideas and beliefs, he set the standard for the Chartists.

After the spring of 1834 Hunt was rarely in good health, and he took no further part in active politics. He suffered a severe stroke which paralysed his left side and deprived him of the power of speech whilst on a business trip to Hampshire: he died soon afterwards at Alresford on 13 February 1835. A week later he was buried in Colonel Vince's vault at Parham Park, Sussex, after Mrs Vince's own family, the Bishops, had refused to allow the body to be admitted to their vault.[25]

Hunt died before he could recapture the popularity he had enjoyed in the Peterloo years and lost during the Reform Bill agitation. 'I am still, and shall die the victim of patriotism', he wrote in one of his last letters to Gilbert Martin, his close friend in the north, casting a sorrowful eye over the folly and ingratitude of the capricious people, the 'bitterest of fruit'.[26] Soon after his death, however, his patriotism was accorded its full due: his reputation was revered and his name became the very touchstone of independent working-class radical endeavour, the symbol of emancipation from the Whigs, liberals, and O'Connellite Radicals. As the various strands of working-class protest were drawn together in an unprecedented unity and strength, united by common hostility to the social and economic policy of the reforming Whigs and parliamentary Radicals—the new Poor Law, the factory legislation and the attack on trade unionism—Hunt was recognized and honoured as the great prophet who had tried to warn the non-represented people of the deleterious consequences of middle-class political reform. Full-length portraits of the radical champion appeared on

[24] *PMG*, 26 Apr. 1834.
[25] *PMG*, 21 and 28 Feb. 1835. Huish, ii, 497–8. A funeral procession was held in Manchester, see Sykes, 'Popular Politics', 397.
[26] Hunt to Martin, 3 July 1834, quoted in Huish, ii, 490.

many public house signs in the north, and radical poetasters eulogized the prescient leader 'Who boldly said in thirty two/ The Bill was a cheat and vain/ Have we not found his judgement true/ We shall never see his likes again.'[27] To Feargus O'Connor, leader of the new Chartist movement, Hunt stood as model and master, the incorruptible and uncompromising champion of the platform, the advocate of radical fundamentalism, the proponent of independent working-class organization. O'Connor, indeed, legitimized his leadership by consciously taking on Hunt's mantle—a recurring image in Chartist iconography[28]—presenting himself as the humble successor to the greatest of all radicals, tragically consigned to an early grave, broken in heart and spirit by the folly and ingratitude of the people:

He (Mr. Hunt) told them that the Reform Bill was all farce; he saw it to be a delusion; and while he was thus stemming the torrents of public opinion thus misled, his enemies were too powerful for him, and they broke his heart. (Hear, hear.) His (Mr. O'Connor's) position was neither so dangerous, nor was his work so arduous. He (Mr. Hunt) was the great architect who taught the people what that edifice should be; he (Mr. O'Connor) was only a humble workman endeavouring to raise the edifice to its completion.

Enshrined in the Chartist pantheon, Hunt was accorded pride of place in the calendar of counter-cultural celebration and observance, the two most important dates being the anniversary of 'never-to-be-forgotten' Peterloo and the birthday of 'ever-to-be-loved' Hunt. 'They would take Hunt for their model and O'Connor for their guide', an Ashton Chartist proclaimed during the birthday celebrations in 1838, 'he should always revere the memory of Hunt, and he hoped all present would teach their children to hold sacred the 16th of August . . . Henry Hunt could not be dead while Feargus O'Connor was alive'.[29]

The Chartists gave physical form to their respect for Hunt by erecting the great monument in Ancoats, first proposed by Scholefield and the radicals in 1835.[30] The dedication ceremony in 1842, planned to coincide with the anniversary of Peterloo, played a crucial role in Chartist history itself: it brought all the major leaders of the movement together in Manchester at the time of the 'plug plot' or 'general strike', a high point of

[27] B. Harrison, *Drink and the Victorians* (London, 1971), 61. Huntite song in *Northern Star*, 10 Nov. 1838, quoted in Sykes, 'Popular Politics', 397–8.

[28] One of the earliest examples was the much admired Wigan banner, first described in *Northern Star*, 17 Nov. 1838: 'A full length portrait of Feargus O'Connor, Esq., in the attitude of addressing the public, holding the People's Charter in one hand, Hunt's monument in the distance. Motto on a scarlet scroll, gold letters—O'Connor Hunt's Successor.'

[29] Epstein, 90–1. *Northern Star*, 17 Nov. 1838.

[30] *PMG*, 26 Sept. 1835. 'A Monument to the Memory of H. Hunt Esq.' (Bolton, 1835), handbill in Manchester Central Library: Henry Hunt, microfiche newspaper cuttings.

working-class political and industrial militancy in early Victorian England.[31] But after the demise of Chartism, Hunt's reputation went into steady decline and the Ancoats monument fell into disrepair. Planned by the radicals, built by the Chartists, it was demolished in the name of civic pride by the Open Spaces Committee in 1888, the stones being sold to a builder for £3.[32] Local historians and Edwardian Liberals later tried to make amends, and a bronze plaque was installed in the Manchester Reform Club in 1908, where it has long since been forgotten by lunching Mancunian businessmen.[33] A more suitable memorial and greater recognition is due to 'Orator' Hunt, the man of the people, the pioneer of working-class radicalism.

[31] For an account of the ceremony, see *Transactions of the Lancashire and Cheshire Antiquarian Society*, vii (1889) 324–6. According to the recollections of John O'Dea, the taverns in Ancoats in 1842 still rang to the refrain of the favourite Huntite song, 'With Henry Hunt we'll go/ With Henry Hunt we'll go/ And wear the cap of liberty/ In spite of Nadin Joe', *Manchester City News*, 12 Mar. 1904.

[32] *Manchester Guardian*, 3 and 6 Oct. 1888, including the poem by Addleshaw, 'Shame! shame on all those busy thousands who/ Profess to tread the path your champion went/ To love that liberal policy he knew/ Yet bury memory in today's content/ And watch, unmoved, men break his monument/ Who risked his all for you at Peterloo'.

[33] Manchester Central Library: Receipt book for the restoration of the Memorial. 'The Henry Hunt Memorial in Ancoats', *Manchester City News*, 19 Mar. 1904. For the unveiling of the plaque by C. P. Scott, see *Manchester Guardian*, 30 June 1908.

Bibliography

This is a select bibliography divided as follows:

A Manuscript Sources
   I Henry Hunt Papers
   II Others
B Printed Sources
   I Parliamentary Proceedings, State Trials etc.
   II Collections of Prints, Newspapers etc.
   III Newspapers and Periodicals
   IV Contemporary Pamphlets, Books etc.
   V Secondary Sources
C Unpublished Theses

A MANUSCRIPT SOURCES

I Henry Hunt Papers

Bodleian Library, Oxford: Montagu Manuscripts, Autograph Letters, iii, two letters from Hunt to John Foster.

Lancashire Record Office: DDX/113, Henry Hunt Correspondence, 31 items.

Manchester Central Library, Archives Department: 3 letters by Henry Hunt.

——, Manuscript journal kept during Hunt's imprisonment in Ilchester Gaol.

John Rylands Library, Manchester: English MS 378/1029, letter from Hunt to William Shepherd.

Somerset Record Office: DD/DN 282, letter from Hunt to William Dickinson.

Stevens-Cox Collection, Guernsey: 4 large volumes of Hunt correspondence and papers, mostly purchased from the Phillipps Collection.

University of Chicago Library, Special Collections: Henry Hunt correspondence and papers, 102 items purchased from the Phillipps Collection.

II Others

Adelphi University, Long Island: Cobbett Papers, 35 letters from William Cobbett to Hunt; photocopies available at Nuffield College, Oxford.

Bristol Record Office: Burgesses, 1812 to 1818.

——, Election Proceedings, 1806–1812.

——, Letters and Miscellaneous Papers, boxes 1811–12, 1812, 1816, and 1817.

——, Proceedings of Mayor and Aldermen, 1785–1820.

British Library: Place Papers, Additional Manuscripts, 27789–797, 27809, 27822, 27827, 27835, 27837, 27841–843, 35148–149, 35152–153, and 37949.

Huntington Library, California: HM 17198, letter from William Cobbett to Henry Hunt.

Manchester Central Library, Local History Department: Henry Hunt Memorial Fund, receipt book for the restoration of the Memorial.

Nuffield College, Oxford: Cobbett Papers, Faithfull Manuscripts, box xi, Hunt versus Cobbett, 1826.

Public Record Office: Home Office Papers:

    HO, 40/3–31: Disturbances, 1816–1833.

    HO, 41/4–11: Disturbances, entry books, 1818–1834.

    HO, 42/183–203: Domestic, Jan. 1819–Jan. 1820.

    HO, 44/4–12: Domestic, 1820–1822.

    HO, 52/4–18: Municipal and provincial, 1824–1832.

    HO, 64/2–19: Police, secret service, 1827–1834.

    HO, 79/3–4: Private and secret, 1817–1844.

——, Treasury Solicitor's Papers:

    TS, 11/695, 1055–56: Cases for the prosecution.

    TS, 24: Seditious publications.

John Rylands Library, Manchester: English MS 1197, Peterloo material collected by the Revd W. R. Hay.

University of Illinois, Urbana-Champaign: Letter from William Cobbett to Henry Hunt.

Wiltshire County Record Office: Savernake Manuscripts, Yeomanry papers, letters from John and Thomas Ward, legal advisers to Lord Ailesbury.

B PRINTED SOURCES

All works are published in London unless otherwise stated.

I Parliamentary Proceedings, State Trials etc.

Howell, T. B. (ed.), *State Trials*, xxxii (1824).

Journals of the House of Commons.

Parliamentary Debates.

Parliamentary Papers, 1822, *Reports and Papers Relating to Ilchester Jail* (Irish University Press Series: Crime and Punishment, Prisons, ix).

Reports of State Trials, new series, i (1888).

II Collections of Prints, Newspapers etc.

George, M. D., *Catalogue of Political and Personal Satires preserved in the Department of Prints and Drawings in the British Museum*, ix and x (1949–52).

British Library: Place Newspaper Collection, Sets 17, 39, 40, 63 and 65.

Manchester Central Library: Henry Hunt, microfiche newspaper cuttings.

III Newspapers and Periodicals

Addresses from One of the 3730 Electors of Preston, to the Labouring Classes of Great Britain and Ireland
Ballot
Black Dwarf
Blackburn Gazette
Blanketteer, and People's Guardian
Bolton Chronicle
Le Bonnet Rouge
Bristol Gazette
Cap of Liberty
Carlile's Journal for 1830
Carlisle Journal
Carpenter's Monthly Political Magazine
Carpenter's Political Letters and Pamphlets
Cobbett's Evening Post
Cobbett's Political Register
Cobbett's Twopenny Trash
Cosmopolite
Crisis, or Star to the Great Northern Union
Democratic Recorder and Reformer's Guide
Destructive
Edinburgh Review
Examiner
Felix Farley's Bristol Journal
Gauntlet
Gentleman's Magazine
Gorgon
Hone's Reformist Register
Independent Whig
Leeds Patriot, and Yorkshire Advertiser
Lion
London Alfred, or People's Recorder
Man
Manchester Observer

Manchester Political Register; Or, Reformer's Repository
Medusa
Midland Representative and Birmingham Herald
Northern Reformers Monthly Magazine and Political Register
Penny Papers for the People
The People
Peter–Loo Massacre
Political Letter
Poor Man's Guardian
Preston Chronicle
Prompter
Quarterly Review
Radical
Radical Reformer or People's Advocate
Republican (1819–26)
Republican; or Voice of the People (1831–32)
Shamrock, Thistle, and Rose
Sherwin's Political Register
Taunton Courier
The Times
Theological Comet
Trades' Free Press
Trades' Newspaper and Mechanics' Weekly Journal
True Briton
Union
Voice of the People
Weekly Free Press
White Hat
Wooler's British Gazette and Manchester Observer
Working Man's Friend

IV   Contemporary Pamphlets, Books etc.

Account of the meeting of the Friends of Civil and Religious Liberty, at the Crown and Anchor Tavern in the Strand, on Monday the 12th of Feb. 1827 (n.d.).

The Addresser Addressed, or a reply to the Townsman of Bolton with other pieces (n.p., 1816).

Addresses, Squibs, etc at Preston Election, 1826 (n.p., n.d.)

Allen, Thomas, *The History and Antiquities of the Parish of Lambeth* (1826).

An Alphabetical List of Persons Who Polled for a Member of Parliament to represent the Borough of Preston, at the contested election which commenced, the 8th of Dec. 1830 (Preston, 1831).

An authentic narrative of the events of the Westminster Election . . . Compiled by order of the Committee appointed to manage the election of Mr. Hobhouse (1819).

An Authentic Report of the Evidence and Proceedings before the Committee of the Hon. House of Commons, appointed to try the merits of the Bristol Election of October 1812 (Bristol, 1813).

Bamford, Samuel, *Passages in the Life of a Radical* (2 vols., Manchester, 1844; rpt. 1 vol. Fitzroy edn., 1967).

Birmingham Meeting. Which took place on Thursday, Sept. 23, 1819, to take into consideration the late unhappy transactions at Manchester (Manchester, 1819).

Birmingham Union Society, *Declaration, Rules, and Resolutions of the Birmingham Union Society established for the Restoration of Human Happiness* (Birmingham, 1819).

Brayshaw, Joseph, *Proceedings of the meeting held at Yeadon, on Monday 28 June, 1819. Containing the speech delivered on the occasion, the resolutions adopted . . . an appeal to the nation, and a defence of the reformers . . . To which is added, Advice to the Labouring Classes* (Dewsbury, 1819).

Bridle, W., *Bridle's letter to the very noble, and most mighty, the aristocracy of England* (1836).

——, *A narrative of the rise and progress of the improvements effected in His Majesty's gaol at Ilchester* (Bath, 1822).

Broadhurst, Nathan (ed.), *The Whigs, v. The People: or the trial of Broadhurst, Ashmore, Curran, Gilchrist, Lomax, Faux, Pollard, and Maskell, for conspiracy, sedition and inflammatory language* (Preston, 1832).

Carlile, Richard, *Addresses to the Reformers of Great Britain*, 3 Mar., 24 June, and 13 Oct. 1821.

——, *An effort to set at rest some little disputes and misunderstandings between the reformers of Leeds* (1821).

——, *A New Year's Address to the Reformers of Great Britain* (1821).

Carpenter, William, *An Address to the Working Classes on the Reform Bill* (1831).

Cartwright, J., *A Bill of Rights and Liberties or An Act for A Constitutional Reform of Parliament* (1817).

Centinel (pseud.), *The First Six Letters of Centinel . . . containing an exposition of the principles of the Trout-Tavern Dinner Club; of Mr. H. Hunt, the President* (Bristol, 1807).

Cleary, Thomas, *A Reply to the Falsehoods of Mr. Hunt* (1819).

Cobbett, William, *Eleven Lectures on the French and Belgian Revolutions, and English Boroughmongering* (1830).

A Collection of Addresses, Squibs, Songs etc. published during the late Contested Election for the Borough of Preston (Preston, 1820).

A Collection of Particulars Relative to the Election of Common Council-Men for the Ward of Farringdon Without in the year 1828; with some preliminary remarks respecting the introduction of Mr. Hunt to that Ward (1829).

A correct report of the proceedings of a meeting held at Newhall Hill, Birmingham, on Monday, July 12, 1819 (Birmingham, 1819).

Cranidge, John, *A Mirror for the Burgesses and Commonalty of the City of Bristol* (Bristol, 1818).

Davison, T., *Smithfield Meeting* (1819).

The Demagogue; or 'Old Harry's' last speech and visit to his constituents; a farce in one act, as performed at Preston, on Thursday the 12th of July, 1832 (Preston, 1832).

Dolby, Thomas, *An appeal to the electors of Westminster on the public characters and pretensions of the six candidates for their suffrages in the present election* (1818).

——, *Memoirs of Thomas Dolby . . . Written by himself* (1827).

Fairburn's Account of the Meeting in Spa Fields, November 15, 1816 (1816).

A Few Little Truths; Or, the Orator HUNT-ed from Spa Fields to his old Earth at the Cottage (Bath, n.d.).

Fitzgerald, J. R., *To the Electors of Preston* (1831).

Fourteen Anti-Reform Pamphlets published at Birmingham, 1819, bound as one volume in Goldsmiths' Library.

French, Daniel, *French versus Cobbett. Cobbett on the Gridiron!! (Grilled to a Cinder!) Being an answer to Cobbett's Register of October 3, 1829* (1829).

A Full Account of the General Meeting of the Inhabitants of Newcastle-upon-Tyne and the vicinity, held on the Town Moor, on Monday the 11th of October, 1819 . . . for the purpose of taking into consideration the late proceedings in Manchester (Newcastle, 1819).

A Full Report of the Speeches and Proceedings of the Westminster General Meeting, Palace Yard, 2nd September 1819 . . . on the late barbarous transactions at Manchester! (1819).

Greville, Charles, *The Greville Memoirs* (3 vols., 1874).

Hobhouse, J. C., *The Speech of John Cam Hobhouse, Esq. M.P. for Westminster, in answer to Cobbett, at the Purity of Election Dinner, Crown and Anchor Tavern, 25 May, 1829* (1829).

Hone, William, *Full Report of the Third Spa-Fields Meeting* (1817).

——, *Hone's Riots in London, Part Two* (1816).

——, *The Meeting in Spa Fields. Hone's Authentic, and Correct Account, at length, of all the Proceedings on Monday, December 2d; with the Resolutions and Petition of Nov. 15, 1816* (1816).

——, *The Riots in London, Hone's Full and Authentic Account* (1816).

Hunt, Henry, *An account of the public dinner of the friends to purity of election, held at the Talbot Inn, Bath-Street, Bristol, on Thursday, January 28, 1813, Henry Hunt, esq. in the chair* (Bristol, n.d.).

——, *An Address to all those who wish to preserve their country from the horrors of a sanguinary revolution. Wherein is introduced the Resolutions entered into at a meeting at the Trout Tavern, Bristol on 2 June 1807, the letter of Sir Francis Burdett, bart. M.P., to the president of the meeting, the letter of Samuel Brooks, esq., chairman of the Westminster Election Committee* (Bristol, 1807).

——, *An Address to the Public of the City of Bristol, in answer to an anonymous letter, signed Centinel, which appeared in the Bristol Western Star, on Friday, August 21, 1807* (Bristol, 1807).

——, *Addresses from Henry Hunt, Esq. M.P. to the Radical Reformers of England, Ireland and Scotland, on the measures of the Whig Ministers since they have been in place and power,* 1–13 (1831–1832).

——, *A brief history of the Parish of Christ Church in the County of Surrey, with its public charities* (1830).

——, *Bristol election: an account of Mr. Hunt's public reception in Bristol, May 18, 1812, with a full report of his second address, delivered to the citizens, from the pedestal in front of the Exchange: also the particulars of the dinner given by his friends at the New Assembly-Rooms, Hotwells* (Bristol, 1812).

——, *Corn Laws, The Evidence of John Benett, Esq. of Pythouse, given before the Committee of the House of Lords on the Corn Bill. An Impartial Report of the Meeting of Landholders at Warminster. Mr. Benett's Letter in answer to that Report. Mr. Bleeck's Letter in reply. Together with an inedited letter from Mr. Hunt on the subject; and a copy of the Petition signed by the farmers at the several market towns in the County of Wilts., for a Corn Bill* (Salisbury, 1815).

——, *A correct report of the proceedings of the meeting held at the Crown and Anchor, Strand, on Monday June 1, 1818 . . . to take into consideration and adopt the best means to secure the election of Henry Hunt, esq.* (1818).

——, *Deep Mourning. Wig v Blackball. Trial of Henry Hunt, Esquire, for defamation, in the Earl Marshal's court, on Monday, October 20, 1828* (1828).

——, *Examination of Henry Hunt, Esq. Joseph Johnson, James Moorhouse, etc at the New Bailey Court-House, Salford on Friday the 27th Aug. 1819* (Manchester, 1819).

——, *Full particulars of the final examination of Mr. Hunt and the other prisoners at Manchester, on a charge of high treason; with Mr. Hunt's reply to the court and the subsequent proceedings* (1819).

——, *The Green Bag Plot* (1819).

——, *Hunt's Letter to the King, Peel's Letter to the Lord Mayor. Disappointment of the Grand Civic Feast. With every particular of Hunt's Lecture at the Rotunda; and all the news of the day* (1830).

Hunt, Henry, *Mr H—t's second Speech without Notes* (Bristol, n.d.), posting-bill.

——, *Investigation at Ilchester Gaol, in the county of Somerset, into the conduct of William Bridle, the gaoler, before the commissioners appointed by the crown. The evidence taken by H. B. Shillibeer. Dedicated, with an address to his majesty, King George the Fourth, by Henry Hunt, Esq.* (1821).

——, *The King's answer to Cobbett's letter on the present state of England; and Hunt's letter to His Majesty, and every particular of the intended Grand Royal Civic Feast* (1830).

——, *Lecture on the Conduct of the Whigs to the Working Classes, delivered at Lawrence Street Chapel, Birmingham, on Wednesday, October 31st, 1832* (1832).

——, *A Letter from Mr. Hunt to the Freemen of Bristol, Upon the subject of the large and numerous Estates, and other Property left them at sundry times, under the name of Charities; and the Rents or Proceeds of which they now receive, or ought to receive. To which is added, a list of those charities* (1812).

——, *Lines Composed on the Immortal Memory of H. Hunt Esq.* (n.p., n.d.), broadside in the Harkness Collection, Preston.

——, *Memoirs of Henry Hunt, Esq. Written by himself in his Majesty's Jail at Ilchester* (3 vols., 1820–2).

——, *A Monument to the Memory of H. Hunt, Esq.* (Bolton, 1835), posting-bill in Manchester Central Library.

——, *National Distress. Speech of Mr. Hunt, made at the meeting of the electors of Westminster . . . September 11th, 1816* (Holt, n.d.), broadsheet in Bristol Record Office.

——, *Oath offered to be taken by Mr. Hunt, before the Sheriffs, Mayor, or Alderman Vaughan, and refused by them on the ground of its irregularity* (Bristol, n.d.), posting-bill in Bristol Reference Library.

——, *A Peep into a Prison; or, the inside of Ilchester Bastile* (1821).

——, *Plain Facts. Is he a Traitor? Being a defence of Mr. Hunt from the calumnies of the London newspapers* (n.d.).

——, *The Preston Cock's Reply to the Kensington Dunghill* (3rd edn., 1831).

——, *The Proceedings at large in the Court of King's Bench in the cause the King against Henry Hunt, Esq. for challenging the Rt. Hon. Charles Brudenell Bruce, commonly called Lord Bruce. Addressed to the Officers and Gentlemen of the Wiltshire Yeomanry Cavalry* (1801).

——, *To the Radical Reformers, male and female, of England, Ireland and Scotland* (2 vols., 1820–2).

——, *Speech of H. Hunt, Esqr. M.P.* (Manchester, 1831), broadsheet in Manchester Central Library.

——, *The Trial of Henry Hunt, Esq. . . . for an alleged conspiracy to overturn the government, etc. by threats and forces of arms* (1820).

——, *The Triumphal Entry of H. Hunt into London . . . September 13, 1819* (1819).

'Huntite, A', *A Letter to the Working Classes of Blackburn* (Blackburn, 1831).

An Impartial Narrative of the Late Melancholy Occurrences in Manchester (Liverpool, 1819).

Johnson, Joseph, *A Letter to Henry Hunt, Esq.* (Manchester, 1822).

——, *A Second Letter to Henry Hunt, Esq.* (Manchester, 1822).

Lee, Thomas, *A Letter to Henry Hunt, Esq. Chairman of a Political Club held at the Lamb and Lark, Thomas Street, Bristol, on certain resolutions lately entered into at one of the usual weekly club-meetings, and signed and published by him. And also, on the inevitable tendency of political clubs, to weaken or destroy every important relation, public and private, in civil society* (Bristol, 1808).

Leeds Reform Meeting. Held on Hunslet Moor September 20th, 1819. (Leeds, 1819).

A List of Persons Entitled to Vote, distinguishing those who voted, at the election of members for the Borough of Preston, commencing Wednesday, 12th Dec. 1832 (Preston, 1833).

Lovett, William, *Life and Struggles of William Lovett in his Pursuit of Bread, Knowledge and Freedom* (London, 1876; rpt. Fitzroy edn., 1967).

Metropolitan Political Union, *An Appeal to the People of England, by the Council of the Metropolitan Political Union. Signed H. Hunt, chairman* (1830).

——, *Authorized Copy of the Resolutions adopted at the Great Public Meeting, consisting of 30,000 people . . . for forming a Metropolitan Political Union, for the recovery and protection of public rights* (1830).

To the People of England. At a meeting of the Deputies from Fourteen Petitioning Bodies of the County of Lancaster, held at Middleton, the 16th Day of December, 1816, the following Resolutions were unanimously passed, and Declaration made (Manchester, n.d.).

Political Tracts 1819 (Volume of pamphlets and newspaper cuttings in the British Library).

Political Tracts 1819–1820 (Volume of pamphlets and newspaper cuttings in the British Library).

Political Tracts 1822–23 (Volume of pamphlets and newspaper cuttings in the British Library).

Prentice, Archibald, *Historical Sketches and Personal Recollections of Manchester* (Manchester, 1851; rpt. 1970).

Preston, Thomas, *A Letter to Lord Viscount Castlereagh; being a full development of all the circumstances relative to the diabolical Cato Street Plot* (1820).

——, *The Life and Opinions of Thomas Preston, patriot and shoemaker* (1817).

Proceedings of the Hampden Club, 1812–22 (bound volume in the British Library).

Proceedings of the Middleton Union Society, for promoting a constitutional reform in the Commons House of Parliament, established Oct. 19th 1816 (Manchester, n.d.).

The Proceedings of the late Westminster Election (1808).

Radical Recriminations. The Correspondence of Hunt, Thistlewood, Blandford and Watson (London, n.d.).

Radical State Papers (London, 1820).

'Reformer, A', *A Letter to the Working Classes of Blackburn, in reply to the answer of 'A Huntite' to a former letter on Parliamentary Reform* (Blackburn, 1831).

A report of the meeting held in Smithfield, on Wednesday July 21, 1819 to consider of the best means of recovering our lost rights (1819).

Report of the Metropolitan and Central Committee appointed for the relief of the Manchester sufferers (1820).

Report of the Proceedings at the Public Meeting of the Working Classes and Others, at the Crown and Anchor Tavern, Strand; to support the people's daily press, The True Sun (1832).

Report of the Proceedings of a Numerous and Respectable Meeting, held pursuant to advertisement, at Stockport, on Monday the 28th Day of September, 1818 (Manchester, n.d.).

Resolutions, and Petition of the Inhabitants of Manchester (Manchester, n.d.).

Romilly, Sir Samuel, *An account of the entry of Sir Samuel Romilly into Bristol, on Thursday, April 2, 1812; with a report of the speeches delivered on that occasion, at a dinner given to him at the Assembly-Room, Prince's Street* (Bristol, 1812).

——, *Memoirs of the life of Sir Samuel Romilly, written by himself* (3 vols., 1840).

Shepherd, William, *Three Letters originally published in the Liverpool Mercury, with the introductory observations of the editor of that truly independent and liberal journal, on the subject of the Ilchester Gaol Investigation* (1822).

Taylor, J. E., *Notes and Observations, critical and explanatory on the Papers Relative to the Internal State of the Country* (1820).

Visits to a Prison; A Peep at the Prisoners; and a description of the interior of Ilchester Gaol (Ilminster, 1821).

Walker, C. H., *An Independent Address to the Electors of Bristol, upon the state of the representation of the people, with free remarks upon the present candidates* (Bristol, 1812).

Watson, James, *A Letter to Viscount Lord Sidmouth* (1818).

——, *The Rights of the People, Unity or Slavery* (1818).

The White Hat, which was lately discovered, like a spot, in the Sun, afterwards greatly enlarged by the telescope of the Times; now made visible, without the aid of glasses, to Whigs, Tories, and Radical Reformers, in the shape of a Garland (Newcastle-upon-Tyne, 1819).

V Secondary Sources

Aspinall, A., *Lord Brougham and the Whig Party* (Manchester, 1927).
——, *The Early English Trade Unions* (1949).
——, 'The Westminster Election of 1814', *English Historical Review*, xl (1925), 562–9.
Barnes, J. C. F., 'The trade union and radical activities of the Carlisle handloom weavers', *Transactions of the Cumberland and Westmorland Antiquarian and Archaeological Society*, new series, lxxviii (1978), 149–161.
Baylen, J. O. and Gossman, N. J. (eds.), *Biographical Dictionary of Modern British Radicals: Volume I, 1770–1830* (Hassocks, 1979).
Belchem, John, 'Henry Hunt and the evolution of the mass platform', *English Historical Review*, xciii (1978), 739–73.
——, 'Republicanism, popular constitutionalism and the radical platform in early nineteenth-century England', *Social History*, vi (1981), 1–32.
Bohstedt, J., *Riots and Community Politics in England and Wales 1790–1810* (1983).
Booth, A., 'Food riots in the north-west of England 1790–1801', *Past and Present*, lxxvii (1977), 84–107.
Brewer, J., *Party Ideology and Popular Politics at the Accession of George III* (Cambridge, 1976).
Briggs, Asa, 'The Background of the Parliamentary Reform Movement in Three English Cities (1830–2)', *Cambridge Historical Journal*, x (1950–2), 293–317.
——, 'Middle-Class Consciousness in English Politics, 1780–1846', *Past and Present*, ix (1956), 65–74.
Brock, M., *The Great Reform Act* (1973).
Butler, J. R. M., *The Passing of the Great Reform Bill* (1914).
Calder-Marshall, A., 'The Spa Fields Riots, 1816', *History Today*, xxi (1971), 407–15.
Cannon, J., *Parliamentary Reform 1640–1832* (Cambridge, 1973).
Cole, G. D. H., *Attempts at General Union: A Study in British Trade Union History 1818–1834* (1953).
——, *The Life of William Cobbett* (1924).
Collins, B., 'Proto-industrialization and pre-Famine emigration', *Social History*, vii (1982), 127–46.
Cookson, J. E., *The Friends of Peace: Anti-war liberalism in England 1793–1815* (Cambridge, 1982).
——, *Lord Liverpool's Administration: The Crucial Years 1815–1822* (Edinburgh, 1975).
Cunningham, Hugh, 'The Language of Patriotism', *History Workshop Journal*, xii (1981), 8–33.
Davis, H. W. C., 'Lancashire Reformers, 1816–17', *Bulletin of the John Rylands Library*, x (1926), 47–79.
Dickinson, H. T., *Liberty and Property: political ideology in eighteenth-century Britain* (1977).

——, (ed.), *The Political Works of Thomas Spence* (Newcastle-upon-Tyne, 1982).

Dinwiddy, J. R., 'Sir Francis Burdett and Burdettite Radicalism', *History*, lxv (1980), 17–31.

Dinwiddy, J. R., 'The early nineteenth-century campaign against flogging in the army', *English Historical Review*, xcvii (1982), 308–31.

——, 'Luddism and politics in the northern counties', *Social History*, iv (1979), 33–63.

——, '"The Patriotic Linen-Draper": Robert Waithman and the Revival of Radicalism in the City of London, 1795–1818', *Bulletin of the Institute of Historical Research*, xlvi (1973), 72–94.

——, *Christopher Wyvill and Reform 1790–1820* (York, *Borthwick Papers, 39*, 1971).

Dobson, W., *History of the Parliamentary Representation of Preston, during the last hundred years* (Preston, 1856).

Donajgrodski, A. P., (ed.), *Social Control in Nineteenth-Century Britain* (1977).

Eley, G. and Nield, K., 'Why does social history ignore politics', *Social History*, v (1980), 249–72.

Ellis, P. B. and A'Ghobhainn, S. M., *The Scottish Insurrection of 1820* (1970).

Emsley, C., *British Society and the French Wars 1793–1815* (1979).

Epstein, James, *The Lion of Freedom: Feargus O'Connor and the Chartist Movement, 1832–1842* (1982).

——, and Thompson, Dorothy (eds.), *The Chartist Experience: Studies in Working-Class Radicalism and Culture, 1830–1860* (1982).

Flick, C., *The Birmingham Political Union and the movements for reform in Britain 1830–1839* (Folkestone, 1978).

Foster, John, *Class Struggle and the Industrial Revolution: Early industrial capitalism in three English towns* (1974).

Fraser, Derek, 'The Agitation for Parliamentary Reform' in J. T. Ward (ed.), *Popular Movements c. 1830–1850* (1970).

Fraser, P., 'Public Petitioning and Parliament before 1832', *History*, xlvi (1961), 195–211.

Gash, N., 'After Waterloo: British Society and the Legacy of the Napoleonic Wars', *Transactions of the Royal Historical Society*, 5th series, xxviii (1978), 145–57.

——, *Aristocracy and People: Britain 1815–1865* (1979).

Goodway, D., *London Chartism, 1838–1848* (Cambridge, 1982).

Graham, H. D. and Gurr, T. R. (eds.), *The History of Violence in America* (New York, 1969).

Gurr, T. R., *Why Men Rebel* (Princeton, 1970).

Halevy, E., *The Liberal Awakening 1815–1830*, trans. E. I. Watkin (2nd edn., 1949).

Harvey, A. D., *Britain in the Early Nineteenth Century* (1978).

Hewitson, A., *History of Preston* (Preston, 1883).

Hill, C., 'The Norman Yoke' in J. Saville (ed.), *Democracy and the Labour Movement* (1954).

Hilton, B., *Corn, Cash, Commerce: the economic policies of the Tory governments, 1815–1830* (Oxford, 1970).

Hobsbawm, E. J. and Rudé, G., *Captain Swing* (Harmondsworth, Penguin edn., 1973).

Hollis, P., *The Pauper Press: a study of working-class Radicalism of the 1830s* (Oxford, 1970).

Holton, R. J., 'The crowd in history: some problems of theory and method', *Social History*, iii (1978), 219–33.

Hone, J. A., *For the Cause of Truth: Radicalism in London 1796–1821* (Oxford, 1982).

Huish, R., *The History of the Private and Political Life of the late Henry Hunt, Esq. M.P. for Preston* (2 vols., 1836).

Mr. Henry Hunt. His Monument Taken Down and Sold, broadsheet in the Manchester Central Library, dated January 1889.

Jephson, H., *The Platform: its rise and progress* (2 vols., 1892).

Johnson, Richard, 'Thompson, Genovese, and Socialist–Humanist History', *History Workshop Journal*, vi (1978), 79–100.

Jones, David, 'Women and Chartism', *History*, lxviii (1983), 1–21.

Jones, Gareth Stedman, *Languages of Class: Studies in English working-class history 1832–1982* (Cambridge, 1983).

Joyce, P., 'Labour, capital and compromise: a response to Richard Price', *Social History*, ix (1984), 67–76.

Kemnitz, T. M., 'Approaches to the Chartist movement: Feargus O'Connor and Chartist strategy', *Albion*, v (1973), 67–73.

Kent, C. B. R., *The English Radicals* (1899).

Kirby, R. G. and Musson, A. E., *The Voice of the People: John Doherty 1798–1854* (Manchester, 1975).

Knox, T. R., 'Thomas Spence: The Trumphet of Jubilee', *Past and Present*, lxxvi (1977), 75–98.

Latimer, J., *The Annals of Bristol in the Nineteenth Century* (1887; rpt. Bristol, 1970).

Linebaugh, Peter, 'Labour history without the labour process: a note on John Gast and his times', *Social History*, vii (1982), 319–27.

Lomas, C. W., 'Orator Hunt at Peterloo and Smithfield', *Quarterly Journal of Speech*, xlviii, 4 (1962), 400–5.

Maccoby, S., *English Radicalism 1786–1832* (1955).

Machin, G. I. T., *The Catholic Question in English Politics 1820 to 1830* (Oxford, 1964).

Main, J. M., 'Radical Westminster, 1807–1820', *Historical Studies (Australia and New Zealand)*, xii (1965–7), 186–204.

McCord, N., 'Tyneside Discontents and Peterloo', *Northern History*, ii (1967), 91–111.

Miller, N. C., 'John Cartwright and radical parliamentary reform, 1808–1819', *English Historical Review*, lxxxiii (1968), 705–28.

——, 'Major John Cartwright and the Founding of the Hampden Club', *Historical Journal*, xvii (1974), 615–19.

Mingay, G. E., *English Landed Society in the eighteenth century* (1963).

Mitchell, A., 'The Whigs and Parliamentary Reform before 1830', *Historical Studies (Australia and New Zealand)*, xii (1965–67), 12–22.

——, *The Whigs in Opposition 1815–1830* (Oxford, 1967).

Moorhouse, H. F., 'Attitudes to class and class relationships in Britain', *Sociology*, x (1976), 469–96.

Morton, A. L. and Tate, G., *The British Labour Movement 1770–1920* (1956).

Murray, J. (ed.), *Lord Byron's Correspondence* (2 vols., 1922).

'Notes and Queries', *Manchester City News*, 12, 19 and 26 March 1904.

O'Gorman, F., *The Emergence of the British Two-Party System 1760–1832* (1982).

Osborne, J. W., 'Henry Hunt, 1815–1830: the politically formative years of a Radical M.P.', *Red River Valley Historical Journal of World History*, v (1981), 177–94.

——, 'Henry Hunt's Career in Parliament', *Historian*, xxxix, (1976), 24–39.

Parkin, Frank, *Class Inequality and Political Order* (1972).

——, *Middle Class Radicalism* (Manchester, 1968).

Parssinnen, T. M., 'Association, convention and anti-parliament in British radical politics, 1771–1848', *English Historical Review*, lxxxviii (1973), 504–33.

——, 'The Revolutionary party in London, 1816–20', *Bulletin of the Institute of Historical Research*, xlv (1972), 266–82.

Patterson, M. W., *Sir Francis Burdett and his Times* (2 vols., 1931).

Peacock, A. J., *Bread or Blood: a study of the agrarian riots in East Anglia in 1816* (1965).

Post, J. D., *The Last Great Subsistence Crisis in the Western World* (Baltimore, 1977).

Price, Richard, 'The labour process and labour history', *Social History*, viii (1983), 57–75.

Proctor, W., 'Orator Hunt, M.P. for Preston 1830–32', *Transactions of the Historic Society of Lancashire and Cheshire*, cxiv (1962).

Prothero, Iorwerth, *Artisans and Politics in early nineteenth-century London: John Gast and his Times* (1981 edn.).

——, 'William Benbow and the concept of the "General Strike"', *Past and Present*, lxiii (1974), 132–171.

Read, D., *Peterloo: The 'Massacre' and its Background* (Manchester, 1958).

Reynolds, J. A., *The Catholic Emancipation Crisis in Ireland, 1823–9* (Yale, 1954).

Rostow, W. W., *British Economy of the Nineteenth Century* (Oxford, 1948).

Royle, E. (ed.), *The Infidel Tradition* (1976).

Rubinstein, W. D., 'The End of "Old Corruption" in Britain 1780–1860', *Past and Present*, ci (1983), 55–86.

Rudé, George, *Ideology and Popular Protest* (1980).

——, *Paris and London in the 18th Century: Studies in Popular Protest* (1970).

——, *Protest and Punishment: the story of the social and political protesters transported to Australia 1788–1868* (Oxford, 1978).

Samuel, R., (ed.), *People's History and Socialist Theory* (1981).

Soffer, R. N., 'Attitudes and allegiances in the unskilled north, 1830–1850', *International Review of Social History*, x (1965), 429–54.

Spater, George, *William Cobbett: The Poor Man's Friend* (2 vols., Cambridge, 1982).

Stanhope, J., *The Cato Street Conspiracy* (1962).

Stevens, John, *England's Last Revolution: Pentrich 1817* (Buxton, 1977).

Stevenson, J. and Quinault, R. (eds.), *Popular Protest and Public Order* (1974).

Stewart, Neil, *The Fight for the Charter* (1937).

Tholfsen, Trygve, *Working Class Radicalism in mid-Victorian England* (1976).

Thomas, W., *The Philosophic Radicals: Nine studies in theory and practice 1817–1841* (Oxford, 1979).

——, 'Whigs and Radicals in Westminster: the election of 1819', *Guildhall Miscellany*, iii (1970), 174–217.

Thomis, M. I. and Holt, P., *Threats of Revolution in Britain 1789–1848* (1977).

Thompson, Dorothy, *The Chartists* (1984).

Thompson, E. P., 'Eighteenth-century English society: class struggle without class?', *Social History*, iii (1978), 133–65.

——, *The Making of the English Working Class* (Penguin edn., 1968).

——, *Whigs and Hunters* (Peregrine edn., 1977).

——, *William Morris: Romantic to Revolutionary* (1976 edn.).

Transactions of the Lancashire and Cheshire Antiquarian Society, vii (1889), 324–6.

Turberville, A. S., 'Leeds and parliamentary reform 1820–1832', *Thoresby Miscellany*, xii (1954), 1–88.

Wallas, Graham, *The Life of Francis Place* (4th edn., 1951).

Walmsley, Robert, *Peterloo: The Case Reopened* (Manchester, 1969).

Weisser, H., *British working-class movements and Europe 1815–48* (Manchester, 1975).

Western, J. R., 'The Volunteer Movement as an anti-Revolutionary Force', *English Historical Review*, lxxi (1956), 603–14.

White, R. J., *From Waterloo to Peterloo* (Peregrine edn., 1968).

Wiener, Joel H., *Radicalism and Freethought in Nineteenth-Century Britain: The Life of Richard Carlile* (Westport, 1983).

Williams, Gwyn, *The Merthyr Rising* (1978).

Wilson, J., *Introduction to Social Movements* (New York, 1973).

Yonge, C. D., *The Life and Administration of Robert Banks, Second Earl of Liverpool* (3 vols., 1868).

Zeitlin, Jonathan, 'Social theory and the history of work', *Social History*, viii (1983), 365–74.

C UNPUBLISHED THESES

Belchem, J. C., 'Radicalism as a "Platform" Agitation in the periods 1816–1821 and 1848–1851: with special reference to the leadership of Henry Hunt and Feargus O'Connor' (Sussex University, D.Phil. thesis, 1974).

Donnelly, F. K., 'The General Rising of 1820: a Study of Social Conflict in the Industrial Revolution' (Sheffield University, Ph.D. thesis, 1975).

McCalman, I., 'Popular Radicalism and Freethought in early nineteenth-century England: a study of Richard Carlile and his followers, 1815–32' (Australian National University, M.A. thesis, 1977).

Newman, W. J., 'Henry Hunt and English Working-Class Radicalism, 1812–1832' (Princeton University, Ph.D. thesis, 1950).

Sykes, R. A., 'Popular Politics and Trade Unionism in South-East Lancashire, 1829–42' (Manchester University, Ph.D. thesis, 1982).

Index

IX
1
2
3
4–6
7. 8
10
12
14

Extract of Place but not I HH
Printing errors

History

c. 400 words   Dr. Bruce Gilbert, Glasgow, History Dept.